+ B + C

+ B + C + D →

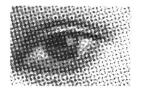

To Kay

BOOK

A
BALANCE HOUSE
BOOK

MARSHALL LEE

MAKING:

The illustrated guide to design/production/editing

SECOND EDITION
Completely revised and expanded

Published by

R. R. Bowker Company

New York

Published by R. R. Bowker Company
1180 Avenue of the Americas, New York, N.Y. 10036
Copyright © 1979 by Marshall Lee
All rights reserved
ISBN 0-8352-1097-9

Library of Congress Cataloging in Publication Data
Lee, Marshall; 1921–
Bookmaking: the illustrated guide to design
production/editing.
Bibliography: p.
Includes index.
1. Books.   2. Book industries and trade.   I. Title.
Z116.A2L44 1979 686 79–65014

Printed and Bound in the United States of America

Prices in text valid to January 1979.

ACKNOWLEDGMENTS

Dozens of experts, specialists, technicians, and generally experienced people were consulted in the preparation of both the First and Second editions of *Bookmaking*. Some were asked only one question; others were asked for and gave considerable portions of their time. Of the latter, particular mention is due: Daniel Melcher, Ernst Reichl, Jack W. White, Leonard Schlosser, Robert Nangle, Alan Duffield, Frank Matonti, Max Tanzer, Kenneth James, Constance Schrader, Donald F. Johnston, and Gladys Carr. A special word of thanks belongs to Chandler Grannis, who not only contributed invaluable suggestions on the text, but completely revised the Sources of Information section in Part III. It is impossible to name each one who helped, but to all of them goes our sincere gratitude.

Despite every effort to check the facts, errors have undoubtedly remained in the text. For these, as well as for the judgments expressed, the author takes all responsibility.

Grateful acknowledgment is made also to: McGraw-Hill Book Co. for permission to use or adapt several illustrations from *Printing and Promotion Handbook*; Strathmore Paper Co. for permission to use the papermaking diagrams on pages 152–153; *Publishers Weekly* for permission to use several pictures from their files.

Read this first

The following paragraphs define the terms and explain the concepts and premises on which this book is based.

BOOK EDITING is the conception, planning, and preparation of the content of a book, in cooperation with the author.

BOOK DESIGN is the conception, planning, and specifying of the physical and visual attributes of a book.

BOOK PRODUCTION is the execution of the design, i.e. purchasing materials and services, scheduling and routing the work, coordinating the manufacture of the book with distribution requirements, and maintaining records.

Book editing, design, and production are not 3 separate functions, but 3 parts of one function, i.e. *to transmit the author's message to the reader in the best possible way*. This means creating a product that can be profitably sold, as well as satisfying the requirements of author and reader. The term BOOKMAKING is used to express the whole function.

The word BOOK applies to many different products. As often as possible, the text refers to a specific category of book (text, reference, paperback, juvenile, reprint, etc.) but when the term is used alone it may be taken to mean *tradebook*, the conventional hardcover book sold to the general public.

A WELL-DESIGNED BOOK means one that is (a) appropriate to its content and use, (b) economical, and (c) satisfying to the senses. It is not a "pretty" book in the superficial sense and it is not necessarily more elaborate than usual.

ECONOMICAL refers to an efficient use of the graphic and material elements of the book and the money spent for its manufacture. This does not necessarily imply the smallest possible expenditure, but rather the smallest expenditure that will achieve the most successful result.

It is assumed that the importance of being PRACTICAL and ECONOMICAL at all times is understood, so reminders to this effect will remain implied rather than stated.

Each technical or special term is italicized the first time it occurs in a significant sense and usually its meaning is given directly or by the context. At the back of the book is a Glossary-Index, in which every italicized term is listed alphabetically, with a definition when one is needed. In the text are references [(CH. 20) etc.] to other chapters in which a term or subject is discussed.

Grammatical usage in the text defers to logic and efficiency more than custom. For example, space and reading time are saved by the use of figures instead of spelled-out numbers and abbreviations for frequently used terms. In punctuation, British practice is followed where it is more logical and no confusion will result. Commas are used wherever they contribute to clarity.

This volume is *an outline of practical information and procedure* for those engaged in planning and producing books, and as such it is quite complete, but no book of this length—or many times this length—could describe in detail *all* the processes, equipment, and materials that go into bookmaking. Part III lists specialized books and other sources of further information on each subject.

Even if everything known about bookmaking was included today there would be something lacking tomorrow, because of the rapid pace of development. Probably, the technological principles on which bookmaking will be based for the coming decade are those in operation now, but there will undoubtedly be a constant flow of improvements and additions. Readers are advised to keep informed through trade periodicals. To help the reader keep up with changes, some pages have been provided at the back of this book for inserting notes and clippings about significant developments.

By enlarging the scope of *Bookmaking* to include editing we have extended in a concrete way the premise expressed in the First Edition—that everyone in book publishing should know something of each aspect of it. Although editing is covered in a separate section, it is hoped that all those concerned with any part of bookmaking will read all of this book.

Preface

When the First Edition of *Bookmaking* was written in 1965, the generally used processes of book production were relatively simple mechanics. They were not so simple compared to the hand operations of two hundred years earlier, but they were in many respects quaintly primitive compared to the sophisticated technology in use today.

With few exceptions, the advanced equipment and processes that now dominate bookmaking existed in elemental form or were in experimental states when the original text was written. If they were not described then, at least the reader was informed of their existence, so it was possible to let fourteen years pass before it became necessary to issue a revised edition. Indeed, until quite recently, the new methods—particularly in typesetting and printing—have had to prove their practical and economic value, struggling for acceptance in competition with the old methods. This struggle is now won, so it is possible to say that a new era in bookmaking has begun—just as a new era was launched with the introduction of printing in the 15th century, and again with the advent of engine-powered machines in the early 19th century, and once more with the invention of typesetting machines in the 1880s.

What is significant today is not so much the extraordinary speed and complexity of the computer-controlled machines that have transformed most bookmaking processes from mechanical to electronic-optical systems, but the almost overwhelming variety and number of these systems. A young person starting in the field at the end of World War II had to learn the operation of only two machines—Linotype and Monotype—to be competent in composition. Today, there are a score of different photocomposing and scanning machines in wide use; each of these varies enough from the others to make it necessary to study individually any machine one intends to use. On top of this, almost all of the equipment is subject to frequent improvement. And it is not even enough to know the composing devices. Each one may be hooked up to one, two, three, or more of a large array of associated keyboard, editing, printing, computing, or makeup devices, no two of which work in exactly the same way. Learning the present technology is an awesome task.

Awesome it may be, and even intimidating, but it need not be discouraging. The capacity of the human brain is far greater than the limited demands we make on it, so even the very considerable increase in knowledge that modern bookmaking requires is a minor challenge in relation to what we can handle. All that is needed is a little more determination and effort than it took our predecessors to learn their trade.

It is the author's hope that *Bookmaking* will make the learning somewhat easier than it would otherwise have been. The guiding principle in this writing has been *careful selection of information* to give a clear picture of what should be known, without overwhelming the reader with information (also useful) that is not necessary for the non-specialist.

What about quality in the new techology? Perhaps it is unfair to assess the performance of the present machines; they will surely be improved in time. However, the developments of the past century have seen a steady shift of control from people to machines, and the recent era has brought a long jump in that direction. The Linotype and electric-powered, sheet-fed presses greatly increased production speeds, but they were still mainly mechanical aids for their human operators—who exercised a continual control over their output. The present machines are *capable* of superb quality because of their precision and sophisticated controls, but their output is dependent largely on advance instructions—with little control by their operators after the starting buttons have been pushed. This works for the general and the simple, which can be accurately controlled by detailed computer programming, but it is rough on the individual and the subtle—which can be dealt with satisfactorily only by programming too elaborate to be feasible. The refinements, then, can be achieved only by either stopping the machines for manual adjustments—thereby losing much or all of their speed advantage—or correcting in a second (or third or fourth) run-through—which also costs the time that the new devices are designed to save.

It would be nice to hold out hope for a return to the quality levels of the former days, but this is unrealistic. The essence of the new technology is speed—super-human speed—and this cannot be reconciled with care and skill. The only hope for good work lies in the extraordinary accuracy and flexibility of the new machines, which can do marvellous things if we demand that they do.

Economy in bookmaking has been defined as spending the least needed to achieve a good result—not the least possible. This calls for *making* the demands that will produce the excellent work of which modern technology is capable.

ML

SOME SPECIAL NOTES

ON TERMINOLOGY

Much time (money) and energy are wasted, countless practical and esthetic calamities are caused by misunderstandings due to our lack of a uniform terminology in bookmaking. The problem would not exist if we had a central publishing school teaching one set of terms and signals; but, since there is none, perhaps this first comprehensive textbook of American bookmaking can help achieve the much-needed standardization.

Thus, it is urged that the terminology found here be adopted by, and disseminated to, all concerned with bookmaking. These terms are not necessarily better than others used elsewhere but they are those most generally accepted. After all, it is not so important *which* term is used, but that the term used is understood by all.

ON METRIC MEASUREMENT

At the time of this writing, the metric system is not yet in general use in the United States. Measurements are given in inches and pounds, but metric equivalents follow in parentheses, so the reader will be fully prepared when the official system changes. Conversion tables are included in Part III.

ABOUT PRICES

To make this book as useful as possible, actual prices, costs, fees, etc., have been given wherever generalities would be inadequate. It should be recognized, however, that these amounts are composite figures prevailing at the time of writing and are subject to variation according to time, locality, individual policy, and various special circumstances. The date for which the figures are valid is given on the copyright page. For a rough updating, add a percentage per year, according to the annual rate of inflation.

Short contents

Contents

PART I: Design & Production

A THE PROFESSION

B BASIC KNOWLEDGE

C   PROCEDURE

PART II: Editing

A THE PROFESSION

B BASIC KNOWLEDGE

C PROCEDURE

PART III: Useful information

PART I Design and Production

A

THE PROFESSION

1 | Background

In its broadest sense, the story of bookmaking goes back to the beginning of graphic communication. The development of writing from the first picture-symbols scratched on bone or stone to the sophisticated alphabets of today is a fascinating study, but, for our purposes, the story begins with the earliest codex, i.e. the first book in the form of bound leaves, as distinguished from the scrolls that preceded it.

No one knows when the first codices were made, but they came into general use in Europe during the 9th century. By that time, paper and printing were known in Asia, and some codices were used, but scrolls were still in favor there. A form of codex was developed by the Aztecs during this period, but only a few later ones survived the systematic destruction of the Spanish conquest.

2nd century Egyptian codex covers

A book printed in Mexico in 1544.

Until the fall of Rome, papyrus had been the common material of books and then it was vellum, the treated skin of animals.

The Arabic art of papermaking came to the West in the 8th century and was ready to serve that voracious consumer, the printing press, which appeared in Central Europe in the mid-15th century. As far as we know, printing in Europe was invented without reference to the Asian craft that had been in use for hundreds of years—perhaps a thousand years—before Gutenberg.

Many of the conventions of bookmaking originated in the manuscript phase, and the general aspects of page form and binding were quite well established by the time printing began. Indeed, the first printed books were made to look as much like manuscripts as possible, largely in the hope that the difference would not be noticed!

Whereas a complex alphabet and unfavorable social conditions discouraged a wide use of printing in China, its spread was relatively explosive in Europe. Within 50 years, presses were established in every major country—and by 1535 printing issued in Mexico City from the first press in the New World. However, another century passed before printing came to the North American settlements.

The book in America

From 1639, when the first printing was done in the American colonies, until the 19th century, the printer was publisher and bookseller as well. Working with presses little different from Gutenberg's, he became increasingly involved in the complexities of publishing until it was impractical to operate these functions *and* the craft of printing from one office. Separation began with the advent of the steam-powered press (about 1815), when printing became a major business in itself.

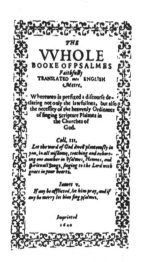

The Bay Psalm Book, the first book printed in the colonies.

The power presses were capable of devouring all the handmade paper produced and more but, fortunately, papermaking machines came along to meet the demand. Then, with the introduction of mechanical typecasting equipment about 1838, mass production of books became possible.

Rapid expansion had an unfortunate effect on typographic development. Where the hand printer was confined to a few basic typefaces (and therefore simple typography), the machine-age printer had types of every description—and many that defied description. The result, beginning at mid-century, was typographic chaos. About 1890, a reaction set in against the machine-made monstrosities. In England, William Morris revived the handcrafts of medieval bookmaking. In America, a few scholar-printers, notably DeVinne, Updike, and Rogers, restored the typography of the 17th and 18th centuries. Although no more inventive than Morris's, this movement introduced the mature traditions of printing to machine technology—and had a far greater effect.

THE CENTAUR. WRITTEN BY MAURICE DE GUÉRIN AND NOW TRANSLATED FROM THE FRENCH BY GEORGE B. IVES.

I Was born in a cavern of these mountains. Like the river in yonder valley, whose first drops flow from some cliff that weeps in a deep grotto, the first moments of my life sped amidst the shadows of a secluded retreat, nor vexed its silence. As our mothers draw near their term, they retire to the caverns, and in the innermost recesses of the wildest of them all, where the darkness is most dense, they bring forth, uncomplaining, offspring as silent as themselves. Their strength-giving milk enables us to endure without weakness or dubious struggles the first difficulties of life; yet we leave our caverns later than you your cradles. The reason is that there is a tradition amongst us that the early days of life must be secluded and guarded, as days engrossed by the gods.

My growth ran almost its entire course in the darkness where I was born. The innermost depths of my home were so far within the bowels of the mountain, that I should not have known in which direction the opening lay, had it not been that the winds at times blew in and caused a sudden coolness and confusion. Sometimes, too, my mother returned, bringing with her the perfume of the valleys, or dripping wet from the streams to which she resorted. Now, these her home-comings, although they told me naught of the valleys or the streams, yet, being attended by emanations therefrom, disturbed my thoughts, and I wandered about, all agitated, amidst my darkness. 'What,' I would say to myself, 'are these places to which my mother goes and what power reigns there which summons her so frequently? To what influences is one there exposed,

ANNALS
OF THE
CITY OF KANSAS:
EMBRACING FULL DETAILS OF THE
TRADE AND COMMERCE
OF THE
Great Western Plains,
TOGETHER WITH
STATISTICS OF THE
AGRICULTURAL, MINERAL AND COMMERCIAL RESOURCES
OF THE COUNTRY
WEST, SOUTH AND SOUTH-WEST,
EMBRACING
WESTERN MISSOURI, KANSAS, THE INDIAN COUNTRY, AND NEW MEXICO.

BY C. C. SPALDING.

KANSAS CITY:
VAN HORN & ABEEL'S PRINTING HOUSE.
1858.

The last basic bottleneck in printing was eliminated by the perfection of typesetting machinery in 1886. By this time, machinery had been introduced into the bindery, although some operations have only recently been mechanized.

The separation of printer and publisher which had begun at the start of the 19th century was far advanced at its end. Where an association remained, it was generally a publisher who owned a printing plant rather than a printer who published books.

New distribution methods created the need for protective wrappers, which developed rapidly from plain paper to the modern full-color jacket. While books changed little in 400 years, jackets evolved entirely during the first quarter of the 20th century.

At the beginning of the second quarter, a distinction between printer and typographer/designer took form. By then, technical developments permitted a wide enough range of expression in book design to attract some full-time designers. The names of T. M. Cleland, W. A. Dwiggins, Merle Armitage, Ernst Reichl, John Begg, P. J. Conkwright, and others became known in the next decades. This was the period that saw book design emerge as a recognized department of publishing. Book design courses, the Fifty Books shows, clinics, and other activities of the American Institute of Graphic Arts (AIGA) grew in influence, and the publishing trade journal, *Publishers Weekly*, began a monthly department devoted to design and production.

World War II interrupted the progress of bookmaking, but one important development did come out of military needs: the technique of high-speed production of paperbacks—which paved the way for the postwar expansion of paperback publishing. The technology was ready when paperbacks began to be distributed through magazine outlets. This made possible very large printings, thus enabling greatly reduced costs and low retail prices. At first, these books were handled like magazines and, like the pulp magazines they soon drove off the stands, they tended toward Westerns and mysteries—with maximum pictorial appeal on the outside and relatively little attention to design inside. Gradually, the publishers and magazine distributors began to treat titles of more enduring interest as if they were books, and the better lines began to find their way into bookstores. An important breakthrough occurred when the *Anchor* books, a line of higher-priced paperback reprints of serious titles, demonstrated that the college market could absorb enough books of this kind to justify their publication. Similar lines followed, thereby creating a whole new segment of publishing. The design of these "quality", or *"trade"*, *paperbacks* got off to a good start and has been in the main excellent, although even their inside pages tend to be neglected.

By the 1950s, many publishers recognized the challenge posed by a generation accustomed to the dynamic graphics of advertis-

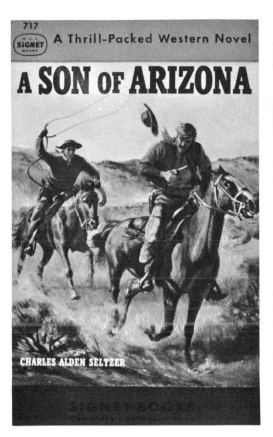

mass market paperback covers of the 1940s

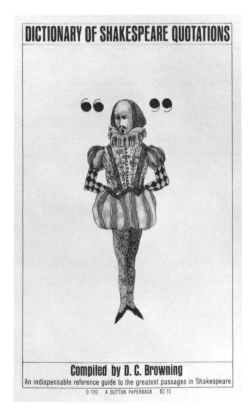

trade paperback covers of the 60s

ing, magazines, and television—and books showed definite signs of responding to the visual esthetics of the 20th century. The design of jackets and paperback covers led the way, chiefly because they are closer to advertising and are often the work of designers whose training and experience were in that field. (A critical survey of individual designers and their work is outside the scope of this book—see "Sources of information" in Part III for further reading.)

The most marked development was in textbooks and children's books, where rapidly expanding markets and keen competition drove publishers to heavy use of color and illustration. At first, the competition was mainly in the *amount* of graphic effects used, but gradually the quality of design became the selling point.

Meanwhile, technical advances in color printing encouraged an already growing interest in art and illustrated books, with many publishers using foreign as well as American color-printing facilities (CH. 29).

At the beginning of the fourth quarter of this century, these trends had created a responsive audience for many books of graphic interest. A major new category of trade paperbacks—large format and extensively illustrated (sometimes with very little text)—were published and sold in large numbers in regular bookstores.

There is still considerable adherence to convention in American book design, but it is becoming weaker. The change is good where meaningless and impractical conventions are dropped, but the blessing is not unmixed. Too many young designers have cast themselves loose from conventional forms without having developed better alternatives. On the whole, however, it seems preferable to open the possibility of creative design than to remain locked within rigid and outworn rules.

2 | Function

Ideally, responsibility for the design and production of books is vested in one person who is well qualified in both aspects, and there are a few successful examples of such an arrangement in publishing houses. Generally, however, the functions are divided, and an imbalance results. Because of its economic role and seniority, the production department almost invariably has a dominant relationship to design. Planning tends to originate in the production department, and often the designer is brought in only after the main decisions are made. This arrangement does not usually bring the best results, although a great deal depends on the particular production manager.

Many publishers have added an "art director" to their staffs. This arrangement is effective where the art directors have some authority, but in some houses they are simply heads of the design department, with about the same relationship to the production manager as the designer had before.

The proper relationship of designer to production manager is comparable to that of architect to builder. The architect (designer) plans the practical and esthetic aspects of the structure and the builder (production manager) carries out the plans. However, no matter how good the builder, the result will not be successful unless the architect has a thorough mastery of the materials and techniques of construction. From this it is apparent that the designer must be expert in production or become merely a "layout artist".

Production people should, of course, learn as much as they can about design, but their role is primarily purchasing and coordination of schedules.

In practice, some of the principal decisions affecting design and production are made by editors. This is inevitable and proper because the editor represents the interests of publisher and author. The weakness of this arrangement, unfortunately, is that the editor

Relationships
DESIGN TO PRODUCTION

DESIGN AND PRODUCTION
TO EDITORIAL

often does not know production or understand design well enough to make the best decisions.

Publishing books is a complex and deeply interrelated operation, in which specialization can easily be carried too far. All members of the staff must know their jobs extremely well, but each should have a working knowledge of all the other operations. The editor functions somewhat like the director of a play, supervising and coordinating the various elements. But, where the theatrical director is expected to be qualified to supervise acting, staging, scenery, costumes, lighting, and music, few editors are sufficiently educated or experienced in the making of books. This is due in great part to the lack of a publishing school in America—a deficiency which, it is hoped, this book will help overcome (see Part II). An encouraging development is the increase in publishing courses noted at the end of CH. 3.

BOOKMAKING TO SALES The bookmaker has 2 basic tasks:

(a) to facilitate communication between author and reader, and
(b) to make the book a successful commercial product.

This book will deal directly with both problems, but for a proper understanding of their background, it is necessary to know something of the way books are sold and distributed and the economics of publishing.

There are various kinds of publishing—direct mail, textbook, technical, medical, law, music, paperback, etc.—and each kind has its own economics, with unique problems requiring special considerations of design and production. As it is obviously impossible to explain every kind of operation here, this discussion will deal only with *tradebooks* [books published primarily for sale through bookstores and circulation by public libraries]. The particular problems of other kinds will be taken up in other chapters.

Publishers often have cultural or personal objectives when they accept a book for publication, but the object of publishing as a business is to sell books. However, it is only in the profit motive that book publishing resembles any other business. It is much more informal, complicated, and hazardous than most.

Toothpaste manufacturers, for example, hire people to create a few products to their desire (after considerable market research), standardize their manufacture, and turn them out in large quantities year after year. They can advertise and promote their products as much as they like, knowing that their campaign will take effect sooner or later. They can concentrate their money and effort on a single campaign that may be good for years. Their products are sold in stores accessible to virtually everyone and their production can be geared to their sales—or at least to an estimate of sales based on thorough research. Most important, a satisfied customer is likely to *continue* buying the same product more or less indefinitely.

The publisher, on the other hand, must sell perhaps a hundred entirely different products-in one year, each one a unique creation by an independent individual who has determined personally what the product shall be. There is no way of knowing how many buyers there will be, so (except in rare cases) the product must be made in an uneconomically small quantity. The amount of money and effort spent on promoting the book will be disproportionately high if there is only one printing (as usually there is), and the campaign must be immediately effective, because most books are highly perishable, like vegetables, and become almost worthless if not sold quickly. To sell the books, the publishing company has only a few thousand outlets in the cities, of which only a few hundred are really bookstores. Even when it sells its products to the stores it is not necessarily ahead, because the stores can return the books if they don't sell them. Worst of all, the sale of a book to a reader doesn't mean that the same person will remain a customer of the publisher's, except perhaps for another similar book by the same author—which may not come in for years, if at all. To survive, the publisher must have other kinds of outlets—libraries, book clubs, etc.—each of which requires special handling and attention.

The sales and distribution problems of publishing are discouraging enough, but the economics are positively forbidding. Of the book's list (retail) price, about 47% is the average (combined) wholesaler's and retailer's discount, and at least 10% is the author's royalty—with the figure usually going to 12% or 15% as sales increase. Of the 43% retained by the publisher, about 20% goes for making the book, about 5% might go into advertising, and 2% is for storing and shipping. A share of the cost of salaries, rent, electric bills, and other items of overhead must be carried by each title—and 16% of the retail price is a realistic figure. With a little arithmetic you will see that at least 100% of the book's price is accounted for and no profit has been mentioned. The picture is *this* bright only because we are assuming that all the books printed will be sold—which is rarely the case. Indeed, there are numerous copies—sometimes hundreds—given away for review and promotion, and some of the expenditures mentioned above are incurred even on books not sold.

From this it can be seen that cost must be held down, and also that one of the most important decisions the publishing company makes is the size of the first printing. If it makes too few books, the unit price will be too high; if it makes too many, to keep the unit cost down, it will be left with many unsold books.

There are 2 factors which may lighten this otherwise black picture of publishing as a business: (a) a sellout of the first printing with the necessity of a second (and more) to meet the demand and

(b) a sale of *subsidiary rights* to the book—reprint rights, translation rights, foreign rights, serial rights, book club distribution rights, television, radio, dramatic, and movie rights, etc. Second printings usually mean profits since some of the initial costs of production are not repeated. Also, in practice, publishers seldom spend the whole advertising budget.

What then is the relationship of book design to the book's sale? It is to be found in the complex of elements affecting the public's reaction to a particular title. This reaction is not only unpredictable, it is usually impossible to rationalize even after it is known.

There are at least a dozen factors that influence sales of a book:

(a) Intrinsic quality or interest
(b) Reputation of author
(c) Reviews
(d) Advertising
(e) Promotion and publicity
(f) Current events
(g) Efficiency of distribution
(h) Price
(i) Jacket design
(j) Local interest
(k) Competition
(l) Availability
(m) Size and weight

A commercial success may be attributed almost entirely to one of these elements, or it may be due to 2 or more of them. Except in the most dramatic cases—such as the extraordinary content appeal that made *Jonathan Livingston Seagull* a best seller despite an almost total lack of initial promotion, favorable review, or author fame; the direct impact that General Motors' well-publicized harassment of Ralph Nader had on the sale of his *Unsafe at Any Speed*; or the obvious effects of the names of popular authors, such as Michener or Mailer, on a new title—the reasons for any book's sale are almost impossible to identify.

The first factor named—intrinsic quality or interest—includes those qualities of the book itself that generate enthusiasm in the reader or browser. This is believed by many to be the most influential single factor because it results in the kind of "word-of-mouth" advertising that begins with "You *must* read . . ." and ends with sales. It is within this area that the book's design operates as a cause of sales.

The importance of the design can vary from *vital*, in the case of the "coffee table" books which are meant to sell as impressive gifts, to *insignificant*, in the case of books which have an appeal of a special, and nonvisual, kind (lurid novels, for example). Between these extremes lies a vast and uncharted area in which design has an unmeasurable but definite effect on sales.

The general public's reaction to book design is, in most cases, subconscious. Except where the visual aspect is spectacular, the nonprofessional browser is aware of only a general sense of pleasure or satisfaction in the presence of a well-designed book and a vague feeling of irritation when confronted by a badly designed one.

While it is impossible to isolate the reaction to design from the other elements of a book's appeal, it is probably safe to say that good design is in many cases influential and, where a buyer is undecided, this influence, small as it may be, can tip the balance in favor of a purchase. This is particularly true in the case of expensive gift books and nonfiction that competes with similar titles. It is also effective in the sale of schoolbooks, where competition among several titles of almost identical content is common.

There are 2 ways in which good book design psychologically aids sales: (a) it gives the buyer an impression that the book is highly regarded by the publisher and (b) it tends to make the book look more expensive than it is.

The importance of design in book publishing has much increased in the past decades as movies, magazines, and television have heightened the competition for public attention, sharpened the public's appetite for visual excitement, and conditioned its taste. During this period, incidentally, it has become apparent that the public tends to *follow* leadership in matters of taste rather than insist on its own preferences. The soundest policy then—both esthetic and practical—is to do what seems *best*, without trying to guess what the public will like.

The truth is that many books are created by editors, production managers, designers, and sales managers, each of whom probably knows little of the work of the others.

In the early days of book publishing this problem never arose. The publisher was editor, printer, and designer. Today, the publisher functions more like the producer of a play, hiring the principal members of the staff and making the major policy decisions. However, publishers are usually not equipped (by time, talent, or training) to direct the work of staff specialists. Most of the directing functions of management have been shifted to editors.

Publishers are coming to regard book designers as industrial designers who can be of help in creating salable products, and they regard production managers as experts who can help them operate economically and profitably. This is a far cry from the time when the "manufacturing man" was little more than a clerk who sent manuscripts to the printer, and the designer was a luxury to be used only for fancy editions.

This new attitude towards professional staff has had positive effects on morale and performance. However, the emphasis on efficiency and short-term goals brought to publishing by the business managers who increasingly dominate many large and conglomerate-owned companies also imposes on publishing professionals unaccustomed disciplines and financial criteria. These sometimes adversely affect decisions that would otherwise have been guided by the entrepreneurial judgment and instinct that are the essence of good publishing.

Schools of design

There is a continuing controversy over the relationship of design to the book. There are 2 distinct points of view:

(a) Book design is concerned only with making an economical, tasteful choice and disposition of the material and visual ingredients of the book.

(b) Book design is a problem in communications, of which the above is only a part.

The proponents of (a) contend that designers should not interpret the content of the book. They should keep their work as neutral as possible, so that it will not "interfere" between author and reader. The other school (to which this author, frankly, belongs) feels that such neutrality, even if it were desirable, is impossible. A book inevitably has graphic and tactile characteristics, and these should be organized to the advantage of author and reader. It is foolish to ignore the reader's senses when the thoughts of the writer are being transmitted through a physical book which can and does affect these senses.

The full powers of visual design are as properly brought to bear in a book as they are in a play or a building. It is true that the essential qualities of a play or the shelter of a building can be enjoyed without sight, but they are certainly better appreciated when seen, *unless* they are badly designed.

Here lies the crucial point. The books of the "neutral" school are often poorly done but they are rarely offensive. On the other hand, a clumsy or tasteless attempt to use the full range of graphic effects in a book can be monstrous. This is not an insignificant point, but more important is the fact that a book produced by a skillful and sensitive designer can rise far above a work that aspires only to be neutral.

3 | Requirements

"Talent" refers to innate capacities rather than acquired skills. The talent required by a production worker is primarily a sense of organization and secondly a superior ability to learn and retain facts. The successful production manager is one who knows the vast array of technical data, material specifications, prices, sources, processes, and equipment that go into the manufacture of books and can organize this knowledge in a smooth and efficient operation. A third talent needed is a knack for getting cooperation from a variety of people. As coordinator, the production manager must extract copy from editors, specifications from designers, materials and production from suppliers—always in competition with numerous conflicting demands.

Patience and calmness under pressure may not properly be called talents, but whatever they are, the production worker needs them.

Failure in production is revealed by late schedules, broken budgets, and faulty manufacture, but a poorly designed book goes unnoticed in the great flood of bad book design. This doesn't mean that it is easier to design books than to produce them, it is simply easier to get away with incompetence.

Fifty years ago the limited possibilities of book design made few demands on the designer. Today, particularly in textbooks and increasingly in tradebooks, the graphic and technical resources available require the highest level of competence in designers. They must (a) be definitely talented in the disposition of form, space, color, and texture, (b) be especially perceptive and analytical, and (c) have some natural ability to assimilate technical knowledge.

In the fullest sense, the designer is a partner (albeit a minor one) of the author and must be capable of analyzing and interpreting the author's intentions. This is most apparent in the creation of

Talent
PRODUCTION

DESIGN

textbooks and other books of exposition in which the graphic part of the presentation is vital, if not equal to the verbal part. This relationship is not as well understood in connection with other books, but it is no less valid.

A talent for graphic representation (and mastery of graphic techniques) is not absolutely necessary because the book designer, like the architect, specifies work that others carry out, but it helps to be able to draw well.

One can design books without even a talent in visual art, but the possibilities are definitely limited. If book designers need not be craftsmen, they should be artists. Book design without art is like building without architecture. However, don't give up if you have never thought of yourself as an "artist". Talent exists in many persons, unknown to themselves or to others.

Background & training

The *ideal* background for a production manager is to have worked for at least some time in shops doing: hot and cold composition, color separation, letterpress, lithographic, and gravure printing, and paper manufacturing. It would help also to have had a stint in an art studio as well as in the sales, editorial, shipping, promotion, and accounting departments of a publishing company. College courses in engineering, math, physics, chemistry, and statistics would come in handy.

It isn't *necessary* to have this work experience and education to run a production department successfully, but the equivalent of a large part of it is very desirable. Most of it can be picked up on the job by reading books and trade publications, taking courses, visiting plants, and asking questions. A good production manager aims to know almost as much about the work of the suppliers as they know themselves.

The perfect background for a designer would include all of the above, plus a liberal arts education heavy on English and literature, a couple of years at a good art school, and at least a year's apprenticeship to a first-class designer. An extremely valuable experience for *anyone* in publishing is selling in a bookstore. This can provide insights not obtainable any other way.

A 4-year college program geared to prepare for either production or design work might begin with 2 years of liberal arts, with English as the major subject and the fundamentals of graphic arts and publishing as minors. The second half might concentrate on technical theory and practice, business administration, and design. During the last year, production students would stress administration and science, while the design students would emphasize design and literature. Such a curriculum, larded with field trips to plants and summer work in publishing houses, could radically improve the quality of American publishing.

A number of schools offer courses along these lines. At this time, intensive graduate-level summer courses in book publishing are offered at Harvard-Radcliffe Summer School, University of Denver, New York University, Northeastern University, George Washington University, Simmons College, and other institutions. Courses or workshops in design, production, editing, selling, and other functions of publishing are also given at Rochester Institute of Technology, Carnegie Institute of Technology, Printing Industries of Metropolitan New York, U.S. Department of Agriculture Graduate School, Graphic Arts Association of the Delaware Valley, Hofstra College, Hunter College, New School for Social Research, Parsons School of Design, School of Visual Arts, University of Chicago, and many state universities. Library schools present courses in the history of the book and the structure of publishing. Comprehensive seminars are held at Rice University, Stanford University, and other locations. In addition, workshop programs are provided by the American Institute of Graphic Arts, Bookbuilders of Boston, Bookbuilders West, Women's National Book Association chapters, and other local book-industry groups.

The Association of American Publishers, One Park Avenue, New York, N.Y. 10017, maintains a current list of book-industry-related courses in the United States. Information about many courses is available in the *Literary Market Place*, an annual directory of publishing (Part III), and *Publishers Weekly*.

4 | Opportunities

Kinds of jobs The nature of each kind of job varies according to the size and organization of the company. In the smaller houses, usually one person does all of the production work and directs, or actually does, the design. In the very smallest operations, the proprietor may handle these functions, although this is possible only when the list is small (a dozen books or fewer per year), and the service departments of other publishers or of manufacturers and other suppliers are used.

In medium-sized houses (30 to 100 titles per year) there is usually a production manager and from 1 to 3 assistants. In such situations, the manager or one of the assistants may do most of the design—giving out only the complicated and "special" books to freelance designers. Some employ a full-time designer.

In the larger companies (100 to 150 titles) the production department may consist of a half dozen persons, or more, and 1 or 2 designers. The largest houses (150 titles and up), of which there are dozens, may employ up to 50 people in design and production. In some, there is a separate design department under an art director or chief designer; in others, the designers work within the production department. There is often considerable specialization in the large production departments.

Besides the size of the company, the nature of its operation is significant. Textbook and reference book publishers require more help in their art departments than tradebook publishers of comparable size. The same is true of children's book publishers, although most books for small children are created by author, illustrator, and editor, without the use of a designer. In mass-appeal paperback houses, design is emphasized less than direction of the cover art, which is handled by editors—except in large houses where art directors are employed.

The design of jackets is usually given to freelancers in the smaller and medium-sized companies—unless the production manager is also a designer. In the largest houses, many of the jackets are designed by the staff.

Another source of jobs is the book manufacturer who employs people not only to handle the production of his various departments, but to coordinate production problems of the publishers with those of the plant. This work is excellent preparation for a good production job in publishing. Some of the larger manufacturers provide design services as well.

Finally, there is a handful of independent production and design services that employ assistants.

Futures

Evaluating the ultimate rewards of each kind of job is a highly personal matter. From the standpoint of money, the maximum can be obtained by working through smaller production jobs to becoming head of production in a giant company. In large firms, such jobs may pay, roughly, from $19,000 to $40,000 a year, averaging in the low 20s, and may include a vice-presidency with stock options and other financial benefits.

The production manager in a small company may have a salary in the $21,000 area, but will usually have, also, the satisfaction of intimate participation in company affairs. How satisfying such an arrangement will be depends to a large extent on the personalities involved. There is little difference in pace and pressure whether 30 or 300 books are produced each year. Much more depends on the efficiency of the operation than on its size.

A production assistant with experience may start at about $200 a week and work up to nearly twice that much. The scale for a production trainee—who will keep records, file, and so on, while learning—will start at a much lower point than an assistant.

For the designer, the ultimate—both financially and in terms of satisfaction—is to become design/production head of a big firm. The same position in a medium-sized company brings less money, but usually more creative opportunity. For the art director of a small company, the salary may range from $13,000 to $20,000. It may run up to $30,000 in a large firm. The satisfaction will depend on the compatibility of the management. For a head of both design and production the pay will probably be about the same as for a production manager. A senior designer's salary may be in the $10,000 to $14,000 range in small companies and up to $22,000 in larger ones. Staff artists may be paid $8,000 to $12,000 in small companies and up to $20,000 or so in large firms.

How to get a job

Book publishing being what it is, a large number of its positions are filled in accidental ways. (In fact, a 1977 Association of American Publishers report on education for book publishing is entitled "The Accidental Profession".) Although there are now several intensive summer teaching programs (CH. 3), there is no central school from which candidates can be drawn and there is no organized pool of applicants. People drift into jobs by knowing someone or being in the right place at the right time. Paradoxically, book publishing is one of the most desired (glamorous) fields, but many of its jobs go to those willing to take comparatively low pay.

To get a first job in production, unless you have worked in a suppliers' shop or know someone who is willing to take you in spite of your lack of experience (either to save money or to train you), you will probably have to start in some relatively subordinate position in the company. As a stenographer, wrapper, clerk, or even messenger, you have a better chance than someone outside. In a small firm it doesn't matter where you work, but in a large one, try to get into the production department, because it is sometimes harder to move from one department to another than to get in at all. If you show yourself intelligent, diligent, and interested, there is a good chance that you will be given a production job in time.

If you live outside the main publishing areas, look around for a nearby university press before rushing to the city. The university presses have few jobs and may not pay the most, but they give good experience and are certainly no harder to crack than any other. The same is true of local printers, compositors, etc. Once you have even a little experience it is much easier to get a job. You should also check the listings of publishers in *Literary Market Place* for companies in your area. Increasingly, specialized and small general publishers are starting business in the smaller cities and towns of America.

Experience with a printer or manufacturer is, rightly, highly regarded as preparation for a production job in a publishing company. A period spent working in the shops and plants where books are made will pay big dividends in better jobs and higher pay later.

The first design job is in some ways easier and in some ways more difficult to get. You can show tangible evidence of your ability, but you are then trying for one of relatively few positions. Also, it is almost essential that you have a considerable amount of knowledge if you are to be given any responsibility.

It is not a bad idea to start by working at any job you can get in a production or design department, with the hope that you can move over into design work later (as suggested for getting into production). Whether you do this or attack the job directly, the best thing you can do is to assemble a portfolio of layouts and sketches that show (a) that you know what you are doing and (b) that you have real talent. Leave out the lovely but unprofessional collages and figure sketches from art school and, after studying this book, make a series of sketches *with specifications* of all the parts of at least one book, and preferably 3 or 4. Be realistic in terms of commercial production, but let your imagination have a bit of play, too. A truly impressive portfolio of this kind will be almost as effective as a bagful of printed books. If you have previously done any graphic work that could conceivably be related to practical book work—such as illustration in woodcut, pen and ink, etc., or your own printing—put in some of this, provided that it shows ability of specific value.

Buy or borrow a copy of *Literary Market Place* and look up the names and addresses of the publishers. It is much more likely that you will get started in a large house than a small one, so try these first. The listings show the number of books published by each company. Start with those over 100. It may do you some good to get in to see the top person, but it really isn't necessary. If the firm is looking for someone, they are just as anxious to find you as you are to find them. In the smaller companies, it is a good idea to look for the name of the production managers or art directors in the *LMP* listing (get the latest edition) and call or write to them for appointments.

From this point on, the rules are the same as for getting any other job. Be prompt, neat, reserved, but pleasant—and don't stay too long.

There are specialized employment agencies in this field, but they are more likely to help you find your second job than your first.

Freelancing

Freedom, like peace, is wonderful. The idea of coming and going as you please with no grouchy old boss to be nice to is very attractive. But, before you decide to freelance, remember that a lot of others like freedom just as much as you do—and the grouchy old boss comes through with a paycheck *every* week.

A fair amount of freelance design work, particularly in jackets, is done by relatively inexperienced people, but there are a great many such people competing and, as book publishing gets more professional, this kind of work diminishes. Generally, the smaller, routine jobs are done in the house, while the more demanding and special ones go outside. These go, of course, to the designers of experience and reputation.

In freelance production work, there is really no room for any but the expert. The large publishers, if they give out production work at all, will do so only for special books that require more attention than they can give them or involve a special circumstance. In either case they want an experienced hand. The small publishers, who have production work done on a freelance basis to avoid hiring someone on a salary, do not feel safe unless they deal with a competent and reputable person.

Generally, it is best to have a number of years of experience before freelancing. For those who want to try this method, the following scale of prices will be useful.

■ *Book design*—The range is from about $250 for an unillustrated book of uncomplicated narrative text, to thousands of dollars for a large picture-and-text book. The prices paid vary considerably according to the publisher and the standing of the designer.

■ *Jacket and paperback cover design*—Prices run from about $300 to $1000, again depending on the publisher and designer involved.

■ *Production work*—This is done on either a brokerage basis—in which case the publisher pays a certain amount over the cost of manufacture (about 10 to 20%) for the service—or on a fee basis—whereby a flat sum is paid for the service, either over a period of time or for a specific number of books. Either way, the amount paid by the publishers should equal a proportionate share of what their production departments cost, or would cost if they had one.

B

BASIC KNOWLEDGE

5 | Composition

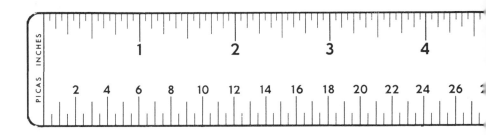

Not so long ago, *"composition"* could have been defined as the assembly of individual metal-type characters into words, lines, and pages. Today, if we are to encompass the great variety of composition methods, we might say that composition is *the transformation of manuscript (or typescript) into a form suitable for printing or for making printing plates*. This would cover the 4 present methods:

    (a) setting metal type by hand,
    (b) setting metal type by machine,
    (c) typewriter composition, and
    (d) photographic composition.

Machine composition—metal type, typewriter, and photo—is now being produced with the application of various electronic aids: punched and magnetic tapes, computers, etc. While these dramatically affect speed and efficiency, the typesetting operation and the product remain the same, so we still have 4 basic methods. One method of photographic composition, *scanning*, differs radically from all the others, but it is still photographic (see "Machine composition—photographic").

In this chapter, each operation will be explained and the various machines will be discussed. However, the standards of measurement of typography are the same for all methods and must be learned first. (These standards are necessarily discussed in terms of the metal-type processes where they originated, although photographic typesetting standards sometimes differ in minor respects.)

Printers measure type and spaces by *points*. One point is .01384", and 72 pts. equal almost exactly 1" (2.54 cm). For an exception, see CH. 16.*

    One *pica* is equal to 12 pts., so there are approximately 6 picas to

Measurement & terminology

MEASUREMENT

---

* Many European countries use the *Didot* point, which is slightly larger than the U.S. point. For example, 30 pt. U.S. is the equivalent of 28 pt. Didot. See equivalent table in Part III.

3 em quad

2 em quad

1 em quad

2 em space

3 em space

4 em space

5 em space

type size

A delight

one inch. Picas and half-picas are used to measure the width and depth of pages or columns, and other distances of one pica or more. Dimensions are given in multiples of picas plus a half-pica when applicable, or plus the appropriate number of points. For example: one picas, 24½ picas, 17 picas 4 pts. Dimensions up to about 6 picas are sometimes expressed in points, i.e. 14 pts., 28 pts., 42 pts., 53 pts., etc.

Note that paper, illustration, and margin measurements are given in inches or centimeters. In general, measurements *within* the type page are given in points and picas, those outside in inches or centimeters.

Another unit of type measurement is the *em*, which is the square of the type size; i.e. the em of a 10 pt. type is 10 pts., of a 12 pt. type 12 pts., etc. (Among the many photographic typesetting systems now in use there are often exceptions to this rule, e.g. the em might be slightly more or less than the type size, depending on the design of the particular typeface.) An *en* is theoretically half an em; in some photosetting systems it is $^5/_9$ of an em. Ems and ens are used as units of horizontal measurement, such as indentions, sentence-, word-, and letter-spacing, and dashes. In writing, the em may be expressed as M or ▢. The en is either N or Ⓝ. In speech, printers call an en a "nut" to avoid confusing it with the similar sounding em.

Horizontal spacing is further divided into multiples and fractions of the em. The multiples are called *quads*. In *Monotype* and in hand-set type there are, in addition to em quads and en quads, 2-em and 3-em quads. The fractions are called *spaces*. One fifth of an em is called a 5-em space, one fourth a 4-em, and one third a 3-em. There is also a *hair space*, which is a strip of copper about ½ pt. thick. In *Linotype* the only spaces available on the keyboard are the em, the en, and a 4-em space called a *thin space*. (This sometimes causes confusion, as the hair space is sometimes referred to as a "thin" space.) There are also ¼, ½, and 1 pt. spaces, but they must be inserted by hand. Spacing with *spacebands* on the Linotype machine will be explained later in this chapter.

The *type size* refers to the distance from top to bottom that includes the highest and the lowest points in an alphabet. For example, in a 10 pt. type there will be a distance of 10 pts. from the top of, say, the "f" to the bottom of the "y". In another 10 pt. face the highest point may be the top of the capitals or the lowest may be the bottom of the "g". In any case, the size refers to the overall measurement. (In large sizes, the face of the type is sometimes a little less than the nominal type size. For example, a 36 pt. type may measure only 32 or 33 pts., although the *body* [see below] is 36. In small sizes there is occasionally a minute variation.)

Note that the apparent size of the characters may vary considerably among faces of the same type size. The height of the *lower-*

case letters exclusive of *ascenders* or *descenders* is called the *x height*. While this is not used as a unit of measurement itself, it is often referred to in the specification of distances. The x height of two 10 pt. typefaces may be quite different.

Alphabet length is the measurement in points of a complete lower-case alphabet in any type face and size. This in itself is not a particularly useful figure, except in comparing the relative width of various typefaces, but it is the basis for determining the average *characters per pica*—an important unit of measurement in typography (CHS.6,17).

In metal type, the *body size* refers to the metal on which the type is cast, both height and width. A 10 pt. type is usually cast on a 10 pt. body, but it may be cast on one 11 pts. or even 9 pts. high. Type may be cast on a larger body in order to provide extra space, or *leading* (pronounced *ledding*), between the lines. This page is set in 10 pt. type on a 13 pt. body. (The additional 3 pts. are usually at the bottom of the line; however, in some photosetting systems the leading is at the top.) This is expressed as 10 on 13, or $^{10}/_{13}$. If there is no extra lead added to the body, it would be *solid*—$^{10}/_{10}$.

The body width of a piece of individual metal type is usually the width of the character itself—i.e. a "w" is cast on a wider body than an "i", although some types are designed with a little wider body on some characters to provide more space between them and others.

Metal type is 3-dimensional, and the third dimension is the height of the type from the surface on which it stands to the printing surface. This distance is *type-high*, which is a uniform dimension in the United States (almost an inch, .918 to be exact) but differs slightly from this in many parts of the world. All *plates* (CH.9) which print with type must be secured to blocks of wood or metal so that their printing surfaces will be type-high. This does not apply, of course, when the type itself has been plated (CH.9).

Leading, the vertical spacing between lines, is measured in points. In metal type, spaces of 1, 2, and 3 pts. are made of strips called *leads*, although a lead is understood to be 2 pts. unless 1 or 3 is specified. Spaces of 6 and 12 pts. are made with *slugs*. All spacing between lines is made with combinations of these 5 sizes. For spaces of less than 1 pt., strips of cardboard are used. Leading, like horizontal spaces, is made less than type-high, so that it will not print. In some photosetting machines, leading can be adjusted to $^{1}/_{10}$ of a point.

The *measure* of a line is its width in picas. To give the measure to which a particular type and size is to be set (and include the leading also), one says, for example, 10 pt. Electra on 13 by 25 picas. This may be expressed as Electra $^{10}/_{13} \times 25$. *Full measure* means that the line is set the full width of the type page, without any indention.

10 pt. Granjon   10 pt. Electra
(enlarged)

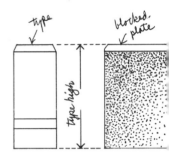

1 Point	
2 Point	
3 Point	
6 Point	
12 Point	

Spacing type

These lines of 24-point Caslon have been set with type-high spaces and leads to show how spacing is done. One lead (2 points thick) was inserted between each two lines.

The paragraphs are indented one em. Between words is the normal "3-em space" (3 to the em). Additional spaces were used as necessary to make the lines come out even.

Some 1½-em and 2-em "quads" were used at the ends of paragraphs. Here is some letter-spacing.

Most of the terms discussed here are defined in the Glossary-Index, but it is particularly helpful to have a knowledge of these in reading this chapter and the next.

The parts of type are described with various terms—some of which relate to the printed image and some only to the metal itself. The adjacent illustration shows and names the parts. There are numerous terms which refer to variations in the design of a particu-

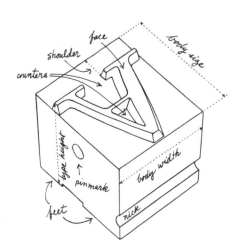

lar typeface. For example, *expanded, wide,* or *extended* means that the letters are made wide in proportion to their height. Exceptionally narrow type is called *condensed* or *elongated.*

A *font* is a complete assortment of types of one face and size including capitals, *small capitals,* lower-case letters, numbers, punctuation marks, etc. Each item in a font is called a *character,* i.e. a capital M, a comma, a 5, are each characters. Small capitals (*small caps* or *s.c.*) are x height, but are not made in every typeface. Numbers are called *figures,* and may be *lining,* i.e. the height of the capitals (approx.), or *old style,* which means that the 1, 2, and 0 are x height, the 3, 4, 5, 7, and 9 descend below the *baseline* [the bottom of the capitals] and the 6 and 8 extend above the *x line* [the top of x height]. Almost all fonts have an *italic* [slanted] variation, and most have a *bold,* which is a heavier weight of the typeface. Capitals are called *upper case* and the other (small) letters are called lower case. (These terms come from the arrangement of *cases* or trays of type in the old printing offices. The case with caps was placed above the case containing the small letters.) Words of small letters beginning with caps are referred to as *upper and lower case* (*ulc*).

EXPANDED

CONDENSED

ABCDEFGHIJKLMNOPQR
STUVWXYZ&

abcdefghijklmnopqrstuvwxyz

1234567890$ Qu ﬆ

. , : ; - ' ' ! ? [ ] fi fl ff ffi ffl Æ Œ

ABCDEFGHIJKLMNOPQRS
TUVWXYZ&

abcdefghijklmnopqrstuvwxyz

A B C D E G J K L M N P Q
R T U W Y &   *hkvwz*

1234567890$ *. , : ; - ' ! ? fi fl ff ffi ffl st*

Font proofs of 24 pt. Caslon 337 and Caslon 337 italic. Note the swash [decorative] characters in the italic font.

A *kern* is a part of a character which extends beyond the body, of the type, overlapping another character. These occur most frequently in scriptlike typefaces. *Kerning* is fitting type to improve the spacing of standard characters that occur in an awkward sequence—such as a cap A following a cap F. Such kerning, or fitting, is usually accomplished by *notching* or *mortising* [cutting away a part of the type metal]. Kerning is easily accomplished in photocomposing systems.

Slugs, besides being 6 and 12 pt. spaces, are the lines of type cast on a single piece of metal, as in Linotype and *Intertype** machines, which are referred to as *slug-casting* machines (discussed later in this chapter).

A *matrix* (or *mat*) is a mold in which type is cast. Originally used to refer to the casting of individual pieces of type, the term has come to be used in connection with the Linotype slug-casting operation, and even with the photocomposition machines in which no type is cast at all. Today, the term refers to any model from which a type character is produced.

Rules are elements of typography such as straight or decorative lines, usually used as borders or separators. They may contain one unit of design or a repeated series of units. In metal type, a large number of straight line rules are available in thicknesses ranging from hairline to 72 pts., in any length up to 144 picas.

Ornaments are individual decorative or illustrative type elements. With a few exceptions, these are not part of type fonts, but are available separately.

---

* The Linotype and Intertype machines are virtually identical. When this kind of machine is referred to hereafter, only the term *Linotype* will be used.

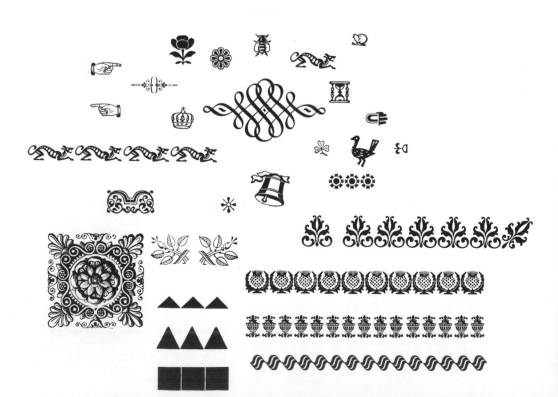

At left, *ornaments*; above, *rules*; below, *ornamental brackets*;
at right, *straight rules*.

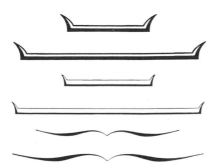

Hairline	
¼ Point	
½ Point	
¾ Point	
1 Point	
1½ Point	
2 Point	
3 Point	
4 Point	
6 Point	
8 Point	
10 Point	
12 Point	
18 Point	
24 Point	
30 Point	
36 Point	

Justified lines are those in which the word and sentence spacing are varied to achieve uniform measure (as these), as opposed to *unjustified* or *ragged* lines, which are set with uniform word spacing and uneven lengths (see page 46).

The *type page* is the area containing all of the printed elements on a page. The term is used mainly in reference to books whose text pages have a uniform overall width and depth. The type page includes the text itself, the *folio* [page number], and any heading, marginal notes, or other elements on the page.

Emage is the area of the text page expressed in terms of ems of the type size of the text, and is used as the basis for pricing much composition (CH. 12).

Sinkage is the distance down from the topmost element *on* the type page, not from the edge of the page itself.

type page

The Patient 95

bills for payment, in the form of serious disease of the arteries or of the liver, or there is a general breakdown.

187

Who serve the gods die young—Venus, Bacchus, and Vulcan send in no bills in the seventh decade.

188

Vulcan plays with respectability, he allows a wide margin—unless one is a college man —he sends in his bills late in life. Venus is heartless—she sends in her bills throughout all decades. Bacchus is a respecter of persons. North of the Tweed he may be disregarded—he sends no bills there.

189

The thermometer habit is a definite sequel of typhoid, especially in children. Throw away the thermometer, discharge the nurse, soothe the parents.

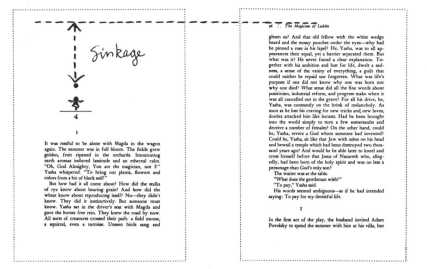

Proofs are printed examples of type and/or illustrations. *Reproduction proofs*, or *repros*, are carefully printed to achieve the best quality of image. They are photographed for making printing plates of various kinds (CH.8).

The "proof" of a photographic film is a print made by one of various processes (explained later in this chapter). These are called *blueprints, whiteprints, Ozalids, vandykes, Brunings*, etc.

The person who actually sets the type is a *compositor*, and the typesetting is done in a *composing room*. In computerized photocompostion the typesetting function is divided into four parts: *keyboarding, computer programming, editing, composing*. Sometimes each part is done by a separate machine, in other cases two or more are combined in one machine. So, too, there may be specialized operators for each part, or (less often) one person may do all the operations.

Type specification

The original material that is to be set (or otherwise converted for reproduction) is the *copy*. In order to have type set as it is wanted, specifications of certain kinds must be given for every line or character. More often than not, one or more of the necessary instructions is missing from the copy received by printers. These omissions result in delay and expense and should be avoided. *Layouts* [the sequence and numbering of the pages] should be used to supplement, not substitute for, specifications.

Here is the information required for *each* item:

(a) typeface,

(b) type size,

(c) whether caps, small caps, cap and lower case, lower case, caps and small caps,

(d) whether italic or *roman*,

(e) *letterspacing*, if any,

(f) vertical position (sinkage, or distance to next item above or below),

(g) leading (if more than one line),

(h) measure (if set on justified lines or to a particular width),

(i) horizontal position (flush left or right, indented, centered, etc.),

(j) word-spacing (tight, normal, or wide),

(k) weight (if the typeface is available in more than one weight, e.g. bold, semibold, etc.).

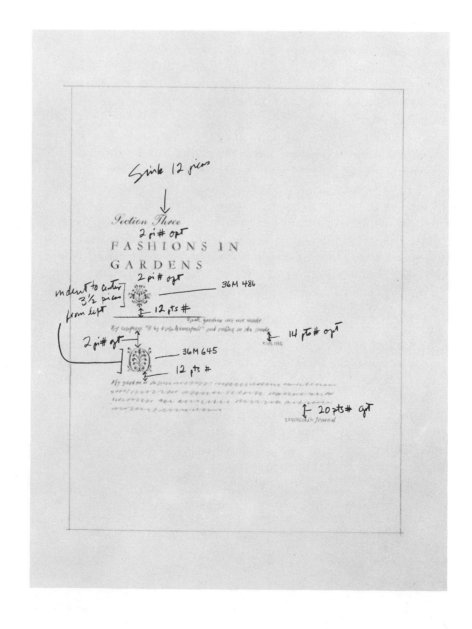

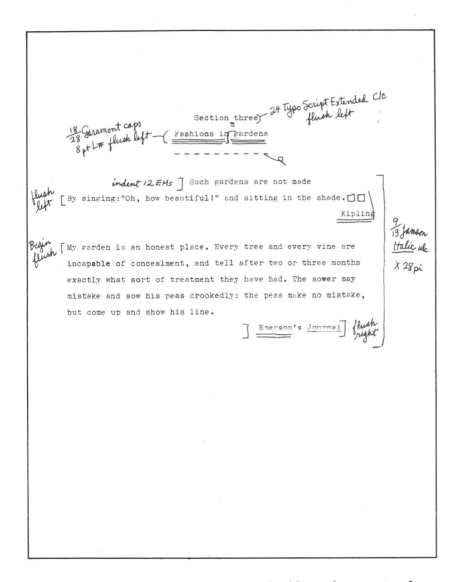

The specifications should be written legibly in the margin of copy or layout with a sharp pencil of a different color than used elsewhere.

Many advanced composition systems provide a wide variety of typographic modifications that did not exist when the original system of type specification was developed. It is now possible to order type altered in height or width in increments of fractions of a point, or even to have it curved into a circle or a spiral. No standard system for giving such instructions has been devised, so it is best to use the usual specifications as far as they apply, and then explain as clearly and simply as possible what is wanted beyond that.

When type is to be set by a coded tape- or disc-operated machine, the type specifications must be translated into the appropriate code language. It would be nice to be able to describe a code here and enable the reader to do this work. Unfortunately, the chance to establish a single coding system was lost in the competitive scramble, so there are now several codes, each of which is incompatible with some typesetting systems. In a composing room with computer-driven typesetters, the person who marks the manuscript with the codes is called a *formatter*.

When specifying leading, or the space between lines, in metal-type composition, it is necessary to indicate whether the space is to be *actual* or *optical*, i.e. whether you want the compositor to insert spacing material in the amount indicated or to insert only enough material to give the *appearance* of the space indicated. Remember that most metal type is made the full depth of the type size, including the ascenders and descenders. In a line of capitals, for example, there will be a non-printing area of metal underneath the line. Your specifications must take this into account. When you indicate spacing, it is taken to mean actual spacing material. If you want optical spacing, the word "optical" or the abbreviation "opt." (sometimes *visual* is used) should be written after the amount.

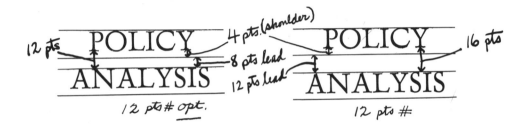

For photographic composition, text leading instructions may be given in the same way, although the space is added between lines photomechanically instead of with metal. Space between lines of *display type* (sizes usually larger than 18 pt., see CH.6) is assumed to be optical.

In letterspacing, where a single line is involved, it is usually better to have the line letterspaced to a specific width rather than to indicate the amount of spacing. This prevents disappointment. In specifying letterspace for a number of small-cap lines that will vary in length (subheads, etc.), give the amount of spacing wanted, preferably in units of standard machine spaces. For photosetting, it is important to find out if the compositor knows about letterspacing. Most do not, and it is necessary to explain carefully what is wanted. In some countries, letterspacing is used to fill out lines in justified setting (and to emphasize names). In the United States, this is considered bad typography and is used only in newspapers.

Chapter titles, subheads, etc. may be set in lower case with caps beginning either (a) all important words or (b) only the first word and proper nouns. The copy should be typed or marked with the capitalization desired (a vertical line through a cap makes it lower case; 3 lines under a letter makes it cap) and the specifications should indicate that this is to be followed. However, it is helpful to have a symbol for each style. Some use *Clc* for "cap all important words" and *ulc* for "cap first letter and proper nouns only". If you use these designations, be sure that your compositor understands what you mean by them. This usage is not widely known, but it would be very good to have it generally adopted, since there is no other for the purpose.

When giving type specifications for printed copy, it is useful to know the standard proofreaders' marking system (CH. 37).

Hand composition

Typesetting is no longer done by hand, letter by letter, as it was before the invention of typesetting machines, except to set display type and occasional small blocks of text. Nevertheless, a knowledge of hand composition is fundamental because much of the practice and terminology of machine composition is based on the original method. Even the most advanced composition systems do not entirely abandon some concepts of metal typesetting by hand.

Like most hand operations, hand composition is relatively expensive. The cost of setting a line of display type by hand may range from $1.50 to $5 or more, depending on the type face and size used, the length of line, the spacing requirements, who does the setting and for what purpose. The cost of hand setting is based on the time required, plus the cost of the type if it must be obtained for the job. While much more type can be set in the same time by machine, it should be remembered that setting up a machine takes time also, and it is often cheaper to set a few lines by hand.

HAND-SET TYPE

Hand composition may involve one of 2 kinds of type: (a) Foundry or (b) Monotype.
■ *Foundry type*—The type cast in relatively hard metal by *type founders* such as ATF, Bauer, Stempel, Stephenson-Blake, etc. and sold to compositors.
■ *Monotype*—Individual characters are cast in a softer metal on the Monotype machine, usually by the compositor.

Foundry type is sold by the fonts or by the pound. The fonts usually have a standard assortment of characters based on normal frequency of occurrence, i.e. there will be many of the common letters such as "e" or "a" but comparatively few such as "q" or "z". The type is stored in wooden trays called cases, each character having a compartment of its own, in a size and position also based on frequency of use.

There are several problems connected with foundry type. It is relatively expensive, particularly the more decorative faces. Being expensive, it is rarely used for printing except to *pull* [print] reproduction proofs. An alternative is to make duplicate plates (CH.9)

upper case

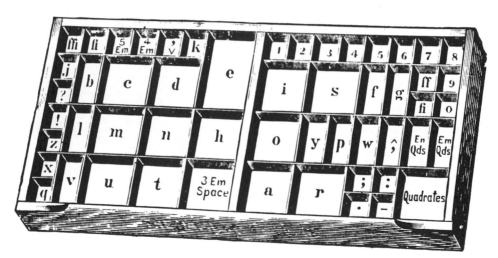

lower case

or else to incorporate the foundry type in a page which is then plated. Any of these operations involves considerable cost. Then, too, the type must be *distributed* [each character returned to its compartment] after use, an expensive hand operation.

Monotype is much less expensive to buy and it need not be stored in cases at all if the printer owns a casting machine. It is almost as cheap to melt down Monotype after one use and recast it as needed as it is to save and distribute it each time. Also, there is then less need for storage space and the type will always be fresh and sharp.

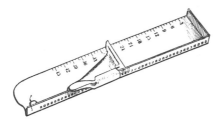

The compositor begins by holding in his left hand a small metal tray called a *stick*, into which he places the type taken from the case. The stick has an adjustable bracket to control the length of line. The type is arranged (upside down) in lines, with spacing inserted as desired. When the stick is full—it holds about 10 picas in depth—the type is transferred to a *galley*, which is an oblong metal tray with an edge about ½″ high. This process is repeated until the hand composition is finished. In the galley, the lines are assembled with other type and/or *cuts* (CH.8) belonging together, and the elements are arranged with proper sequence and spacing. This is done on a table or cabinet called a *bank*.

Machine composition— metal type

All mechanical methods of setting metal type are basically the same—the copy is typed out on a keyboard and another device casts the type in accordance with the *keyboarding*. The use of tape controls and computers has speeded the process, and in some cases the keyboard is separated from the caster to the extent that it may not even be in the same city; nevertheless, someone must tap a key for each character and the type must be cast. Indeed, metal-type composition is rapidly giving way to phototypesetting, but it is important to know the former to understand the latter.

There are 2 kinds of metal type set by machine: (a) individual type characters and spaces assembled into lines—the Monotype method—and (b) entire lines consisting of a single bar of metal

Type being assembled in galleys on the bank. Note storage of galleys at right.
Cabinet at left holds strips of wooden spacing material called furniture.

(slug) on the face of which the characters appear—the Linotype method. Slug composition is the fastest, and therefore the least expensive way of setting large amounts of metal type.

Monotype has certain advantages over slug composition—it is more practical for setting complicated material, it can be corrected by hand, its typefaces are generally better designed, and its metal is harder—but it is more expensive for straight, uncomplicated composition.

The Monotype caster is used also for setting display sizes or type for which the mats are hand assembled, and there is a special Linotype machine—the All-Purpose Linotype (APL)—which casts large sizes and extralong slugs. However, when one speaks of machine composition what is meant is the mechanical production of *text type* (CH.6).

LINOTYPE   The Linotype machine combines keyboard and caster. Their link is the *magazine*, a flat metal box containing the mats. Each mat (and there are several of each kind in the magazine) is in a separate *channel* or slot. When the operator taps a key, the appropriate channel is opened and the mat drops into position in a rack called a *rail*, on which the desired width of line (in picas) is set. The consecutive mats drop into place until the line is almost filled. At the end of each word, a key is struck to drop in a *spaceband* [a thin metal wedge]. When it becomes clear that another full word or syllable cannot fit on the line and leave enough space between the words and sentences, the operator stops and sends the row of mats to the casting element, where the spacebands are pushed up until the line is wedged out to full width (justified). Hot-type metal is then injected into the molds on the face of the mats, and the slug is formed. It is trimmed to size by knives and ejected onto a tray

At left, Linotype mats *(edge views of 1-letter mat and side view of 2-letter mat)*; below, *a line of mats assembled with spacebands between words.*

Diagram showing operation of Linotype machine.

1. Keyboard
2. Magazines
3. Mats dropping out of channels
4. Mats and spacebands on rail
5. Line at caster
6. Ejected slug
7. Line elevated after casting
8. Mats being lifted to distributor bar
9. Mats dropping back into magazine

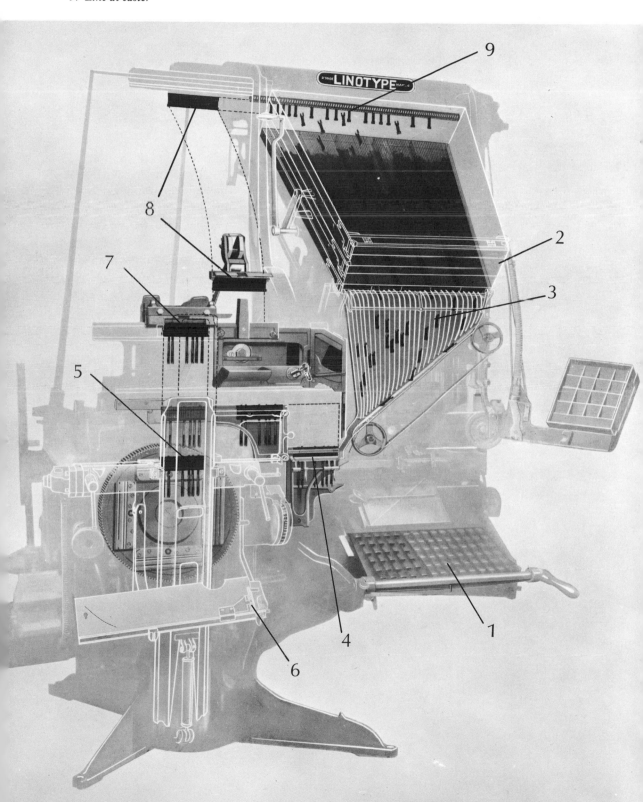

Newly ejected slug being examined by operator.

similar to a galley. While the slug is being cast, the mats are lifted onto a *distributor bar* which drops each one back into its own channel. This is accomplished by notching the edge of each mat in an individual pattern (as on a latch key) so that it can fit into its own channel and no other.

Each mat has 2 characters on it. They are usually the roman and italic form of the same letter, although some fonts have a boldface instead of the italic. To change from one character on the mat to another (say, roman to italic) the operator moves a lever which raises the mats to bring the lower characters into position to be cast. This is like the shift key on a typewriter, which enables typing the capital or other alternate character on the key.

The standard Linotype machine cannot set a slug longer than 30 picas. For longer slugs, up to 42 picas, a special machine must be used. One can set wider than 30 picas with the regular machine by setting each line on 2 slugs and *butting* them together.

Any requirement that slows an operator increases the cost of setting. It is more expensive to set a great many italic or small cap words interspersed with roman, due to the frequent shift from upper rail to lower and vice versa. Setting a large number of centered lines involves more time unless the lines are set with a *quader*, which automatically centers. Other causes of additional expense are the use of hand spacing, and the use of *pi mats* or *side sorts*. These contain special characters (such as brackets, accented letters, etc.) that do not run in the magazine, and must be picked out of a special box on the machine and inserted in the line by hand. Characters of different point size can be set on the same slug, but they will align at the top rather than at the bottom.

The Intertype machine operates on the same principle as the Linotype. Both Linotype and Intertype have models which can be operated by coded tapes produced on a separate keyboard machine.

M ᴹ

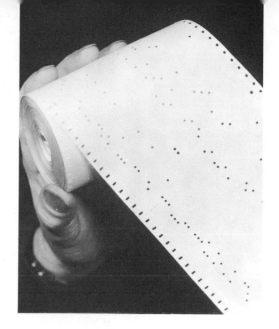

At left, Monotype mat case; at right, roll of coded tape.

In Monotype, the keyboard and the casting machine are entirely separate. Instead of the keyboard arranging mats directly, as in Linotype, it produces a perforated roll of paper (which is actually a coded tape) which is then "played back" in the casting machine. The mats, which are contained in a rectangular frame *(matrix-case)*, are moved into place according to the pattern on the roll and then are cast in individual characters. The completed lines are ejected onto a galley.

Justification is accomplished by a means somewhat similar to the Linotype spaceband system. The keyboard machine indicates when the line is nearly full and how much is needed to make it full. The operator presses a button and the word spaces are automatically divided evenly into the remaining space.

On the Monotype caster it is possible to set roman, italic, and bold on one line or to mix typefaces without the additional handling required for such work in Linotype. For this reason, some complicated books can be set at less cost by Monotype. Also, the Monotype machine will cast lines up to 60 picas in length without any difficulty.

Because the Monotype is operated by an encoded tape, this machine might be regarded as the true progenitor of modern coded-tape-driven typesetting systems. And, as the Monotype exceeded the Linotype's flexibility, so the photocomposing machines can outperform the Monotype.

The impulse behind development of typewriter composition was economy, but it was the simultaneous development of (photo-) *offset lithography* printing (also originally an economy measure, see CH.9) that provided a practical basis. The hot-metal typesetting machines produce type from which high-quality proofs (repro proofs) must be made in order to provide copy for a litho camera.

MONOTYPE

Machine composition—typewriter

The typewriter, with the same keyboarding, produces *camera copy* [type and/or artwork ready to be photographed for reproduction] directly. Not only is the repro proof step eliminated, but the cost of keyboarding is greatly reduced by the use of less-skilled operators than are needed to handle Linotype or Monotype machines. In addition, the machines cost very much less and take up much less space.

The absence of any step between the keyboard and the product is another advantage over photocomposing. The typewriter composition operator strikes a key that prints a character of reproduction quality by impressing metal type through a special ribbon, as in an ordinary typewriter. In photocomposing, the keying produces only a coded tape that must then activate a photounit which produces a type image. Composing typewriters differ from standard machines mainly in that they produce a higher quality impression, are capable of more variation in typeface and arrangement, and are capable of justification, with a special attachment. Some have computer memory capacity. This means that the copy keyboarded is stored by the computer and may be treated in many different ways according to the instructions fed into the computer, either immediately or later. Thus, if the copy is set 24 picas wide, and it is decided after proofing to change the width to 26 picas, the computer is reset for 26 picas and a new proof of the entire book is produced (in minutes) with the new width. Depending on the particular computer's capabilities, any other characteristic of the typography can be similarly modified.

When practical typewriter composition machines first appeared in the late 1940s, the term *cold type* was coined to distinguish this method from *hot-metal* typesetting. The term cold type (or *cold composition*) is still used, but it now applies generally to any method of composition that involves no casting of metal type.

Justification is the most difficult technical problem in typewriter setting. It is accomplished either by keyboarding the copy twice, once manually and once automatically, or by using a minicomputer that justifies lines while they are being set on the keyboard. Computer-equipped machines cost many times more than those requiring 2 keyboardings.

Typewriter composition is used today mainly for noncommercial publications (theses, scientific papers, government publications, etc.), for limited-interest books of university presses, for pamphlets, workbooks, and other ephemeral printing, and for reference books in which the composition may be done much more economically than by any other method.

The use of typewriter composition *must* be warranted by economy, as it is severely limited typographically. The typefaces available are generally inferior to those of more sophisticated systems. Although these types are not always limited to the single

delight to meet
ot ready to go on
B.O. says he can't
enclosing my
ler took it in place
h, Mr. Pixie, we
something fierce.

body-width of the standard machines, on most models there are no italics, small caps, or bold face available without a change of font.

It should be noted that "typewriter composition" refers only to the use of machines that have a standard keyboard and are not equipped to store coded data on tapes or discs. Machines with the latter features are used to produce input for tape- or disc-operated typesetting machines (see "Machine composition—metal type" and "Machine composition—photographic").

The most economical composing typewriter is probably the IBM Executive. It is, in fact, merely a superior office machine with a few special features which enable it to serve as a composing machine, provided its limitations are acceptable. Its economy derives from its low price (about $1000) relative to other machines and the ease and speed with which it can be operated with little special training. Because the operator is paid hardly more than a typist, the final typing of the manuscript and the composition may be economically combined—thus saving one complete keyboarding. This saving could offset the additional operation needed to justify.

The IBM Executive has more than 15 typefaces available, but the one chosen when the machine is purchased cannot be changed, except for a few special characters, and there is only one size. The faces are relatively well designed and have more proportional spacing than any other such machine.

A more advanced machine is IBM's Stand Alone Composer, which has 11 faces available on golf-ball size spheres that can be changed in seconds. Justification requires double keyboarding as on the Executive. A still more accomplished device is this company's Electronic Selectric Composer. Justification is automatic, as are several other functions, such as centering and column makeup. Its 11 faces come in each size from 6 through 12 pt. Much of the machine's cost (about 8 times that of the Executive) is in a computer memory that can store 8000 characters. This is very useful for work involving 3 or 4 pages, but is much too limited for book use.

IBM Selectric

useful for work involving 3 or 4 pages, but is much too limited for book use.

Another composing typewriter is the Varityper made by the Addressograph-Multigraph Company. The Varityper, although it offered several sizes of type, at first used the single-width body, whereby narrow and wide characters are designed to fit the same space, as in the standard typewriter. (This is considered a deficiency by typographers accustomed to conventional Roman type design. But if one regards the matter pragmatically, it is really much more useful to have all characters the same width, so the type should be designed to look good with that system. Instead, we have gone to a great deal of trouble to devise systems that will accommodate variable-width type design. This is turning design backward, creating a practical problem to fit an esthetic decision.) Later models of the Varityper use variable-width type, and have the double keyboarding justification feature. (Manufacture of the Varityper stopped in 1978.)

In the same vein, tremendous sums have been spent to achieve justification of lines on composing machines of all kinds, when there is really little value in justified composition. It is slightly more economical of space, and in some publishing situations this is important, but it is usually possible to accommodate the extra width (approximately 5%) needed for unjustified (ragged) lines— particularly since they are visually more open on the ragged side, and can be set wider without seeming more crowded. There is no cost advantage in setting justified lines.

From an esthetic standpoint, unjustified lines are preferable because word-spacing can be made uniform. Even such a conservative designer as Eric Gill advocated unjustified composition, and so set his own essay on Typography. Readability is improved by the reduction of word-breaking as well as by more even spacing. The only possible argument in favor of retaining the squared-up page* is that we are accustomed to it; but then, we are also accustomed to the unjustified lines of typescript and few, if any, editors complain of difficulty in reading typewritten pages. It is unfortunate that at the technological turning point in bookmaking we missed the opportunity to discard an unnecessary convention. And what a price we are paying to preserve it!

Machine composition—
photographic

There are advantages in phototypesetting that would have warranted its development in any case, but, as in typewriter composition, the basic impulse behind its rapid flowering was the growing use of offet lithography. Here the connection is closer yet. A photocomposing machine can not only produce a type image

---

* The First Edition of this book was set with justified lines (except this page) because it was designed for setting by Linotype, which favors justified lines. Although the Second Edition was set by a photocomposing machine, the design was retained because it has worked well for its purpose.

ready to photograph, it can deliver a *film* ready for use in making a *photomechanical plate* (CH.9).

Photocomposition can produce a sharper image than even the best reproduction proofs, it is more flexible and versatile than hot-metal composition, and it is capable of faster production, but its most significant economic value is in its elimination of the repro-proof *and camera* stages in making plates for litho and *gravure* printing (CH.9).

Photocomposition does have some drawbacks, particularly the expensive procedure for making corrections in film by *stripping* [cutting out the error and taping in its place the corrected piece of film], but there are now electronic *editing devices* (discussed later in this chapter) that can sometimes overcome this problem, and the advantages mentioned above have made photosetting so much more efficient than Linotype that it is now economically competitive. In fact, its advantage in both price and capability is increasing at a rate that is rapidly driving metal typesetting into obsolescence.

The most sophisticated high-speed composition equipment was designed for the newspaper industry, and its capabilities far exceed the needs of most book publishers. So, while the performance of some machines is dazzling, it is not necessarily economical to use them. A machine that sets a book in seconds instead of minutes (or even hours) may not be giving a publisher enough extra value to be worth its cost. As long as the keyboarding and proofreading of a book take days, it doesn't seem that the saving of minutes is very significant, particularly if greater cost is involved. The significance increases, of course, with the volume.

This is particularly relevant to the present, and growing, tendency toward the installation by publishers of in-house type composition equipment. As the cost of such devices comes down, publishers find it increasingly feasible to produce either part of, or their entire, composition output in their own offices. Since these devices can usually be operated by easily-trained office workers, the labor cost is lower than buying the services of more highly paid technicians and paying the overhead and profit of a composition house. Obviously, however, these advantages need to be balanced against the investment in equipment and the publisher's own overhead and ability to fully utilize the production of the machines. Here is where it is important to avoid expensive high-speed systems that cannot be kept busy. On the other hand, the benefits to the publisher of having complete possession and control over the composition materials can be considerable in some circumstances, and must be weighed in the decision.

A practical option is the use by the publisher of only a keyboard machine that delivers the "manuscript" to a composition house in the form of an *"idiot" tape* or *disc* [one that has the copy and some setting instructions encoded, but without justification commands.

This tape or disc is then fed into the compositor's computer, which adds justification and the other commands needed for typesetting. (The term *floppy disc* is often used to distinguish between the small, flexible discs used for such information storage and transmittal and the larger, rigid discs used for type storage in typesetting machines.) However, as the page format increases in complexity the savings from publisher-keying go down, since codes will probably have to be added by specialists at terminals in the composition house. In any case, it is significant that keyboarding accounts for only 8–10% of the composition cost.

THE MACHINES In contrast to the few metal composition machines, there are a very large number of devices involved in photocomposition. However, while there are dozens of pieces of equipment, they fall into 4 main categories: (1) *input devices* that record manuscript onto coded tapes or discs that enable the setting of type, (2) *editing devices* that enable (a) correction of the composition either before or after typesetting, and (b) some page *makeup* (see "Makeup"), (3) *computers* that enable (a) storage of information, including the copy itself and instructions for its editing and setting, (b) retrieval of this information for use and manipulation in various ways, (c) operation of other pieces of equipment, (4) *typesetting devices* that transform the information on tapes or discs into type composition on either paper or film—or even directly onto printing plates.

The equipment available includes separate "stand-alone" units of each of the 4 main kinds, which may be linked in various combinations, and devices that combine several or all of the 4 kinds in a single unit. In addition, there are various auxiliary units that perform some of the functions included in the larger machines. For example, there are *lineprinters* that produce a *printout* of a tape or disc for use in proofreading prior to composition, and there are computers that can be attached to almost any composing machine to give it capabilities that are not built in.

Because of the complexity of the systems and the many varieties of devices, it seems best to explain each *kind* of machine and name examples rather than to describe particular pieces of equipment, each of which may vary only a little from the others of its kind.

■ *Input devices*—These are usually keyboards that deliver to a computer or typesetting machine perforated paper tape, a magnetic tape, or a disc containing magnetic (*digitized*) codes for the copy, plus, in most cases, codes that give various typographic instructions (commands), including page makeup. Some keyboard machines produce only an idiot tape (non-counting keyboards); others have built-in computers that justify the lines (counting keyboards). *VDT* (Video Display Terminal) editing devices are also used to produce input (see below).

Another kind of input device is the *OCR* (Optical Character

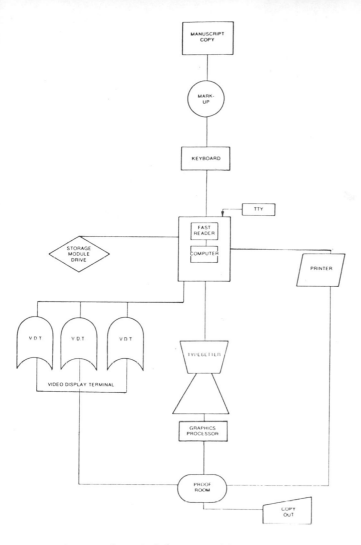

diagram of a typical photocomposition system

AlphaComp II direct entry system. The phototypesetter is activated directly by the keyboard, rather than by a tape or disc produced by the keyboard.

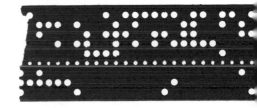

Mergenthaler Linotype MVP 2 input keyboard with VDT

Mergenthaler OCR 100 scanner

Recognition) *scanner* (ECRM, Mergenthaler, etc.). Just as bank machines read the specially designed account numbers on a check, this machine reads with electronic eyes the characters of a specially typed manuscript page, translates them into magnetic code, and delivers a tape or disc like those produced by keyboards. This seemingly ultimate typesetting method was expected to sweep the field, but it has not, so far, overcome its need for copy typed with characters that are not often available on authors' typewriters. If the manuscript is *not* so prepared, and it is not virtually error-free, it must be retyped, and then it might as well be keyboarded on a machine that will produce a coded tape or disc directly, as well as a readable printout. The problem is being eased by enabling the machines to read more typefaces. Some can handle up to 10—the U.S. government has one, which is still too expensive for commercial use, that can read about 100 different faces—and there are some in development that can read any face. But it may be that advances in other input methods (particularly the use of in-house input machines by publishers) will overtake the solutions. However, as in most such situations, the particular needs of each publisher will determine the choice of method, and OCR may be ideal for some—especially those whose copy is produced in-house, as is done in some reference and technical book companies.

There are also scanning machines that produce digitized magnetic codes of illustrations—both *line* and *halftone* (CH. 8)—that are transmitted electronically to photocomposing machines for inclusion with type, so that first proof may have both type and illustrations in position.

■ *Editing devices*—These are sometimes called VDT stations. They have a small—usually about 14″ (36 cm)—television screen on which the operator can read both the copy and the typographic or editorial instructions that are encoded on a tape or disc produced by an input device. If a correction or change is desired, the new copy or instructions are keyed and, with the push of a button, the original tape or disc is altered and the change becomes visible on the screen. This kind of device is also used for arranging material visually—breaking copy into columns, drawing rules, arranging equations, etc.—and for page makeup (see "Makeup"). The VDT screens show varying numbers of lines, ranging from only one up to 24. VDTs can sometimes be used as keyboard or input devices.

The lineprinter, too, may be considered an editing device. It is activated by a coded tape or disc, like a VDT, but instead of showing the copy on a screen, it prints out the copy on paper, i.e. it produces a proof of the data on the tape or disc. This proof is used by the compositor for an initial reading by in-house proofreaders. It shows the coded instructions, but the type is one of the standard faces used by the machine, and on most machines the lines are unjustified—although the hyphenation is indicated. Usually,

V.I.P. lineprinter

computer printout

```
01Y0070623.2S     PAGE NO. 002

023 023,01 therapy?<QL>

023 023,05 *1B>

024 024,00   MD, Illinois<Y>

024 024,02 *1A>

025 025,09 A

026 025,08    I am replying to your questions in the order in which

027 026,07    they are posed: (1) You should have another PPD test

028 027,06 done, and if a dose of 5 tuberculin units results in induration

029 028,05 greater than 10 mm, then a one-year course of isoniazid

030 029,04 would be advisable. (2) You should test all the monks; the

031 030,03 tine test is satisfactory for such a screening procedure.

032 031,02 Those who have a positive test reaction should have a chest

033 032,01 roentgenogram taken, and only those whose reactions are

034 033,00 markedly positive or those whose chest x-ray films show an

035 033,11 abnormality should be considered for isoniazid treatment.

036 034,10 (3) If you perform skin testing at regular intervals and
```

this printout is not shown to the publisher, but if the publisher, and author, are willing to read it, the tape can then be corrected and used for typesetting, so that the first type proof will be error-free (or as much so as any proofread material is). This has considerable value when using typesetting machines capable of not only page makeup but platemaking (see "Typesetting devices" below). The lineprinter printout thus replaces the galley proof—in effect, enabling a direct transition from manuscript to page proof.

■ *Computers*—The word "computer" tends to inspire paralyzing awe, but, in spite of their almost incredible capacities, these devices are quite simple in principle. The computer's strength is in numbers. By increasing its number of simple yes/no switches into the millions, it can handle problems of a complexity far beyond the capacity of the human brain, and perform in seconds what would require hours, days, or even years of a person's time. If data is fed into a computer it remains there until it is needed—which gives it the equivalent of memory. If the activity of one of its switches sets off the activity of another, it can set into motion not only its own functions but the operation of another device—according to extremely complex instructions with correspondingly complex results. Of course, the performance of a computer is no better than the instructions or commands (*program*) given it by the operator.

In composition technology, a single computer may be programmed to handle the entire process of typesetting (usually by converting a coded tape produced on input and editing devices into magnetic discs or tapes that drive typesetters)—including typographic arrangement, justification, some *copy editing*, and page makeup (APS-5, Videocomp, Fototronic, etc.). In other cases, there may be several smaller, so-called "minicomputers" programmed to do each part of the work in separate machines.

For example, a keyboard machine may have a minicomputer to justify the lines (AKI, Compographic, ATEX, etc.); the more sophisticated of these machines have computers that memorize the "proper" hyphenations for as many as 150,000 words. (There is actually no agreement among grammarians as to a correct system of word division. Even if a system were to be adopted, a large number of exceptions would have to be memorized. The effort and expense put into solving this problem is particularly appalling in view of the fact that there is no real value in justification, and without justification there would be little, if any, need for word division.) An editing device may have a minicomputer able to modify the spelling of certain words wherever they occur throughout a book (MGD, Tal-Star, DEC, etc.). A lineprinter may have a computer that searches out all footnotes and places them at the ends of pages made up according to a programmed page depth. In each case, the computer carries out—at unbelievable speeds—instructions given it and activates the parts of another device .

The economic advantage of high-speed computer operations is limited by the relatively slow speed of the keyboard operator. Keyboard machines can now produce much faster than any human could possibly operate them, so the only way of utilizing the capacity of computer-assisted typesetters is to have many keyboards feeding each one.

Very complex operations can be performed by computers with extreme rapidity and consequent savings—*provided* that programming the machine is not so involved that the time gained in operation is lost in preparation. Obviously, it is necessary to choose very carefully *which* jobs are to be put on the machine. When one programming can be applied to numerous titles or editions, or to a very large amount of copy (as in newspapers), the economy is substantial. But this situation is relatively rare in book publishing, with its multiplicity and diversity of products. Except in some textbook and reference book areas, the author is not part of the team but a lone individual producing a unique manuscript according to personal needs and inclinations. By and large, the publisher produces the book as written. This diversity, which gives book publishing its strength and charm, has defeated much standardization in book manufacturing and tends to limit efficient application of computers to the field.

Computers are expensive, so the time savings they produce must be major to warrant the investment (and maintenance). Yet, studies have shown that none of the numerous operations of book composition represents more than 10% of the cost. Thus, speeding up 2 or 3 operations may result in a large saving in those steps, but would mean only a very small reduction in the overall cost of composition—which is, in turn, only part of the total production price of a book. A major economy, therefore, must come from complete new systems, in which some steps are eliminated and the rest combined.

The present development of composition is concerned with the manipulation of code symbols within a computer so that all operations are programmed before any product is delivered—i.e. a single program is put into the machine that includes correcting, typesetting, and makeup instructions. All of these functions are coded by the computer on one tape or disc that is fed into a phototypesetting machine that delivers proof of made-up pages, or even a complete *form* [all the pages being printed on one side of the sheet at one time]. If an electronic scanner is connected to the system, it is possible to include illustrations in the proof.

■ *Typesetting devices*—There are basically 2 kinds of photocomposing machines:

(a) The ones that use photomechanical processes (Linofilm, Fototronic TxT, V.I.P., etc.): These devices employ a variety of mats, grids, drums, or discs on which glass or film negatives of type characters appear. These character negatives are moved into position in various ways to project them onto photographic paper or film at the correct place. The negatives are made in different faces, and in several sizes for each face. The machine can reduce or enlarge to produce in-between sizes. The speed of these machines is limited by the mechanical action of the positioning device to about 20 characters per second.

V.I.P. film font being placed on drum

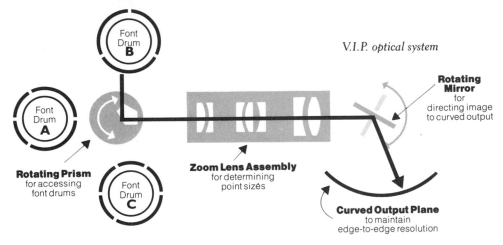

V.I.P. optical system

Font Drum **B**

Font Drum **A**

Font Drum **C**

Rotating Prism
for accessing
font drums

Zoom Lens Assembly
for determining
point sizes

Rotating Mirror
for
directing image
to curved output

Curved Output Plane
to maintain
edge-to-edge resolution

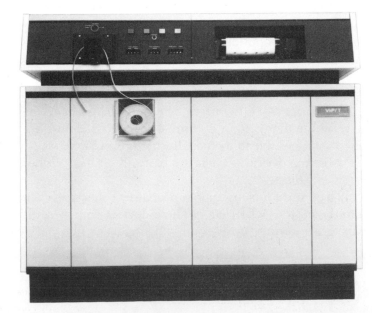

V.I.P./T phototypesetter

Harris Fototronic TxT phototypesetter

segmented disc for DYMO Pacesetter

discs for Harris Fototronic TxT

(b) The *CRT* (Cathode Ray Tube) machines (APS-5, Video-comp, Fototronic 7000, etc.): These generate images by giving instructions from a magnetic tape or disc to a CRT that forms and projects characters onto photographic film or paper at a rate of up to 1500 per second (the practical speed of operation is usually about 1/10 the maximum speed). The CRT is actually a small television tube with a screen divided by a line pattern similar to, but much finer than, the one that forms the pictures on a TV screen (up to 1200 lines per inch against about 220 lines in the TV screen). While it is true that the resultant type is formed of parallel lines and is not solid, the line pattern is so fine that it is not visible unless the type is magnified many times. These machines also reduce and enlarge type. However, the *resolution* [number of lines per inch] changes with the type size and cannot be made too fine (by reduction) or too coarse (by enlargement). Generally, half-size and double-size are the limits.

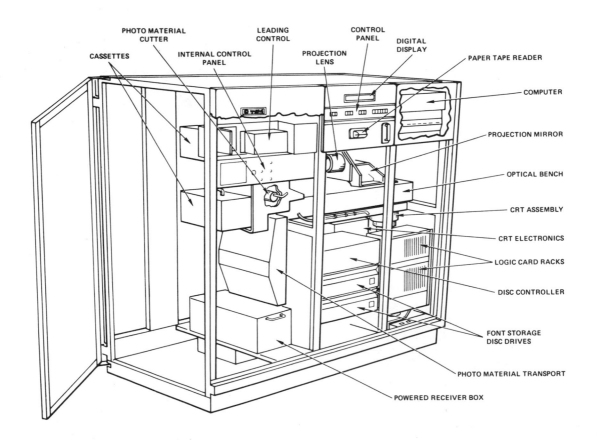

interior of Harris Fototronic 7000 series phototypesetters

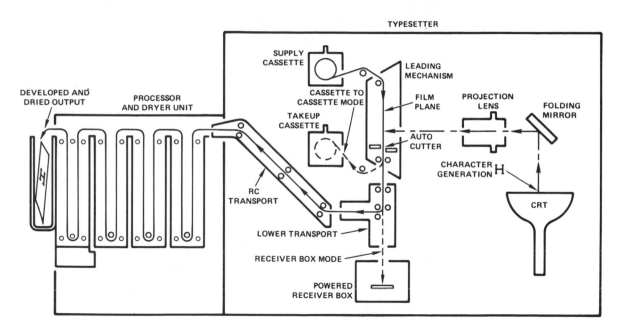

Harris Fototronic 7000 series CRT photocomposition system

Advanced models of photocomposing machines are designed to project the type by *laser beams* [high intensity light that travels in a straight line without diffusion] rather than CRTs. The most interesting of these project type directly onto printing plates, thus bypassing the paper or film stage. This is feasible because the editing devices and lineprinters enable all necessary proofreading and correction, so that no further proofing is necessary when the typesetting stage is reached. This assumes, however, that author and editor are willing to read proofs in the typeface provided by the lineprinter. Also, the designer must be willing to go directly from layouts to plates without seeing intermediate proofs in the chosen type. Because of technical problems and a lack of distinct advantages over CRT typesetting, the development of laser systems for composition petered out in 1978. Except for a laser machine made by Monotype, and used only in England, the use of lasers seems unlikely for this purpose unless some future technical development improves their prospects.

Even the need for film and plates is being eliminated by typesetting computers that are connected to *web-fed presses* (CH.9), with electronically-activated *ink jets* (CH.9) that print each character in position on the paper as soon as it is generated in the typesetter. Such machines are being used in commercial printing, but will eventually be made feasible for book work.

There are some relatively simple and inexpensive machines, such as the Alphatype, that have 2 elements: a typewriter-like keyboard machine and a somewhat larger photo unit that turns

Phototypositor 3000

FRAMPTON KING
★ Standardization Committee of Bottlers of Coca-Cola ★

CARBON WEB

For Men and Women

**PURE
SHORTENING**
ARTIFICIALLY COLORED
MADE FROM HYDROGENATED VEGETABLE OILS AND MEAT FATS
WITH MONO-GLYCERIDES AND DI-GLYCERIDES ADDED: WITH NOT MORE
THAN 1/100 OF 1% BUTYLATED HYDROXYANISOLE ADDED AS A PRE-
SERVATIVE. ARTIFICIALLY COLORED WITH CAROTENE.

keyboard-produced tape into positive proof or film. Later models, such as Compset, have a VDT attached.

A number of photographic machines have been produced to set display type only (Phototypositor, Headliner, etc.). Generally, the assembly of characters is more or less manual, while production of the result is (photo-) mechanical. In all cases, the product is a strip of film or photographic paper on which the image appears. These machines were designed for advertising use, and the typefaces available are generally of the more flashy kind, but some are perfectly acceptable for book work. By using special lenses, some of these machines can distort type to virtually any degree. The *photo-*

Controlled Type

Controlled Type

Controlled Type

Controlled Type

Controlled Type

lettering services make these distortions available by the word or line. Curving, undulating, tapering, shivering, and slanting type are all possible. The use of such facilities in books is limited, but it is helpful to know that they exist.

New photocomposing machines and improvements on existing ones are coming along rapidly. Between this writing and your reading there will undoubtedly be developments of this kind and there will be more later, but a knowledge of the machines described here will be a helpful base for keeping abreast of those to come.

NOTE: The rapid proliferation of typesetting equipment has resulted in an unfortunate lack of compatibility between systems. Copy prepared for one machine cannot be set on another because the codes are different. This situation greatly reduces the publisher's flexibility and limits the economy of the composition field. It would be beneficial to all if the publishers would get together and insist on a single coding system. The equipment makers would have to comply.

Makeup

Makeup is the assembly of all elements of a page in their proper relationships. This may mean the arrangement of metal type and cuts (CH. 8), the arrangement of proofs and illustrations, or the arrangement of *film negatives* or *positives* (see "Makeup with film") of the various parts. In terms of metal type, makeup is a stage of composition and the work is done in the composing room. Much or all of the makeup done for litho or gravure printing may be done in an art studio, in the publisher's office, or a printer's shop. The procedure varies considerably and so does its position in the production schedule, but makeup is a fundamental phase in bookmaking which must take place one way or another—even when it is called by another name.

Makeup begins when the *castoff* (CH. 20) has been made to determine how many lines should be on the text page. This information, with the *sample page* specifications (CH. 18), will provide the information on which makeup will be based. All corrections are then made, and *running heads* [book, part, chapter titles, etc. repeated on text pages] and folios are set. At this point the compositor's *makeup man* will take the galleys of type from the bank and insert the space necessary to arrange all the elements properly.

Each page is measured to be sure that it is the proper depth. Theoretically, every page has the same number of lines of text (except, of course, the beginnings and ends of chapters), so the makeup should be very simple. Actually, there are several complications.

this line would be a widow if it were the top line of a page

so would this one

■ *Widows*—The most common cause of difficulty is the *widow* [a line of less than full width occurring at the top of a page]. In a page of justified lines, widows do give a ragged appearance, and it is a typographic custom to eliminate them by one means or another. A short line of conversation is not usually considered a widow, but the end of a paragraph is. Some printers will allow a widow of $4/5$ of a line, others will tolerate ¾, but purists insist on a full line. Granted that a *very* short line at the top of a squared-up page looks awkward, it is doubtful that the not-quite-full line warrants the effort required to remove it. (Of course, if we did not insist on justified lines there would be no widow problem at all.)

The simplest way (from the printer's standpoint) to correct a widow is to have the editor or author add words to fill out the line, or delete words to eliminate the line. Sometimes this is possible, sometimes not—for example, in reprints. Otherwise, the usual procedure is to take the preceding line from the bottom of the last page and make it the first line of the new page, instead of the widow. This creates a short page. The solution then is to make the facing page one line short also. Here the plot thickens. If the offending widow occurs on a right-hand page *(recto)*, all that is needed is to leave that page one line short and it will match the preceding left-hand page *(verso)* from which the rescue line was taken. If, however, a left-hand widow occurs, the 2 preceding facing pages must be made a line short, thus providing 2 full lines over the widow—that is, if the 2 preceding lines are full width. If not, the complications extend farther back. If making the adjustment necessary to eliminate the widow creates a widow on another page, a half-dozen or more pages may become involved.

Facing short pages may be left that way, or they may be *carded* [strips of thin cardboard are inserted between the slugs to fill the pages out to full depth]. This practice is frowned upon because the lines do not then back up those on the other side of the page. Considering that the average page has about 36 lines, and the lines are about 12 pts. deep, only ⅓ pt. is added to each line. On the facing pages themselves this is imperceptible to almost anyone, and the misalignment on backup can scarcely be observed.

An even naughtier practice is to card only the one short page so as to leave the facing page undisturbed. Here the misalignment may be detected by an expert, but considering that this much or more misalignment generally results from inaccurate folding or sewing, the imperfection is not likely to be noticed at all.

These remarks may sound like incitement to the lowering of standards, and in a sense they are. But the relatively meaningless refinements insisted upon by some, at the cost of considerable efficiency, seem a waste of good intentions, when there is so much improvement needed in spacing, presswork, binding, and engraving—where the faults are glaring and only a little care is required for relief.

When the type fits very tightly into the desired number of pages, the makeup may be ordered with facing pages a line *long*, instead of short, to avoid widows. Too many short pages may result in added pages at the ends of chapters in which the last page is full, or almost so.

The widow problem—and makeup problems in general—are eased when the book contains many subheads, illustrations, and other opportunities to adjust space. When the "opportunities" are so numerous that they create their own problems, a *dummy* is made by pasting up rough proofs on pages of correct size and number (CH. 21). This avoids taking expensive composing room time and gives designer and editor a chance to experiment with the arrangement. Once the dummy is turned over to the makeup man, the problem of makeup is purely mechanical—provided the dummy is accurate.

■ *Run-in breaks*—Another problem inherent in page makeup is what to do when subheads, *spacebreaks* [1- or 2-line spaces in text], or *run-in chapters* [chapter openings that occur on the same page as the end of the preceding chapter] (CH. 16) fall at the bottom, with insufficient room for a minimum number of text lines underneath. It is best to settle these questions in advance. Neither schedule nor budget fare well if the printer must phone for instructions while the makeup is underway. The considerations involved are discussed in CHS. 20 and 24.

■ *Running heads and folios*—Practices of inserting running heads and folios (CH. 18) vary. Sometimes they are set separately even if they appear on the same line. Other compositors prefer to set them on one slug. The difference affects design to some extent. A standard Linotype slug should be at least 2½ picas long in order to include enough *ribs* to give stability, so, if folios are set on separate slugs, their relationship to the running heads will be affected by the minimum slug length. Some compositors, however, now have molds which cast slugs that are solid for the first 3½ picas on one end, so the minimum length may not be required. In photocomposition, no such problem exists.

Running heads can be set in advance on the basis of the castoff and dropped in as the galleys of type are divided into pages, except where the running heads refer to the content of each page, as in dictionaries, directories, and other reference works. Here, pages are made up first and the running heads are set and inserted later.

■ *Heads in text*—Captions, subheads, and chapter heads not already in the galleys are also set in advance and dropped in place as the pages are made up. All type (except hand-set display) is set on slugs the width of the text, so that the horizontal position of each element on the page is controlled by its position on the slug (centered, flush left or right, or indented). Typographic arrangements that involve cutting and fitting slugs slow the makeup considerably.

■ *Odd-depth spaces*—When all pages must be made up to the same depth, problems may arise when spaces other than full lines are used. For example, the use of half-line spaces above and below poetry causes trouble when the poetry begins on one page and ends on another. Each half-line space must be increased to a full line or eliminated entirely, unless some lines are carded to take up the other half-line of space. The problem is usually complicated by the odd space resulting when the poetry is set on a body size different from that of the text.

Before makeup begins, it must be known whether the book is to be printed from (a) the type itself, (b) plates made by molding the type, or (c) plates made by photographing repro proofs made from the type (CH.9). When the type is used for printing or for pulling repros, all spacing material must be lower in height than when plates are being molded, and the blank ends of slugs with short lines must be sawed down to the lower height *(low-slugging)*. This is done to prevent picking up ink in blank areas and transferring it to the paper. On the other hand, the high spacing material facilitates platemaking by molding, and the open areas can later be *routed* [cut away by a revolving cutter similar to a drill] on the plate.

MAKEUP WITH PROOFS When the book is to be printed by a process using photomechanical plates (most often lithography), the final form of the pages before photographing is usually black-on-white (positive) proofs adhered to a white board or heavy paper, with all elements in correct position relative to each other and to the edges of the page.

This is called a *mechanical* and the preparation of it (CH.8) is the equivalent of makeup. Very often, when the mechanical is made with repros of metal type, part of the makeup is done in type before the repros are pulled. It is much easier to adjust spacing around subheads, etc. or to insert folios and running heads with slugs than with proofs—which must be cut apart, squared up, aligned, and adhered.

To the extent that the page arrangement is formal and uniform, the makeup problems with proofs are the same as in metal type. When complicated layouts are involved, a dummy with rough proofs is prepared first and the position of each element is specified on it (CH.21). The mechanical follows these instructions (CH.8).

MAKEUP WITH FILM

The output of photocomposing machines may be positive paper proofs suitable for mechanicals, but often it is positive film, i.e. the type is black. When such film is exposed in contact with unexposed film, the result is ordinarily a negative, but it is also possible to *contact* to positive film.

Makeup with positive film is done page by page in the same way as a mechanical, except that pieces of film are *stripped in* on a sheet of transparent film instead of proofs being adhered to an opaque board. When an entire form is made up, it is exposed to a single sheet of light-sensitive film and a negative is made. Negatives of the illustrations are then stripped in and the whole form is exposed against the plate. When high quality, *deep-etch* offset plates are to be made, the final film must be positive (CH.9).

One advantage of this method is the ease of inserting rules for tables and charts. With negative film, these may be made by *scribing* [scraping off the emulsion with a pointed tool] or, with positive film, by setting the rules on the machine and superimposing this film over the film of the type.

In general, makeup with film is likely to be more precise than mechanical *pasteup* but, again, the cost per hour is much higher. Against this may be weighed the saving in camera work. As in most comparisons of cost, there are many variables, so the particular conditions of each job must be considered.

MAKEUP WITH COMPUTERS

The main hope for substantial economy in computer composition lies in the perfection of integrated systems that automatically produce corrected, made-up pages from *typescript* copy. The necessary machines do in fact exist, in the sense that a computer can be programmed to code the required procedures, and machines are available which will manipulate various elements of film and place them into position according to instructions. These not only place pieces of film as directed by an operator, but can enlarge or reduce any part of the copy. Although such machines are used primarily for making up newspaper pages, they are suitable for book page

Mergenthaler Page View Terminal for page makeup

makeup. They are activated by coded instructions, with the help of operator intercession as needed. Other machines do not actually place the illustration film, but can leave space in the type for illustration.

The problem of programming can be very formidable. Simple matters such as the placement of running heads and folios in uniform position present no difficulties, but in a complicated book with irregular layouts on every page, the trouble of programming might be economically prohibitive. Certainly, the difficulties have to be considered in relation to the particular circumstances of each job. If the proportion of manually controlled operation is too large, it might be cheaper to do the whole job manually. Makeup machines are expensive, and the cost of using them is high. Nevertheless, for a large number of pages of relatively uniform layout—say an encyclopedia or a law book—such computer operated makeup can be very economical.

An auxiliary device called a *data tablet* is a flat, glass-topped box that is connected to a VDT and a computer. The image of a whole page or group of pages is projected on the face of the tablet in reduced size and in diagrammatic form—i.e. blocks of type appear only as outlined boxes, and illustrations appear in very simplified form. The elements of the page or pages shown can be moved around by the use of a kind of light pen. The operator points the "pen" to a part of the page and presses a button on the "pen" to instruct the computer to move that part in a certain way. These commands are taken from the computer's memory on a tape or disc and put into a composing machine that makes the changes. If the operator wants to see an enlarged segment of text, a button can be pressed to bring that material up on the VDT screen.

The discussions of galley, page, book club, foundry, plate, and repro proofs which follow refer to metal typesetting practice. Proofs of cold composition are discussed separately, after the others. This section deals with the purpose and production of proofs. Proofreading methods are explained later in this chapter, and in CH 37. For a discussion of the use of proofs, see CHS. 20 and 24. Color proofs are covered in CH.9.

Proofs

When the galleys on the bank are ready to be filed in a cabinet, a *galley proof* is pulled on a *galley press* or *proof press*. The galley is set on the bed of the press, with the type held firmly by wooden wedges. An inked roller called a *brayer* is passed over the type and then a sheet of galley paper—usually a fairly smooth stock—is placed on top of the type. An *impression cylinder* then passes over the paper, applying enough pressure to transfer the ink from type to paper.

GALLEY PROOFS

The purpose of the galley proof is to enable authors, editors, and designers to check for typographic errors (*typos*) and to make minor corrections in copy, spacing, etc. The printing should therefore be clean, but need not be of high quality.

Vandercook proof press

After the corrections indicated on the galley proofs have been made and makeup completed, *page proofs* are pulled, usually on the same proof press as the galleys. The type is still in the galleys, with pieces of *furniture* [wooden blocks] separating the made-up pages. Normally, 2 or 3 pages fit on one galley.

In England, it is customary to print page proofs on large sheets *imposed* [arranged for printing, see CH.9] as they would be in the finished book. The sheets are then folded and bound in paper covers. This is a pleasant and practical way to handle page proofs—particularly for the designer, who can see how the pages will look while there is still a chance to make changes. Alas, the custom has never been adopted in the United States. (*Book blues* [blueprints folded and trimmed as in printing imposition, see "Cold-type proofs"] are the equivalent in offset printing.)

The purpose of page proofs is to enable the checking of galley corrections and the accuracy of the makeup. Not only the corrected lines themselves, but the sequence of lines must be checked, as there is sometimes a transposition of slugs during the makeup. Remember, too, that this is the first reading of running heads and folios. As with galley proofs, page proofs are not necessarily well printed. Corrections in pages are much more expensive than in galleys.

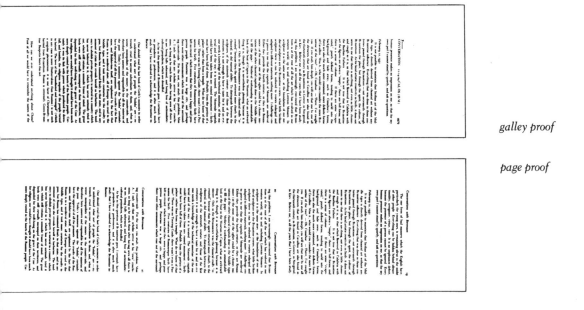

galley proof

page proof

Publishers submit books for consideration of the various book clubs as soon as possible, in order to get a decision before the book goes to press. A book club edition will usually be printed with the regular run, but sometimes the original publication schedule is changed entirely to accomodate the club.

Occasionally a manuscript is submitted, but the clubs prefer the convenience of handling printed and bound copies. This is arranged by pulling special proofs of the galleys (sometimes called *BOM proofs* because they were first used for Book-of-the-Month Club) on each of which half the galley appears. This relieves the judges of handling awkwardly long galley sheets and yet minimizes extra work and expense. The proofs are then given a paper cover with a printed label and bound with a plastic, spiral wire, or other *mechanical binding* (CH. 11), or bound with adhesives.

Book club proofs are printed on the proof press except when the publisher wants a large number to use for promotional purposes, in which case the proofs may be duplicated by some photo-reproduction process—often by a service company engaged specifically in making such copies.

If a book is to be printed from type, page proofs are the last ones submitted before the job goes to press. Ordinarily, there are few corrections on pages and the publisher is sent corrected proofs of only those pages involved. When *electrotype plates* (CH. 9) are to be made, *foundry proofs* [proofs of pages locked up ready to be electrotyped] are pulled after pages are corrected, to enable checking of these corrections.

FOUNDRY PROOFS

When plates are made, either plastic or electrotype, proofs are pulled to check the quality of the plates as well as to check page corrections.

PLATE PROOFS

After pages have been corrected, if repros are wanted, the pages are locked up, usually 4 or 6 in each form, and printed on a *repro press*—which is a fine, electrically operated press with all the adjustments necessary to do first-class printing. The repro press is, in fact, really a miniature of those on which books are printed (CH. 9).

REPRO PROOFS

Coated paper, either glossy or dull (CH. 10), is used, and it may have a pressure-sensitive adhesive backing for convenience in making mechanicals. For special circumstances, usually where a second color is involved, repro proofs may be pulled on transparent plastic sheets, either with or without adhesive backing.

Repro proofs should give a perfect image of the type, which means a perfect impression, perfect inking, perfect choice of ink and paper—perfect everything. This perfection is, of course, impossible to achieve, and even the closest thing to it is very difficult to obtain. Certainly, the images produced by photocomposition are sharper than any printed proof can be, but a *good* repro proof is quite satisfactory for any printing requirement.

Cold-type proofs are required at the same stages of composition as in metal typesetting, but they take different forms and are produced by different methods.

COLD-TYPE PROOFS

"I will pick up

You will see so

Two things. A1

right reading

the book.

mething new.

1d I call them

wrong reading

Typewriter machines produce a positive proof on paper. Photo-composing machines deliver either positive photographic prints on paper or images on film. These may be positive or negative and may be either *right-reading* or *wrong-reading*, i.e. the type on the emulsion side reads properly from left to right or runs backward (as in a mirror) from right to left. It is important to think the whole job through in advance, so as to order the product best suited to the plate-making process being used. In most cases, any product *could* be used, but the object is to reduce the number of steps between composition and the finished plate (CH. 9).

The considerations involved are: (a) with what kind of illustration or type material will the product be combined and (b) what method of makeup will be used? For example, if halftones are involved, it might be best to make wrong-reading negatives which could then be stripped up with negatives of the halftones. If same-size line illustrations or repro proofs of display type are to be included, a mechanical with right-reading positives on paper would be preferable. Another consideration is the kind of plates that will be made. Some offset plates are made from negative film and others require positives.

Even the most sophisticated cold-composition machines generally deliver only one reproduction-quality proof (some typewriters can make a few copies), so additional copies must usually be produced by another process. This must be kept in mind when corrections in mechanicals are needed. With only one set of proofs, the correction or replacement of even a single character can become a problem. Additional sets of repro proofs can be made, but they are relatively expensive.

■ *Blueprints*—The most direct method of obtaining a proof from film is to make a blueprint, or one of its variations. The blueprint is actually a contact print of the film. It is less accurate (and less expensive) than a photoprint, but is adequate for proofreading purposes. Blueprint paper is treated chemically so that when a strong light strikes it through the transparent (or translucent) part of the film, the blue color becomes fixed. The paper is then passed through a chemical bath and the blue is washed away where no light came through. This gives a negative image of the film. When a negative film is used, the blueprint is, of course, a positive. The paper shrinks irregularly when it is washed, which makes it unreliable for checking sizes and register. A vandyke print is brown instead of blue.

The whiteprint is an improvement in that it makes a positive from a positive (the *un*exposed parts are fixed) and it is developed by ammonia fumes instead of a liquid wash, so it does not shrink or warp. Whiteprints are also known as Ozalids, from the machine on which they are made. There are also other kinds of prints with various trade names.

■ *Duplicating*—The blueprint or whiteprint methods are relatively cheap if only a few prints are needed, but they are not well suited to quantity production. For large numbers of proofs, duplicating machines, such as the Multilith, must be used. These are primarily office machines but they are actually small offset lithography presses (CH.9). In the hands of good operators they can produce results comparable to much larger presses but, in any case, can turn out any number of very satisfactory proofs of type. These machines generally use a paper plate, which can be made from the film copy. A metal plate, which produces better printing quality, can also be used.

■ *Photocopying*—Duplicating machines are the answer also for larger numbers of proofs from typewriter composition. For a few copies, a photocopying machine, such as Xerox (CH.9), is practical. These machines require no film and are best suited to making copies from positive proofs and other *reflective* [not transparent or translucent] *copy*.

KEYBOARD & COMPUTER PROOFS

Most lineprinter proofs from keyboard encoding machines and editing devices are unjustified and of limited value, for the composition is subject to further error in the justification and typesetting processes. Their main purpose is to enable the operator to catch and correct errors before the tape or disc goes into the next machine. The printout from lineprinters was discussed earlier in this chapter under "Machine composition—photographic".

Proofreading & style
PROOFREADING CUSTOMS

The first reading of any set of proofs is done by proofreaders employed by the compositor. Their notations are marked on the *Master Proof*, and include printer's errors, queries carried over from the Ms or foul [previous] proofs, and queries on corrections such as spelling, punctuation, grammar, or even factual errors. When coded tape is used, the first proof is usually the printout from a lineprinter (see above). However, when high-speed photosetting systems are used, it is sometimes more economical to bypass the lineprinter and read photo unit output, since the greater speed of reading actual type may offset the cost of producing it. (In practice, the first proof is usually corrected and cleaner proof is sent out as the "first" proof.)

The Master Proof and at least one duplicate are sent to the publisher, who sends the duplicate to the author for reading. Sometimes proofreaders' queries are transferred to the duplicate set so that the author can answer them, and occasionally the Master Proof is sent to him or her, but this is a risky practice. Not only might this master set be lost, but it may be spoiled by some incorrect marking. Many authors do not take the trouble to learn proofreaders' marks.

With the proofs to the publisher go the Ms and the foul proofs, if any, for checking. The foul proofs are sent back to the compositor with the corrected Master Proof to enable a determination to be made as to which corrections are printer's errors (*PE*), and which are author's alterations (*AA*), chargeable to the publisher.

Some publishers rely on the compositor's proofreader and are satisfied to have the author check the proofs with a final once-over by the editor. Other houses insist on all proofs being checked carefully by their own proofreader. It certainly seems true that no matter how many times a set of proofs is read, more errors can be found.

Whatever is done about reading proofs, the final results are clearly marked on the Master Proof. Conflicting instructions are resolved, proofreaders' queries are answered, corrections are collected from all copies and combined. There should be no omissions or ambiguities. Only one set of proofs should be returned to the compositor (plus, of course, the foul proofs).

Whether or not previous instructions exist, it is a good practice to include, with any proofs, instructions as to the next step. If revised proofs are required, this and the number of copies should be indicated. If the next step is makeup, indicate the number of page proofs required, etc. In the absence of specific orders, the compositor will send the regular number of copies—which may be fewer than you need. In any case, include *some* orders—don't send back a set of proofs without instructions.

MARKING PROOFS   Proofreading is nominally an editorial function, and is covered in detail in CH. 37, but in practice, designers frequently find it necessary to read and mark parts of the text in order to make the proofs consistent with the design specifications, and they often spot typesetting errors that escaped all the other readers. Further, it is not uncommon for editors to phone last-minute corrections to the designer, who is expected to insert them properly in the proofs. For these reasons, designers and production people should know how to mark proofs.

You may boast about your illegible handwriting, but don't use it on proofs. Clarity is the first requirement of corrections and any delays caused by unclear writing are inexcusable. Use a writing tool with a fine point—a sharpened pencil is acceptable if it is not too soft and is *kept* sharp, and a ballpoint pen (or a very fine felt pen) is ideal—if you are not inclined to change your mind.

Use a color different from any other markings on the proof. Avoid blue or green as they do not show up on most copying machines. Initial each proof in the color used.

All marks must be at least partly, and preferably entirely, in the margins, as markings entirely within the text might be overlooked. The location of a correction is indicated in the text usually with a *caret* [a small wedge ∧], a line, or a circle, but instructions are written in the margin *opposite the line affected*. The marks must therefore be quite small so as not to intrude on another line— which may also require a correction.

When 2 or more corrections are made on one line, they are written alongside each other and separated by a vertical or diagonal line *(slash)*. In extreme cases, some corrections may be written in the left margin and some in the right. When doing this, be sure it is clear where each correction belongs. If you want someone to approve your correction, put a question mark after the slash. If the correction is approved, the question mark is crossed out. If not approved, the entire correction is crossed out.

Corrections that require setting more than about one line should be typed on a separate piece of paper and partly taped to the galley. Where the makeup is seriously disarranged, a new layout should be attached. In general, use all means to insure clarity.

The special markings developed for proofreaders should be *learned* and *used*. As are all such codes, this one is designed to achieve maximum accuracy and efficiency. It is almost universally understood and any departure from it entails the risk of confusion.

For a chart of proofreaders' marks, and further information about proofreading and marking proofs, see CH. 37.

As used here, *style* refers mainly to the optional points of grammatical usage. Normally, this is a concern of the editor, but there are circumstances in which the designer or production people become involved and they should be aware of the problems.

Until fairly recently, book printers had a large part of the burden of editorial as well as typographic labor. Printers had their own style, the publishers knew what it was and, if they agreed, they left the matter in the printer's hands. Even today, many printers and compositors have issued booklets indicating the style they use in the absence of specific instructions. Most large publishers have their own house style and make this known to their printers. Where there is no definite set of rules, the publisher must either (a) give specific instructions with the composition order, (b) permit the compositor to follow a particular stylebook (the most commonly used are those of the University of Chicago and *The New York Times*), or (c) as is often the case, give *some* specific orders and designate a stylebook to settle the remaining questions.

The various considerations involved in style—points of disagreement, schools of thought, authorities and references, etc.— are discussed in CH. 36, which should be read by all designers and production people.

6 | Typography

Introduction
This chapter deals with typography in the sense that it is the art of arranging *printed* type. We say "printed" because typography refers also to the physical setting of the type itself (CH. 5). Firms that set type are called typographers, as are also the designers who arrange printed type.

The term "typography" is very often used synonymously with book design, and book designers sometimes are called—and call themselves—typographers. This is a mistake, because typography is only one of several parts of book design, although the most important and obvious part.

TRADITION & CHANGE
The design and use of type is deeply involved with tradition. Some typographers feel that any departure from traditional forms in type design or arrangement is distracting and therefore inefficient. This contention would seem to be supported by the findings of many psychologists, who invariably discover that people read most easily the type to which they are accustomed. It is debatable, however, that this truism is a strong enough basis for the retention of old forms.

Mankind is not a single, continuous entity with one permanent set of habits. A child born today is no more accustomed to the Roman type forms than was a child of the Paleolithic era. A new form would not be strange to children growing up with it. For adults, a change would be a temporary inconvenience, the extent of which would depend on the nature of the change. The traditional view is that no inconvenience to the reader can be tolerated. Most changes in typography have been very gradual, but the pace of development in almost every aspect of life has accelerated far beyond anything considered possible a generation ago, and typography may have to change accordingly. Certainly, we must be receptive rather than resistant to change.

Tradition has enshrined the appearance of the Roman alphabet and the process of printing it, but it is dangerous in our dynamic era to remain committed to this tradition (except in a scholarly sense). Computerized photocomposition, lithographic and electrostatic printing (CH.9) are, in principle, entirely different from letterpress printing with hand-set metal type, so it can no longer be argued that our typographic forms must remain as they are because they relate to the technical process.

The new technology suggests certain changes. Easier character recognition features are needed for scanners; a simpler system of set widths would ease justification problems—abandonment of justification itself would be a boon; typefaces suited to both computer printout and photomechanical reproduction are desirable; and so on. High-speed, automated composition methods using oral as well as written copy would surely benefit from long overdue reform of the Roman alphabet. Today, at least 8 different sounds are given the letter "a" and it has two different printed forms—"a" and "*a*". Worse yet, the use of the letter is only partly covered by rules. The story of the other vowels is about the same.

The significant point is that type is nothing more or less than a device for communicating thought, and the nub is the thought—not the forms or processes of transmittal. We must be ready to modify these when they no longer serve their purpose efficiently.

With this willingness to change must go a recognition of the possibilities for esthetic improvement. These possibilities become obvious when we look at the abstract design of some other alphabets, such as Arabic, Chinese, Sanskrit, or even Cuneiform. The Roman alphabet can have great beauty in the hands of a fine typographer, but these others seem to look well in any arrangement at all.

(The foregoing paragraphs were written for the First Edition in 1965, when the new technology was only beginning to emerge. More than a decade later, the new technology is predominant, but no type design changes of the kind proposed have been made, and the opportunity to incorporate them in the emerging technology has passed.)

PRACTICAL & ESTHETIC LIMITS

In typography, as in other aspects of bookmaking, it is necessary to reconcile the esthetic and practical demands. Economic danger lies in the fact that it is physically *possible* for a compositor to accomplish almost anything a designer requests—even though the request may be extremely impractical. Many designers go on for years repeating expensive mistakes because compositors seldom (for a number of reasons) bring such matters to the customer's attention. It is most important for a designer to understand the practical limitations of typesetting (CH. 5).

Esthetic limitations unfortunately do not exist, except in the form of conventional rules that stop far short of the creative needs of the designer. The only insurance against visual excesses is *taste*, which is basically innate, but which can be trained and sharpened. An effort to develop one's taste is indispensable to the study of typography. Typographical trouble can be avoided by following good models, but creation of excellent work depends on a highly developed perception.

The discussions of typefaces that follow are based on type designs that originated in the era of metal type. There were comparatively few type founders and for the most part they had their own designs—although most had their own version of the best classical faces. Today, each maker of a typesetting machine, and there are many, has its own list of typefaces—most of them being slightly modified versions of the metal-type faces. For this reason, it was decided to retain the typeface names used in the First Edition. To try giving all of the alternate names used for imitations of these designs would be impractical and invidious. It is best for the reader to become familiar with the faces discussed here, and then examine critically the substitutes offered by the makers of the various photocomposing machines. Regrettably, almost all of them will be found inferior to the originals.

Type classification

Systems of type classification are based generally on relatively insignificant variations of historical rather than visual interest. They classify type according to the time and place of design, even though these factors may have no particular effect on the appearance of the face. Because of the burgeoning of the printing arts during the first 300 years after their invention, much is made of minor changes during this time, and quite dissimilar groups of later faces are either lumped together in catchall classes or ignored entirely. In any case, from a graphic standpoint, the chronological or geographical origins of a typeface are less important than its visual character. In Germany and France there are type classification systems based on visual characteristics, but they are quite complex. True, the variations of type design *are* very complicated, but it is necessary to make a simple division at first, and go into the complications later.

Visually, there are 4 broad classes of type (see CH. 5 or Glossary-Index for type terminology):

■ *Roman*—The classical letter with serifs and graduated thick and thin strokes based on writing with a square-edged tool.

■ *Abstract*—Letters based on mechanical drawing, with more or less straight edges and lines of uniform thickness, having no serifs *(sans serif)* or square serifs of the same weight as the letter *(block serifs)*.

■ *Cursive*—Letters based on slanted writing with a more or less continuous line, including the italic forms of Roman.

■ *Decorative*—All the faces that have exaggerated characteristics of the other 3 classes, or distinctive features that place them outside the other classes.

Ultimately, details of type design and subtleties of character are important if first-rate typography is to be produced, but *first* the major characteristics of the typeface must be considered. For broad design purposes, it hardly matters which typeface within each class is used. The graphics of design involve combining lines, forms, and spaces—and the details are less important than the general characteristics.

Variations in Roman type are largely in the shapes of serifs, and to some extent the relative weight of thick and thin strokes. Groups are named for their historical sequence or geographical origin, but it is their visual characteristics that count. The most significant subdivisions are:

ROMAN

■ *Old Style*—Based on rather freely drawn manuscript writing, there tends to be a flowing passage from thicks to thins and strong brackets on slanted serifs. The types of Jenson, Garamond, and Caslon are typical. This is the style used for the first 3 centuries of printing. A separate category is usually reserved for "Venetian", but this hardly seems warranted. (Much is made of the minor fact that the Venetian lower case "c" has a slanted crossbar.)

Garamond
Caslon
Baskerville
Bulmer

■ *Transitional*—The types of Baskerville and Bulmer were designed in the middle of the 18th century to be printed on smoother papers. The faces of this group are generally more angular, with sharper contrast between thick and thin strokes. The serifs are straighter, brackets less pronounced.

■ *Modern*—These faces are a logical development of the Transitional, but are no more "modern" than they, having originated with Bodoni and Didot shortly afterward. They further accentuate the contrast between thick and thin and eliminate entirely the brackets on serifs. Serifs and the other square strokes are perfectly straight, as though mechanically drawn.

Bodoni

■ *Egyptian*—A 19th century development, this group has particularly heavy serifs with brackets. There is little contrast between thicks and thins, the serifs are usually at least as heavy as the thins and squared off at the ends. Examples are Fortune, Clarendon, and Consort. This group borders on Abstract. The distinctions are discussed in connection with the related group, block-serifed.

Fortune
Consort

■ *Miscellaneous*—In the ever-expanding catalogue of typefaces, there are some that do not fall exactly into one of the above groups. Examples of these will be given in the discussions of both text and display types.

The main subdivisions of Abstract faces are (a) serifed and (b) non-serifed. The serifs in this class are simply short strokes of about the

ABSTRACT

Futura Light

Futura Medium

Futura Bold

Futura Ex Bold

Lydian

Optima

Beton

Memphis

Karnak

Garamond Italic

Bulmer Italic

Bodoni Italic

Typo Script

Kaufmann Script

Brush Script

PROFIL

Ornata

RUSTIC

same thickness as the main parts of the face and have no brackets at all, or only a slight rounding at the junctures. If the bracket becomes pronounced, and a variation of thickness occurs within the curved lines, the face is then better classed Roman (Egyptian) than Abstract.

■ *Sans serif*—These may have strokes of uniform or varying thickness. The strokes may have perfectly straight edges, as in Futura, or be slightly curved, usually with a slight swelling at the ends of straight strokes and the middle of curved ones. Examples of these are Lydian and Optima. Almost all of the sans-serif faces have various weights—some varying from a spidery fineness to a heavy black.

■ *Block-serifed*—The variations in this group are somewhat smaller than within the sans serif. Typical are Beton, Memphis, Karnak, and Cairo. Each has numerous weights. This is the group that borders on Egyptian, and is considered Egyptian (note the names) in most systems. However, there is an important distinction visually between the faces of almost purely mechanical design (Abstract) and those that are strongly modified in the direction of Roman. So, although there are borderline cases, the extremes are far enough apart to justify the distinction, as the examples show.

The primary graphic features of these faces are the slanted letter and the generally continuous feeling. They vary mostly in the character of their line, usually indicating the kind of tool used.

■ *Italics*—A slanted form of Roman faces, based on the handwritten books of Italy at the beginning of printing. Early types designed by Aldus Manutius were italic and resembled a slanted writing done with a narrow, square-tipped pen. Almost all the italics are variations of this Aldine type.

■ *Scripts*—These are faces drawn to look as though they were handwritten, and have no serifs or other resemblance to Roman type. They vary from very formal pointed-pen scripts based on 18th century models (Typo Script or Bank Script), through round-pointed pencil or pen scripts (Kaufman Script or Mistral), to the most informal brushwriting, such as Brush Script.

Some faces based on free lettering are vertical in feeling and cannot be classed as Cursive. These belong in the next group.

There is no way to subdivide these faces as they are usually exaggerated or embellished forms of the other classes. Some, such as Rustic or Astur, are so bizarre as to be unique, but even the others can be treated as individual graphic elements of a special character without reference to their antecedents. Examples are Ornata, Profil, Saphir, etc.

One Decorative group that deserves special mention is *Text*, *Black Letter*, or *"Old English"*. Now obsolete, this group of faces was the common form of writing in Northern Europe well past the Middle Ages, and persisted in German printing into the 20th century. Today, it is used only to imitate or suggest antiquity (or Germany), mainly on newspaper titles, churches, and schools.

Text types are those used for the body of a book and are generally considered to be no larger than 18 pt. Display types are any size of any type that is designed for use in headings, titles, initials, etc. These may be made in sizes from 12 or 14 pt. up to 72 pt., 86 pt., or occasionally larger. In photocomposition, of course, the sizes may be modified. However, the modifications are made from base sizes that vary according to the system, and it is important to know what degree of magnification is involved. It is possible to enlarge to, say, 60 pt. from an 18 pt. matrix, but the result will be much heavier and clumsier than a 60 pt. that was designed for that size. Magnifications which more than double the base size should be avoided.

Theoretically, the only difference between text types and display types of the same name is size. In metal type, it is often true that a name is all they have in common. The two are usually made by different manufacturers, of different materials, by different processes, and created by different designers. It seems logical that they should be studied separately. In photocomposition, as noted above, the display types are often just enlargements of the text types, but in the better systems they are separate designs.

Foundry text types are still used in an occasional private press book, but in most cases, metal text type is produced by Linotype and Monotype machines. While no physical type is made by the photocomposing machines, they do create type images, so they may be said to produce text type.

The problems of *copyfitting* (CH. 17) tend to divide text faces into groups according to width (characters per pica, see CH. 5). Some are exceptionally thin for their height (Linotype Granjon, Electra, Times Roman, Bodoni Book, Intertype Garamond and Weiss), some are normal in width (Linotype Baskerville, Caledonia, Caslon, Janson), and some are particularly wide (Intertype Waverley, Linotype Primer). The difference in width of individual characters is minute, but multiplied by a half-million or so this difference will seriously affect the length of a book. For example, in a book of 500,000 characters, with an average page size, a shift from 11 pt. Caledonia to 11 pt. Granjon will save 24 pages. Remember, however, that the *appearance* of 2 faces of the same body size can differ greatly (CH. 5).

The various phototype faces based on these designs vary in their widths, so it is best to check the width for each face you want to use in a photosetting system.

𝕺𝖑𝖉 𝕰𝖓𝖌𝖑𝖎𝖘𝖍

Type characteristics

TEXT TYPE

Bookmaking
Bookmaking
Bookmaking

top to bottom, *14 pt. Granjon, Caledonia, Waverley*

Times Roman
Weiss Roman

Baskerville
Janson
Granjon
Caledonia
Times Roman
Electra
Fairfield
Bodoni
Waverley

Text types vary in general character just as much as display types, but the differences are not as noticeable because of the smaller size. While readers may not consciously perceive the distinctive nature of a text face, they are affected by it and the face must be chosen for its harmony with the text.

One of the most discernible differences in types is in their degree of masculinity or femininity. Some are definitely strong and rugged, some are definitely light and delicate, some are, of course, in between. Here, as in other areas of classification by character, there will be differences of opinion due to varying subjective reactions. It is reasonably safe to say that almost everyone would find Caledonia, Times Roman, and Monticello masculine; Granjon, Weiss, and Bodoni Book feminine; but even with these, and certainly with the borderline faces, a certain amount of the feeling conveyed depends on the way the type is used.

Type faces—like people's faces—have distinctive features indicating aspects of character. Some features are quite pronounced, some are very subtle and subject to individual interpretation. Here are some text faces with capsule character analyses.

Baskerville—Classical and elegant
Janson—Round and warm
Granjon—Round, warm, and graceful
Caledonia—Clean, firm, businesslike
Times Roman—Stiff, cold, formal
Electra—Light, cool, efficient
Fairfield—Fussy
Bodoni—Dramatic
Waverley—Round and cool

In choosing type it is better to consider these characteristics than to follow historical or conventional rules. After all, it is the type's character, not its history, that affects the reader.

No primarily cursive faces are in regular use for book texts. The British Monotype Company cut an italic face called Blado, which is rarely used except as the italic of a roman face called Poliphilus, and a face called Arrighi, which is used as the italic of Centaur.

There is a general reluctance to use italics for large amounts of text. It is said that italic is harder to read than roman, but this is true (if at all) only in the sense that people are less accustomed to reading italic. As with most statements concerning readability of type, this will never be proven. The only valid study would be one that neutralizes the factor of experience, and this would require a controlled experiment with subjects who had *always* been exposed to italic and roman in reverse of the present proportion—a most unlikely occurrence.

An attempt to overcome the problem of reading italic was made by W. A. Dwiggins in 1935 when the Mergenthaler Linotype

Company introduced Electra with an italic that is actually a slanted roman, lacking the cursive feeling of other italics. Probably because it makes too little contrast with the roman, Electra Italic (or "Oblique", as it is generally called) was not accepted as an italic, and Electra Cursive was issued later. While "Oblique" is useful where large amounts of type must be set in a style distinct from, yet similar to, the main text, it was not carried over into Mergenthaler's photocomposing systems.

Among the other text faces, the italics vary somewhat in their cursiveness and style, the most distinctive being Linotype Janson. Some italics, such as Linotype Baskerville, Caslon, and Granjon, contrast with the roman particularly well. This is a factor in choosing type for books in which italic is much used for emphasis.

There are about a dozen Abstract text types in general use. Among sans serifs are Spartan, Metro, Erbar, Optima, Helvetica, and Standard. A number of the older text "gothics" have been little used recently, but fashions in type run in cycles and interest in these is being renewed. In block-serifed faces there are Memphis and Cairo.

Each of the Abstract faces has variations of weight in both roman and italic. The italics of these types are actually obliques, having no cursive feeling. They do not contrast well with the romans.

The block-serifed faces are quite similar to each other, but the sans serifs vary considerably. The contrast between Roman and Abstract type is so striking that people tend to ignore the differences among individual sans-serif faces (the way that people tend to think that those of another race "all look alike"). Yet, there is at least as much difference among sans-serif types as among Romans. In general, Spartan, Metro, and Helvetica are more uniform of thickness and straight of line than the others. Optima in particular has characteristics that make it almost a serifless Roman rather than an Abstract.

There is a much larger variety of display types than of text types, but relatively few are frequently used in books. Some of the others are used occasionally, and some hardly at all.

The rarely used faces tend to be in the Decorative class. Most of them are produced for advertising typography and are slow in getting accepted for books. There is some justification for this disdain in that advertising display types are designed to attract attention, which is not the purpose of book typography (except on jackets). However, many of these faces are well designed and can be effectively utilized where they are suitable.

A skilled designer can use such types in a way that exploits their special qualities yet avoids a blaring effect. The general idea is to use them as an *accent* to the rest of the page rather than as the

Electra Italic
[Oblique]
Electra Cursive

Janson *Janson*
Baskerville *Baskervill*
Caslon *Caslon*
Granjon *Granjon*

Spartan
Metro
Erbar Light Condensed
Optima
News Gothic
Helvetica
Gothic Condensed No. 2
GOTHIC NO. 31

Memphis
Cairo

Spartan Heavy
Spartan Heavy Italic

DISPLAY TYPE

dominant element. Their impact can be diminished by reduction in size, by letterspacing, and by counterbalancing with contrasting blocks of space or type. Even where a decorative type is the only element on the page—on a part-title, for example—it can be restrained in its relationships to the space around it.

It is almost impossible to achieve a successful page using a poorly designed display face, even though the type is appropriate and is skillfully used. One poor element in a design tends to spoil the whole as the rotten apple spoils the whole barrel.

In the Roman display types, Monotype Janson, ATF Baskerville, and ATF Caslon 471 are fairly close in design to the Linotype faces of the same name—but Monotype Garamont, Bodoni 175, and Caslon 337 are quite different from their Linotype namesakes.

Not all of the text faces have display types of their name, but there are display faces of sympathetic character for any of them. For example:

Caledonia—Scotch, Bulmer
Electra—Corvinus, Bodoni Book
Fairfield—Garamond, Deepdene
Granjon—Garamond
Waverley—Scotch

Baskerville
(Monotype)

Baskerville
(ATF)

Garamont
(Monotype)

Garamond
(ATF)

Some confusion is caused by the practice of naming typefaces after the designers of earlier models. There may be several versions of one face produced by the same foundry, as the numerous ATF Caslons or the various Monotype Bodonis. In other cases, different companies have made their own cuttings of one early design, such as the quite dissimilar Baskervilles of ATF and Monotype, the Garamond of ATF and Monotype's Garamont, and the many variations of Bodoni and Caslon designs made by American, English, and European foundries. Thus, in using display faces named after early designers, consider each face on its own merits. For example, Caslon 540 (ATF) is one of the most beautiful of the Roman types, while New Caslon (ATF) is a crude affair. Bauer's Bodoni sings, Monotype's Bodoni 275 is a simple oaf.

There are a number of Roman display faces that have names unlike any of the metal composing-machine text types. Among these are:

- *Old Style*—Elizabeth, Orpheus, De Roos, Trajanus
- *Transitional*—Columbia, Horizon, Mademoiselle
- *Modern*—Corvinus, Normande, Modern 20, Torino
- *Egyptian*—Egizio, Consort, Fortune

Besides the italics of the Roman faces, the Cursive display types most used in books are those based on Spencerian script (Typo Script, Bank Script, Royal Script, Excelsior Script, etc.). In general, the other Cursive types are too informal for most books. However, not all books are serious works of classical stature, so even the least formal letter may find an appropriate use. Below is a selection of miscellaneous Cursive display types:

Stationers Semiscript

Slogan

Constanze

Commercial Script

Legend

Excelsior Script

Mistral

Maxime

Scritto a Lapis

Lydian

Charme

Bernhard Tango

Reiner Script

Murray Hill

Stradivarius

Salto

Virtuosa No 1. and 2

Ondine

Champion

Gavotte

Royal Script

Of Abstract display faces there are large numbers and a great variety. The variations of weight and style are about the same as for text types, *plus* open, shadowed, extended, and condensed forms.

Sans-serif faces range from the relatively hand-lettered feeling of Lydian or Post Title to the mechanically drawn regularity of the numerous Gothics—Franklin, Airport, News, Alternate, etc.— and the more recent Helvetica, Venus, Standard, and Microgramma series.

The block-serifed faces are less numerous and range less widely in style, as they tend to run into the Egyptian group once they form brackets. Below are some examples:

OUTLINE

LINED

SHADOW

Extra Condensed

Extended

Memphis Medium

Stymie Medium Condensed

BETON OPEN

Tower

Girder

Garamond

Garamond Bo

Venus Light Extende

Venus Medium Exter

Venus Bold Exten

Venus Extrabolc

Bodoni

Bodoni Bold

ni, Ultra

Typographic design

The desire for contrast in type weight, to make distinctions in style or to create graphic interest, has led to a demand for "boldfaces". With rare exceptions, bold forms of Roman faces are unsuccessful designs and are best avoided. The reason is that they are not new faces at all, but simply thickened versions of the regular face. The overall dimensions of the type are altered hardly at all, but the relationships of weight, form, and line—so carefully balanced in the original design—are distorted far from the ideal in order to achieve the desired "color". If no attempt were made to retain the appearance of the regular weight, it would be possible to produce a boldface of good design, but the need to combine the new proportions and the old characteristics dooms Roman boldfaces to ugliness.

The Abstract faces seem to withstand fattening much better. Some of them range from wire thin to heavy black—with each weight as successful as any other. This is due in part to the absence of distinctive details, such as brackets, serifs, etc., to be retained as the weight of the face changes. Also, where the Roman faces have a special character related to their origin in writing, and cannot be modified too far before they lose that character, the Abstract faces are original constructions that can be modified almost indefinitely with success—provided each variation is individually designed.

The modern "fat faces" (Ultra Bodoni, etc.) succeed because the original design is based on a sharp contrast in weight between thicks and thins, so the extreme contrast creates a different and interesting form while retaining the basic features of the regular design. On the other hand, Bodoni Bold simply disturbs the happy proportions of the regular face and fails to create a valid new design.

In addition to the photo typefaces available, there is another source of display type—*transfer type*. This is the type that is printed on plastic sheets so that it can be transferred to another surface by rubbing the plastic sheet against that surface. The number and quality of the typefaces available in these systems (Normatype, Letraset, etc.) are very high, but the technical quality of the transferred image varies according to the brand, the age of the sheet, and the technique of the user. This is a useful method where a small amount of display copy is needed.

While it is true that the vast majority of readers are neither aware of nor informed about typefaces, it is wrong to assume that they will fail to respond to good typography—even in its more refined state. Their reactions are subconscious, but are no less definite for being so. Indeed, the conscious choices of laypersons frequently differ from their responses as revealed by psychological tests. This casts some doubt on the importance of habit in typography and suggests that the designer should strive for maximum excellence by visual

In combining type it is better to use very close *harmony* or definite *contrast* than to mix faces that are only slightly dissimilar. The near-miss relationship creates a sense of uneasiness, even among those who are not familiar with type. They sense a difference and get a feeling that something is wrong because they are not consciously aware of the difference. As an example, the use of a Roman Old Style face like Janson with a Transitional like Baskerville in text sizes would usually create this effect.

The use of an Abstract face with a Roman, or any other combination of types of different classifications, provides a contrast that has a settling effect because it leaves no doubt as to the designer's intentions.

The surest and safest procedure is to use the same face throughout, but it is possible to mix faces of the same category without disturbance if they are *close enough* in appearance (Granjon with Garamond, Bulmer with Baskerville, etc.).

A judicious use of both contrast and harmony is usually the best solution. The cardinal sin in design is to be equivocal and vague. Relationships may be subtle, but there must never be any doubt that the relationship was intended. Design *is* intention, the deliberate creation of order.

Variety is essential in design, but not necessarily in large amounts. As indicated above, an entire book can be printed in one typeface—or even one size of one face—with great success. On the other hand, it is possible to make a mess using many different faces, or using too many variations with few faces. There is no one "right" way to use variety. The degree of activity or restraint that is proper depends on 2 factors: (a) the nature of the book's content (CH.15), and (b) the visual requirements of the design. In both cases, the only guides are intelligence and intuition.

COMBINING TYPE

Baskerville
Janson

Univers
Janson

Garamond
Granjon

Bulmer
Baskerville

To establish a relative order of importance, or to lead attention to an element of copy, it is necessary to give type various degrees of emphasis. There are many ways to do it, because type has so many aspects. Emphasis can be achieved by the choice of:

- *Typeface*—A decorated or cursive face will take more attention than another, all other things being equal.
- *Type weight*—A boldface is more prominent than a lighter one. A strong face will dominate a thin, weak one.
- *Type size*—Large size is, of course, more important than small.
- *Italics*—In most cases, italics imply emphasis.
- *Capitals*—Size for size, capitals have more importance than lower case.
- *Position*—This is a difficult point about which to generalize,

EMPHASIS

but there are a few broad principles. Emphasis may be achieved by isolating an element, placing it at the top of the page, placing it adjacent to the most important element or in any unique situation—at right angles to the rest of the type, on a slant, upside-down, etc.

■ *Color*—The ability of certain colors to advance may be utilized (CH. 15).

■ *Spacing*—Letterspacing is used in Europe sometimes to emphasize proper names. A block of copy can be emphasized by increasing or decreasing leading.

The attention-getting power of *contrast* is a key factor in establishing emphasis. Any element will become conspicuous (and therefore emphasized) if it is unlike any other. A word in 8 pt. type can be made most important in a page of 30 pt. A line of lower case will stand out if every other line is in caps. Roman stands out among italics. Even a gray blue will outshine bright red if it is unique.

KINDS OF ARRANGEMENT

No general style of typographic layout is better than another. The only criterion is success, and it is just as possible to do a bad job with a centered arrangement as with an asymmetrical one.

However, symmetrical arrangements are relatively simple, and the centered style has the fewest problems. The moment that dependable central axis is left behind, designers find themselves in an unmarked expanse, without guidelines or conventions. It is the difference between traveling on roads and navigating the open sea.

The asymmetrical arrangement permits a far greater range of expression, but it also requires much more skill. The problem is not only to make a visually pleasing and effective arrangement of type and space, but to achieve a solid structure with unequal balance. With a central fulcrum you know that each side must have the same weight. When you move the fulcrum off center, you must be able to determine how much weight is needed on each end to prevent collapse. In graphics there is no way of computing this. Everything depends on the designer's sense of balance. The difficulty of creating such a structure with complex copy is not to be taken lightly.

While the centered arrangement is easier because a structural framework or skeleton is present, the use of this style by no means guarantees success. The *worst* disasters (common in asymmetrical layout) will be avoided, but the achievement of an excellent page still depends on a superior choice and disposition of the various elements of design.

It is *possible* for a combination of symmetrical and asymmetrical elements to be used successfully in a book, but this requires such mastery of design that it is extremely improbable. Since there is rarely any need to have such a combination, there is really no

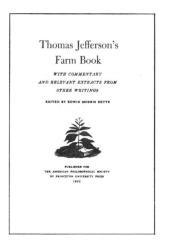

symmetrical

asymmetrical

reason to attempt it. This is not a "rule" (there is only one rule in design: *If it works, it's good*), it is a logical conclusion. As soon as an unsymmetrical element is introduced into a symmetrical arrangement, the design ceases to be symmetrical. A centered element in an asymmetrical layout does not of itself make the design symmetrical, but it does introduce an ambivalence that is just as unsettling and out of character. A single centered line in an asymmetrical layout is usually absorbed by the overall plan and doesn't seem to be centered at all. When there are 2 or more centered lines together, they create a sense of conflict that is death to design. This is true even if the centered lines appear on a separate page.

A formal arrangement may be centered, but it may also be aligned to one side or the other. "Formal" implies a certain *regularity* of arrangement, rather than any particular one.

An informal style results from the placement of elements according to caprice rather than a rigid structure, and from the use of elements that suggest a topical approach rather than an effort to count eternity. This includes typefaces and illustrations that have a light, fresh touch—even a bit of eccentricity—as opposed to classical forms.

formal

THE STONES OF
FLORENCE
BY MARY McCARTHY

PHOTOGRAPHS BY EVELYN HOFER AND OTHERS

NEW YORK ✿ HARCOURT, BRACE AND COMPANY

ITALIAN FABLES

The Orion Press
New York

informal

by ITALO CALVINO
translated from the Italian
by Louis Brigante
illustrated
by Michael Train

There are many ways to convey dynamism in graphic design. Strong contrast is dynamic, and so is strong movement. Sharp curves are more dynamic than gradual ones, diagonals are generally more dynamic than horizontals, short lines more than long ones, and an informal arrangement is more dynamic than a formal one. The converse of these axioms are applicable to placidity. The choice of elements is not as significant in this respect as their interaction—the result of their combination and arrangement.

The masculine and feminine characteristics do not need to be described, but it is worth pointing out that any kind of design—symmetrical or asymmetrical, formal or informal, dynamic or placid, etc.—can.be either masculine or feminine in feeling. Certainly, there are both men and women with any given combination of attributes who are, nevertheless, masculine or feminine respectively.

CHANGES

The elements of typographic design are numerous, and their interaction complex. No element can be introduced, deleted, or changed without affecting all the others. The successful design is a perfectly balanced construction of type—with its many variations of style, size, weight, and category—illustration (if any), and space. In some cases, a change can be countered with a corresponding modification in another part of the design, but in a simple and delicately balanced composition any change may require a new start. (One of the designer's worst frustrations is to have the sketch come back with the notation "O.K. as corrected", when a subtitle or an author's middle name has been added or deleted.)

THE SHAPES OF WORDS

One of the least understood principles of typography is that the visual form of the copy is a vital factor. For example, many designers, particularly beginners, are fond of making a vertical arrangement of the words in a title. This has been done with great success and will be again, but only when the words *in the particular title* lend themselves to such a scheme. The words must be of such length as to form an interesting pattern when disposed vertically—either aligned to one side or centered on each other. (They may sometimes be staggered with satisfactory results.) Also, if a large size of lower case display type is used, a great deal depends on what the words are, as the occurrence of ascenders or descenders in the wrong place can be ruinous.

Any combination of words and letters can be beautifully and effectively arranged, but they must be arranged to suit their own form—not squeezed into a designer's arbitrary scheme. The decision to use caps or upper and lower case, the choice of size, placement, or style of type must be based *first* on the nature of the copy, as this is an unchangeable element. It is not a bad idea to begin by

HOLIDAYS
IN
THE
SUN

awkward

THE
OLD
LIDO
SUN

less awkward

IN
SUNNY,
SOUTHERN
ITALY

pleasant

Thy
Only
Myth
of
Logic
Holy

awkward

Thy Only Myth of
Logic Holy

less awkward

THY
ONLY MYTH
OF LOGIC
HOLY

better

simply sketching out the display words in *both* caps and ulc. Often, the words will take a shape that suggests the most natural arrangement.

The design of any flat surface consists of 2 parts—the covered and the uncovered areas. In a sense, one is no more important than the other. When we print a word in black ink on a rectangle of white paper, we are creating a composition in black and white. While the

USING SPACE

type's primary value is in its symbolic and graphic (black) pattern, it is also delineating areas of space around and within itself. In a well-designed page, the white areas are effective elements interacting with the black—the page is alive. In poor typography, the type seems printed *on top of* a white background—the page is dead.

ITALIAN

MANUSCRIPTS

IN THE

PIERPONT MORGAN

LIBRARY

Descriptive Survey of the principal Illuminated Manuscripts of
the Sixth to Sixteenth Centuries, with a selection of important
Letters and Documents. Catalogue compiled by Meta Harrsen
and George K. Boyce. With an Introduction by Bernard Berenson.

THE PIERPONT MORGAN LIBRARY
NEW YORK 1953

live page

GUNS
of
ARIZONA

Originally published as
BREED OF THE CHAPARRAL

NELSON C. NYE

KLEY PUBLISHING CO
• New York

dead page

LETTERSPACING

LATIN

LATIN

Both capital and lower case letters in our alphabet vary so much in shape that a nasty visual problem can arise from an unlucky sequence. The occurrence of capital IN together creates an entirely different pattern of space than the combination LAT. Yet these combinations make one word—LATIN—which is by nature uneven in "color". It is difficult to reduce the space between LAT, but we can add space between IN to make an evenly spaced LATIN. This word is an extreme example, but a problem arises to some degree in any line of caps (or small caps). If the amount of copy is small and the size of type large, spacing between letters can be adjusted as shown. Where optically adjusted letterspacing is impractical (for example, in Linotype cap or small cap subheads and running heads [CH. 18]), some uniform spacing should be added, and as much as possible. The addition of 10 pt. letterspace to L A T I N doesn't eliminate the irregularity of space, but the latter becomes proportionately less significant.

The problem is even more acute in the lower case alphabet and grows with the size of type. The word "billowy" in 60 pt. is almost hopeless, but can be saved with considerable letterspacing.

billowy billowy

There is a prejudice in America against letterspacing lower case, although the stricture wouldn't be applied against selective spacing as shown above. It is really directed against the practice of using letterspacing as a means of filling out a line of text. This is a common procedure in newspapers, where the narrow column often creates awkward problems. If a line starts with 2 long words and the next one is an unbreakable word such as "through" that doesn't quite fit on the line, the alternatives are: (a) leave a giant space between the 2 words or (b) letterspace them. Of the 2, letterspacing is probably the less objectionable solution. The *best* procedure is to reset a few previous lines to get a better break. (In photocomposition it is possible to distort the type to make a line fit.) Repeated occurrences of lines with excessive word space results in unpleasantly loose composition and noticeable *rivers* [jagged vertical white lines caused by a series of wide spaces in about the same place on successive lines].

The relationship of typography to content in books is discussed in CH.15. In principle, it is best to avoid the kind of allusive typography that is nothing more than imitation of the style of another period or place. There is nothing wrong with *suggesting* another time or place, but imitation is neither honest (which should rule it out) nor effective. Typographic imitation becomes more unsettling the better it is done. One begins to wonder whether it is an imitation or the real thing. The best practice is to express the *spirit* of the period or subject, rather than to make an imitation of its typography.

Readability and legibility are sometimes considered synonyms; actually, they are not. There is a tendency (hastened by the regrettable W3 "dictionary") for the distinctions among words of similar meaning to blur and disappear, but in an increasingly technological society we need all the precision of language possible. The terms readability and legibility are needed to describe 2 quite distinct qualities.

Legibility is the quality of type (or writing) that makes it *possible*

enlarged word spaces

seemed so irrelevant at the time, had been eliminated! Unquestionably, Germany would then have conquered all Europe, and would still have been ruling it today. From the

letterspaced

seemed so irrelevant at the time, had been eliminated Unquestionably, Germany would then have conquered all Europe, and would still have been ruling it today. From the

reset

seemed so irrelevant at the time, had been eliminated! Unquestionably, Germany would then have conquered all Europe, and would still have been ruling it today. From the Atlan-

ALLUSION

Readability

to read. Readability is the characteristic of a body of type that makes it *comfortable* to read. Both are relative terms. For example, 4 pt. type used for a credit line under an illustration may be legible because it *can* be read at the normal reading distance for a book. For reading on a billboard atop a building, the smallest legible size of letter may be 6″ (15.24 cm) high. Similarly, 8 pt. type with no leading may be readable for an encyclopedia in which the text for each item is only a paragraph or two, but it would not be readable for a 320-page novel, although it would be legible in both cases.

Both readability and legibility are so fundamental to the design of books that there is no more need to praise them here than to praise structural strength in discussing architecture. The desire for these qualities may be taken for granted. Our concern with them is not *should* they, but *how* are they to be achieved. In this, we may assume that legibility has been achieved when readability has been.

There has been a considerable amount of research in readability, but the problem has too many subtleties to ever yield to rational study alone. Nevertheless, where many tests are in agreement with each other *and* with the observations of experienced designers, it is fair to assume that some truth has been found. Thus, the opinions expressed in this section, while those of the author, relate to the scientific data available.

The readability of a page is affected by no less than 9 factors:
(a) typeface,
(b) size of type,
(c) length of line,
(d) leading,
(e) page pattern (which includes "margins"),
(f) contrast of type and paper (which includes color),
(g) texture of paper,
(h) typographic relationships (heads, folios, etc.), and
(i) suitability to content.

Some factors are more significant than others, but it is their combined effect that gives the page its character, and it is only when all are in perfect balance that a truly readable page results.

Paper is covered in CH.10, typographic relationships are discussed elsewhere in this chapter and in CH.18. Suitability to content is referred to in CH.15 and elsewhere throughout the book. The following discussion deals with the remaining factors of readability.

TYPEFACE We have seen that typefaces—even text types—have individual characteristics that can be matched with corresponding characteristics of the text. The choice of typeface should be made initially on this basis. If it becomes apparent that the face chosen cannot

compromise may be necessary. As always, begin with that which
seems best and give up only what you must.

It is the apparent, or *visual*, size of type with which we are con-   SIZE OF TYPE
cerned first. The *actual* type size (CH. 5) will affect the book's
length, but it is the appearance of the face that affects readability.

Readability is relative to the reading ability of the book's user.
Within the limits of normal book use—that is, with a general audience of adult readers—minor differences in type size are not
significant. When the potential readers are either very old or very
young, type size becomes an important factor.

It is generally recognized that larger sizes are desirable for children who are learning to read, but most children's book editors in
America favor extremely large type in comparison to the sizes ordinarily used in England and other countries. In the lowest age
group—say 5 to 7—the 18 pt. faces in use are probably not excessive, as the children are still having some difficulty recognizing
letters. From 7 to 8 up to about 10 there is probably no need for
anything larger than an average 12 pt. face, although 14 pt. is often
used. Between 10 and 12, a good reader needs no more than a large
11 pt. and over 12 years old an average child does not have any
difficulty reading the 11 pt. faces commonly used for adult books,
as long as the other elements of the text page are selected for particularly good readability. Some editors and teachers feel, however,
that larger sizes are necessary to make reading seem easier.

The use of large type for children is based more on psychological
than optical reasons, and these are somewhat debatable. With elderly readers, larger sizes may be needed because failing sight requires them. Yet, little attention is given to this consideration. (It is
true that proper eyeglasses would eliminate the problem, but the
book designer's function is to accommodate the readers [and the
author and publisher], not to drive them to the optometrist.)

In books intended primarily for people over 60, the text type
should not be smaller than a large 11 pt. Where space permits, 12
pt. is preferable. The other elements of the page should be chosen,
as they are for small children, for maximum readability. There are,
of course, books published in large type size especially for the elderly and those with poor vision. Here we are discussing books for
the general reader which are expected to have an audience of older
people with average vision for their age.

For adults whose sight can be presumed to be normal, the larger
10 pt. faces are adequate, if the other elements of readability are
favorable. Most hardcover books are set in 11 pt., although paperbacks have enjoyed a tremendous public with 10 and 9 pt. text
types, and sometimes 8 pt.

Readability is relative also to the *kind* of reading. Normal sizes of type are needed for sustained texts such as novels, etc., while brief texts, as in encyclopedias, can be set smaller without impairing readability.

LENGTH OF LINE There are few aspects of readability that are truly measurable, but length of line is one. In view of this, it is insupportable that the most frequent destroyer of readability is excessive length of line. The reason is quite obvious. Long lines of type, especially when well leaded, look graceful—just as tall, slender models do. But the models are too skinny for anything but modeling, and long lines of type are not efficient for reading.

rooms (when the normal day ending at 10 p.m. would be much prolonged) girls have asserted . . . that they enjoy the excitement of such nights, unless too often repeated; the furious haste with which the work is pushed on, the speculation as to whether it will be finished in time, and the additional refreshments provided on such occasions,

Tests have shown many disadvantages in long lines: (a) the eye must blink at intervals during reading. After each blink, an optical adjustment and refocus of vision takes place. The longer the line, the more frequently blinks occur within, rather than at the end of lines; (b) there is the time and visual effort lost in traveling back to the beginning of the next line; (c) when the measure is too wide, there is momentary difficulty in determining which *is* the next line (sometimes the wrong one is selected). Each interruption—the blink, the trip back, and the search for the right line—causes loss of reading efficiency, or poor readability.

Another optical factor that affects reading comfort is the span of vision. Without moving your eyes or head you can see clearly straight ahead and about 2° to each side. Naturally, the less movement necessary, the less fatigue. (A very small amount of movement is desirable, but more becomes tiring.) Consequently, there is a maximum comfortable measure for each distance from eye to object, the ideal width becoming greater as the distance increases. At the normal book-reading distance—about 16″ (40 cm)—the maximum comfortable measure is about 5″ (12.7 cm). At the billboard-reading distance, a line of 20 feet in length can be read with no more muscular effort than required by a 5″ line in a book.

All the factors of visual comfort tend to suggest a *maximum* of about 70 characters per line in a page of average size. Fewer characters is better—down to about 50, where it becomes difficult to set justified lines without excessive hyphenation of words and irregular word-spacing, both of which reduce readability. The ideal is probably between 55 and 60 characters per line, at a length of about 4″ (24 picas) for justified text. For unjustified lines, 45 characters is about optimum. It may be necessary to vary from the ideal for economic reasons, but then it is better to make a radical change in the basic decisions than to exceed by very much the maximum and minimum limits. However, the limits depend on the reading capabilities of each audience. For children, the elderly, and the visually or mentally handicapped, the lower limits are applicable. For the experienced reader and the mentally gifted, the upper limits may be used.

LEADING

Neither size of type nor length of line can be selected independently of leading. The larger the type the more leading is needed to avoid confusion. If the space between lines is not sufficient in relation to the space between words, the horizontal movement of the eye is disturbed. The longer the line, the more leading is needed to distinguish the lines and facilitate finding the beginning of the next one.

every page at full width

Up to a point, the more leading the better. Beyond this point, additional leading may detract from readability. The optimum amount depends on the typeface, its size, and the measure. Where word-spacing is unusually large, as in books for young children, the amount of leading should be in proportion. With so many variables involved, the choice of leading is more a matter of visual judgment than mathematics.

In general, average 10 pt. and 11 pt. faces on measures up to 22 picas can do with 1 pt. of leading; from 22 to 25 picas with 2 pts.; over 25 with 3. Types of 12 and 14 pt. generally need a minimum of 2 pts., require 3 when set wider than 25 picas, and read better with 4 pts. on 28 picas or over. Small sizes, such as 8 and 9 pt., need proportionately more leading than the larger sizes, to compensate for their lower readability. When set in narrow measures, this need diminishes. For example, 8 pt. set 12 picas wide can be read quite comfortably with 1 pt. (or no) leading. On a 20-pica measure it might need 2 pts., on 23 picas, 3 pts. Remember, however, that the x height of each face greatly affects the leading desirable. For this reason, a table indicating the proper leading for each size and measure would not be practical.

When I wrote the following pages, or rather the bulk of them, I lived alone, in the woods, a mile from any neighbor, in a house which I had built myself, on

8/9 x 12

When I wrote the following pages, or rather the bulk of them, I lived alone, in the woods, a mile from any neighbor, in a house which I had built myself, on the shore of Walden Pond, in Concord, Massachusetts, and earned my living by the labor of my

8/10 x 20

When I wrote the following pages, or rather the bulk of them, I lived alone, in the woods, a mile from any neighbor, in a house which I had built myself, on the shore of Walden Pond, in Concord, Massachusetts, and earned my living by the labor of my hands only. I lived there two

8/11 x 23

When there is too much space between lines, there is a loss of efficiency (readability) because the reader expects to find the next line at the customary distance. His eye goes first to this point and then makes an adjustment. When the adjustment is small, the loss of efficiency is probably not significant. Where the leading is very large—say, 8 pts.—the disturbance is probably considerable and may persist throughout the reading of the book.

In this matter, as in other aspects of readability, habit and experience are larger factors than is generally conceded. Most psychological testers of reading acknowledge these elements to some degree but, in the end, they usually draw conclusions from the performance of their subjects without giving much weight to the influence of training. Since peoples of other cultures learn to read easily in alphabets very different from our own, it is reasonable to assume that we would respond very differently to reading tests if we had been otherwise trained. Thus, the testers' conclusions are not empirical facts so much as observations of conditioned behavior. For example, if it is a fact that more than 3 or 4 pts. of leading hampers reading—as many psychologists claim—why do typesetters prefer double-spaced typescript having about 12 pts. of leading? Even allowing for the large size of typewriter type and the usually wide measure of typescript, double spacing is proportionately the equivalent of about 9 pts. of leading in a page of 11 pt. type set 24 picas wide.

PAGE PATTERN

The term "*page pattern*" may seem unfamiliar in this context, but it is used deliberately to avoid the word "*margins*". The concept of a page as a block of type surrounded by a frame of "margins" is a vestige of hand-press days. Then the page was indeed a rectangular block of metal arranged on the page so as to leave enough paper on each side to meet the printing and binding requirements of the time. The proportions of these margins were determined largely by the need to minimize the size of the 4-page forms generally used in the early days of printing. This meant reducing the head and inside margins to get the pages as close together as possible, so that a good impression could be obtained with a minimum of effort. This left plenty of paper on the outside and bottom edges of the printed page. The practical necessity soon became an esthetic dogma and the conventional margin proportions have been taught to apprentice printers ever since.

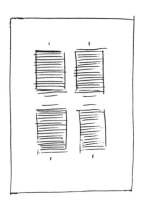

To see what bookmakers would do without the mechanical restraints of printing, look at the early manuscripts. In these, the pages were regarded as areas to be filled in the most beautiful and effective way with words, pictures, and space arranged over the entire *spread*, rather than the individual page. The manuscript maker's criteria were visual and functional, not conventional and mechanical—at least in the beginning.

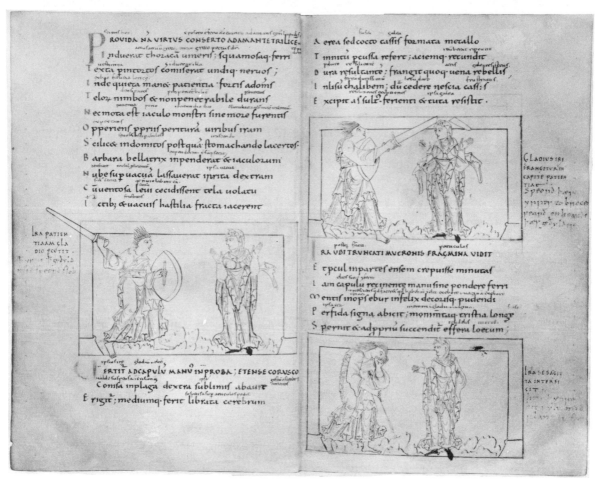

8th century manuscript.

The graphic freedom of the manuscript books is available again. In any method of printing in which photomechanical plates are used—and they are used in all—the mechanical limitations of the hand-press no longer apply. There *are*, sometimes, extra costs involved in nonconventional page layouts, but there is no significant reason—esthetic, practical, or economic—to remain bound by the obsolete conventions of "margins".

It has been suggested that the type page should not come too close to the outside edge in children's books because young readers have a tendency to swing off the page at the end of a line. Whatever the merits of that claim, there is certainly no such consideration in adult books. Millions of paperbacks are sold and read with outside margins of minimal size. In defense of the conventional arrangement it has even been claimed that a large foot margin is necessary to provide room for the reader's thumb! Aside from the obvious fact that anyone able to read would have sense enough to move his thumb if it happened to cover the next word, no one is likely to hold a book at the bottom unless reading while walking—an uncommon and risky practice.

This is not to say that a conventional page pattern is bad. It may very well be the best. The point is that the size, shape, and position of the type areas and other elements on the page should be determined by the visual, practical, and economic requirements of the individual problem, not by the application of a rigid formula. If the problem is well analyzed and solved, any arrangement is fully justified.

In conclusion
A truly personal style in typography takes many years—decades—to develop. There are some who feel that in book typography the designer's personality should be completely submerged. It is doubtful, however, that the personality of a designer, as it is revealed in a well-done book, is any more detrimental to the content than the personality of an actor is to a play or that of a conductor to a symphony. As long as the interpreter's personality does not *dominate* or *alter* the work, it can enliven and enrich it.

The heights attainable in typography are limited by talent and experience. In the beginning, simplicity is best because it is necessary for success. Later, it becomes an essential part of the designer's outlook. In between, experiment has its place.

This chapter has dealt with typography in general—later chapters will discuss typography in relation to particular phases of bookmaking.

7 | Illustration

Far from simply "laying out" pictures supplied with the Ms, the designer may initiate the idea of illustrations and suggest their character. Few authors think in graphic terms—and fewer still are well acquainted with the techniques of visual expression. The book designers operate as graphic engineers, utilizing the science and art of visual presentation to achieve optimum communication, so it is appropriate for them to advise on this aspect of books. Therefore, the very conception, inclusion, and selection of the illustrations—as well as their placement and reproduction—are parts of book design. Properly, these matters are discussed by author, editor, designer, and production manager jointly—with a view to producing the best book possible.

Relation to design

In tradebooks, the use of illustration is considered less often than it should be, due to the impression that it necessarily involves great expense. This is not so, as will be shown.

There is a wide range of visual material included in "illustration". This becomes clear when the kinds of illustration are divided by function. There are 4 kinds: (a) Informative, (b) Suggestive, (c) Decorative, and (d) Representative.

Kinds of illustration

■ *Informative*—Those whose purpose is to explain or depict facts, circumstances, characters, things, or places. Included here are the realistic drawings commonly used in teenage fiction, the photographs, drawings, diagrams, etc. found in many technical and other nonfiction books.

■ *Suggestive*—These include all graphic elements designed to establish or enhance mood or atmosphere.

■ *Decorative*—These are graphic elements whose purpose is simply to ornament the page.

■ *Representative*—These are pictures being shown as works of art, for the purpose of producing an approximation of the pleasure of seeing the original. This includes the reproductions and prints in art books and other illustrated books in which works of art are included for this purpose. In our visual age, more and more books fall into this category—and many are created around such illustrations. Not only is the public attuned to graphics by television and movies, but the technology of picture reproduction has greatly enhanced the quality and economy of illustrated books.

Some illustrations fall into more than one category, but a dominant purpose can usually be defined. Realistic illustrations may have such evocative power as to place them in the suggestive category. If they are more valuable for the moods they induce than for the facts they impart, they may be used accordingly. Some decorative material may be particularly allusive and find its way into the suggestive group. Hardly anything less abstract than type rules and some stock ornaments can fail to suggest subject matter, although the medieval and Renaissance illuminators used floral decoration with no subject relationship to the text on the page.

One picture may be used for different purposes and thus fall into a different category in each case. The distinction is in the intent, which is important because it determines how the illustration is used and reproduced. For example, a fine photograph of Wall Street used in a guidebook would be informative. In a book of poems about city life the same picture could create atmosphere (suggestive). In a book of photographs, it might be reproduced just to give the reader pleasure and thus would be in the representative class.

Ways of introducing illustration

INFORMATIVE

It is sometimes desirable to use a map or diagram to clarify a point in fiction or narrative nonfiction. The simplest sketch can do the trick. It need be no more elaborate than the kind you would make to show someone the way to your house. Drawn directly and simply, such a sketch can be very effective. Another possibility is to use antique maps.

ILLUSTRATION   99

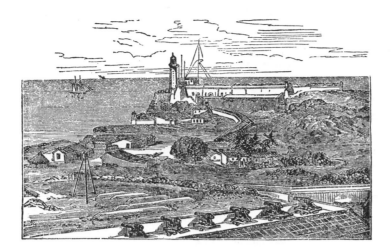

Illustrations of objects, characters, and places can be useful and interesting. These too can be rough sketches by the designer (or the author) or they can be taken from existing pictorial material. For example, some charming and accurate engravings of carpenter's tools were taken from an old hardware catalogue and used in a new book on finishing cellars and attics. Many travel books of the 19th century had pen-and-ink drawings of various places. These could be used in travel books, biographies, fiction, etc.

Here the opportunity for illustration is truly unlimited. The whole range of symbolism, from literal to abstract, is at the designer's disposal.

SUGGESTIVE

Of literal symbols there are all the insignia, emblems, and devices of organizations, nations, families, societies, companies, etc. A book about submarines can use the submarine officer's insigne, a book with England as its subject can have a British lion or even a royal coat of arms, and so on. Other symbols can be created from type ornaments and rules. Anything that establishes or enhances a mood or atmosphere can be used. The most abstract device can have suggestive power. A classic example is the black border that effectively creates a funereal mood.

arthur daley

RANDOM HOUSE

NEW YORK

tımes at bat

A HALF CENTURY OF BASEBALL

Pictures can be used to enhance atmosphere. Among the thousands of works by artists over the centuries there are some expressing virtually every state of feeling. Gay, sad, tragic, bucolic, orgiastic, tender, terrible, pictures abound—many by great masters. These can be your background music. Old Chinese drawings of bare trees were used to create a wintry feeling, bacchanalian scenes from Greek pottery have been used to set a gay mood. Countless wood engravings and other pictures have been used to provide the flavor of a particular period characterized by a style of illustration. The possibilities are endless.

DECORATIVE   An excess of decoration in the late 19th century led to a severe functional attitude in the second quarter of the 20th. It can be argued that pure decoration, without informative or suggestive

ILLUSTRATION 101

value, is meaningless and therefore superfluous. Yet, the total absence of decoration in architecture has brought a new demand for decorated surfaces, and a recognition that decoration need not be at odds with function. (Louis Sullivan, one of the prophets of the "form follows function" school of architecture, used decoration extensively—as did his follower, Frank Lloyd Wright.) It is, however, quite difficult to use decoration functionally—and very easy to use it as pointless gaud. In any case, it must not be allowed to take precedence over other aspects of the book.

Where decoration is used to suggest the style of a period related to the text, it ceases to be decorative illustration and becomes suggestive. Any decoration using elements of a distinctly allusive nature is suggestive. It hardly seems worth using decoration that has no suggestive value, but it can be done. There is a great deal of typographic ornament available (although it is decreasing because of disuse), ranging from purely abstract rules, dots, squares, etc. to the most elaborate florets. These may be combined in infinite ways to create a pattern on a whole page—one of the more interesting uses of decoration—or a spot on a chapter opening or title page.

For the most part, this kind of illustration is an integral part of art and photography books. However, a reproduction of a picture can enhance the beauty (and value) of almost any kind of book— poetry, biography, history, etc.

When a picture is used whose subject is related to the text, the illustration has suggestive value, but if its main purpose is representative, it must be so treated. An abstract or nonobjective picture presents no such problem.

A single reproduction may be used as part of the frontmatter or several may be scattered through the book, either at random or at specific places, such as part-titles (CH. 22).

Sources of illustration

There is a huge store of graphic material available to the designer who has the imagination and knowledge to use it. Illustration can be obtained in 4 ways: (a) by commissioning an illustrator, (b) by paying for reproduction rights to existing pictures, (c) by using graphic material in the public domain or available without charge, and (d) by doing it yourself.

ILLUSTRATORS

It is desirable to keep a file of the names of illustrators who do a variety of work. A folder for each, with some photostats of his or her work is worth the trouble and space. Such a file can be developed by interviewing artists and by clipping interesting illustrations from magazines and newspapers or making photocopies of illustrations from books. A useful source of artists is the *Illustrators' Annual*, a catalogue of the yearly exhibitions sponsored by the Society of Illustrators. Also, there are agents who specialize in representing illustrators.

In general, younger artists charge lower prices and sometimes do work that is fresher and less commercial looking than that of the more experienced illustrators. It is possible to get attractive work (at even lower prices) from art school students. The disadvantage here is in the comparative uncertainty of the results. It takes long experience to develop a reliable technique and a sure approach. It is not enough to have the *ability* to do an excellent job, one must be able to deliver a good job in a very high percentage of tries, under the pressures of time and stringent requirements. This comes with years of practice.

The question of how much to pay an illustrator involves several intangible factors: the artist's experience, talent, and reputation; the job's difficulty, complexity, magnitude, and use. Then, what prices are asked by comparable artists? Is this an isolated job or one of many the same artist will get? Also, is it a rush or not? There is no easy way to get to the right answer. It must be worked out with goodwill on both sides.

Book illustration is an artistically attractive assignment, and many first-rate artists prefer this (at least occasionally) to advertis-

ILLUSTRATION   103

ing or magazine work. Consequently, they can sometimes be persuaded to accept little or no more than what a mediocre professional illustrator would be paid. This seems like an exploitive attitude, but it is not, when one considers that the economics of (most) book publishing will not permit the kind of fees paid in advertising and magazines. The choice is not between high and low fees, it is between small payment (in comparison with advertising) and no illustration.

It is good to support and encourage living artists, and a lot more could be done in this respect than is being done, but sometimes this is not possible. Then it becomes necessary to look to other, less costly means of finding illustration.

REPRODUCTION RIGHTS

If the illustration needs of the book can be met with pictures that already exist (thus eliminating the uncertainties of made-to-order illustrations), the rights to use such material can usually be obtained for much less than it would cost to commission the work initially.

How much the fee will amount to is a matter to be settled for each case. It can be very little, or the artist/photographer/owner may ask for a lot. If the price is too high there is usually no need to accept the terms, although sometimes a particular picture is so desirable it becomes necessary to pay an excessive price for it. Photographs by contemporary photographers are usually available from them directly or through a picture agency. The prices tend to be the same in either case, as they often are based on the standard fee schedules of the American Society of Magazine Photographers (ASMP). Since the economics of magazines and advertising are entirely different from those of book publishing, these prices are painfully high, although they are somewhat adjusted for book uses. Generally, fees vary according to use—more for jackets or covers than inside pages—with a sliding scale according to size: full-page, half-page, quarter-page. Of course, color is much more expensive than black & white (although the photographer's cost may be less). Some agencies relate fees to the number of books printed. The fee is generally for one-time use in one edition—with additional fees for reprint editions and foreign language editions.

"Fine" artists are much less organized than photographers. Their work is not done for reproduction, and it is relatively rarely reproduced outside of art books (except for a few very popular works by artists like Warhol, Johns, Oldenburg, etc.) so they are less dependent upon reproduction fees and less concerned about them. Since they often see a book reproduction as a valuable advertisement for the sale of their work they sometimes ask no fee at all. Exceptions to this are the artists who belong to the French organization SPADEM, which is similar in practice to ASMP in that it sets reproduction fees, but different in that it *collects* fees on behalf of the artists and their estates. Most of the artists listed by SPADEM are French, but some are other nationalities. SPADEM collects fees for publication in the United States as well as in Europe. Some publishers who use many pictures by SPADEM artists make special fee arrangements with the organization.

In the cases of SPADEM and the ASMP, the cost of their fees plus the administrative handling can make it economically unfeasible to publish a book with many pictures. Fortunately, there are often less expensive alternatives.

There are 2 kinds of material for which reproduction fees are paid: that which is in copyright and that which is not.

■ *Copyrighted material*—The old U.S. copyright law replaced in 1978 was in many ways inadequate, but it was quite simple on duration of copyright. The period was always 28 years, with one renewal for another 28 (extended during the gestating years of the new law). Unpublished works were protected indefinitely by common law. The new law is more fair to authors, but it is more complex. Following is a simplified outline of some relevant features:

For works created

1. before September 19, 1906: all U.S. copyrights of published works are expired; unpublished works are protected as in 2(c) below.
2. from September 19, 1906 through December 31, 1977:
   (a) Copyrights not renewed by the end of the 28th year after publication are expired.
   (b) If renewed, add 47 years (instead of 28) for a total of 75.
   (c) Works that are unpublished and unregistered have the same protection as works created *after* 1977, but are protected at least through 2002. If they are published before 2003, protection extends 25 years more (through 2027). If unpublished but registered, (a) and (b) above apply. Their status once their registration expires is not clearly defined.
3. For works created after December 31, 1977:
   (a) All works have copyright protection for the life of the author plus 50 years, except:
   (b) Works by anonymous or pseudonymous authors and "works made for hire", i.e. made by someone employed or commissioned by the copyright owner, which are protected for either 75 years from first publication or 100 years from creation, whichever occurs first.

(The term "author", as used in the copyright law, refers to all creators of original copyrightable works, including painters, sculptors, photographers, etc.)

When the maximum term of "old law" copyright was extended from 56 to 75 years, a provision was made for the author to get the benefit of the extra 19 years. If a work had been licensed for the full ILLUSTRATION 105 term before 1978, the author can (by complying with some complex formalities) get the rights back when the 56 years expire, even though the term is now 75 years.

Another new provision in favor of authors allows them (again, with considerable effort) to get most of their rights back after 35 years, even though they have granted them under the new law (after 1977) for their own lifetime plus 50 years.

Under the present law, all copyrights expire on the last day of the calendar year. Formerly, the expiration was on a particular day, so it is not possible to tell from the notice—which gives only the year of copyright—exactly when the renewal began, since there was more than a year during which renewal was possible. The Copyright Office will search its records and report on the copyright status of a particular work on request and payment of a modest hourly charge.

Under the old law, a work that was published in the U.S. without a proper copyright notice ordinarily lost its copyright forever. The new law still requires the notice, but allows for some curative steps in case it is omitted—provided they are taken within 5 years after publication. Note that once a work has passed into the U.S. public domain, for whatever reason, it can never be restored to copyright status. Thus, a work published without a notice under the new law is not in the public domain as long as it is subject to the remedies allowed.

Note that the copyright notice in a book is considered to cover the illustrations within the book, i.e. no separate notice is required on the illustrations. However, since the notice is usually in the name of the author or publisher, complications can arise if an artist or illustrator wants to defend a picture right.

Registration of a work with the U.S. Copyright Office is not *essential* to protection, so long as a notice appears on the work, but with registration the legal protection is better.

The law provides that the author, as the initial copyright owner, has the exclusive right to grant reproduction rights. If a work is sold—a painting, for example—in 1978 or later, the rights of the buyer to authorize reproduction are nil unless the painter specifically grants some. Non-exclusive reproduction rights can be conveyed verbally (a shaky basis), but if the buyer is to get exclusive rights, the artist must grant them in writing. With the exclusive right to reproduce the work goes copyright ownership to the extent necessary to protect that right.

Under the old law, some courts presumed that, generally, copyright was transferred along with physical ownership of a painting in the absence of anything specific to the contrary, while others took other positions. The present law is clear enough, but applies only to transfers taking place after 1977. Since transfers of ownership before 1978 are not covered by federal law, they are subject to the individual laws of the 50 states. Add to this the ambiguities of situations involving long-deceased artists and it becomes apparent that the question of reproduction rights is murky indeed. Even under the present law, when a living artist assigns exclusive rights to a purchaser, and the new owner gives authorization to a publisher, it is customary for the latter to ask the artist's permission out of respect for artistic integrity. Whether this courtesy extends to the estate of a recently deceased artist is a matter for personal decision.

Whatever the actual legal rights of a museum to grant—or withhold—reproduction permission in a particular case, as a practical matter one must either respect their requirements or risk being denied access to their collections thereafter.

All of the foregoing discussion applies only to U.S. law and publication in the U.S. To the complexities of domestic copyright law must be added the international problem. Under the Berne Convention (1886), works protected in one contracting nation are protected in each, according to its own laws. Most Western countries belong to this agreement, but the United States does not. However, its terms are generally respected by American publishers—who expect similar treatment in the other countries. Under the UNESCO Universal Copyright Convention, of which we *are* a signatory, protection in all participating nations usually is obtained by publication in any one, provided the proper notice is used (a "c" in a circle ©, the year, and the name of the copyright owner) in the proper place. Again, the protection given in each country is the same as given to works published under that country's laws.

There is an important exception in the U.S. copyright law known as the "manufacturing clause". This is a protectionist measure, inserted in the old law at the insistence of the U.S. book manufacturing industry and its labor unions, whereby a work by an American author could lose copyright protection if it was printed outside the United States. In the present (1978) law, these provisions are eased to allow printing in Canada, but the basic restriction remains. There are several complicated modifications, but in any case this rule expires on July 1, 1982. In the meantime, care must be taken whenever a book is planned for foreign manufacture, as the rule applies to pictures as well as text. The law is not specific as to what constitutes manufacture abroad, and there are some who interpret it to allow composition and film preparation outside the country. Certainly the copyright owners should be consulted if any risk to their protection is involved.

The copyright owner has a right to demand a fee for reproduction or to refuse permission altogether—and violation of copyright is punishable by law. When there is genuine doubt about the

ILLUSTRATION 107

copyright status of a particular work, inquiries should be made on the assumption that there *is* copyright protection.

Copyright law—both domestic and international—is not only often imprecise, it is riddled with exceptions and special conditions. The foregoing outline is meant to provide a general view of the subject, not a legal definition. It is a good idea to become familiar with current copyright requirements and to check whenever in doubt.

■ *Non-copyright material in private ownership*—A vast amount of graphic material not protected by copyright is yours to use—if you can get it. There are several kinds of agencies that collect such material for the purpose of charging reproduction fees. These include picture agencies, photographic agencies, some private museums, libraries, etc. Most of these will search their files for pictures you request, and then charge a fee for supplying them for reproduction. Your payment is almost always under an agreement that it is for one use only. Fees generally start at about $25 for one picture and go up from there according to the difficulty of finding the material, the use, etc. It is the owner's picture, and he can charge whatever he wants.

This can be a relatively expensive way to illustrate a book, but it usually costs less than hiring an illustrator, and sometimes the material is unobtainable otherwise. The larger picture agencies, such as Culver, Bettmann Archive, etc., have excellent facilities. There are dozens of sources of picture material, some quite specialized.

By far the greatest quantity of picture material in existence is available without charge. Man has been creating pictures for thousands of years, and much of this output is of excellent quality. There is no reason why it should be dormant when it can be effectively used. The problem is simply to find it. One publisher, Dover Publications, has made a business of selling, in book form, reprints of old pictures. Their quality is excellent, and the pictures are available for reproduction to anyone. However, Dover has merely scratched the surface—and could never reprint more than a cupful from the oceans of picture material extant.

FREE MATERIAL

There are 2 kinds of free graphic material: (a) that in the public domain and (b) material in private ownership.

■ *Material in the public domain*—This includes all uncopyrighted material obtainable without charge and without permission. Again, be careful about determining what is in the public domain. For example, nonmechanical (handmade) *reproductions* of works in public domain may be protected by copyright.

The primary sources of free illustration are old books. The great libraries are treasure houses of such material, but you need a special key. Except for some specialized collections, the books are catalogued according to their literary content and a great deal of searching is required to discover pictures among them—unless you know in advance of specific titles containing the pictures you want. Librarians can be very helpful in this respect, but most are not trained to think in terms of illustration, and their time is limited. It is best to go first to a specialized source or to someone familiar with the subject.

The print collections of libraries, historical societies, and museums are excellent sources of free pictures. (In almost all cases, a charge of between $1 and $6 is collected for photostats or photoprints supplied, but this is so small compared to the value of the pictures that they may be considered free.) The curators are usually able to guide you to material by subject, although most collections are catalogued by artist, title, number, etc. Some very old and rare prints and books may be unavailable for reproduction because of their condition. Many institutions that formerly charged no reproduction fees now do so.

There are several general picture collections that arrange material by subject and lend pictures for reproduction or similar use at no charge. The best of these are at the Main Building of the New York Public Library and the Library of Congress in Washington. The latter combines the features of a print collection and a picture collection, while the former confines itself mainly to clippings, movie stills, and some magazines. There is a good collection at the Philadelphia Free Library and others of varying size elsewhere. The use of pictures from these collections usually requires no fee to the lender, but the borrower is responsible for getting permission from copyright owners where necessary.

Old books, magazines, catalogues, prints, etc. can be bought in secondhand bookstores cheaply, if you count the value of the pictures they contain. With luck—and time—you can pick up good picture material at country auctions. A few cents will sometimes buy a boxful of old publications of no value to anyone but a picture user. Old postcards are also a valuable source, although many are in copyright.

One of the most valuable (and extensive) sources of public domain material is the U.S. government. This includes any work prepared by an officer or employee of the U.S. government as part of that person's official duties.

■ *Privately owned material*—Thanks to the desire of many business and other organizations to publicize themselves, there is a tremendous amount of free picture material available to anyone who can provide a credit line. Almost any medium-sized or large company will gladly supply pictures of their products, and some of the largest corporations maintain picture libraries of considerable scope. The public relations department is the place to ask. Another good source is the promotion department of a country, state, or resort anxious for publicity to attract visitors.

ILLUSTRATION   109

Movie stills can be purchased for small amounts (rare ones are not cheap) at shops in the larger cities or directly from the movie companies. Most picture agencies, and some museums and libraries, will supply them for a fee. The question of copyright for movie stills is quite complicated, but many of the older ones are out of copyright, even though the movie companies ask reproduction fees for their use. It is best to check with an expert.

It is possible, also, to obtain *color-separation films* (CH. 9) of illustration material under certain circumstances. Museums, art galleries, book and magazine publishers, have films of pictures which they have used, and will sometimes supply these at cost plus a fee that varies according to the owner. Usually, the fees are a fraction of the cost of making a new set of color separations. Reproduction permissions and fees are not affected by such arrangements. If films are obtained from someone other than the owner of the reproduction rights, the latter must still be approached for permission.

Some museums reserve the right to deny permission if the quality of reproduction fails to meet their standards. Again, there may be no legal right involved, but it is unwise to cross a great museum whose facilities may be denied in the future.

It is worth repeating that the real problem in getting illustration material is finding it. No one who has not done picture research personally has any idea how much time it can consume. To make use of existing pictures feasible, you must be able to go to the proper source without too much trial and error. Study the history and development of illustration to become familiar with general and specific sources. When looking for pictures, keep in mind the possibility of future use. Some excellent material may be discovered in the course of a search for something else. It is a good idea to build up a picture collection of your own. Save your old magazines, catalogues, etc. and cut out usable or unusually interesting graphic material. File your pictures by subject and you will sometime save yourself a trip and some money. Always remember that the picture you want to use may be someone else's property and that the copyright laws are to be observed. Speaking of people's rights, it is important to consider getting written releases *(model releases)* from anyone identifiable who appears in a photograph you want to reproduce. The right of privacy is very strongly protected by the courts, even where no apparent injury is involved. Professional models, as well as others, should be asked to give their signatures to a simple form you can prepare. This is sometimes difficult to arrange (even someone in a crowd scene can claim invasion of privacy under some circumstances), but every effort should be made. If you rent a picture, the owner should provide releases. It is not easy to know exactly when releases are needed, so unless you are very experienced in this matter it is best to get legal advice before deciding that a release is not necessary.

DO-IT-YOURSELF A certain amount of illustration may properly be considered part of the design. If designers introduce minor decorative elements into a title page they should, under most circumstances, execute the drawing as part of their function. If the illustration is at all extensive, and the designer is capable of producing it, he or she should be considered as an illustrator and paid accordingly.

Even those who are not trained or experienced in illustration can execute simple drawings and diagrams. There is a minimum of talent required, however, if the work is not to sink below the general level of the book. If you are in doubt, get some competent outside opinion before you include your own drawing in a book.

Treatment of illustrations Illustrations must be treated according to their nature and purpose and to the considerations arising from their physical relationship to the text. The factors involved are:

(a) editorial requirements of position (CH. 16),
(b) methods of binding (CH. 11),
(c) the processes of platemaking and printing (CH. 9),
(d) the paper (CH. 10),
(e) layout (CH. 21),
(f) preparing the illustrations for camera (CH. 8).

How these factors are taken into account is discussed in CH. 16.

8 | Preparation for camera & press

The emergence of offset lithography as the predominant method of printing has raised the subject of preparation for camera and press to a level equal to the other main departments of bookmaking. "Preparation" involves 2 basic areas of work: (a) the preparation of material to be photographed, and (b) the production and assembly of platemaking film. The former is generally done in the publisher's or designer's office, the latter is done in the shop of the printer or a specialized preparation (*prep*) house. For convenience, the one is called "preparation for camera" and the other "preparation for press", although this is not entirely accurate because the printer is also involved in preparation for camera. Nonetheless, this chapter has been divided into those two areas, with the functions described in the order that seems logical, regardless of who performs them. Thus, the "preparation for press" section is given first, because this knowledge is necessary to do preparation for camera properly—even though the latter is actually done before the former.

General

This section is concerned with processes that are basically photographic—which is true of almost all the steps in the preparations for printing by offset lithography, gravure, *silk screen*, or *xerography* (CH.9). ("Photographic" in this sense includes the various technologies that use optics and light—cathode ray, laser, etc.—as well as conventional photography.) Preparation for *letterpress* printing (CH.9) involves photomechanical processes in platemaking and *photoengraving* (see below), but otherwise the work is largely in giving instructions for the disposition of plates on the press (see "Imposition" later in this chapter). Since the use of illustrations in letterpress is now almost entirely a matter of using existing engravings, this section is, in effect, concerned only with offset printing and other processes using photomechanical plates.

Each aspect of preparation will be described separately, but keep

Preparation for press

in mind that the tendency is toward *systems* rather than individual operations. Because the systems coming into use include the generation of all graphic elements—type and illustrations—as well as printing plates and even finished printed images, there is necessarily some overlap with chapters dealing with each part of the process. Duplication is avoided as much as possible by making reference to other chapters.

TYPE The steps in the production of final film ready for making plates are described in CH. 5. The point at which this process becomes preparation-for-press is when some form of imposition for printing is involved. In the systems approach, the line between makeup and imposition blurs as it becomes possible to encode a single tape with both imposition *and* makeup commands, and as devices become available to do both in the same operation. However, since makeup may involve illustrations as well as type, discussion of this phase of type production is deferred until after illustration production is described.

ILLUSTRATIONS:
PHOTOENGRAVING

Photoengraving is the name applied to a branch of photomechanical platemaking concerned with making metal relief plates for letterpress printing. These plates were used mostly for reproducing illustrations and are referred to as *cuts*. There are basically 2 kinds: *line cuts* [which reproduce artwork that has only black & white, i.e. no gray tones] and *halftone cuts* [which reproduce copy with continuous tones (photographs, etc.)].

Modern offset lithography can print illustrations—particularly halftones—so much more efficiently than letterpress that the use of photoengraving has been reduced to very limited special applications. The photomechanical procedures for making illustration plates for offset are virtually identical to those for making photoengravings. The difference in the two processes is in the making of the plate itself.

In photoengraving, the photographic negative is exposed against a photosensitive coating on a metal plate, which is then acid-etched to a suitable depth. Offset platemaking is described in CH. 9 under "Lithography". The method of producing the films used for making illustration plates of both processes is described below.

ILLUSTRATIONS: BLACK & WHITE

■ *Line illustrations*—These are photographed with maximum contrast to produce a negative that has no intermediate tones—only solid positive or negative areas. The process for making a line negative is no different from that for shooting type. In the scanning machines or CRT devices (CH. 5) line illustrations can be generated in the same way as type characters. (See "Camera copy" later in this chapter.)

■ *Halftone illustrations*—*Continuous-tone* copy (see "Camera copy") is photographed through a glass plate containing a grid of very fine lines. In the printed image this breaks up the subject into thousands of tiny black squares, each one varying in size according to the amount of light reflected by the subject at that point. Theoretically, black reflects no light, so the squares will be full size; white reflects the maximum light, so no square will appear at all (they usually appear in very small size); a middle tone of gray will produce a square of half size, and so on. The effect of light rounds off the corners of the squares so that they look like round dots to the naked eye. The overall impression conveyed by these thousands of tiny dots of varying size is an illusion of the tones of the subject.

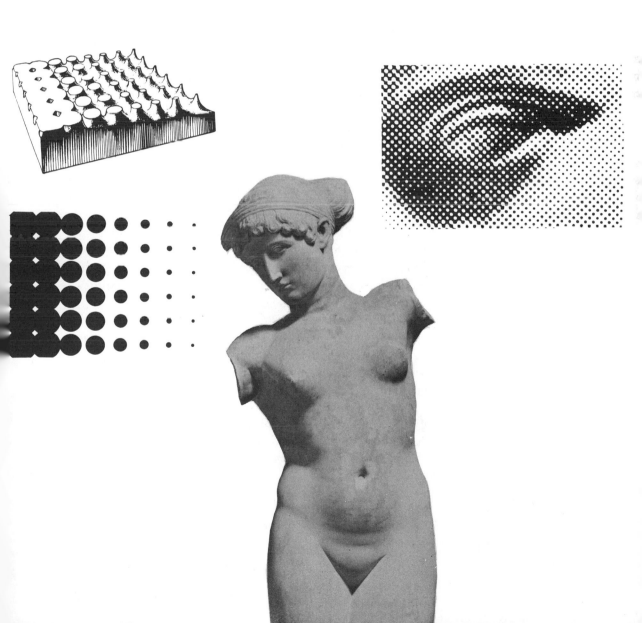

60   85   100   120   133   150

The finer the grid (*screen*) the better the illusion. Halftone screens range from about 50 lines to the inch up to 300. The sizes generally available are: 50, 60, 65, 85, 100, 110, 120, 133, 150, 200, 300. Of course, in the film *negative* the black dots are clear and vice versa in film positives.

There are several variations possible in making illustration films. A halftone can be combined with a line illustration (*combination*); the background can be eliminated in a halftone, leaving only a figure or object (*silhouette*); the background can be made to fade away (*vignette*); or the screen can be dropped out of areas in which pure white is desired (*highlight* or *dropout halftone*); screen patterns (*bendays*) can be added to line illustrations; halftones can be made with straight, wavy, or circular line screens instead of dots. It is also possible to shoot halftone copy with such contrast that it becomes line illustration and to make line copy look like halftone.

A particularly important variation is the *doubledot halftone*. This is made by shooting the copy twice, with different exposures, then *contacting* the 2 negatives by placing one over the other and exposing the two against a third piece of sensitized film to make a single negative (or positive). The result is a greater range of tones and richer shadows. Efforts are made to improve the results by changing the angles of the screens and varying the exposures.

A related variation is the *duotone*, which is similar to doubledot in preparation. Instead of combining the 2 negatives, each one is used to make a separate plate, one of which prints in black while the other prints in a color or a gray ink. Of course, this requires 2 press runs whereas doubledot is a one-color method.

Benday tone or *tint* screens are measured according to their size (as halftone screens) and their degree of darkness (tint). The tint is determined by the size of the dots or lines and is usually specified in percentages of solid black. Thus, a request for a benday tone must include both screen size and tint (for example, 120 screen, 70% tint, etc.). Tints are also designated by letters from A (about 10%) to H (about 90%), but it is probably safer to use the percentage method.

Most of the special effects are achieved by skilled craftsmen working with the negatives on a translucent glass table lighted from underneath. The negatives are assembled on a paper, glass, or plastic sheet (called a *flat*) to be stripped in. Silhouetting, highlighting, and other effects in which the screen is eliminated are ac-

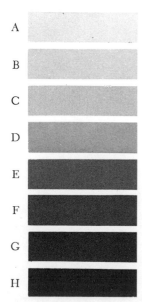

tints, 120 screen

A
B
C
D
E
F
G
H

silhouette

dropout

vignette

Aphrodite

combination

circular screen

benday

complished by *opaquing* the negative [painting out the unwanted areas] or by *masking* areas to reduce the light admitted. This is expensive work, and some of it can be done on the copy by an artist or retoucher at less cost and with more control over the results.

Preparation of film for making photomechanical plates for *simple (non-process) color printing,* regardless of the kind, is exactly the same process as preparing for printing in black. Provided the copy is *pre-separated* (see "Mechanicals" later in this chapter), the cameraman proceeds without regard for color at all. If the colors do not overlap (*overprint*) and are on the same board, the entire copy is photographed 4 times, once for each color, and the negatives are opaqued so that each film is left with the copy for only one color. When the colors overlap, the copy for each is on a separate mechanical and is photographed individually. Either way, in the end there is separate film for each color.

Color process (full-color reproduction) (see "Camera copy") involves 3 distinct operations—each of which must be performed well or the result will be poor. Full-color reproduction is at best a compromise, so there is not much room for failure. The 3 operations are: (a) color separation, (b) color correction, and (c) color proofing.

■ *Color separation*—The copy is photographed 4 times, once with a special lens to get black, the other 3 times with colored filters that exclude all but blue, yellow, and red, respectively. (Sometimes the black shot is omitted. Theoretically, the 3 primary colors will combine to produce all others, but in practice the addition of black is usually needed to add depth and brilliance.) (See front endpaper.)

The separation films are usually continuous-tone negatives, i.e. there is no screen. To correct color imbalances and various deficiencies in the copy, the separator may use *film masks* [a set of separation negatives made with special filters which are combined with the primary set] to control the densities in each film. (The Kodak Tri-Mask film accomplishes this with one shot.)

The corrected separation negatives may then be contacted to make positive films, which are exposed against another film with a halftone screen grid placed between. The result is a set of 4 screened halftone negatives which are used to make plates. Some offset plates require positive films (CH.9), which are made by contacting the screens to the original separated negatives. The final film may be made by various combinations of contacting, depending on the preference of the separator and/or the printer. The halftone screens are placed at different angles for each color, so that the dots for each color will print alongside, rather than on top of, each other. This creates a "rosette" pattern which should be present in all color process proofs if a good result is to be expected. This pattern is evidence of proper *register* [the correct placement of printing plates in relation to each other].

There are *color-scanning* machines that electronically separate the colors without the use of a camera or masks. An operator sets the appropriate exposures for each color, making allowance for deficiencies in the original or for desired modifications. With an attachment called a Chromoscope, the operator can see the results of such corrections and thus can control them better. The machine produces a set of film separations in a fraction of the time required for camera separation. When scanners were introduced in the 1950s their work was used mainly for inexpensive, large-volume work. More recent machines, like the laser-operated Hell DC 300L, produce excellent screened or continuous-tone separations in about 7 minutes.

Before separation is begun, it is important that the separator be informed of the paper to be used, and of the printer's ink color, sequence, and *density* [the degree of coverage] requirements. These considerations must be taken into account when making the separations or there will be difficulties on press.

■ *Color correction*—It is extremely difficult to obtain fine quality reproduction with color-separation photography or scanners alone, so it is often necessary to modify the films by hand. This operation demands highly skilled technicians, and requires considerable time. The work is usually done on the screened film. To *decrease* the strength of a color, a positive is chemically etched to

Hell DC 300L scanner

make the dots smaller (*sharpening*). To *increase* the color, a negative is etched to make the dots larger. The corrected film is then contacted as necessary to produce either positives or negatives for platemaking. Such correction can be either general—over the entire picture—or local—in only one area. It is best to make general corrections first, to get all the colors in balance, before making local corrections. Some color correction is done by the separator before the proofs are pulled for the customer. Further correction is made after, when marked proofs are returned.

■ *Color proofs*—Proofs of simple color are used to check register and color (particularly the effects of overprinting).

Proofs of color process films, usually made on a 38″ one-color or 4-color press, are shown singly for each color and in combination, using the *process inks*—a more-or-less standard yellow, violet-red (magenta), green-blue (cyan), and, of course, black. These *progressive proofs* are usually presented in the sequence of printing—for example, first the yellow plate alone, then red alone, then yellow plus red, blue alone, yellow and red plus blue, black alone, all 4 together (see front endpaper). Where more than 4 colors are used, the same procedure is followed. To be useful, the proofs should be pulled on the same paper with the same inks that will be used for the production run. It is also best to see that the ink densities and color sequence are coordinated.

In checking color process proofs, compare the copy with the final proof to see if the balance of color is correct. Defects in color may be corrected in 3 ways—by modifying the separation films, by changing the sequence of colors, or by altering the color of ink. The latter 2 are not recommended unless the change would be suitable for *all* the color illustrations in the book. If you are not quite expert in such matters, it is best to simply complain to the separators about what seems wrong and leave the choice of remedy to them.

There are several contact-image systems for checking color process that are less expensive than pulling proofs on a press. One of these is the 3M *Color Key* proof, which delivers separate film positives in color of each color separation negative. The colors obtained by placing these films over each other are not a true indication of the final effect, but the proofs are useful for checking size, register, blemishes, etc., and they are very good for making presentations. A better method is the *Chromalin* proof. This is made by exposing each separation film to a sheet of photosensitized clear plastic treated so that a dust of the appropriate process color will adhere to the printing areas (the dots). Each color is applied this way. The 4 plastic sheets are then placed over each other in register and laminated for protection. The color can be quite accurate, although it is subject to some variation in the process of application.

No matter what the method of proofing, remember that register can affect color, so the proofs must be in perfect register. The separator should provide proofs with register marks on all edges of the sheet, and with *color bars* on one long edge. Color bars are small printed solid panels that show each color separately, so that it is possible to check that the ink density is sufficient and even over the entire sheet. This insures that the separator did not correct color deficiencies by manipulating the ink on the proofs (in ways that cannot be matched by the printer).

Ink density can easily be measured by an instrument called a *densitometer*, which is part of the equipment of all color separators and printers. If the density is not sufficient, it may be difficult for the printer to control the color because there will not be enough ink flow to permit the normal fluctuations. Normal ink density varies with the paper used, but the range is usually from 80–90 for yellow, 110–120 for blue and red, and 125–135 for black.

IMPOSITION

Regardless of the method of composition, platemaking, or printing used, a certain number of pages will be printed at one time. This number is determined partly by press size and binding requirements (CH.11). A large page—say 9 × 12″ (22.9 × 30.5 cm)—may be printed with only 8 pages on each side of the sheet; with an average page—say 5½ × 8¼″ (13.97 × 20.96 cm)—there may be 64 on each side. (One factor is printing quality, which is easier to control on a small sheet.) While any number of pages can be *printed* in one form, *binding* requires a multiple of 4—and preferably 8. Most books are printed in forms of 16, 32, or 64 pages, but some have 12, 24, or 36 page forms.

Imposition is the arrangement of the pages in a form so that they will be in correct order when folded. The plan is determined by the binder according to the folding equipment to be used. The imposition also involves placing the pages so that the margins will be correct.

The designer should have an imposition diagram (CH.11) in hand while making illustration page layouts (CH.21). In cylinder press printing (CH.9), one edge of the sheet is held to the cylinder by *grippers* requiring about ½″ (1.27 cm) space, so there can be no *bleeds* [illustrations running off the edge of the page] on the gripper edge, unless a larger sheet is provided.

work-and-turn

sheetwise

Sometimes, 2 small forms are printed together on one side of a sheet and kept on the press while the pile of sheets is turned over lengthwise and the other side is printed. Thus, form 1 backs up 2 on one end of the sheet, and 2 backs 1 on the other, so that 2 complete units are printed with the number of impressions required for one, with only one form to make ready instead of 2. This is called a *work-and-turn* imposition. A normal imposition, in which a single form is backed by another, is called *sheetwise*.

When small units, such as endpapers, are printed in large quantities, they may be imposed with 4, 8, 12, or more units in one form (4-*up*, 8-*up*, 12-*up*, etc.), provided the reduced number of impressions required justifies the increased plate cost and the larger press.

Making photomechanical plates with multiple-unit impositions means making as many negatives as there are copies wanted, combining them in position, and then exposing them as in making a single plate. Even where only one color is involved, the several negatives (and there may be 20 or more) must be accurately positioned so that when the printed sheet is cut apart, all copies will be square and have correct margins. When the copy has several colors, the problem of positioning becomes formidable because of the importance of registering each color (see "Illustrations: color"). Most printers now use high-precision *step-and-repeat* machines to achieve the positioning required, at much greater speed and with more accuracy than by hand.

Sometimes, books are imposed for printing 2-up in order to facilitate 2-up binding. This is a very economical practice, provided that large quantities are involved.

The imposition requirements of *web presses* differ in detail, but the principles are the same as for *sheet-fed* presses. Since most webs have *in-line* folding [a machine is in-line when it is attached to the machine that performs the preceding work, so that no handling of the material between operations is required] (CHS.9, 10), there is no problem of coordination between printer and binder.

Preparation for camera

The key attribute in this work is *accuracy*. Neatness is highly desirable—and its absence can cause some problems—but it is possible to produce the desired results with sloppy work *if it is accurate*. The preparation of copy is essentially the same for all kinds of material and all processes. There *are* differences, and these will be taken up later, but the basic considerations are similar and are discussed in this section.

CAMERA COPY

There are 2 kinds of camera copy: line and continuous-tone.

■ *Line copy*—This is photographed with maximum contrast—that is, every mark is solid and everything in the background is eliminated entirely. Even where there is the appearance of intermediate tones, as in halftone screens, benday tints, etc., there are really only solid dots or lines with white space between.

Thus, the essential characteristics of line copy are sharpness and contrast. Each dot, line, or mass should have clearly defined edges and every mark should be as close to black as possible, the backgrounds as close to white as possible. Anything short of the ideal black against white necessitates a compromise in the camera work, and there will be a loss of quality in the result. Faint lines and gray areas *can* be picked up, dark backgrounds *can* be dropped out, but the measures required to compensate for deficiencies in the copy will create other deficiencies in the result. To some extent, these problems can be overcome by skillful etching, finishing, etc., but it is best to avoid the problems by providing good copy.

■ *Continuous-tone copy* (photographs, etc.)—This copy cannot be reproduced exactly, but something pretty close to perfection is theoretically possible. However, to achieve the best results it is necessary to have an ideal combination of perfect plates, paper, and press work, and these are rarely available. It must be anticipated that some loss of fidelity will result, so the copy should be of the highest quality possible. While some qualities lacking in copy can be faked by the prep shop, it is much better (and cheaper) to start out with good subjects.

Each piece of copy has its own requirements and characteristics. Following are some notes on the most frequently used kinds:

■ *Reproduction proofs*—The sharpest proofs are made on a gloss-coated paper, but some cameramen prefer dull-coated stock because it makes less glare. Examine repros carefully for broken letters, etc. Proofs are not necessarily first-rate just because they are called repros. Reject those that are not sharp and clean. The positive prints that are made by a phototypesetter are also repros. These are usually perfect, but not always. Sometimes exposure or development is too long or short, and the result is type that is too thin or too heavy. This is particularly worth watching when corrections are being put in as *patches*, when the patch might not match the rest of the type.

■ *Photostats*—The main problem with photostats is distortion caused by shrinkage of the paper in drying. Some attempt is made in the camera work to compensate for this, but the trouble is that the shrinkage is irregular. For most purposes, the distortion is negligible, but it can be serious where register is involved. The larger the size, the worse the problem. It is now possible to get stats on non-shrinking plasticized paper.

Don't expect good duplication of continuous-tone copy by photostat. The process is primarily a means of reproducing line copy cheaply. To get good line copy duplication, ask for *glossy prints* and indicate that they are for reproduction. However, use original copy whenever possible, as even the best stats are 2 steps away and there is some loss in each step. Out-of-focus prints should be rejected. *Matte* [soft finish] *prints* are cheaper and are good enough for dummies and sketches. Remember that the first step is a negative. To get a positive print, 2 stats are needed.

■ *Direct positives*—These are photoprints that reproduce the copy in one step. The process is ideal for line copy, but produces too much contrast for tone copy. A single print costs a little less than a positive stat plus a negative, so it is economical if only one copy is needed. For multiple copies it is cheaper to make positive stats from a single negative. Like almost all photoprints now, direct positives are made on plasticized paper that does not shrink or stretch.

■ *Photographs*—For good reproduction, monochrome photographs should be glossy prints, preferably with a wide range of tones from light to deep shadow. The reproduction process tends to flatten out the tones (the lights get darker and the darks get lighter), so it is best to begin with rich contrasts.

Everyone knows that one shouldn't write heavily on the back of a photograph or use paperclips without adequate padding, but a large proportion of photographs carry the bas-relief marks of those offenses. Don't.

■ *Line drawings*—The time to worry about the suitability of drawings for line reproduction is before they are made. Experienced professional illustrators need no warning, but those who are not familiar with the problems of reproduction should, when possible, be told the basic considerations:

(a) Use *black* ink, paint, or pencil on white paper.

(b) Faint lines won't show in the reproduction (except pencil lines that shouldn't).

(c) All lines tend to get heavier in printing.

(d) Reduction may cause small spaces to close up completely, but it is best to provide for some reduction, as this tends to minimize imperfections.

(e) The printed result will probably be off-black on off-white.

(f) When the drawing is to print in more than one color and register is involved, use accurate register marks.

■ *Continuous-tone monochrome drawings and paintings*—The same requirements as for monochrome photographs.

■ *Continuous-tone color copy*—Reproduction of continuous-tone (full-color) color copy is called color process (see front endpaper). There are 2 kinds of copy for color process: (a) opaque (reflection) copy (drawings, color photographs, and original paintings or prints) and (b) transparent copy, i.e. the *transparency* obtained from some color film (Kodachrome, Ektachrome, etc.). For fidelity, the original subject (painting, etc.) is the best copy; the next best is a transparency or a color photoprint. From the standpoint of the mechanics of color separation, there is little difference. In most situations, the transparency is easier to use, particularly when the separations are to be done by scanners. Any copy to be used on a scanner must be flexible enough to wrap around a cylinder (see "Illustrations: color").

■ *Simple (non-process) color copy*—This includes: (a) type, rules, borders, solid or benday areas in illustrations, and illustrations themselves (including where several colors are used, and even where colors are produced by overprintings) and (b) halftones to be printed in a single color.

■ *Screened photoprints*—A contact print on paper of a screened halftone negative is known as a *velox*. It looks like a proof of a halftone plate. Being just black dots and white paper, a velox can be used as line copy, so it is possible to save part of the cost of halftones by having a velox made (by a photoprint company) and then a line negative. This is effective only when coarse screens are used (up to 110). There is too much loss of quality with the finer screens.

Another advantage in using veloxes is the opportunity to incorporate them in camera copy with other elements—thereby saving high stripping and finishing charges. They also enable the original artist to do dot retouching rather than leaving this to someone else.

Scaling [determining the final size and shape of reduced or enlarged copy] is a simple matter, once understood. There are 2 methods—one mechanical, the other mathematical. The mechanical one seems easiest, but it is slower and less useful for complex problems. Both methods are described below:

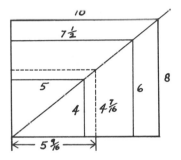

■ *Mechanical scaling*—This is based on the geometric fact that all rectangles of the same proportions have the same diagonal, i.e. a rectangle 8 × 10″ will have the same diagonal as one 4 × 5″, 6 × 7¹/₂″, etc.

Thus, to reduce a horizontal 8 × 10″ photograph to a width of 5⁹/₁₆″, lay a sheet of tracing paper over the copy and draw a line between diagonally opposite corners. Then measure 5⁹/₁₆″ along the 10″ side and draw a line from this point perpendicular to the edge. When this line touches the diagonal you will have the height of the reduced picture.

It is possible to buy, and very simple to make, a transparent plastic device that eliminates the need for drawing lines and measuring. This is very desirable because there is much room for error in the mechanical process.

■ *Mathematical scaling*—You don't have to be good at mathematics to use this method, because it is really just another mechanical process. The basic principle is mathematical proportion, but with the use of an engraver's *proportional scale*, or slide rule, it is simply a matter of setting 2 dimensions in alignment, and then finding a fourth by reading it on the scale opposite the third. So, to find the height of an 8 × 10″ picture being reduced from 10″ to 5⁹/₁₆″ wide, align 5⁹/₁₆ with 10, then find 8 on the same line as 10. The number opposite 8 will be the answer (4⁷/₁₆). Not only will you have the dimensions, but you will be able to read off the percentage of original (linear) size of the copy after reduction (55+%) and the fractional proportion (9 to 5) at the same time. These are extremely useful for economical *ganging* [combining for simultaneous shooting] of pictures with identical *focus*. The principles of propor-

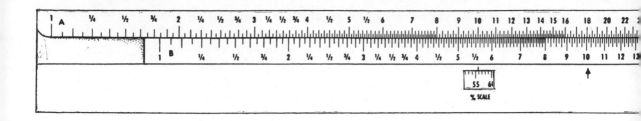

tion are, of course, the same for either inch or metric measure.

For use with inches, get an engraver's slide rule or proportional scale calibrated in eighths, rather than the engineer's, which is divided into tenths (and has other complicated scales not needed in this work). A slide rule seems rather formidable at first, but with a few minutes' practice you can do simple problems very rapidly, and complicated ones with hardly more trouble.

There is another type of proportional scale that is favored by many. This is the *proportion wheel* which has 2 discs revolving independently on the same center. The 2 discs have calibrated circumferences with a small window cut out of the top disc to enable reading percentage scales on the bottom one. The principle of operation is the same as for the slide rule, but the latter has somewhat more versatility.

Ratios and proportions can also be worked out easily by using a calculator. This method has several advantages over the others—particularly ease of reading.

MECHANICALS   A mechanical is a piece of camera copy consisting of one or more elements, arranged and marked for maximum accuracy and

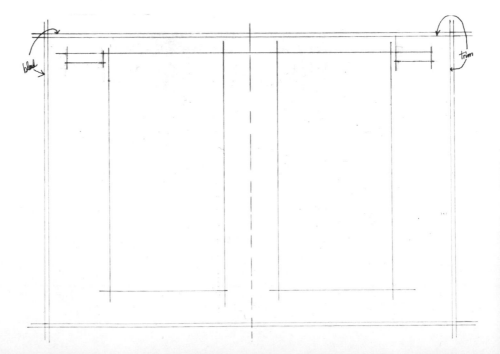

economy in platemaking. To make a mechanical of a single page, a few pages, a jacket, or a cover, draw the outlines (trimmed and untrimmed) in light blue pencil on a board. When a whole book is being prepared for camera, it is worth having mechanical boards—about 50 lb. (136 gr) cover weight, see CH. 10—printed in non-photographing light blue ink with the outlines of a 2-page spread and whatever guidelines, corners, etc., would be useful in speeding the pasteup and increasing accuracy. For small numbers of pages, the printing can be avoided by working on a light-table, with a transparent *guide sheet* [a sheet with guide lines drawn in black] taped to the glass. In any case, *trimming guides* [lines that indicate where the printed sheets are to be trimmed] outside the page area should be printed or drawn in black or red so they will show when the mechanical is photographed.

Economy in mechanicals means minimizing the amount of camera and stripping work required. To this end, it would be best to combine *all* the elements of each intended printing plate into one unit, which could be photographed in a single shot and the film exposed onto the plate without further handling. This is not always possible, but the closer you can come to the ideal the better.

There are 3 requirements for single-shot copy:

(a) each part of the copy must be in the same scale,

(b) the parts must be in the proper position in relation to each other, and

(c) there must be no part that requires a different screen or exposure than any other.

If part of the copy does require a different screen but is in the same scale as the remainder, it can be placed in position and the mechanical will then be shot twice—once for the screened copy, once for the other. The 2 negatives will then be combined to achieve the desired result. In practice, artwork (photographs, drawings, etc.) is usually larger than the finished size, and is not in position with type—which is usually *same-size*. In this case, the artwork is shot separately and the film is stripped in with the films of the same-size copy, in a position indicated by either an outline or a photocopy made the correct size and pasted on the mechanical. The positions of process-color illustrations are also indicated on the mechanical by either an outline or a photocopy. If time permits, proofs or blueprints of illustrations can be pasted onto mechanicals.

If one part of the copy overlaps another, it can be pasted on a transparent acetate *overlay* in the correct relative position. Copy that overlaps (overprints) may be black & white—a tint, a halftone, or a line drawing—or color, either simple or process. As far as the camera is concerned, each element of simple color is either line or continuous-tone black & white copy. It is only the ink used to print it that distinguishes it as color copy.

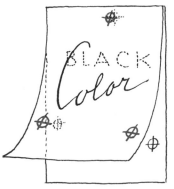

1. *one-shot mechanical; all line copy in one focus*

2. *two-shot mechanical; line and halftone copy in one focus*

$4\frac{1}{8}$"

3. *one shot mechanical; all line copy in one focus,*
   with halftone to be reduced and stripped into
   position indicated on mechanical

If more than one color is involved but none overlaps, all the copy may be pasted into position on the board or on an overlay. If the colors overlap, separate black & white copy is prepared for each. The most important color (usually black) is pasted on a board as the *key plate* and the other colors are pasted on overlays to register with the key plate. This is called pre-separated copy.

Whenever overlays are used, there should be at least 3 widely separated register marks on the base copy, and corresponding marks on the overlays. If there is no overlapping and all copy is in the same scale it is better to put everything on one board. This eliminates the need for register marks and results in maximum accuracy.

There are numerous tricks of the trade in making mechanicals. These can be learned by experience, talking to experienced hands, and reading books on the subject. Copy can be adhered with rubber cement—*regular* or *one-coat*, tape, a melted adhesive *(dry mounted)*, or by use of pressure-sensitive adhesive-backed paper. Squaring can be done with a T square, a light-table, or a transparent grid device. Each method has its advantages and disadvantages. The only important thing is *the result*—which should be accurate, secure, and clean copy. Remember that paper edges, cuts, cement excess, dirt, or anything else visible that is not part of the copy may be picked up by the camera.

MARKUP

Even perfect copy will not bring a good result if it is not marked properly. Instructions must be clear and complete. And remember, what may seem clear to you may not be clear to others— particularly if they are being rushed. Everyone has a tendency to omit what seems obvious, forgetting that these things are not obvious to someone unfamiliar with our *intentions*. To compensate for this tendency, try writing your instructions as though they were directed to an idiot. You might be surprised to find that you no longer have trouble from confused instructions—and no one will complain.

Here are some of the markings that should appear on camera copy (when appropriate):

■ *Register marks*—Place them outside the copy.

■ *Indication of bleeds*—Write "Bleed" wherever one occurs. (Extend bleed copy 1/8" outside trim.)

■ *Indication whether line or halftone.*

■ *Size of halftone screen*—To be indicated only if a screen is wanted that differs from the standard screen used by the printer. (Most offset printers use 133 or 150.)

■ *Size and tint of benday screen*—(85 screen, 20% tint, etc.).

■ *Trimming guides*—Make clean, fine lines *outside* the copy in black or red.

■ *Folding guides*—Same as above.

■ *Dimensions*—Clearly indicate whether sizes and distances are before or after trim.

■ *Scale* (same-size, how reduced or enlarged)—This is a confused area. Cameramen work with the relative percentage in *linear* size of the finished work to the copy, i.e. if 8 × 10″ copy is to be made 4 × 5″, the percentage is 50. If 8 × 10″ becomes 12 × 15″, the percentage is 150. Same-size is 100%, etc. The marking should be: Focus 50, Focus 150, etc. (or F50, F150, etc.). Ideally, everyone would use this system and there would be no trouble. However, some say "reduce 50%" in the first instance and "enlarge 50%" in the second. Others say "reduce ½″" and "enlarge 1½ times" (1½X). Still another method—and probably the safest in view of the confusion possible with percentages—is to use proportions. The first example is expressed as "reduce 2 to 1", the second is "enlarge 1 to 1½". Another advantage of this system is its flexibility. For example, "reduce 17 to 9" can be instantly translated into percentages with a proportional scale.

Whatever system you use, it is best to let the printer know about it in advance. With work coming in marked in several ways, it is understandable that there might be confusion.

When practicable, give the actual dimensions to which the copy is being reduced or enlarged. A dimension with arrows pointing outward on each side (← 5⁹/₁₆″ →) indicates that the entire copy is to be made that size in that direction. If the copy is to be reduced so that a certain *part* of it is to become 5⁹/₁₆″, a mark should be made in the margin opposite each end of the part concerned, and the indication 5⁹/₁₆″ BM (Between Marks) written between them.

In no case should more than one dimension be given, unless the printer is permitted to *crop* [cut away part of the picture] as necessary to maintain both (as when illustrations must align). In that case, one should indicate *where* to crop. In general, it is best to indicate one dimension and scale the subject so that the other dimension will be correct after reduction or enlargement.

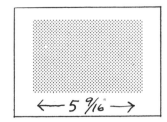

- *Cropmarks*—These should be clean lines in the margin indicating the places for cutting. An arrow should point to the mark in the direction of the portion of the picture being retained. If there is no margin, attach a slip of paper to the edge. Cropmarks on the back of a picture are a source of trouble.

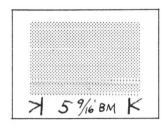

- *Color*—Indicate which color for each part of the copy. Supply a sizable (at least 1 × 2″) swatch of flat, even color to be matched, or refer by number to a color system such as *PMS*.
- *Silhouetting*—Unless the outlines are obvious, make a tissue overlay and indicate how the silhouetting is to be done.

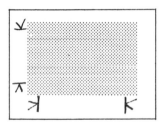

All markings except register, trim, and fold marks—which must be black—should be made in color so that they will stand out and not be confused with copy. Light blue is best for markings that must not photograph. On photographs, mark with a grease pencil or tempera paint. Ballpoint pens make permanent marks.

DUMMIES

For material to be printed by offset lithography, silk screen, gravure, or any process that uses photomechanically-made plates, it is best to make a mechanical for each page or item. However, for books in which there are no more than 2 elements on each page, or in which none of the elements can be shot together, it is usually sufficient to make a dummy. The preparation of a dummy for use by a photomechanical shop is the same as the procedure described in CH.21 for making a dummy for makeup, except that only final (fully corrected) proofs must be used, and the repros must accompany the dummy. Margins may be given for each piece of copy or, if the pages are uniform in design, a general instruction for margins may be given at the beginning.

When giving instructions, one margin must be the top or bottom, the other, the inside or outside. When giving the distances between elements on a page, at least one vertical and one horizontal measurement is left out. This permits minor inaccuracies to be absorbed. The omitted measurement is usually one of the outer margins in each dimension, but not necessarily. Shown are 2 alternatives.

FILM ASSEMBLY   The completion of film containing type and illustrations (black & white and/or color) is followed by a series of procedures to assemble the film so that it is in the final arrangement for making plates. The steps are: (a) page makeup, (b) form makeup, (c) *compositing* [contacting to make a single piece of film comprising all the film on a flat]. Generally, these operations are performed by hand by strippers who tape the various pieces of film into position on large plastic sheets and make the contact films needed to complete the work. However, some or all of the operations are sometimes performed by systems of machines. The operations are described in CH. 5.

Note that CH. 5 also refers to procedures that completely bypass some or all of the operations. These systems will undoubtedly be used, but they will be limited by the need of publishers to make changes and control results at intermediate stages. This is why the main thrust of research now is in *software*—the improvement of devices and procedures that enable effective use of the enormously sophisticated production machines that we already have. The availability of a system that can turn a manuscript and illustrations into printed sheets without the use of film or plates is marvelous, but only if the publisher is given ample opportunity to be sure that the printed sheets contain exactly what is wanted. This is where that cranky human element collides head-on with the incredible machines it has created. Presumably, the brains that invented the machines can find ways to avert this collision, or at least soften its impact.

9 | Plates & printing

Successful bookmaking requires a knowledge of both the principles of printing and the equipment. A design must be matched to the press available or a press must be found that is suited to the design. An eighth of an inch more in a book's page size could add much to the cost of printing—planning a book for one press instead of another might mean a saving of 20% or more in printing, paper, and binding cost. A printer is not likely to let you put a job on an unsuitable press, but it is best to know enough about printing yourself to insure against a costly mistake.

Unless printing is done directly from metal type or slugs (increasingly rare), it involves plates of some kind. The plates being merely an adjunct of the presses, albeit the most important one, each kind will be discussed within the section devoted to the printing process in which it is used. The basic processes of printing and platemaking are explained below. (Although book printing is rapidly coming to mean offset lithography, other processes—particularly letterpress—are still being used and so they are covered in this book to the extent that their present use requires.)

There are many kinds of plates, but they divide into 2 basic categories: (a) duplicate plates molded from type and (b) photomechanical plates.

■ *Molded plates*—The metal type is covered with a substance which forms a negative (female) *mold* which is filled with the plate material. When this material hardens the mold is stripped away, leaving a positive (male) duplicate of the printing surface. Molded plates are made for letterpress only.

■ *Photomechanical plates*—A film negative or positive is made by some means: (a) by a photocomposition machine, (b) by photographing black & white copy (repros, photoprints, artwork, etc.), or (c) by printing (or drawing) an opaque image on any transparent or translucent sheet. The film is placed against a photosensitized plate and exposed to light. The plate is then treated with chemicals that affect the exposed parts differently from the rest. This results in a distinction between the printing and nonprinting parts that makes printing possible. Such plates are used in all printing processes.

There is another method of making a plate, by xerography, but this is more a method of printing than platemaking, so it is explained under printing processes. The use of xerography in platemaking is merely a substitute for a *part* of the photomechanical process, whereby the copy image is transferred to the plate by static electricity rather than through the use of a photosensitive coating.

PRINTING PROCESSES

There are numerous variations of the basic printing techniques. The fundamental principles of the 3 dominant methods are:
■ *Relief printing (Letterpress)*—The printing parts are raised on the plate and are inked. The ink is transferred to the paper by pressure.
■ *Planographic printing (Lithography)*—The printing parts are virtually level with the rest of the plate, but they are treated to accept a greasy ink, which the nonprinting parts repel. The process is based on the antipathy of grease and water. The ink is transferred by contact.
■ *Intaglio printing (Gravure)*—The printing parts are etched into the plate and are lower than the rest. They are filled with ink, which is transferred to paper by pressure and suction.

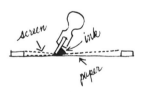

Three other principles are of interest. Although they are not (at present) used in printing the text of books, they are used in some bookmaking operations:
■ *Screen printing (Silk screen)*—A fine mesh screen is stretched taut and the nonprinting areas are blocked out. The screen is placed over the paper and ink is squeezed through the open parts.
■ *Ink jet printing*—A coded tape controls a battery of tiny laser-activated jets that propel ink onto paper in patterns that create type and other graphic images called up by the tape (CH. 5).
■ *Electrostatic printing (Xerography)*—The printing image is photo-projected onto the paper where it is electrostatically charged. The ink is oppositely charged and is thus attracted to the image.

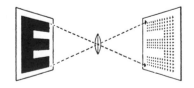

1. *The paper is given a positive charge.* 2. *The image is projected onto the paper. Where there is no image, light strikes the paper and removes positive charge.* 3. *Negatively charged powdered ink is applied to paper, sticks only where there is positive charge.*

One variation of the basic printing methods is indeed very significant—*offset*. Generally associated only with lithography (offset lithography is usually referred to as "offset"), the offset method can be applied to any printing process and has been used with letterpress (*letterset* or *dry offset*) and gravure. In offset printing, the plate transfers its ink not to the paper but to a rubber-covered cylinder which in turn "offsets" the ink to the paper.

Letterpress

This is the oldest method of printing and it remained remarkably unchanged for hundreds of years before the advent of power presses. Until the 1950s, it was unchallenged as the leading method of printing books. Today it has lost its place to offset lithography. And, except for *belt presses* (see below), once the existing machines break down, it will continue in use only for special applications, almost all of them involving only type. Making letterpress plates of illustrations is no longer economical, and such plates that exist are usually converted to offset lithography.

There are 4 different techniques of letterpress printing:

■ *Platen*—The type form is held vertically and the paper is fed onto a metal plate that is hinged below the form and swings against it, much as a clam shell would close. Ink is applied to the form by rollers which pass alternately over it and a flat ink plate above it.

■ *Cylinder*—The type or plates are held on a horizontal or vertical plane (*bed*), while ink rollers and sheets of paper (carried by a cylinder) alternately pass over it. Horizontal beds are called *flat beds*.

■ *Rotary*—Curved plates are clamped to a cylinder which revolves against a revolving cylinder on which the paper is carried. Ink rollers revolve against the plate cylinder on another side. The paper may be fed in sheets or from a roll. When a roll (web) of paper is used the process is called web-fed rotary.

■ *Belt*—Flexible relief plates are mounted on 2 continuous belts that revolve against a web of paper. The principle is similar to web-fed rotary, with a belt of variable length—60–640″ (1.5–16.3 m) —instead of a cylinder of fixed diameter. (The belt press is generally known by the trade name of its inventor, *Cameron*.)

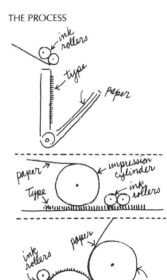

In general, rotary is faster than cylinder, which is faster than platen. Web-fed rotary produces more impressions per hour than any other process. Belt presses are faster than any but web rotaries.

By adding cylinders, rotary and cylinder presses can print 2 or more colors with one run through the press, or may print both sides of the paper in one run. Presses equipped for the latter are called *perfectors*, and are actually 2 presses in one. Belt presses are also perfectors.

Makeready is the preliminary process of adjustment to compensate for irregularities of the press and the type or plates. This involves placing sheets and pieces of paper on the bed and/or cylinders of the press at the low points, to make the impression equal all over. The quality of letterpress printing depends more on the makeready than any other single factor.

Linotype slug metal is hard enough to print the number of copies in the first printing of an average book, but if a large number of copies is to be printed, page plates are usually made from the type. The kinds of plates available are described below.

■ *Molded plates*—The first and most common of the molded plates was the electrotype (or electro), but these are no longer made. They were copper-faced, lead-backed plates that were superior in quality but were displaced by less expensive kinds.

Plastic plates are made by pouring a *thermosetting* plastic powder [it softens when heated, but once cold will not soften again] into a plastic mold. These plates are quite satisfactory for type and fairly simple line illustrations.

Rubber plates are made in the same way as plastics and provide an even lower quality of reproduction. In durability they are much superior, however, and they require less care in printing than any other kind of plate. Rubber plates are ideal for printing large runs in which quality is not paramount. For that kind of work they are often made curved to run on rotary presses. These hard rubber plates used for book printing should not be confused with the soft, hand-cut, "rubber stamp" kind used for printing cartons and rough-surfaced materials.

Many other kinds of molded plates have been developed, some of them superior in quality to plastic plates, but the decline of letterpress printing has slowed these developments. The only significant effort is in the development of flexible *"wraparound"* plates that can be used on belt presses.

■ *Photomechanical plates*—Much hope was invested in the development of letterpress plates that could be photomechanically made, so that letterpress printing could compete with offset lithography by making etched plates from photocomposition products. The procedure is about the same as for making lithographic plates, except that exposure of a sensitized coating makes the printing areas resistant to an acid that eats away the nonprinting areas to a depth necessary for relief printing.

The most promising of such plates are the *photopolymers*. Here, the entire thickness of the material, not merely a coating on it, is affected by exposure to light. This enables the etching to go down as deep as desired, and almost at right angles to the surface. The photopolymer process was developed under the trade name Dycril, but there are other brands. This is the kind of plate generally used on belt presses.

The various considerations involved in choosing presses for a particular printing job are discussed under "Lithography". The use of letterpress is now limited to a choice of 3 main kinds of presses: (a) the standard cylinder machines, (b) rotary machines, and (c) belt machines. The first two kinds survive because of the existence of letterpress plates and the fact that the cost of the presses has long since been amortized. As plates wear out and the machines need replacement of parts that are no longer available, this kind of printing will, for all practical purposes, disappear. Certainly, the metal-type composition that fed them is not going to be available.

Belt presses, which use photomechanical plates, have some advantages over offset for books that have only type and line illustration. The principle one is the ability of these presses to print small runs (as few as 2000 copies) economically, due to the relatively little makeready they need, and to their high speed. Since belt presses produce folded and collated signatures in one pass through the machine, their economy is outstanding even for larger runs. They are also economical in paper use, since the length of the belt can be adjusted, thus eliminating the waste of paper that sometimes occurs when using rotary presses with fixed cylinder diameters. In addition, their short makeready time reduces paper spoilage. The Cameron press is developing toward a capacity to print quality halftones and to do multicolor work—including color process. The key to much of this is plate improvement. Even the

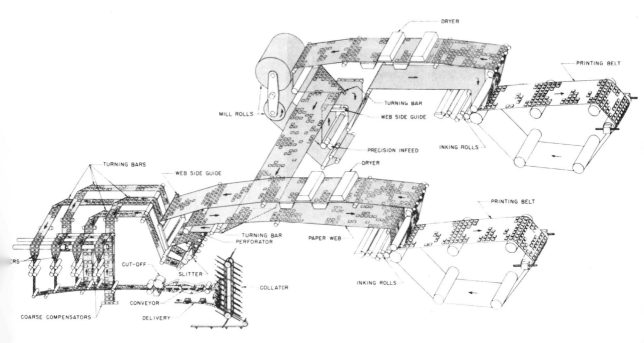

Cameron belt press

original press, however, is capable of printing halftones up to 110 screen, and can produce attractive books at low cost when they are designed with the machine's capabilities—and limitations— in mind.

Lithography

While lithography has been used in some form since 1798 when it was invented by Senefelder in Bavaria, its application to mass production is comparatively recent. The necessary techniques were developed in the early part of this century, but it was not until the 1920s that any considerable commercial printing was done by this method, and it was not until after World War II that it became a major book-printing industry.

The method would have had more use in its early days had it been able to deliver a better result, but the skills were not well enough advanced to avoid the gray, flat quality that marked lithography as a "cheap" process. Good lithography depends on achieving a perfect balance of water and ink, and it was not until the 1950s that this technology was perfected to the point where it is now possible to do the best quality of printing—in both black & white and color—by offset lithography.

With the advent of photographic typesetting, lithography was given a major boost. Since the lithographic plate is photomechanically produced, the product of photocomposing machines can be applied directly to the plate—thus bypassing the repro proof and camera steps. This not only reduces the cost of lithography, it improves its quality.

While there are still some situations in which letterpress printing has advantages (see discussion of belt presses above), it is likely that before long offset will be used for all printing except some special situations.

THE PROCESS

Lithography means "stone-writing" in Greek, and it was originally a method of printing by (1) processing the surface of a flat, smooth stone into grease-receptive (printing) and water-receptive (nonprinting) areas, (2) wetting the stone with water (*dampening*) so that the nonprinting areas would repel a greasy ink which (3) was spread over it, and (4) pressing paper to the stone to transfer the ink from the printing areas.

Stones were used until the end of the 19th century. By that time, lithography was a popular medium for artists because it was much easier than engraving in wood or metal and permitted a wider range of graphic techniques and effects. Many lithographed posters and magazine illustrations were produced by leading artists. The stone is still used (on flat-bed presses) by artists, but for commercial printing it has been replaced by metal sheets treated to duplicate the stone grain.

Another important change in the technique of lithographic

printing is the use of the rotary offset method. Several advantages are gained by printing on a rubber blanket first instead of directly on paper: (a) the plates last longer, (b) less water comes in contact with the paper, (c) the resilient rubber cylinder permits printing finer copy on rougher paper, and (d) speed is increased. All of these are essential to the commercial success of lithography, which has come to be known as offset lithography.

In offset lithography, 5 kinds of cylinders or rollers are involved:

(a) *the plate cylinder* around which the plate is wrapped,

(b) *the blanket (offset) cylinder* around which the rubber blanket is attached,

(c) *the impression cylinder* which carries the paper,

(d) *ink rollers*, and

(e) *water rollers*.

As the plate revolves, it comes in contact first with the water rollers, then the ink rollers, then the blanket cylinder. The impression cylinder presses the paper against the blanket from which the inked image is offset (printed). On commercial-size presses there are several water and ink rollers for better distribution and control.

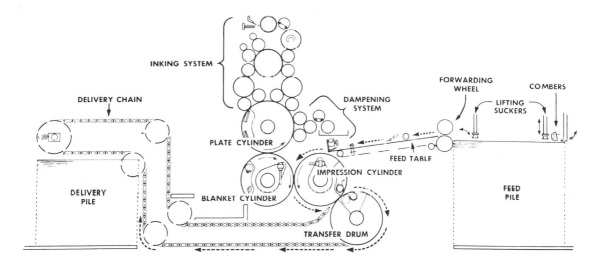

Diagram of an offset lithography press used for printing large sheets.

Since the paper is printed by the rubber blanket rather than the plate itself, there is relatively little makeready done in offset lithography. Quality of plate and correct adjustment of inking, dampening, and press are the main factors in the result. However, in color process printing the makeready time is usually several hours, as it includes adjustment for register and color.

Two factors that affect quality and *can* be controlled are halftone screen size and paper. Because of the light impression (*kiss impression*) of the rubber blanket, 133 and 150 screens can be well printed on comparatively rough-surfaced papers; on smoother papers, up to 300-line screens can be used. Provided that the choices of paper and printer are right, a finer screen will produce better results.

Paper will be discussed in CH. 10, but it should be noted here that paper characteristics tend to affect lithographic printing quality very strongly. Because of the use of water in the process, excess moisture may enter the paper and gray the ink, and it may cause a certain amount of paper distortion—with resultant problems in register. Another factor is the tendency toward *picking* [pulling fibers or pieces of coating from the paper surface], due to the tacky inks used.

PLATES   The lithographic stone was a thick and heavy fixture immobilized on the flat bed of a press. A modern offset lithography plate is a thin sheet of lightweight metal wrapped around a rapidly turning cylinder. There are many variations on these plates, but they are the same in principle—the printing areas accept ink, the others repel it. The only essential difference is in the materials used to form the printing and nonprinting areas.

The platemaking process is photomechanical. Unlike letterpress, where the plates are usually individual pages, the lithographer strips-in all the pages of a form on a single plate.

There are a great many kinds of lithographic plates, with improvements and variations being developed constantly. However, these divide roughly into 3 groups: (a) surface plates, (b) deep-etch plates, and (c) multimetal plates.

■ *Surface plates*—A metal sheet is coated with a light-sensitive, ink-receptive substance. When this is exposed to light through a negative film, the coating hardens in the (printing) areas where the light hits it and remains soft in the other (nonprinting) parts. The soft parts are then washed out and a coating of water-receptive material is applied. This adheres only to the bare metal, so that the plate is divided into ink-receptive (printing) parts and water-receptive (nonprinting) parts. Surface plates differ in materials and, to some extent, processes. The main varieties are *albumens*, *presensitized*, and *wipe-on*. These are used for most printing purposes.

■ *Deep-etch plates*—While surface plates leave the printing areas on the surface (thus subject to wear), deep-etch plates are made in reverse with film *positives*, leaving the printing areas slightly *below* the nonprinting areas (somewhat like an intaglio plate). These plates are used for longer runs and for especially fine work in color-process printing. Their cost is somewhat higher.

■ *Multimetal plates*—For even longer runs and better quality, there are *bimetal* plates. These have a light-sensitive protective coating on an ink-receptive metal base. After exposure, development removes the coating from the nonprinting parts, which then receive a plating of water-receptive metal in an electrolytic bath. Another bath washes away the remaining coating, exposing the ink-receptive base metal in the printing areas. On some plates, the metals are reversed, i.e. the plating is ink-receptive while the base is water-receptive. Bimetal plates are rarely used for runs under 100,000 because of their high cost.

On *trimetal* plates, the base metal is given a plating also. Such plates appear to be virtually indestructible.

Small offset lithography machines (such as the Multilith) can print with plates made by typing or drawing on a specially treated paper. The ink used will stick to the carbon image produced by the typewriter, while the paper repels the ink. Only a few hundred copies can be obtained in this way. *Paper plates* can also be made photographically in the same way as metal ones. Some of these are capable of quite long runs. Another method of making paper plates is by xerography. A grease-receptive, negatively charged powder is applied electrostatically to the printing areas on a positively charged, water-receptive paper. In general, paper plates are used for office duplicating work rather than commercial printing.

An offset lithography plate room. In foreground: light-table and tools for stripping film. At far corner; film being exposed onto plate in vacuum frame.

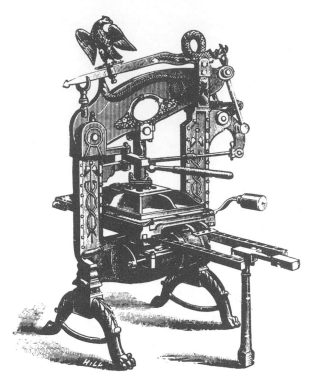

Left, *a Columbian hand press. These were still widely used at the beginning of the 20th century.*

Below, *a 2-color, sheet-fed rotary press.*

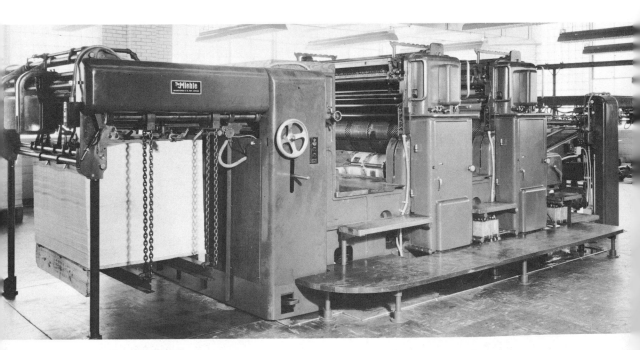

PRESSES An offset press is actually a rotary press, with all its potential advantages—speed, multiple-color printing, and web-feed. It is not surprising that the search for these properties points in the direction of offset lithography.

A sheet-fed offset lithography press. This size is generally used for printing jackets and other work on small sheets.

Harris M1000 web-fed 4-color offset press

Unlike letterpress, offset lithography presses are basically the same, whether large or small. Except for the difference between web- and sheet-fed, the essential distinction between the smallest office machine, such as the Multilith, and the largest sheet-fed press—about 55 × 78″ (139.7 × 198.12 cm)—is the control mechanism. The larger presses have computer-monitored devices to control register and inking. The same 5 kinds of rollers and cylinders are used in all, although the larger presses will have more of each to increase efficiency and control. In lithography there are also perfector presses, both sheet- and web-fed. Small sheet-fed presses usually run at 5 to 9000 impressions per hour, the larger machines at 4 to 6000. The larger web presses can run high quality color-process work at 16,000 to 20,000 impressions per hour.

Speed is a major consideration in choosing presses, but size is paramount. Size in a press means the maximum size sheet or roll it can take. For large orders, paper can be made in special sizes, but in most cases it is best to use one of the standard sizes carried in stock (CH. 10). When a stock size of paper is used, there will probably be a press to fit it, and this is almost certainly the press to use. A smaller press would require cutting the paper and printing a smaller form—which means more forms and more impressions—and a larger press means paying a higher rate than necessary because the hourly cost of running a press increases with its size.

The cost of presswork is the charge for use of a press for a period of time, so the running speed is not as significant as the amount of work the press can perform per hour. Press A may not run any faster than Press B, but it may be printing 4 colors, or both sides of the sheet in one color, while B is printing only one color on one side, and it may deliver folded sheets while B delivers them flat.

It does not necessarily follow that Press A is the one to use, because the more a press can do the higher the cost of using it. Not only is it a more expensive piece of equipment but being more complex it requires more makeready time and may require more help to run. Multicolor presses will usually do a multicolor job much more cheaply than a single color machine.

In all cases, the speed at which the press is run will depend to some extent on the kind or quality of work it is performing. Half-tones on coated paper or very detailed illustrations on any paper will be run more slowly than type on regular book stock. In general, the higher the quality desired, the more slowly the job is run. Quality printing requires frequent examination of sheets to see when adjustments, plate cleaning, etc., are needed.

Small work, such as jackets, endpapers, illustrations, etc., is generally printed on presses which handle sheets of about 17 1/2 × 22 1/2″ (44.45 × 57.15cm) or 19 × 25″ (48.26 × 63.5cm). Unless the run is very short, say under 10,000, a duplicate set of films will be made and the work will probably be printed 2-up. For example, the sizes mentioned will accommodate 2 jackets for average-sized books. If the run is very long, say 25,000, 3 sets of films may be made and the job will be run on a 22 ½ × 35″ (57.15 × 88.9 cm) or 25 × 38″ (63.5 × 96.52 cm) sheet.

The text is most likely to be imposed in 32- or 64-page forms, and be printed on a sheet-fed press ranging from 38 × 50″ (96.52 × 127 cm)—32 pages 6⅛ × 9¼″ (15.56 × 23.5 cm) to 50 × 76″ (127 × 193.04 cm)—(64 pages 6⅛ × 9¼″ (15.56 × 23.5 cm). The commonly used sizes are discussed in CHS. 10 and 16. For economical printing of simple black & white books, perfector presses may be used.

Substantial savings are possible with high-speed, web-fed rotary presses, provided the job is suited to the equipment. Formerly, this meant long runs. Unfortunately, most of book printing consists of runs too short to effectively utilize these presses, some of which can turn out 30,000 impressions of a 64-page form in one hour. A first printing of 5000 copies (very common for tradebooks) would thus be completed in 10 minutes of running time—and the time needed to make the press ready could be 15 times as long. Paper spoilage tends to be high and, when color is involved, can go up to 60% or more. However, runs as short as 7000 are feasible if the number of forms is large enough to effectively utilize the roll of paper.

In most cases, however, such short runs are uneconomical, especially for multicolor books. Furthermore, even when the first printing is long enough to economically use a web press, thought must be given to the possibility that a reprint of a much smaller quantity may be needed later.

Mini-webs (also called *quarter-size* or *half-size* webs) using narrow width rolls are providing an answer to the problem of fairly short-run book printing by web offset. These rolls have widths of 22½ to 26″ (57.15 cm to 66.04 cm) as compared with widths up to about 61″ (155 cm) on the largest web presses.

Web-fed rotary presses usually have folders and slitters built in. This means that a sheet can be printed with 64-page forms on both sides and be delivered as 4 completely folded 32-page *signatures* ready for the next bindery operation (CH. 11). One limitation is the thickness (*caliper* or *bulk*) of the paper. Most web presses have trouble handling paper that has a more-than-6 pt.—.006″(.015 cm)—thickness (CH. 10).

Another aspect of web printing that is crucial is the *cutoff* [the length of sheets cut from the roll], which is determined by the circumference of the impression cylinder and in turn determines the final *trim-size* [page size]. One dimension of the page size must be divisible into the cutoff size or there will be wasted paper. For example, with an 8½ × 11″ (21.59 × 27.94 cm) page, the 11″— 11¼″ (28.58 cm) including trim—will fit two times into a 23″

(58.42 cm) cutoff. It would not fit into a 40″ (101.6 cm) cutoff, except by wasting about 6″ (15.24 cm)—some 15%—of the paper. When choosing a trim-size for a web, remember that the grain of the paper runs the length of the web, i.e. around, not across the roll (CH. 10).

On all presses there is a maximum printing area which is somewhat smaller than the maximum sheet size. This is due to the space required for guides, grippers, and other mechanical features of the machine.

Gravure

Printing from an engraved plate is an ancient process, perhaps older than letterpress. Engraving in wood and metal was a highly developed art thousands of years ago, but it was not until the application of photography that gravure became feasible for commercial printing, although many book illustrations were printed from engraved copper and steel plates in the 18th and 19th centuries.

The gravure process is the most difficult and complicated of the 3 major printing methods and is consequently the most expensive.

Like offset lithography, gravure is by nature a rotary process readily adapted to web-feed. Web-fed gravure, letterpress, and lithography cost less per impression than sheet-fed when runs are long enough to justify their use. In gravure, however, the high cost of platemaking accentuates the difference to the point where sheet-fed printing in moderate quantities (say 6 to 10,000) is possible for only expensive illustrated books, while web-fed gravure in the long runs of magazine printing (say 200,000 and over) is no more expensive than any other method.

Gravure is at its best in reproducing continuous-tone copy, particularly photographs. Its attraction for newspapers and magazines is its ability to print pictures well on relatively cheap paper. For fine-quality picture reproduction in books, gravure appeals to those who prefer not to use coated paper. However, with doubledot and duotone methods (CH. 8), offset lithography can achieve results comparable to gravure (except, perhaps, the rich velvety black that gravure can produce with its heavy application of ink), so the latter is disappearing from commercial use in books.

The weakness of gravure is that it must print type with a screen. Gravure screens are very fine, ranging from 150 to 300 lines, and the black tone is solid, but there is always a fuzziness on the edges of type due to the sawtooth pattern of the diagonal screen. For fine books, it is best to print the text in letterpress or lithography, even if the illustrations are printed by gravure.

THE PROCESS

The entire area of the gravure plate is covered by a grid similar to a halftone screen. The lines are level with the surface and the square spaces between the lines are etched to varying depths. The darker the tone, the deeper the square is etched and, consequently, the

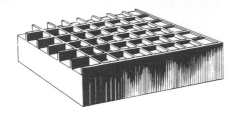

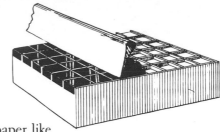

more ink it holds. The squares—which appear on the paper like dots—are all the same size, but they vary in tone according to the amount of ink deposited, i.e. they vary in opacity. Thus, gravure is a true halftone process, whereas letterpress and lithography only simulate tones by optical illusion. The only flaw in gravure reproduction of tone is the grid of white lines, but this is virtually invisible due to the fine screens used. In the darker tones, so much ink is deposited that the dots run together and eliminate the white lines altogether.

There is a process (News-Dultgen) in which a combination of the gravure and letterpress halftone screens is used. The wells between the lines vary not only in depth but in size.

Gravure printing is mechanically very much like rotary letterpress. A plate cylinder revolves against an ink roller and then against the paper which passes between it and an impression cylinder. The one important difference is due to the nature of the gravure plate. After the plate is inked, a flat bar, called a *doctor blade*, wipes the ink off the surface, leaving it in the recesses only.

Because of the need to wipe the ink cleanly off the plate surface on each impression, a thin, fast-drying ink is used. This ink tends to spread on the paper and helps close the spaces between the dots. The ink must be thin also because it acts as a transparent wash— letting the paper show through in varying degrees according to the amount deposited.

The offset method is used in gravure as well as in lithography and letterpress, but mainly for printing on plastics and other specialty materials.

Gravure plates have a screen, but it is not used when the copy is photographed. A continuous tone negative is made and, because a gravure plate is the opposite of relief plates in that the *printing* areas are etched, a film positive is made from the negative. PLATES

The screen (not the lines but the black squares between) is printed on a sheet of tissue which backs a sheet of photosensitive gelatin. The gelatin (called a *resist*) is exposed to light through the screen, then it is turned over and exposed through the film positive. The gelatin is soluble in water, but becomes less so as it is exposed to light. So, when full light strikes it (as through the lines of the screen), it will not dissolve at all; it remains soluble in varying degrees according to the tones in the film positive. After exposure, a warm water bath washes away the gelatin in proportion to the amount of light it received in each square.

The sheet is then laid on the copper plate or cylinder, the printed tissue is peeled away, and an acid etch bites into the metal according to the thickness of the gelatin. This leaves the screen lines as walls around millions of tiny square wells of varying depth.

Gravure plates are made up in complete forms from flats of stripped-in film, in the same way as for lithography.

PRESSES

Sheet-fed gravure presses range in size from 12 × 18″ (30.48 × 45.72 cm) to about 30 × 44″ (76.2 × 111.76 cm). Their speed is slightly slower than that of comparable offset and cylinder presses. They tend to be slowed by the need for strong pressure against the plate to enable the paper to draw all the ink from the wells. However, on smoother papers less pressure is needed.

Web-fed gravure (known as *rotogravure*) is very advanced in equipment due to its use by newspapers and magazines. Very large presses are available for single color and multicolor printing, and most have built-in folding machines. The plates for rotogravure presses are copper cylinders (rather than copper sheets wrapped around cylinders). Rotogravure runs at very high speeds.

Silk screen

Until quite recently, silk screen was a process for producing rather simple designs in small quantities. It was essentially a handcraft used to make posters and prints (called *serigraphs*) in runs of a few hundred or less. With the introduction of machinery capable of relatively high-speed production, silk screen became feasible for long-run commercial work.

Even now, silk screen is much more expensive than the other methods of printing, but it has certain unique advantages which make it worth the price when its special qualities are needed. Two features are outstanding: (a) any kind of surface—including rough cloth—can be printed and (b) the ink may be completely opaque "paint" which can be built up to a thickness comparable to embossing. These attributes are obviously of interest in relation to covers, and will be discussed further in CH. 26, but there is also use for them in printing endpapers, jackets, and illustrations.

There are many silk screen printers, but few are equipped with machinery to do book work, and prices may vary considerably. It is worth some investigation to find a printer suited to the work needed.

THE PROCESS

The nonprinting parts of the screen may be blocked out by application of a liquid filler, but the most common method is to use a sheet mask or *stencil*. Simple masks can be cut by hand, but for most work, film is used and the image is cut photomechanically. Although the process is best suited to printing fairly large areas of flat color, it is possible to reproduce small type, and even halftones, provided conditions are suitable.

The mask is applied to a very fine screen (it may be silk or metal mesh) which is stretched tightly on a frame. This is then mounted horizontally on a press and the paper is fed underneath, where it receives ink squeezed through the screen by a *squeegee* [a rubber-edged bar]. A separate mask is made for each color, although it is possible to print more than one color at a time if the design is properly prepared. Inks may be bright metallics or rich, flat finishes. They may be applied very thin or thick enough to cast a distinct shadow.

Xerography

Static electricity is not new to printing, but it existed only as a nuisance until recently. Letterpress and offset printers have to contend with sheets sticking together and the attraction of unwanted particles because of the tendency of oppositely-charged matter to draw together. This phenomenon has now been turned to advantage. An entirely new printing process (xerography) has been based on the principles of electrostatic action.

The idea was first put forward as a practical possibility about 1948. Within a few years, the process was commercially available as a means of making copies of letters and other documents in small quantities, and for making inexpensive master plates for small offset duplicators. The quality of reproduction was good when the machines were perfectly adjusted, but they required frequent attention. Some machines produce copies at high speed on a continuous roll and can reduce or enlarge. This puts the process in competition with the other printing methods, but it remains to be seen whether the quality and cost of copies made on such machines will also be competitive. There are dozens of machines using this process, and almost as many variations of the method.

THE PROCESS

A specially coated paper is given a positive charge of static electricity. The printing image is projected onto the paper through a lens. Where the image strikes the paper the positive charge remains, but the light reflected from the nonprinting areas removes the charge. The paper is then covered with a negatively charged black powder (ink) that adheres to the positively charged printing area only. Heat then fuses the powder, which hardens when cool.

Some machines use the offset principle. The ink first adheres to the image on a selenium drum and then offsets to the paper. The advantage here is that an untreated paper may be printed.

Collotype

This is a little-used process, but it is capable of extremely fine reproduction of illustrations under limited conditions. No screen is involved; the tones result from varying amounts of ink. The printed surface, which has a barely perceptible grain, gives an effect of continuous tone. While these tones can be very delicate, and fine detail can be held, the process does not permit strong contrast or a wide range of values. The ink is transparent and type tends to look weak.

The process is similar to lithography in that it is based on the antipathy of grease and water, but in collotype the entire plate accepts ink *in varying degrees*, rather than being divided between ink-accepting and ink-repelling areas. The surface of the plate is a sheet of photosensitive gelatin which becomes impervious to water to the degree that it is exposed to light through a film negative. Before printing, the plate is soaked in water. The darker tones hold more ink because they accept less water, while the lighter tones hold more water and less ink.

Printing by collotype is a precarious matter, in which room temperature and humidity are critical. The plates get damaged easily —usually after a few hundred impressions.

This process is expensive for long runs because of very slow press speeds, but the plate cost is low and runs of 100 to 1000 copies are the most economical. Rotary collotype runs faster and is practical for somewhat larger quantities. Collotype is sometimes called *Photogelatin*.

Color printing

■ *Simple Color*—In simple (non-process) color printing, the only extra cost is the ink *washup*. The previous color must be completely washed out of the press before the new color is used. On short runs there may be a small charge if a color is specially mixed. Otherwise, the presswork is about the same as printing black. Thus a 2-color job costs about twice as much as one color, 3 colors cost 3 times as much as one, etc., provided, of course, that the printing problems in each color are otherwise equal, and each color is run separately. However, most multicolor work is run on 2-color, 4-color, or 5-color presses and the cost per color is much less than if each color is run separately.

On any press run, more care is required when halftones or very fine line copy are involved, but printing with 2 or more colors brings in the problem of register. The register may be very simple or extremely fine. Assuming that the copy and plates were properly aligned, there are still several obstacles to perfect register. Poor feeding, faulty plate mounting, irregular trimming of paper are causes of trouble, but the most difficult problem is distortion of the sheets due to moisture. This may result from excess water in lithographic printing or from a change in general humidity between impressions. Because the paper is likely to expand or shrink more in one direction than the other, a serious problem in register may occur, especially in large sheets. Preventive measures include sizing the paper to resist moisture (CH. 10) and using pressroom air conditioning, but these are sometimes not enough. Moisture causes the least amount of trouble when all colors are printed in one run through a multicolor press.

A method by which colors may be used at less than the usual cost is *split fountain*. On cylinder and rotary presses, ink is picked up by the roller from a trough called a *fountain*. The fountain can be divided into sections of any width and a different color ink put in each section. The roller is then inked with the different colors along its length and transfers the colored inks to the corresponding parts of the plates or type. Thus, if the fountain were divided into 3 parts, with black on the left, red in the middle, and blue on the right, everything on the left side of the sheet would be printed black, everything in the middle red, and the right blue.

If a printing job is designed to take advantage of this arrangement, a quite spectacular multicolor effect may be obtained at very little more than the cost of one color. Theoretically, there is no limit to the number of colors possible with split fountain, but there are some practical limitations. Unless the ink roller is actually cut into sections so that the colors cannot meet, there is bound to be some mixing of color where the inks come together. The vibrating of the ink rollers normally spreads the mixed area to about 2½″ (6.35 cm), although it is possible to reduce the vibration to much less. The mixed color can be avoided entirely if no printing appears in the border areas. This may cause the designer some difficulty, but the cost of cutting a roller is quite high, unless a long run is involved.

■ *Color process*—In color-process printing, the problem of achieving register is acute because the dot pattern of each color must be perfectly related to the others (CH. 8), and the inks must be properly chosen and applied or the color will not be true. Assuming that the causes of misregister discussed above are avoided, in process printing the main problem is color correction of the films (CH. 8). If this is right there should be little trouble in the plates or the presswork. It is possible to compensate for some inadequacies in the films or plates by controlling the amount of ink in the makeready, by using modified inks, by using specially selected paper, or by changing the order of printing the colors (each printer has a preference for this order), but the effectiveness of such measures is limited and they cannot fully overcome the handicap of poor films or plates.

If the bookmaker wants to have control of the printing result, there is no practical alternative to checking production press sheets against progressive proofs at the pressroom (it is rarely feasible to let a press stand idle while press sheets are sent out for approval) as the job is made ready. On a 4-color press, checking is comparatively simple because the results are apparent immediately. A weak or too-strong color in one part of the sheet can often be corrected by increasing or decreasing the amount of ink flowing into the fountain at that point. The problem here is that there may be another illustration in the same row that needs the opposite treatment.

Often it is necessary to compromise, or to improve one subject at the expense of another. On large presses there may be 6 or 8 illustrations in each row—and compromise is a necessity.

Compromise may be necessary in register also. If one subject on the form is slightly out of register it can usually be corrected by an adjustment of the plate positions on the press. However, this will introduce a certain amount of misregister in other subjects. If this is not acceptable, it may be necessary to take the plates off, re-register the films, and make new plates. Before such a drastic measure is taken, it should be determined whether the problem is paper distortion. If so, compromise will be necessary unless the printing is done later under more favorable conditions.

10 | Paper

From the time it was invented (probably in China in the 2nd century A.D.) until the introduction of machinery in the early 1800s, the varieties of paper were comparatively few. The technique of making paper of rags by hand determined its character, and there was so little paper produced that it barely met the needs of bookmaking. There was then neither the demand nor supply of this precious commodity for the fantastic variety of its uses today, from fish wrapping to computer printout. The subject of paper is tremendous, but even the book uses alone are too numerous to be covered here. Of these, many items (such as shipping cartons) are purchased as finished products, and others—proof papers, the paper used to reinforce bindings, etc.—are purchased by suppliers according to their needs. This chapter will deal with only the book uses of paper in which the bookmaker exercises a choice.

A knowledge of paper is important for 2 reasons: (a) paper has properties that affect the success or failure of a design and (b) a large part (usually about 20%) of the production cost of a book is in its paper.

With a few exceptions, printing paper is bought from distributors rather than from manufacturers. The distributor takes a small profit in return for providing service—stocking and delivering the paper, giving advice, and supplying samples as needed. The paper merchants' advice should be sought, not only because it is being paid for but to take advantage of their special knowledge.

Each kind of paper is made a little differently, but the basic process of papermaking is common to all. Variations are more in the ingredients and finishing than in the method of manufacture. The essentials of this method are described below.

The process

The chief ingredient of most papers is wood. The better papers contain cotton fiber and the best are made entirely of cotton. The

INGREDIENTS

character of a paper depends to a large extent on the kind of wood used, but the major distinction is between the long-fibered woods used for strength (*kraft* paper) and the shorter-fibered woods used in quality printing papers. The cotton fibers used are taken from waste in fabric manufacture and discarded fabric articles such as mail bags, uniforms, work clothes, etc.

Water is the other main ingredient. Dyes and pigments for coloring, rosin and alum for *sizing* to resist penetration of ink and water, titanium and clay *fillers* for opacity and surface improvement, and a few other chemicals are added as required.

PREPARING THE STOCK

Stock is the term for fiber when it is processed. The wood pulp and/or the rags are chopped up, soaked, cooked, bleached, beaten, and mixed with the appropriate chemical ingredients until they are a slushy mass. In this process, the fibers have been reduced to the proper size and shape for the kind of paper being made. Cheaper papers are made with finely ground, uncooked wood pulp. These fibers deteriorate more rapidly. A paper free of groundwood is called a *free sheet*.

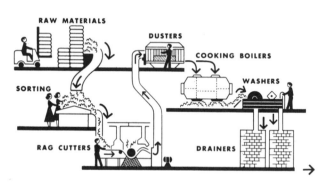

1. *Processing the raw materials.*

THE PAPER MACHINE

Around 1800, the Fourdrinier brothers in England produced a papermaking machine, the principles of which are still in use. The stock (or *furnish*, as it is called when all ingredients have been added) is introduced at the *wet end* where it is poured onto a wide —6–25′(1.82–7.62 m)—endless belt of fine wire screen. The *wire* carries it over a long—sometimes 50′ (15.24 m)—distance, constantly vibrating so that the pulp fibers mesh and the water drains away. Despite the vibration, the fibers tend to lie in the direction of flow, and this is the way the *grain* of the paper runs. The top side of the paper is laid down by the *dandy roll* [a cylinder of finely woven wire cloth which revolves over the wire and affects the surface characteristics]. By the time the end of the wire is reached, the stock has dried enough to become a sheet of very soggy paper. The sheet then passes over a felt blanket onto a series of rollers that squeeze out a large part of the water, and then it passes over heated drums that reduce the moisture content to the proper level.

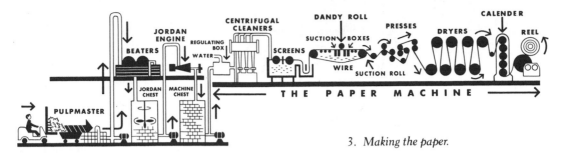

3. *Making the paper.*

2. *Preparing the stock.*

The paper then goes through a *calender*, where it is pressed between a series of steel rollers to give it the desired degree of smoothness. The side of the paper that ran over the wire (*wire side*) is usually a bit rougher than the other, or *felt side*. Considering that the furnish is 99% water and the paper that comes off the machine has only 5% water, it is apparent that the machine is basically a moisture-removing device.

FINISHING

Some finishes are applied during the process of manufacture, either by pressure from a dandy roll or by the texture of felt blankets on which the paper is pressed. Other finishes are applied by separate machines after the paper is made. Textures are made by pressing the paper between special rollers; coatings are generally flowed on. *Sizing* is applied to papers in 2 ways. It may be mixed with the stock (*internal sizing*), in which case it becomes part of the paper itself, or it may be applied to the surface. Most papers have some sizing in them to retard penetration of ink and water. All plain lithographic papers are *surface-sized* to prevent penetration of water and to increase surface strength, as the tacky offset inks tend to pick the surface from the paper. Surface sizing is applied by running the paper through a vat of sizing material.

4. *Finishing and packing.*

Papers intended to be used on web-fed machines are, of course, shipped in rolls, but other paper is cut into sheets. Large orders are shipped on *skids* [wooden platforms] that hold about 3000 lbs. (1360.8 kg). Most printing paper is stocked in *cartons* of about 150 lbs. (68.04 kg), and some of the better papers are wrapped in *packages* of 250, 500, or more sheets, depending on their weight and size.

Some papers are stocked with a *deckle* edge [the feathery, untrimmed edge] on 2 sides.

The varieties and finishes, qualities, weights, etc. of papers seem almost unlimited, but there are 3 main kinds of manufacture, of which all others are variations.

ANTIQUE

These are relatively soft-finish, "toothy" papers. In the antique category, *eggshell* is a fine-textured finish and *vellum* is even smoother. Some antique papers have a *laid* finish, which is a pattern of close parallel lines crossed by a series of widely spaced lines pressed into the paper by the dandy roll. Paper without laid marks is called *wove* finish.

MACHINE FINISH

Most papers are made more compact by calendering on the paper machine. Some are given a little extra calendering to achieve a smoother surface. This is called *machine finish*. Stocks intended for this finish have very short fibers and a heavy mineral content, which produce a rather shiny smoothness when calendered.

COATED

Finishes of still greater smoothness require coating with fine clays which are flowed onto the surface of the paper with adhesives and then supercalendered with extremely smooth rollers. Some coated stock is made with clays that finish dull and are less calendered. These are called *dull coated*, the others, *gloss coated*. Some papers are coated on one side only, others on both sides. A relatively new group of papers called *pigmented* or *matte-coated* papers have generally replaced *supercalendered* sheets. They are actually lightly coated papers—very smooth, but less expensive than fully coated.

The designation of papers as surface-sized is no longer used; virtually all papers are now either coated or surface-sized for offset printing.

USE CLASSIFICATIONS

Since the same kind of paper may be used for different purposes—for example, coated paper may be used for the illustrations in a book or the cover of a paperback—the sale and distribution of paper is organized according to use rather than kind, although with some exceptions. Thus, the papers commonly used for the pages of books are classified as *book papers*. The more expensive book papers are often made in colors (for use in promotion pieces, pamphlets, etc.) and are designated *text papers*. A category of thicker papers of all kinds and finishes called *cover paper* is used for the covers of pamphlets and paperbacks. Some papers are made with the characteristics required for *endpapers*. These and others are sometimes stocked in rolls and are designated *binding papers*. Surface-sized papers used to be classified as *offset* or *litho papers* but this designation has been dropped. There are no unsized papers being made for letterpress use. The grades that include both the former offset and letterpress sheets are now referred to as *plain paper*.

Any of these categories can be and are used for purposes other than the one named, but this is how they are generally listed in catalogues and price lists, and this is the basis for some of the standards used in paper distribution.

The term "weight" is sometimes used to refer to thickness of paper, but this is misleading because paper is sold (mostly) by its actual weight in pounds and this does not always correspond to its thickness. Obviously, a supercalendered paper will be much thinner than an antique eggshell weighing the same amount. Pick up a book of coated paper and notice how heavy it feels in contrast to a book of the same thickness with antique stock.

The weight of paper is determined and specified by a system that seems complicated but is really quite simple. It is usually possible to leave the matter entirely in the hands of the paper merchant, but people who buy paper should understand the weight system themselves, in order to make their own calculations.

When a paper is called "60 lb." (more properly *substance* 60), it means that 500 sheets (a *ream*) of it in a certain size (*basic size*) weigh 60 lbs. (*basis weight*). The basic size of book papers is 25 × 38″ (63.5 × 96.52 cm), but for cover papers it is 20 × 26″ (50.8 × 66.0 cm). Since paper is not always sold in its basic size, it is sometimes necessary to know the *actual* weight of the paper being used or shipped. If the sheets were 38 × 50″ (96.52 × 127 cm) (*finished size*), 60 lb. basis weight, then the actual weight (*finished weight*) per ream would be 120 lbs.—that is, exactly twice the basis weight because the finished size (in area) is twice the basic size (area). Thus, basis weight to basic area equals finished weight to finished area (W:A = W′:A′).

The billing and shipment of book paper may refer to reams or sheets, but prices are based on weight, usually using 1000 sheets as the unit. The weight of 1000 sheets is referred to as M *weight*. To find this, use the above formula and multiply the ream weight by 2. In the example, M weight (finished size) would be 240 lbs. (expressed as 240M). With the formula, one can always find basis or ream weight if M weight is known, and vice versa.

The weight of a particular paper may be expressed in terms of its basis weight—44 × 66″ sub. 50—or, much less frequently its M weight—44 × 66″, 306M—or both—44 × 66″, 306M, sub 50. (The term *"basis"* is used generally for weight and *"basic"* is used with size, but sometimes the words are interchanged.) When paper is shipped in rolls, reference is usually made to the basis weight, the roll width, the total weight, and sometimes to length in feet.

Note that the weight of European or other foreign papers measured in grams relates to a basic size (a square meter) different from those used in the U.S., so it is not correct to use the gram conversion of pounds for basis weight. For example, the Italian equiva-

Weight, bulk, size, & grain

WEIGHT

lent (approximately) of 60 lb. text paper (25 × 38″ sub 60) is called 89 gram (see table of equivalents in Part III), but the conversion of 60 lbs. to grams is 27220. The gram weight refers to the weight of one sheet of one square meter.

BULK   The proper term for thickness in paper is caliper, but the term used in book publishing is "bulk", although the word has come to suggest an artificial, blown-up character. (Whereas paper is improved in printing qualities by being compressed to a harder, smoother sheet, many book papers are sold in the least compressed state possible to satisfy the publishers' demand for fatter books [CH. 16].)

Bulk depends on fibers as well as manufacture, so the more fiber there is, the thicker the paper, given the same manufacture. More fiber may mean bulkier or additional fibers. The latter results in heavier paper (100 lb. paper has about twice as much fiber as 50 lb. of the same grade) while bulky fiber may add thickness without weight. This is because the fillers are heavier for their mass than the fibers.

Paper manufacturers and distributors print bulk tables showing the number of pages to the inch of each weight and finish in almost all grades of paper. Obviously, the more calendered sheets will have less bulk than others of the same weight, but there is also considerable variation among different makes of paper in each category. The table shows the approximate range in the most common grades and weights.

G R A D E	50 lb.	55 lb.	60 lb.	65 lb.	70 lb.	75 lb.	80 lb.
Antique	380–400	350–370	320–340	290–310	270–290	250–270	220–250
Eggshell	430–450	390–410	350–380	330–350	300–320	280–300	260–280
Vellum	440–480	410–450	370–420	350–400	330–370	310–350	290–320
Machine finish	490–560	440–510	410–470	380–440	355–400	330–370	300–350
Matte coated	620–700	570–630	520–560	480–520	440–470	400–430	370–390
Coated	800–850	730–790	640–740	590–680	530–620	490–580	440–530

SIZE   The paper merchant keeps hundreds of items in stock—different brands, kinds, qualities, finishes, colors, weights, and sizes. Obviously, he wants to reduce this number to the fewest possible. The printer has presses of various sizes, but the number is limited. Presuming that publishers want to utilize the full size of the presses, they need mainly the paper sizes that fit the presses available. Consequently, paper is made in a few standard sizes and any others must be made to order (*making-order*). Each paper mill has its own minimum quantity requirements for making special sizes in each grade of paper, but the average for book papers is 5000 lbs., and for text and cover papers 2000 lbs. These minimums may often be cut in half but may require payment of a 10% penalty.

In book papers, the stock sheet sizes and the page size (trim-size) to which they fold are:

35 × 45"—5½ × 8½" (88.9 × 114.3 cm—13.97 × 21.59 cm)
38 × 50"—6⅛ × 9¼" (96.52 × 127 cm—15.56 × 23.5 cm)
41 × 61"—5 × 7⅜" (104.14 × 154.94 cm—12.7 × 18.73 cm)
44 × 66"—5⅜ × 8" (111.76 × 167.64 cm—13.65 × 20.32 cm)
45 × 68"—5½ × 8¼" (114.3 × 172.72 cm—13.97 × 20.96 cm)
46 × 69"—5⅝ × 8⅜" (116.84 × 175.26 cm—14.29 × 21.27 cm)

The first 2 would take 32-page forms, the others, 64s (CH.9). The line under one number in each size indicates that the grain runs in that dimension.

Text and cover papers are stocked in generally smaller sizes:

23 × 35" (58.42 × 88.9 cm)
25 × 38" (63.5 × 96.52 cm)
26 × 40" (66.04 × 101.6 cm)
and sometimes in:
35 × 45" (88.9 × 114.3 cm)
38 × 50" (96.52 × 127 cm)

Paper in rolls is generally stocked in the following widths:

22½" (57.15 cm)
23¼" (59.05 cm)
23½" (59.69 cm)
25½" (64.77 cm)
26" (66.04 cm)
33" (83.82 cm)
34" (86.36 cm)
44" (111.76 cm)
45" (114.3 cm)
50" (127 cm)

The stock sizes given here are American. Other sizes are used elsewhere.

When paper is folded against the grain, the fibers break, the surface cracks, the fold is ragged, and the pages won't lie properly. These effects are more pronounced in some papers than others, but it is always desirable to fold with the grain. For this reason it is important to know how the sheet is to be folded when ordering paper.

Book papers are frequently stocked with a choice of grain directions, while the more expensive text papers are usually available only one way. In making-orders, it is usually possible to get the grain in either direction. In rolls, the grain *always* runs with the length of the paper; around, not across the width of, the roll.

Ordering paper

Choice of paper should be made in consultation with both paper supplier and printer, because many judgments are involved and the specialists can be of great help. In *ordering* paper, a knowledge of the system should be sufficient, but it is such a complex system that it pays to check your calculations with the paper supplier, even if you think you have the answer.

Papermaking is no longer the art it was when done by hand, but neither is the manufacture so precise that it can be depended upon for perfect uniformity. Some variations of color, finish, weight, etc. may occur and cause trouble. To a certain extent this is to be expected, but when the acceptable limits are exceeded, a complaint is in order. At such times (and many others), it is good to be dealing with a reliable merchant. And bear in mind that difficulties with the paper may be due to faults in the pressroom as well as in the mill.

CALCULATING QUANTITIES

When buying paper in sheets for the pages of books, determine how many pages will *cut out* of [divide into] each sheet (twice the number in each form) and divide this into the total number of pages in the book to get the number of sheets needed per book. Multiply this figure by the number of books to be printed and add a certain percentage of the total for *spoilage*. This percentage varies according to the number of colors, difficulties of printing, and length of run. Most of the spoilage occurs during makeready, when trial and error is the rule. On short runs (3 to 5000), this may be 5 to 7% per color, on long runs perhaps 3 to 5%, depending on the printing problem. The amount of extra paper provided should allow for some spoilage in binding too, usually about 3%. The printer and binder should be asked what they require for spoilage in each case.

Example: An edition of 5000 copies of a 256-page book with a trim-size of 5⅜ × 8″ (13.65 × 20.32 cm) being printed in 64-page forms, with 2 colors on each form.

(1) To print 64-page forms of 5⅜ × 8″ requires sheet size 44 × 66″ (111.76 × 167.64 cm)

(2) 64 pages on each side of sheet = 128 pages per sheet

(3) 128 pages per sheet requires 2 sheets for a 256-page book

(4) 2 sheets per book × 5000 books = 10,000 sheets

(5) 5% printer's spoilage per color × 2 colors = 10%. Binder's spoilage of 3% makes total of 13%

(6) 10,000 sheets plus 13% (1300) = 11,300 sheets to be ordered

The same principle applies when ordering paper for jackets or for any other purpose. The size of the sheet required is always decided with the printers, partly because it must fit on one of their presses and partly because they may be printing 2 or more up and will need a correspondingly larger sheet. Also, there are allowances to be made for grippers, bleeds, guides, etc.

Ordering paper in rolls for web-fed printing or binding machines is not very different in procedure. From the size of each page or unit, the size of the form is determined, and this decides the width of the roll—although either dimension may be used for the width, depending on the way the grain is to run. The other dimension is multiplied by the number of impressions involved and this figure is multiplied by *half* the number of forms to be printed (the other half back up). To this amount is added spoilage.

Thus, if the book used in the preceding example were being printed on a web-fed press in a quantity of 50,000 copies:

(1) To fold properly, the grain must be the long way of the page, so the width of the roll will be 44″ (111.76 cm)

(2) Every 66″ (167.64 cm) of length will contain 64 pages. 50,000 × 66″ = 3,300,000″ (838.20 m)

(3) There will be 4 forms of 64 pages, of which 2 will back the other 2, so 3,300,000″ is multiplied × 2 for 6,600,000″, or 550,000′ (167,640 m)

(4) Spoilage of 15% (web spoilage runs higher) makes a total of 632,500′ (192,786 m).

Actually, such a book would probably be printed with 2 webs running together, each with a 32-page form on both sides. The rolls would then be 22″ (55.88 cm) wide, and each would be 632,500′ long. Except for lightweight papers, it is more common to order rolls of paper by weight rather than length. To calculate the weight needed, simply find the sheet size and figure as though ordering sheets (but add the extra web spoilage).

When paper is ordered from stock, the exact amount required will be delivered. When the paper is made to order, it is not possible to be sure of the quantity because the paper machine runs so fast it cannot always be stopped at precisely the point desired, and spoilages in the various papermaking operations are indefinite. The smaller the amount made, the larger will be the percentage of variation. Paper trade customs provide that the customer must accept and pay for a certain percentage more or less than the amount ordered, or elect to specify "not more than" or "not less than" a certain quantity. In the latter case, the variation in one direction that one must accept is considerably larger in percentage than otherwise. In large quantities, the percentage of variation (*overrun* or *underrun*) is not likely to be serious—perhaps 1 or 2%. On small orders, say 1000 lbs., the amount delivered may be as much as 20% off. (Only a few mills will even make orders so small.)

It is easy to make a drastic arithmetical error in calculating paper quantities, and even the most experienced people get a trifle nervous about ordering large amounts. Although the paper suppliers check your figures, they may make the same mistake you made, so use this simple practical test: Take a book of about the same size and kind as yours will be and weigh it. If it weighs 1 lb. (.4536 kg) and you are making 5000 books, you know that you should be ordering about 5000 lbs. (2268 kg) of paper. (The cover on the book you weighed will account for spoilage and then some. A more accurate result can be obtained by using a paperback.) This won't show up a minor mistake, but you will certainly know that you shouldn't be ordering 500 or 50,000 lbs., nor 2500 or 10,000 lbs.

CALCULATING COST The price of book and cover paper is based on weight. For each brand and grade of paper there is a sliding scale of prices per pound according to the amount ordered, with the lowest prices for the largest quantities. The range is considerable, the highest prices being 2 or 3 times as much as the lowest, so it is vital to know the exact amount of paper needed. A small difference in quantity may shift the price into another bracket and make a difference of 15% or more. Because of this, it is quite possible for a larger amount of paper to cost less than a smaller amount.

The price brackets vary somewhat from paper to paper, but the most commonly used are: 1 carton, 4 cartons, 16 cartons, 5M lbs. (2268 kg), 10M lbs. (4536 kg), 40M lbs. (18144 kg) *(carload)*. (M=1000.) The amount of paper in a carton varies according to the size and weight of the sheet, but it is usually about 150 lbs. (68.04 kg). Large quantities may be bought on skids or may be packed in cartons at a slightly higher price.

A price list will give prices for each bracket and show the M weight and number of sheets per carton for each size of sheet in stock. Thus, if we are buying paper for the book used in the previous example, the table will show that there are 500 sheets per carton for the 44 × 66" 306M, sub. 50 item. We had calculated that we should be ordering 11,300 sheets, which is 22.6 cartons. This puts us in the 16 carton bracket (anything from 16 cartons to 5000 lbs. (2268 kg)). Let us say the price per lb. is $.3160 (the price is usually given per 100 lbs. (45.36 kg), but it is easy to move the decimal point). Now it is necessary to know how many pounds are needed. If 1000 sheets weigh 306 lbs. (138.80 kg), then 11,300 will weigh 11.3 × 306 or 3458 lbs. (1609.37 kg). Multiply this by $.3160, the cost per lb., and you have the total cost of the paper, $1092.73. If a making-order were involved, there could be additional charges for special size, finish, grain, or color, or a variation due to an under- or overrun. (Very lightweight papers also carry a price penalty because of the extra fillers needed for opacity.)

While the base price of paper made to order is no higher than stock paper (if the quantity is sufficient), the color or finish may not come out exactly as hoped for, there may be an overrun to pay for, or the delivery time may be a problem. Worse yet, a strike or accident may make it impossible to deliver the order at all. Also, bear in mind the problem that might arise if a reprint is needed in a quantity too small to warrant a making-order. If the printing is sheet-fed and there is a stock size larger than the sheet required, there is only the cost of extra paper, but the problem could be serious if no larger size is made. The same would be true of a roll order.

Against these considerations may be weighed the advantage of having a special color or finish, and the money saved when a special size prevents a waste that would occur if the stock sheet were used. For example, if the page size of a book is 5¾ × 9¼" (14.61 × 23.5 cm), there would be an unused strip 3" (7.62 cm) wide and 38" (96.52 cm) long on a standard 38 × 50" (96.52 × 127 cm) sheet. Thus, 8% of the paper cost is wasted. It can be saved by having the paper made 35 × 50" (88.9 × 127 cm).

Selecting paper

It might seem more logical to put "selecting paper" ahead of "ordering paper", but it is necessary to know the problems of paper buying in order to make practical selections. Unless a making-order is feasible, availability may have as much effect on paper choice as price and preference. Where price is a consideration (and it usually is), it is much easier to choose between a half dozen possibilities if you can roughly calculate the prices yourself.

The selection of paper involves esthetic factors in the choice of color, texture, etc. (CHS. 15, 16), but the first consideration must be suitability to the technical requirements. This is discussed in terms of the printing processes.

■ *Letterpress*—Although virtually all papers are sized for lithography, they can all be printed by letterpress, if sometimes with some difficulty. For all practical purposes it may be assumed that in letterpress only type is involved, so any of the plain papers will be suitable.

The considerations of weight, bulk, and opacity discussed under "Lithography" (below) apply to letterpress also.

■ *Lithography*—For color process or halftone printing it is best to have maximum contrast between the color of paper and ink. Since modern papers are made with halftone printing in mind, they tend to be relatively hard of surface and bright white. In some lines, fluorescent dyes are used to increase the brightness. For books in which the halftones need not dazzle, there are off-white papers available (such as this one).

Any litho-sized paper will take 133 screen, and most sheets will handle 150 well. For 175-line and finer screens a matte-coated stock is best. Perfectly good halftones—and even color process—can be printed on papers with *embossed* (raised) textures.

Books are usually printed on 50 to 70 lb. paper. Most common is 55 or 60 lb. antique, with 50 lb. (and occasionally 45 lb.) used for books with very many pages, and 70 lb. (and occasionally 80 lb.) for those with few. In general, the trade publishers like as thick a book as feasible (CH. 16) up to the point where there is no longer much sales advantage and it becomes desirable to keep the paper cost down. However, if the use of bulky paper fails to produce the thickness wanted, it is necessary to increase the weight. Some illustrated books with relatively few pages and a high retail price may use 100 lb. or heavier paper to get enough bulk, since they need a matte-coated or full-coated stock for reproduction quality. In books of very many pages, the lighter weights of paper are used, but it is best to use a more calendered finish to reduce bulk rather than extremely light weights. The latter are not only expensive, but they cause difficulty in printing, especially in large sheets. Most printers charge a penalty for handling paper below 40 lb. substance.

Opacity is related to weight and is usually affected by bulk. Bulking antiques have good opacity, because the light is scattered by the loose construction, and heavier weights have better opacity due to more fiber and/or filler, although a heavily calendered 60 lb. stock may be less opaque than a bulky, loose fibered 50 lb. sheet. Two sheets of the same weight and finish may vary in opacity if their ingredients differ. Papers coated on both sides are very opaque because of the density of the 2 layers of clay. Coated-one-side, which is usually used over an opaque surface (labels, jackets, etc.), tends to poor opacity because the base stock needs, and has, very little. Opacity is important in books with halftones or with pages of irregular layout in which type or illustrations back up areas of open space.

■ *Gravure*—There is no connection between screen size and paper in gravure printing, as the finest screens can be printed on any kind of paper. Indeed, since the only bar to reproduction of continuous tone is the grid of white lines separating the dots, it is desirable to have the ink spread over the lines. Formerly, this was accomplished by printing on dampened antique paper with heavy pressure. However, the tendency of the antique stock to absorb the ink produced a relatively soft effect, which is not always desirable. Today, much gravure printing is done with lighter impression on coated or pigmented sheets—on which the ink spreads more by surface flow than absorption. The results are more brilliant.

Dull-coated paper is generally preferred over gloss, particularly since there is a tendency for the coating to be damaged by the relatively heavy pressure of gravure printing. Some, but not all, litho-sized papers can be used. Almost any other kind of paper is usable, including the cheapest groundwood sheets (witness the rotogravure sections in some Sunday newspapers). However, although it is possible to get quite good results on almost any surface (including acetate) by this process, the results do vary, so it is best to check with the printer before selecting.

The color of the paper is particularly important in gravure because the ink is transparent. A darker shade will give a softer effect, but as long as the color is clear and bright the result is good. For the most brilliant results, a white paper is best, although the fluorescent whites cause trouble. Avoid light weights of uncoated paper (under 60 lb.) as there is a serious possibility of the thin gravure ink bleeding through.

■ *Xerography*—In the offset method, any paper with characteristics suited to the printing machine can be used. In some copying machines, the direct method requires that the paper be coated with a zinc oxide compound. Other machines using the electrostatic process (CH.9) can use plain papers, and this is the kind of technique that will certainly prevail if the process is used in book printing.

■ *Silk screen*—Any paper can be printed.

■ *Collotype*—As in lithography, water is used and there is also danger of *picking* due to very tacky ink, so the paper requirements are similar. There are 2 main differences: (a) collotype has no screen, so a difference of surface is not so significant and (b) the ink coverage is even less than in lithography, so clarity of paper color is very important. Sharp contrast is quite impossible in collotype, so whiteness is not necessary. The soft, luminous effect is best achieved with a sheet having the characteristics of gravure paper.

11 | Binding

Binding is a complex process. Hardcover binding involves about 18 different operations and uses a dozen materials, most of which are chosen individually for each book. This multiplicity provides many possibilities for variation—with both esthetic and economic significance. Such possibilities are discussed in CH. 26. This chapter describes the mechanics and materials themselves.

There has been little radical innovation in binding compared to composition, platemaking, and printing. Since the hand operations were first converted to mechanical processes in the 19th century, there have been very few changes in the principles by which they are performed.

The main area of improvement today is in reduction of handling between steps. Machines are being built to perform several operations, and new plant layouts have a continuous line of machines, with the product of one feeding automatically into the next.

Electronics and computer technology are improving the efficiency of binding machinery and make possible a considerable degree of automation, but there is nothing in sight comparable to the revolutionary effects of photography on composition and printing.

If any change can be called major, it is the strong swing toward adhesive rather than sewed binding. This is due less to a technological development than to a new surge of confidence in *"perfect-binding"*—aided, certainly, by improvements in the adhesives and techniques used.

The term "binding" without further qualification is taken to mean conventional (hardcover) book binding, and it is to this that the foregoing comments generally refer, but there are some fairly radical departures in technology when other kinds of binding are considered.

There are basically 3 kinds of binding: (a) *case* (or *hard binding*, or *hardcover*), (b) *paper* (or *paperback*, or *softcover*), and (c) *mechanical* (including "spiral" binding, etc.), with many variations of each kind. The distinctions will be discussed later in this chapter. Up to a point, however, the binding process is the same for all kinds. This is the basic operation described below.

For each job, the method of folding printed sheets is determined before the pages are imposed for printing (CH.8). There are many methods, each one based on (a) the number of pages on the sheet, (b) the arrangement of signatures desired, and (c) the characteristics of the paper. An imposition is selected by the binder with the concurrence of the printer, so that all their requirements, as well as the conditions listed above, are met.

The fewer signatures there are in a book, the less its cost. This would suggest making signatures with as many pages as possible, but the number is limited by the bulk and flexibility of the paper. Too many pages in a signature cause wrinkling, buckling, and a tendency to spring open. Generally, antique stock up to 70 lb. (103.5 gr) is folded in 32-page signatures, from 70 through 80 lb. (118.3 gr) in 16s, and over 80 lb. in 8s. These limits should be lowered as more sizing, filling, and calendering are present. Very lightweight papers may be folded in 64s, up to about 30 lb. (44.4 gr).

Given a certain number of pages per signature, the sheet may be folded in different ways. The more pages on the sheet, the more variations possible. Successive folds may be parallel or at right angles to each other, the sheet may be cut into 2, 4, or 8 sections on the folding machine, the sections may each be folded in a variety of ways, and, finally, the sections may be inserted into others to become parts of larger signatures, or they may become complete signatures themselves.

The chief reason for choosing one imposition over another is binding efficiency, but the choice may also be a means of distributing color throughout the book more effectively. For example, if a second color is printed on only some forms, the imposition can be arranged so that the pages with color will be in different parts of the book rather than all together, or they may be imposed to fall consecutively in some places rather than alternately. Considerable flexibility is possible, but any deviation from the simplest imposition usually adds to the cost of binding.

Too much space would be needed to describe all the standard impositions, and there are innumerable special impositions used in unusual circumstances. A simple 16-page example is described below to illustrate the principle.

To make a 16-page signature from a sheet with 8 pages on each side, using 3 right-angle folds, each form would have 2 rows of 4 pages each printed head to head, i.e. one row would be upside-down. The arrangement of pages would be:

front

ϛ		ϛl	6		8
4		13	16		1

back

L		ol	11		6
2		15	14		3

Take a sheet of paper and mark it this way. It will be seen that 1 backs 2, 3 backs 4, and so on. Fold the sheet in half, then again in half at right angles to the first fold, then again at right angles to the previous one, and you will have a signature in which the 16 pages are in consecutive order.

Folding machines vary according to the kind of folding done, the size of sheet handled, and the principle of operation. Most book folding is done by the *tape-and-knife* method. The sheet is carried on a set of narrow endless belts or *tapes* until it is in position for a dull blade to drive it between rollers which press the fold to a sharp crease. This operation is repeated until the sheet is finished. The machine slits or perforates certain folds to prevent *gussets* and wrinkles and to allow the trapped air to escape. On the larger machines, a sheet can be cut into sections (*slit*), each of which is folded separately but simultaneously. Thus, a 128-page sheet may come out of the folder as eight 16-page signatures, four 32s, etc. The machine may deliver a 32-page signature folded from a single sheet (*straight 32*), it may consist of two 16s, one inserted in the other (*double 16 insert*), or the two 16s may be in consecutive order (*double 16 straight*).

tape-and-knife fold

Small units, such as endpapers and inserts, are folded on a *buckle* or *loop folder*. The sheet is passed between 2 plates until it hits a stop which causes it to buckle at the proper place. Two rollers grab the buckle and press it to a sharp fold.

buckle fold

Most web presses have coordinated folders built-in at the end of the press so that the printing of the paper (both sides) and its folding are virtually simultaneous. This may mean folding at a speed of about 25,000 sheets per hour instead of the usual 3 to 4000. The tape-and-knife method cannot work fast enough, so a different principle is used. It is too complex to be explained here, but it is based on high precision manipulation of the sheets by grippers and reduction of the number of right-angle folds needed, by cutting the sheet into small units.

Unless a continuous line of machines is used, the signatures delivered by a folding machine are *bundled* [subjected to pressure and tied tightly between boards] and sent to the *gathering* department, where they are assembled into books. Before they are gathered, the endpapers, if any, are *tipped* onto the first and last signatures, and any illustrations not comprising a separate signature are tipped, *inserted*, or *wrapped*, at the proper place.

■ *Tip*—Tipping means pasting onto a page with about ⅛" (.3175 cm) of paste along the inside, or *gutter*, edge. Tips may be a single leaf or a 4-page fold (as are the endpapers). Pasting tips onto the outsides of signatures is simplest, in the middle of signatures is more difficult, and most difficult is tipping within a signature— which usually requires slitting open a fold by hand. Outside tips are done by machine, but the others are hand operations.

■ *Insert*—Inserting into a signature means placing 4 or more pages in the middle or elsewhere, thereby enlarging it by that many.

■ *Wrap*—Wrapping is the reverse of inserting; here the pages go around the *outside* of the text signature. Mechanically, the process is the same as inserting. A wrap can be placed around certain of the pages within a signature (for example, around pages 5 and 12 in the 16-page signature described earlier in this chapter) but this is a slower operation, performed by hand.

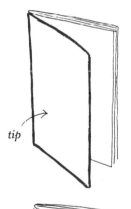

tip

In sewed books, tips are much weaker than inserts or wraps because no stitching goes through them. To avoid tips it is possible to make 2-page (single leaf) wraps by leaving an extra ½" (1.27 cm) of paper on the inside edge of the leaf to wrap around the signature, but this is not very practical for large edition binding, and the short pieces are unsightly where they protrude between pages.

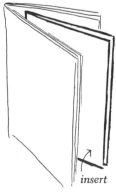

insert

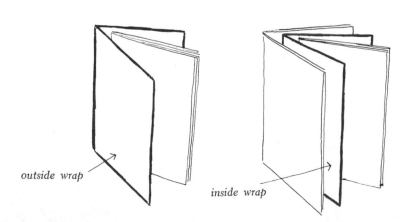

outside wrap

inside wrap

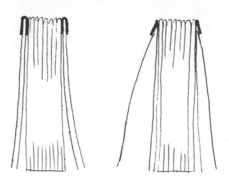

2 methods of reinforcing

REINFORCING

Reinforcing of signatures, when required, is usually done at this stage. There are several methods. Generally, these consist of pasting a 1″ (2.54 cm) strip of cambric cloth along the back folds of the first and last signature after the endpapers are on, or pasting it on the outside of the endpapers only, without going around the signatures—depending on the sewing used. Sometimes, books are specially reinforced and bound for library use *(prebinding)* separately from the regular edition. Libraries also have regular trade bindings *rebound* with extra reinforcement. Another kind of reinforcement is *whip-stitching*; one or 2 extra rows of stitching on the first and last signatures. On very heavy books, 2 or 3 strips of cloth tape may be sewed across the back and extended onto the covers.

GATHERING & COLLATING

The completed signatures are piled in successive hoppers on the gathering machine. A mechanical arm takes a signature from the first hopper and places it on a conveyor belt, a second arm places a second signature from the next hopper on top of the first signature on the belt, and so on down the line until the book is completed. Thus, if the book has 10 signatures, the belt would always have 10 piles—one with all 10 signatures, one with 9, one with 8, and so

on back to the first "pile" which would have only the first signature.

As the completed sets of signatures come off the machine, they are *collated* [checked for correct sequence and position]. In small editions this can be accomplished by an operator fanning through every fourth or fifth set to see that the first and last folios of succeeding signatures correspond, and that none are missing, duplicated, upside-down, or backward. Ordinarily, small marks (*collating marks*) are printed at certain places on the sheets, so that when folded, each signature has one along its back edge. A straight or diagonal line across the back results when the book is properly gathered, so any error is immediately apparent.

At this point, the process varies according to the kind of binding required, although some later operations are used in more than one method.

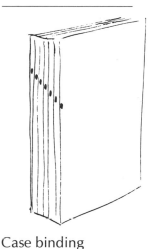

Case binding

This is the conventional method of making a book, whereby the signatures are enclosed in a more or less rigid cover, to the inside of which they are attached by pasting the endpapers, or the first and last pages (*self-lining*). There are several variations in case binding, both in the manner of holding the pages together and in the nature of the cover. Any of these variations may be combined.

The pages may be held together (a) by sewing the signatures together, (b) by the use of wire staples, or (c) by adhesives (perfect-binding). These procedures follow immediately after collating.

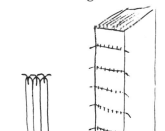

SEWING

There are two methods:

■ *Smyth sewing*—For tradebooks, this is by far the most common method. The thread is stitched through the gutter of each signature and passed through the other stitches at the back to join them. Being held this way, the pages are free to open without hindrance. The newer machines paste the back edge of the first and last signatures to the adjacent ones.

If the book has only one signature and the stitching goes through the gutter, it is called *saddle stitching*.

■ *Side sewing (Singer sewing)*—The thread is passed through the entire book about ⅛″ (.3175 cm) from the back, just as it would be if sewed on a home sewing machine, as a hem is on a tablecloth. For books over ¾″ (1.905 cm) bulk, another machine is used and the process is called *McCain sewing*.

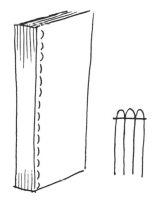

WIRE STITCHING OR STAPLING

This is a cheaper method of holding pages together when there is just one signature. Two or 3 wire staples are passed through the gutter (*saddle wire stitching*), as in a pamphlet. *Side wire stitching* is similar in principle to side sewing, except that metal staples are used instead of thread. Side-sewed books have 2 wire staples put through them in the gathering machine to hold the signatures together for sewing, although these may be omitted on thin books.

This method did not deserve its laudatory name until quite recently. The process consists of trimming off the folds at the back of the book and applying an adhesive to hold the pages together. Essentially, this is the same method as that used to make pads, and in its early days the results were about the same also—the pages were easily pulled out.

Subsequent improvements have made perfect-binding comparable in performance to sewed binding. There are many minor variations in the methods used, but they all involve trimming in such a way as to increase the amount of paper surface to which the adhesive can be applied—usually by notching or roughening the back of the book—and some kind of flexible, quick-drying adhesive.

A more sophisticated type of perfect-binding—which may indeed be perfect—is done by electronically welding the molecules of paper together. The book is then not so much a series of pages adhered or sewed together, as a single piece of paper in the form of a book. The paper must be specially made for this purpose.

NIPPING

Sewed books must be given a heavy, rapid squeeze to eject air, compress the paper, stitching, and folds, and generally produce a compact unit. This is called *nipping* and is applied at the end of the sewing machine where the sewed signatures are pressed between two metal plates. During the perfect-binding operation, enough pressure is applied to the book to compress the pages firmly. No more is necessary because there are no folds left to hold air.

GLUING-OFF

This is the first operation in *forwarding*.

Even though sewed tightly, the back tends to loosen a little after nipping, so a thin coat of flexible glue is applied to hold the signatures in place. This is done by running the books, backs down, over a series of glue-carrying rollers, and then, usually, over a heating element that dries the glue so that it is hard enough to make the book firm in time for the next operation. Perfect-bound hardcover books are glued-off after the back folds are cut off and before the other 3 sides are trimmed. On these, a cloth lining is applied to the back.

TRIMMING

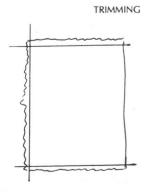

After being glued-off, the book is trimmed. Heavy knives chop off approximately ⅛″ (.3175 cm) at the *head (top)*, *front (fore-edge)*, and *foot (bottom)*, thus opening all folds (or *bolts*) except those at the back. This is called a *smooth (or full) trim*. If a *rough trim* is desired at the foot, the knife takes off only enough to open the bolts, which are made to protrude slightly beyond the slit edges during folding. For a rough front, all folds are slit on the folder and there is no trim. The result is a more or less ragged edge somewhat resembling that of a book printed on handmade or deckle-edged paper. This adds about ⅛" (.3175 cm) to the trim-size of the page.

On case-bound books, the edge color is applied only to the top ordinarily. The color is an aniline dye and is sprayed on stacks of books about one foot high. The spray is directed at an angle from the back so that no excess color will get on the front. It may be applied by hand or by machine.

Gold edges are applied by hand in the same way as gold leaf is applied to frames. It is now possible to have an imitation gold applied by machine at much lower cost. The process is similar to the leaf-stamping operation used on covers (see "Stamping").

Sewed, and some perfect-bound, books are put through a machine which (a) nips the back to a uniform width, (b) rounds the back with a set of knurled rollers (thus producing the concave shape of the front), (c) clamps the book sharply *except* at the very back, thus allowing the back to flare out slightly, and (d) shapes the back with curved backing irons.

The ridge caused by the flaring of the back is called the *joint* and is very important to the structure of a book. It is at this point that the cover hinges and the pages bend when turned. The joint is also a locking device that tends to keep the book from slipping out of its cover. Books can be made with flat backs, but they are not as strong as those with round backs, particularly when the bulk is large and the paper is heavy. Very thin books are usually made flat-backed, because there is not enough bulk for rounding and backing.

This operation is usually performed on the rounding and backing machine.

Lining-up is the major reinforcing process. First, a coat of glue is applied to the back. On top of this is placed a strip of *crash* or *super* [a gauze] extending almost the length of the back and about 1" (2.54 cm) over each side. Rollers press the crash into the wet glue and then apply another coat of glue on top of it. On this is applied a strip of tough paper cut to the length and width of the back.

The crash is very important, being the only link between cover and book other than the endpaper. On books requiring unusual strength, an extra-heavy crash *(legal crash)* or a double layer may be used. On a bound book, the crash can be detected underneath the endpaper.

Headbands are the decorative strips of colored cloth that protrude slightly at the back on top and bottom. They are applied during lining-up, being glued to the back between the crash and paper.

On completion of lining-up, the book is ready to be inserted in its cover. The cover is made while the folding, gathering, and for-

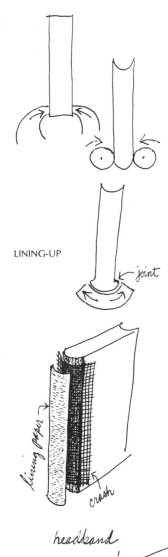

warding are in progress, so that it will be ready at the same time as the book.

The conventional case (or cover) of a hardbound book consists of a more-or-less rigid board on each side and a strip of paper or board at the back, all covered with a decorative/protective material. The characteristics and varieties of these materials are discussed later in this chapter. The process of putting them together is *casemaking*.

The boards and the backstrip are cut to the height of the trim-size of the book *plus* ¼" (.635 cm)—which provides for an over-hang of ⅛" (.3175 cm) at head and foot—but the boards are made ⅛" *less* than the width of the trim-size. The backstrip, for a round-backed book of normal bulk, is made about ⅜" (.9525 cm) wider than the bulk of the pages *(paper bulk)*, to allow for the flare of the joint. For very thick or very thin books, more or less than the ⅜" is added. A useful formula is to make the backstrip 1.33 times the bulk. For flat backs, the backstrip will equal the paper bulk plus the thickness of the boards. In a flat back, the backstrip is generally a rigid board rather than paper. This partly compensates for the lack of strength at the back and gives a neater appearance.

The cover material is cut to the height of the boards plus 1¼" (3.175 cm)—which allows ⅝" (1.5875 cm) at the head and foot for *turn-in*, i.e. for the material to wrap around the edge. In width, the material is made the width of both boards and backstrip, plus 1¼" turn-in, *plus* ¼" (.635 cm) for the joints on both sides. At the joint (or hinge), a space of ¼" is left between the boards and the backstrip. A diagonal cut is made at each corner of the material to prevent excessive bunching of the turn-in. Laid out in position for casemaking, the boards and cover material for a 7 × 10" (17.78 × 25.4 cm) book, bulking ¾" (1.905 cm), with a rounded back, would appear as follows:

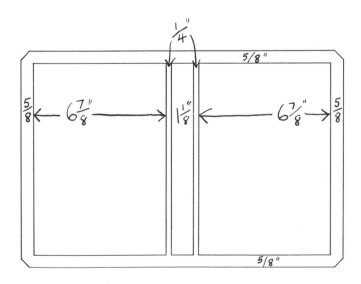

A cover such as this could be made in 2 ways: with precut pieces on a *sheet-fed casemaker*, or on a *web-fed casemaker* with only the boards precut, the cover material and backstrip paper being in rolls.

On the sheet-fed machine, the material is glued on its inside surface, the boards and backstrip are dropped onto the wet glue in the proper position, and small rollers push the turn-ins over and press them down, to complete the cover.

In web-fed casemaking, the material passes over a glue roller and then, glue side up, under a hopper which holds the boards. Pieces of backstrip paper are automatically chopped off a roll to the proper length and dropped into place on the glued material. The boards are dropped into their positions at the same time. As the web moves along, the corners are cut, the material is cut off to the proper length, and the edges are turned in.

On some machines, the width of the web is the height of the material, so that board, backstrip, board, fall *successively (side feed)*; on others, the web is the width, so the 3 pieces drop *simultaneously* alongside each other *(end feed)*.

side feed

end feed

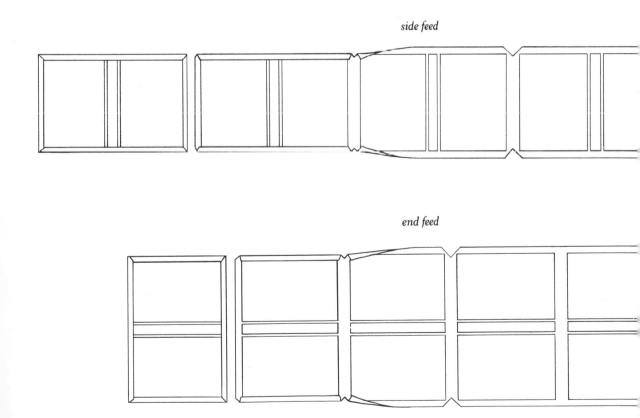

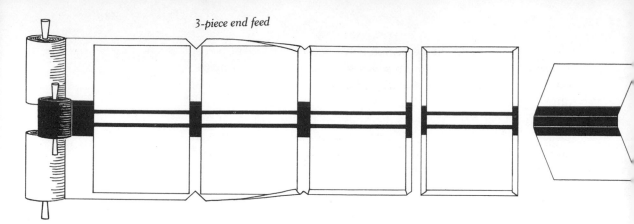

This distinction is of no significance when a cover is made with a single piece of material, but it is of primary importance if a cover is to be made with 2 or more pieces. When such covers are made by running material simultaneously from 2 or more rolls, it is obvious that on a side-feed machine the strips of material would run *across* the cover and on end-feed they would run *up* the cover.

The most common use of this technique is the 3-piece cover made on end-feed machines, with one material for the sides and another for the back (with some extending onto the sides and over-lapped by the side pieces).

Almost any combination of materials is possible in this method, but each strip must be wide and strong enough to withstand the tension used, and to prevent difficulties caused by the almost 15-foot length of the web. For average materials, at least 2″ (5.08 cm) width is usually required, but more may be needed in some cases. Regardless of how much of the back material is supposed to *show* on the sides, at least ⅜″ (.9525 cm) should extend onto the boards to insure sufficient strength. It is, after all, this piece that holds the cover together and provides the structurally vital joint. The side materials, which have virtually no structural importance, may overlap the back material by any amount, with ⅛″ (.3175 cm) the minimum, to allow for inaccuracies in the casemaking.

The same method may be used on the side-feed casemaker, but here each piece forms part of the hinge and must have the requisite strength.

Multi-piece covers can be made on sheet-fed machines, but not in one operation. The standard 3-piece case is made by putting the back material on first, then putting the 2 side pieces on in a second run.

Efforts have been made to find a less expensive way of producing covers, but the only prospect for significant economy is in the direction of molded covers made of a single piece of material. For this purpose, plastics—mostly vinyls—are being used.

Despite the savings effected by the much simpler casemaking, the cost of these covers tends to be high because of the relatively expensive plastic. The problem here is the need to have flexibility in the joint and rigidity in the sides. This can be accomplished by molding a sheet of plastic with the necessary variations in thickness, but no cheaper material (of which paper is the most likely one) would have sufficient strength at the hinge if the thickness were reduced enough to provide flexibility. Experiments toward finding a suitable and cheaper material are in progress. "One-piece" plastic covers are made also by laminating pieces together instead of molding, often with a piece of board between layers of plastic. The edges are then *heat-sealed* [melted together].

Semi-rigid covers are made by using a single piece of plastic just heavy enough to provide some rigidity yet thin enough to bend. These are usually made with a paper adhered to the back in order to reduce the amount of expensive plastic needed (see "Binding materials"). In effect, such covers are virtually the same as paper covers, differing only in the way they are joined to the book itself and in the degree of rigidity. Even the materials are the same as some paperback covers, which have a thin sheet of clear plastic laminated to the printed paper. The difference then is only in the proportion of paper and plastic. Indeed, some "paperbacks" have been produced with covers of paper-lined vinyl.

There are 3 methods used to apply lettering and other designs to covers: (a) printing the material before the cover is made, (b) printing on the cover by silk screen, and (c) *stamping* on the cover. The techniques of the first 2 methods are explained in CH.9 where the printing processes are discussed. (When the material is preprinted, it is possible to web-print and then make cases from the roll, but this is feasible only for long runs.) It is the third—and by far the most common—method which is described here.

There are 2 kinds of stamping: *cold* and *hot*.

■ *Cold stamping (ink stamping)*—This is very much like letterpress in that it involves the application of ink by impression with a raised surface. The basic difference is in the amount of impression. Where the letterpress plate or type lightly "kiss" the paper, the stamping press drives the raised image into the material hard enough to place the ink definitely below the surface. This is necessary to prevent the ink from getting rubbed away too quickly as the book is handled, slipped in and out of spaces between books on shelves, etc. The hard impression is needed also to flatten the relatively rough-surface materials used for book binding. A light impression on a natural finish cloth, for example, would transfer ink to the top of the threads only and not make a solid mark.

Ink stamping is done on a platen press differing only slightly from those used for printing. The stamping plate must be of hard enough material to withstand the heavy wear. It is made of ¼" (.635 cm) thick material and is etched deeper than is necessary for printing. The extra thickness provides more strength and the extra

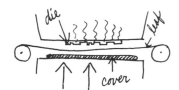

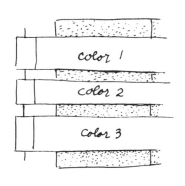

depth allows for the deep impression in the material. These plates *(dies)* are discussed later under "Binding materials".

Because of the hard impression and frequently rough material, ink stamping cannot give the fine results possible in printing on paper. When the cover material is comparatively smooth, however, small type, fairly fine line drawings, and even coarse-screen halftones may be stamped satisfactorily. Light inks on dark materials are not usually satisfactory unless 2 or more impressions are used, although more contrast improves the results.

■ *Hot stamping*—This is used to apply *leaf*, for making *blank* impressions *(blind stamping)*, and for *embossing*. The process is substantially the same as ink stamping, except that the die—which must be metal—is heated by contact with a heating element in the press. Heat is necessary to transfer the leaf from its carrier (see "Binding materials") to the material, and to help mold the material and boards in blind stamping or embossing. The amount of heat used varies from 200° to 275° F. (93.3° to 117.3° C) according to the kind of leaf, the cover materials, and the kind of stamping.

Leaf stamping once meant the application of genuine gold from small sheets or "leaves", and this is still the method used in making cover designs with hand tools. On a stamping press, a roll of leaf (metallic or flat color) just wide enough to cover the die is mounted on one side, and the leaf ribbon is drawn across the die by an arm on the other side, with the pigment side facing away from the die. The leaf is pressed against the cover by the heated die and the pigment is transferred. The pressure not only impresses the leaf below the surface, but forces the pigment into the weave or grain of the cover material. After each impression, the arm pulls the leaf just enough to move the stamped part past the die.

It is possible to mount several rolls of leaf of different colors on the press at a time, and stamp from all of them at each impression. (Some machines have side-feeds enabling them to run rolls at right angles to each other.) The number of colors is theoretically limited only by the amount of space available to mount the rolls, but the loss of time involved in mounting and running more than 4 or 5 is so great that it would probably be more economical to use half as many colors in each of 2 impressions. In making designs using multiple leaf colors in one impression, be sure that the printing image of each color is at least $^5/_{16}$" (.7938 cm) from that of any other color. Each ribbon must extend $^1/_8$" (.3175 cm) on both sides of the die to insure that all of it is covered. Another $^1/_{16}$" (.1588 cm) is needed for a divider to keep the ribbons apart. These paper-thin ribbons being pulled over a span of about 3 feet are not very stable—particularly if they are narrow.

Blank or blind stamping is done by the same process as leaf stamping except that no leaf is used. The visual effect is caused by changes in color and texture of the material due to heat as well as by the impression. Because heat is required, blank stamping cannot be done together with an impression of ink (even if the ink could be kept from part of the plate) but is usually done with leaf stamping. To be effective, blind stamping must be impressed into the board as well as the cover material.

Embossing is similar to the other hot-stamping operations, but the image produced is raised *above* the surface instead of pressed into it. This usually requires use of a male and female die. The latter is stamped on top of the cover while the other is positioned on the press so that it will be under the cover when the impression is made. This means that a negative image will be pressed into the inside of the cover. If this is too large and/or deep, it can interfere with pasting the endleaf onto the board. Where the image is fairly simple, the male die may be omitted, using in its place a piece of cardboard cut to the proper shape. This saves the cost of a die (these are very expensive) and reduces the height of the embossing. The effect of embossing can be obtained without any embossing dies by making a negative image or reverse die, i.e. a background is stamped, leaving the image raised on it.

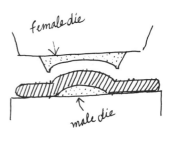

embossing

When leaf has been used, each cover is given a light brushing with fine steel wool to wipe off the excess leaf. (This can cause smears if a dark-colored leaf is used on a very light material.)

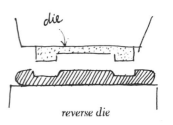

reverse die

With both books and covers made, the next operation is *casing-in* [putting the book in its case or cover]. The books are fed into the machine, backs up, astride flat sheets of metal. The endleaves are given a coat of paste just before the books pass under a hopper of covers. As each book goes through, a cover drops over it and is clamped from both sides, thus pasting the endleaves to the inside of the cover, with the crash in between.

CASING-IN

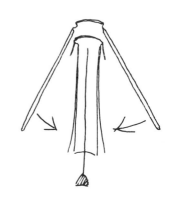

Casing-in a self-lining book is no different. The paste is applied to the first and last pages (where the endpapers would otherwise be) and these are pasted to the cover.

Before the covers are dropped into place they are formed by a heated bar to correspond to the shape of the round-backed book.

Some books are made *tightbacked*, i.e. the spine of the cover is glued to the back.

The cover would warp badly if the endleaf paste was permitted to dry by itself. To prevent this, the books are *built-in*. This is one operation that has been radically improved. The old method—still used for oversized books—was to put the books between wooden boards which were then piled on other layers of books and boards up to about 5′ (1.52 m) in height. A projecting metal rim around the edges of the boards pressed into the joint to hold the shape. The pile was then kept under pressure for 6 to 24 hours while the paste dried.

BUILDING-IN

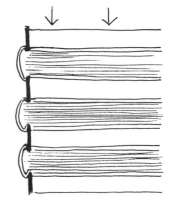

There are now building-in machines which apply pressure and heat from both sides, accomplishing in seconds what formerly required a day. The basic principles of all building-in machines are the same, but they vary in the heat, pressure, and dwell used. This is important to know when using cover materials of differing thermal properties.

INSPECTION

A certain amount of inspection is done at each step in the binding process, but in spite of this some imperfections remain undetected, so a final check is made just before the books are wrapped. This inspection covers the entire range of possible faults—even those created by composition and printing. Composition errors will, of course, appear in all copies, but if serious enough (say, omission of the author's name from the title page) may cause rejection of the whole edition. Printing faults are also likely to affect many copies. In binding, a great many things may go wrong but, because of the relatively slower speeds of binding machines and the numerous occasions for inspection and rejection, the faults at this stage are likely to be limited to a few copies. The most common problems are: sheets folded on a bias, corners folded in, inverted signatures, endpapers stuck together (due to oozing of excess paste), books cased-in upside-down, endpapers not centered or square in covers. Occasionally, imperfections in paper are discovered (holes, tears, stains, etc.).

Imperfect books are sent to the *repair department* where they are made acceptable, if possible. Skillful repair work can restore a remarkably high percentage.

JACKETING, SLIPCASING,
& PACKING

Almost all books are given some kind of individual wrapping. Tradebooks almost always have a printed paper *jacket* [a separate wrapper, as distinguished from the cover which is attached to the book] or a clear plastic one. Technical and school books usually have a jacket of plain paper or *glassine* [a rather brittle, translucent paper]. Until about 1948 all jackets were put on by hand, but there are now jacketing machines in use. These can increase production greatly, but only on long runs.

It is important to provide instructions for positioning printed jackets on the books, because it is not always clear how they should fit. This is particularly necessary with off-centered designs, for there is a tendency to center the type on the spine of the book when wrapping.

If the books are to be inserted in *slipcases* [boxes] or individual mailing cartons this is usually done by hand, although very large editions may be cartoned by machine. In any case, these are fairly slow and expensive operations.

Expensive books are usually cartoned individually or in bulk cartons containing from 35 to 50 lbs. (15.88 to 22.68 kg) of books.

Most books are packed on skids on which from 800 to 1000 average-sized books are piled, with a sheet of paper between layers. A wooden cover is placed on top and metal bands are wrapped around from top to bottom to keep the books under pressure, both to prevent warping and to keep them from slipping out.

Paperbacks

Paperbacks divide into 2 categories of significance to their manufacture: (a) *trade paperbacks*, which are sold through regular book outlets in quantities roughly comparable to hardbound tradebooks —say 6000 to 20,000—and (b) *mass-market paperbacks*, distributed through magazine outlets and printed in runs of 50,000 or more. The retail prices of these categories differ considerably, reflecting fundamentally different methods of production which are, in turn, related to the quantities involved.

TRADE PAPERBACKS

These are sometimes the same trim-sizes as hardcover books— often being printed from the same plates as a hardbound edition, sometimes simultaneously. The basic operations of binding are performed in the usual way. Most of these books are perfect-bound, although many are sewed—particularly when the run is small. The sewed books are fed into a machine which applies an adhesive to the back, drops a preprinted paper cover into place on the book, then trims book and cover together. Sometimes the books are nipped first. If an edge stain is used, this is sprayed on after trimming.

When paperbacks are perfect-bound, they go directly from collating to the binding machine, which trims off the back, applies an adhesive, and then completes the operations described above.

MASS-MARKET PAPERBACKS

To describe the process of binding mass-market paperbacks it is necessary to refer to their printing, because the entire manufacture of these books is integrated. It is only because they are so efficiently produced that they can be sold at such low prices.

The most advanced paperback production equipment can take a roll (or rolls) of paper at one end and turn it automatically into bound books at the other. The web press has a fully coordinated folder built in, which feeds signatures to a gathering machine. A binding machine takes the gathered signatures and completes the books (as described for perfect-bound trade paperbacks) at a rate of about 200 per minute. In quality, the books produced in this way are not always perfect, but they are remarkably good under the circumstances. Many paperbacks are produced on belt presses, which may have paperback binders in-line.

Mechanical binding

The term "mechanical binding" refers to a binding that uses a mechanical device, not to a binding process. In fact, mechanical binding is much less automatic than case binding.

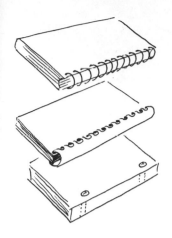

There are many kinds of mechanical bindings, both metal and plastic. All of them involve a device that joins single sheets by passing through holes on one edge. Some snap on, some wind through the holes, some have posts or rods, others have rings, etc.

Although the mechanical devices differ considerably, the binding process varies only in the way that each is attached. The basic operations of folding and gathering are the same as in all binding. The gathered books are then trimmed on all 4 sides, holes are punched through the pages, and the metal or plastic binding apparatus is attached. There are no endpapers needed on mechanically bound books, but the covers—2 separate pieces—are gathered with the signatures.

Slipcases, plastic jackets, & cartons

SLIPCASES

Slipcases are the open-end boxes in which books are sometimes sold and referred to as "boxed". Usually, 2 volumes are boxed together, but sometimes one is presented in a slipcase alone, and occasionally 3, 4, or even more may be in a single box. The construction varies according to the number and weight of the books.

Slipcases are made of boards similar to those used in hardcovers and are usually covered with paper of about the weight and strength of a good text. The box is made of 2 pieces of board, *scored* [blank stamped along the folding line], folded, and held together with paper tape. The cover material may be preprinted or plain. In the latter case, there is usually a printed label pasted on the side(s) and/or edge. Sometimes the covering is put on in several pieces, with the printed label constituting one or more of them. The material is turned in about ½″ (1.27 cm) on the front edges.

For extra-heavy books, some panels may be reinforced with another layer of board. It is customary to die-cut half-moon finger openings on the front edges to facilitate removing the book, but this is not as necessary with a heavy book, which is inclined to come out of its own weight.

The standard kind of slipcase is usually made by machine, but special variations are almost always hand operations. Especially on small runs, the 35 to 50¢ cost of an average slipcase can easily double when a special requirement must be met.

PLASTIC JACKETS

Clear plastic jackets are made of acetate in several thicknesses. The most used is 5 pt.—.005, or 5 thousandths of an inch (.0127 mm)—but 7½ pt. (.019 mm) and even 10 pt. (.025 mm) are used when the book is very heavy and/or very expensive. In all cases, the folds must be preformed with heat. The material is too resilient to fold cold without springing open, and if a cold fold is made too hard it is likely to crack. This is true to a lesser extent of 3 pt. (.0076 mm), but this weight is too thin to be heat formed. Because of the forming, it is necessary to give the supplier a bound dummy of the book on which to base the measurements.

Mailing cartons for individual books must be able to protect their contents well enough to bring them to their destinations in perfect condition. Particularly when the books are expensive, they will be returned if damaged due to inadequate packing. The rigors of going through the mail are severe enough for average-sized books, but very large and heavy ones are subject to considerable stress. (Mechanically bound books are a special problem.)

CARTONS

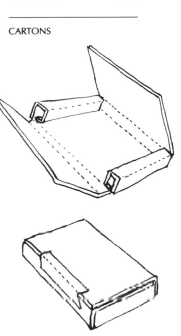

Numerous attempts have been made to achieve maximum protection at minimum cost. One of the most successful is the corrugated paper "bumper end" carton. It is made from a single piece and die-cut. The ends are folded over 4 times to make bumpers that effectively protect the corners of the book—and it is the corners that take the most abuse in mailing. The sides are turned over on top, so that only one edge need be taped closed. One flap is the full width of the carton and overlaps the other, so when the tape (at the corner) is cut, the knife will not harm the book.

There are 2 weights of corrugated paper in general use for this purpose, 200 lb. (90.72 kg) test and, for extra-heavy duty, 275 lb. (124.74 kg) test. These are made in the standard brown color or sometimes in white. Printing is done on the cartons when flat, using soft rubber plates. The results are fairly crude.

Binding materials

In cooperation with the various state agencies that buy books for public elementary and high school use, 4 industrial and educational groups, including the Book Manufacturers' Institute (*BMI*), have established a set of minimum standards for making books to be used in schools. These standards, known as *NASTA* (National Association of State Textbook Administrators) specifications (formerly called BMI specifications), have relieved the textbook purchaser of having to determine acceptability in each case, and have simplified the problem for publishers and manufacturers. The NASTA standards cover almost all aspects of production, but among the most significant features are those having to do with binding materials. In general, these requirements are in excess of what is necessary for satisfactory performance in tradebooks, but they are often met in making tradebooks of interest to libraries. Library books are not ordinarily treated as strenuously as elementary-school books, but they are used continually over long periods, and the librarians, understandably, want them to last as long as possible.

The NASTA specifications are revised frequently as conditions change. The most important recent revision was the acceptance of non-woven materials for binding. Only cloth was accepted before.

COVER MATERIALS—LEATHER

For hundreds of years, animal skins—vellum, leather—were virtually the only materials used for book binding. In the 19th century, some decorative papers were used on sides to make "*quarter-*

bound" [3-piece binding] and "*half-bound*" [3-piece plus separate corner pieces] books. It wasn't until the latter part of the century, when mass production of books by machinery came about, that leather fell into disuse. The individuality of animal skins does not lend itself to large-scale automatic processes. Thus, for general use, leather was replaced by cloth, which is not only relatively uniform, but which may be produced in rolls for use on web-fed casemaking machinery. Today, leather is still used for covers on bibles and on special editions of classics. The modern tanning methods, as well as polluted air and dry heat, tend to shorten the life of leather, so most fine-quality leather-bound books use skins from England, where the old tanning method is still in use. However, the large-scale use of leather generated by the successful mail order sales of leather-bound classics in the mid-1970s created a market sufficient for the development of a domestic book-binding leather industry of good commercial quality.

There is also a *bonded* leather, which consists of small leather particles compressed and bonded with a resin. This material looks, feels, and smells like leather (which it is). Made in rolls, bonded leather (the first of these was called Cabra) can be used on casemakers just like cloth or paper. While economical from a labor standpoint, and much less costly than using whole skins, this material costs about 3 times as much as the most expensive cloth.

COVER MATERIALS—CLOTH
The cloth used for book binding is entirely cotton, despite the use of such terms as "linen" and "buckram". The material without any processing is called *greige goods* (pronounced gray) and comes in various qualities and grades. These are measured mainly in terms of the weight of thread and *thread count* [the number of threads per square inch]. In 1936, the U.S. Dept. of Commerce established specifications for grades of cloth from A to F. After World War II, however, the demand for cheaper cloth and the competition of paper substitutes (which came into being when cloth became scarce during the war) inspired the book-cloth manufacturers to produce a lower grade—and later, a still lower grade.

The way that the greige goods are processed varies also. The main distinction is in the *filler* used. Some cloth is filled with a composition consisting chiefly of starch, while others have some plastic—usually pyroxylin or vinyl—in them. The starch-filled cloth is easily damaged by moisture, while the *plastic impregnated* has enough water resistance to take wiping with a damp cloth. NASTA standards for schoolbooks call for at least a C grade plastic-impregnated cloth.

Some cloth is *plastic coated* rather than impregnated. These materials are just as water resistant as the others, as long as the coating lasts. NASTA specifications provide for the use of coated grades of cloth also.

Book-cloth finishing is done by running the material through various vats and rollers that apply the color and surface characteristics. The chief distinctions are between *natural finish, vellum finish,* and *linen finish.*

In vellum-finish cloth, the goods are dyed first. Then the filler is applied to both sides of the material. The face is given a coating that includes the coloring, while the back has sizing suitable for the adhesives used in casemaking. To make a linen finish, the goods are undyed and the face coating is scraped so that the white threads show partly through. Steel rollers smooth the surface and emboss if required. Natural-finish cloth is dyed, then is filled and sized from the back only, leaving the face in its soft, natural state.

Rolls are put up in widths of 38″ (96.52 cm) and 42″ (106.68 cm), which makes it possible to cut out for most books economically. The usual length of a roll is 250 yards (228.6 m).

The prices of cloth are quite uniform from one supplier to another. They range from about 70¢ per yard (.9144 m)(38″ wide) for the poorest grade to approximately $2 per yard for the best. In A grades and better, most materials may be obtained plastic-impregnated, at about 9¢ per yard more than starch-filled. The price per yard varies with the size of the order, going down 2 or 3¢ in each larger quantity bracket.

The cloth manufacturers stock a large (but diminishing) number of colors and finishes of several grades of material and can usually deliver an order within a few days. They will make special colors and finishes for orders of reasonable size. All companies stock white cloth specially prepared for lithographic printing. Sample sheets 11 × 15″ (27.94 × 38.1 cm) or 12 × 18″ (30.48 × 45.72 cm) and swatch books are available from the principal manufacturers—of which there are only two major and two or three others. The larger binders stock quantities of the more popular cloths for sale to their customers.

COVER MATERIALS—NON-WOVEN

Under the pressure of escalating cloth prices, affected by the fluctuations of a cotton market over which book-cloth manufacturers had almost no control, the standards for textbook covering material were revised by NASTA in 1965 to allow the use of substitutes for cloth—generically called non-woven materials. The pressure for this change existed for decades, but it took the development of an acceptable material to bring it about. The breakthrough was made by Dupont's Tyvek, a 100% synthetic fiber material which met the requirements for a C-grade pyroxylin cloth—the minimum standard for textbook use. It was not until 1976 that NASTA approved another class of non-wovens, made of acrylic-reinforced cellulose and known as "Type II" material. (Tyvek is actually a Type *III* material. Type I is coated paper, which is not acceptable for textbooks.) The non-wovens are about ⅔ the price of equivalent cloth.

The plastic materials available now are mostly vinyls of 4 to 7 pt. (.0102 to .0178 mm) thickness with backings of paper. The backing provides rigidity to enable working the material on bindery machines, and it facilitates gluing. Vinyl is not without problems, however. While it *can* be fabricated with almost any qualities desired, it is difficult to keep these qualities in balance without creating undesirable features. For example, if the material is made to resist the heat used in stamping and building-in, it may lose too much cold resistance *(cold-crack)* and shatter when a carton of books is dropped on a loading platform in midwinter. Other problems sometimes encountered are stretching, sticking together, repelling ink or leaf, etc. These can be and have been overcome, but not without some difficulty. Pyroxylin and other plastics are also being used as binding materials, usually in combination with paper.

COVER MATERIALS—PAPER

Paper was used widely as a cover material when cloth was scarce during World War II. For one-piece covers it was found to be adequate for tradebooks of small to average size, where no hard use was involved. Libraries, however, objected strenuously. When cloth became available again, the use of these papers continued, because of their economy. Even when the lowest grades of cloth were introduced, their price was still double that of the cheapest paper substitutes. The best of the papers are still below the price of the cheapest cloth.

There are 2 kinds of paper used in binding. One is the kind mentioned above, which is strong enough to be used for one-piece cases, the other is used only for the sides of 3-piece cases. Of the former kind, one grade, selling at about 30–40¢ per yard, is made of kraft paper with resin impregnation and a coating of lacquer or pyroxylin (sold as Duroid, Kivar, Sturdetan, Permacote, etc.). These are strong enough for most tradebook purposes.

Several lines of cheaper binding papers sell for around 25–35¢ per yard (.9144 m). These are dyed-through kraft papers with some resin impregnation but without coatings and are adequate for small books with light handling probability. The papers in this group (Deauville, Sierra, Permalin, etc.) represent the minimum quality acceptable for one-piece cases.

There are some paper materials with special formulations that make them unique. One is Elephant Hide, which has a marble-like appearance, considerable strength, and surface resistance to moisture, soiling, and scuffing—without any coating. This material is manufactured in West Germany by a secret process. It comes in a large number of colors and patterns of unusual appearance, is strong enough for most tradebook uses, and sells for around 50¢ per yard. Another material is Linson, made in Scotland of especially tough impregnated fibers. It, too, requires no coating to per-

form satisfactorily and comes in colors with or without embossing.
It is in the same price range as Elephant Hide. A lower-priced version at 30–35¢ is Econolin.

In addition to the lines mentioned there are a number of others with special finishes and patterns. Some lines have a considerable variety of effects available, both printed and embossed.

All of the products mentioned thus far are sold in rolls—generally 40″ (101.6 cm) or 42″ (106.68 cm) wide—or in sheets. While they are intended primarily for one-piece covers, they can be and are used as sides of 3-piece cases. Any paper of about 70 lb. substance and reasonable strength may be used on sides, as there is no structural requirement, but the only lines classified as binding papers are those available in rolls.

Several of the better text papers, such as Curtis' Tweedweave and Stoneridge, and Strathmore's Grandee, have been made available in rolls in their most suitable colors. These are 80 lb. text papers of superior printing qualities and appearance, but their price is low in comparison with even the cheapest papers made for one-piece bindings. They were put up and stocked in 25″ (63.5 cm) or 26″ (66.04 cm) rolls, but rolls are available now only on order.

Also available in rolls are Multicolor and Colortext, 2 lines of colored stock developed primarily for endpapers, but very satisfactory for sides, and even usable as one-piece bindings in some circumstances. These are slightly lower in price than the text papers mentioned above. Both the text paper and endpaper lines are colored through. Neither have any coating.

A 10 pt. (.025 mm) coated-one-side stock is used for most mass-market paperback covers. For larger-format trade paperbacks, 12 pt. (.0305 mm) or even 15 pt. (.038 mm) is used. Such paper may be obtained in all grades. It is flexible enough to fold, yet provides reasonable protection (considering price) for the pages. Less expensive, although not as scuff resistant, is an uncoated stock of the same thickness. It costs less, not only because it has no coating but because it requires no varnish or other finish over the printing. **COVER MATERIALS—PAPERBACKS**

There are several papers which are tougher and thicker than the regular stocks and are intended to provide longer life for the book (Kivar No.3, Lexotone, etc.). Their cost is several cents more per copy on an average trade paperback edition.

New cover material lines and modifications of existing lines are in almost constant development. Contact with suppliers and regular reading of trade periodicals are necessary to keep abreast of these changes.

Endpapers have distinctive and significant strength requirements, since they are the main agent in holding hard cover and book together. All material sold as endpaper stock is made to specifications **ENDPAPERS** required by the NASTA standards for schoolbooks, which call for an 80 lb. kraft. For a discussion of endpaper use, see CH. 26.

DIES   For many years the best dies for leaf or ink stamping were made of brass. They were hand-finished, were cut to more-than-adequate depth, and had excellent resistance to long-run pounding. With handcraftsmanship an increasingly expensive (and rare) commodity, it became necessary to find a cheaper way of producing dies of satisfactory quality.

The fully-etched *copper alloy die* has provided the answer. The metal is claimed to be harder than brass and it etches very well. For most work it is entirely satisfactory, and the cost is far less than that of brass dies.

Brass dies will always be needed for embossing, as it is necessary to sculpt the subject in bas relief—both positive and negative—and this must be done by hand. (Even a pantograph engraver requires an original sculpted by hand.)

It is impossible to rate dies in terms of impressions, because there are a number of variables involved. A die may give 10,000 satisfactory impressions on one job but only 6000 on another. The material being stamped, the nature of the subject, the heat required, the speed of stamping, all affect the die's performance. A more elusive variable is the amount of wear inflicted during the setting-up process. An initial miscalculation of pressure needed may give the die a pounding equivalent to a thousand impressions after the pressure is properly adjusted. Accidental feeding of 2 covers can have the same effect.

LEAF & INK   The ink used for stamping is similar to printing ink, but is heavier and thicker. More ink is deposited than in printing and there is proportionately less absorption by the material, so more drier is used to hasten air-drying. This gives the ink a shiny look. If desired, a flatter look is possible, but this requires running at slower speed. Special inks are required for printing on plastic or plastic-coated materials.

Leaf is a paper-thin (or thinner) layer of colored mineral powder or metallic powder laid on a gum and wax base, which holds it to a carrier of plastic (acetate or Mylar). Over the layer of powder is a layer of resin which bonds the pigment or powder to the material on which it is stamped. Leaf is made up in master rolls 24″ (60.96 cm) wide and 400 to 600′ (121.9 to 182.88 m) in length. These are cut into narrower rolls as needed by the stamper. Special *panel leaf* is available with an extra thickness of pigment.

Metallic leaf includes not only the conventional gold in several shades, but aluminum, bronze, and a number of metallic colors. These were subject to rather rapid deterioration (fading or darkening) until *anodyzing* was introduced. The anodyzed imitation gold is supposed to keep its appearance almost indefinitely. The old imitation gold is inclined to tarnish in a few years—depending on the materials with which it comes in contact.

Colored pigment leaf varies considerably in its stamping qualities. There are chemical differences that prevent some leaf from "taking" on certain materials: the amount of pigment needed to cover varies with the color; the degree of heat needed varies with color, backing, and lot; and the colors vary greatly in their light fastness. On top of this, the performance of leaf varies according to the manufacturer. It is advisable to make sample covers whenever possible (CH. 26).

The variation in heat required is particularly significant when covers are being stamped with more than one color per impression. Sometimes, the quality of one part of the stamping must be sacrificed for another.

Each leaf supplier has a card showing samples of the colors carried in stock. The cards, the names, and the numbers vary, but the colors are about the same from one to another. Special colors can be made, but only for large orders.

COATINGS & LAMINATIONS

It is usually necessary to apply a finish to protect a printed surface on cover materials. There are some materials, such as natural finish cloth and antique paper, that absorb so much of the ink that they need no protection because the normal abrasion of use would not penetrate below the ink. Also, there are special inks of such hardness when dry that they resist scuffing to a considerable extent. Whether these inks are adequate protection or not depends on the amount of wear to which the book will be subjected.

There are 2 kinds of protective finish. One is the application of a transparent liquid coating, of which there are many kinds; the other is *lamination* [adhering a sheet of clear plastic to the surface of the base material]. There is also "liquid lamination", which consists of applying a layer of plastic in liquid form, but this is really more coating than lamination.

Coatings may be applied by spraying, by roller, or by a printing plate. The least expensive coating is the *press varnish* [a coat of varnish applied on a printing press just like an impression of ink]. There are specialized plants called *finishers* which can apply a large variety of varnishes, lacquers, liquid plastics, and other concoctions designed to provide protection for various materials in varying degrees. It is always best to ask the finisher to recommend a coating for a particular job.

Sheet lamination is quite expensive, several times the cost of press varnish, but it gives the maximum protection and a glossy finish matched only by an acetate jacket. The only hazard in lamination is the tendency of the plastic sheet to come loose. For this reason it is not advisable to laminate on a rough material. The smoother the base, the firmer the adhesion.

In using protective finishes, particularly on color process printing, take account of the slight discoloration they cause—varying from almost none with lamination to a distinct yellowing with varnish. Consider also the possibility of *using* the varnish as an overall film of color, at no additional cost. This is available on a press varnish. Any color may be used.

It is important to inform the printer of the finish to be used, as special inks are required in some cases.

BOARD There are 4 kinds of board used for hard covers:

■ *Binder's board*—This is the best and the most expensive. It is made much like paper, as a solid sheet of fibers, and is less likely to warp or crack than any other. NASTA standards require this board for textbooks.

■ *Chip board*—This is made somewhat like binder's board but it is not as dense and is made not more than about 65 pt. (165.1 mm) in thickness. While it is the cheapest board, it is relatively weak and is little used for tradebooks.

■ *Pasted board*—It can be made in any thickness, being 2 or more layers of chip board pasted together. This is the kind used for most general book purposes.

■ *Red board*—This is a thin, tough, flexible board used for "limp" or flexible covers, mainly on books meant to be carried in pockets.

The boards used in most books are between 70 and 90 pt. (.1778 and .2286 mm) in thickness, with 80 to 85 pt. (.2032 to .2159 mm) the most popular size. Red board is usually 36 pt. Large, heavy books may use 110 or 120 pt.

THREAD, CRASH, & LINING PAPER These 3 items are selected and purchased by the binder, but it is useful to know that extra strong grades of each are available when their use is indicated. The decision to use heavy grades should be made in consultation with the binder. An alternative in the case of crash and paper is to double the amount of regular weight. Sometimes nylon thread is used rather than heavier cotton thread, to avoid excessive bulking at the back. There are, however, some technical problems connected with nylon thread that tend to limit its use.

ADHESIVES This, too, is a technical matter best left to the binder. Production people should be aware, however, of the very large range of adhesives available and the need to fit the adhesive to the job. Particularly in perfect-bound books, the adhesive is all-important.

Adhesives fall into several categories: the *pastes* (similar to library paste) used to adhere endleaves to cover, the *glues* used to adhere cover material to boards, and the *flexible glues* used in backing (gluing-off) and perfect-binding. Considerable experimentation was carried out to find the ideal adhesive for perfect-binding. The range has extended from the animal glues originally used in book-binding to "hot-melt" glues made of plastic compounds. The problem was to find an adhesive that is fluid enough to penetrate the interstices of the paper fibers, that dries fast enough to match the speed of the machines, that is very strong and flexible when dry, and will not become brittle and crack with the passage of time. Most binders feel that this search has been successful.

Headbands are made in long strips of cotton cloth about ⅝″ (1.58 cm) wide. The cloth is like a good canvas and has a rolled edge, which is sometimes woven with colored threads, making a pattern of alternating stripes. Some headbands are solid colors. About a dozen choices are usually available. Headbands may be regular or *mercerized* [having a silky gloss] (CH. 26).

HEADBANDS

12 | Estimating cost

A basic knowledge of the subjects covered so far is satisfactory for most readers of this book because: (a) the rudiments are all that can be absorbed at one time, (b) there is no need to know more because you are not actually having to do the things described (such as operating a photosetter or folding machine), or (c) where you do have to apply this knowledge you can usually get help from the suppliers involved. You *should* know more, but this knowledge can come in time as you gain experience.

Estimating cannot be done properly without a *deep* knowledge of the subject, and a thorough knowledge of the art of estimating. It is simple enough to use a table or chart to arrive at the cost of basic operations and sometimes this is very useful information, but once details, complexities, and variations enter the picture, nothing less than an intimate acquaintance with all aspects of the problem will keep you out of trouble. Approximations are extremely dangerous in cost estimating. The profit margins in both book manufacturing and publishing are very small, and a slight error or miscalculation can easily doom your company to a loss. A seemingly minor deviation from the usual procedure in any operation may turn out to be a major problem, involving the use of a larger machine, a hand operation, or a time-consuming adjustment.

Because estimating requires more knowledge than can be gotten from this (or any one) book, and the consequences of even a small error can be disastrous, this chapter makes no attempt to enable you to perform the function yourself. The information given is meant simply to provide enough familiarity with estimating to make it possible to deal effectively with those engaged in it. No reliance should be placed on your own estimates until you have had much practical experience in book production and in estimating itself.

Finding the probable cost of materials is relatively easy, but even this has booby traps. Price increases, penalties, extra charges, spoilage allowances, shipping charges, taxes, over- and under-runs—any or all of these can cause trouble for the unwary estimator. It is in estimating the cost of manufacturing processes, however, that the real dangers lie. The time required to perform a routine operation is known—but how long will it take to make up that special running head, or to make ready to print those unusual illustrations, or to insert books in that special carton? Not even the man in the shop knows exactly how much time these things will take, and your guess is likely to be less accurate.

A rough guess about cost is usually worse than no figure at all. No important decisions should be based on such guesses, because they could be, and usually are, wrong. There is a tendency to guess *under* the actual cost—which may lead to the obvious disaster—and rough figures obtained from a professional estimator are likely to be high—which may discourage a perfectly sound project. Professional estimators usually decline to give rough estimates at all, but if pressed they generally add a substantial percentage to their own guess in order to cover themselves. Even when a figure is thoroughly understood by both parties to be only a guess and not a contract, bad feeling often ensues when the bill comes to more than the guess. Moral: Don't operate on anything but a formal estimate in writing.

This warning having been given, it must be admitted that publishers often want and use rough estimates in the early stages of planning a project. These frequently are in the form of comparisons with the cost of previously published books, and sometimes they are prices on dummy specifications, but in either case they are based on actual costs, not guesses. However, the danger remains, because the new book will rarely come out like either the previous one *or* the dummy specs. Such preliminary figures can be very helpful, provided they are used with caution—and are replaced by detailed estimates before final decisions are made.

Some of the estimating problems and practices encountered in each area of bookmaking are discussed in the sections that follow. Additional information on costs is included in the chapter dealing with each subject.

Composition

There are 3 kinds of composition prices. One is a price based on emage (CH. 5), another is a price based on *time charges,* and the third is a price based on *keystrokes* (or characters, which comes to the same thing).

EMAGE

Emage is computed by multiplying the *overall* width and height of the text area in ems of the type size—the overall area being a rectangle parallel to the edges of the paper, with its sides encompassing the *outermost* elements included in the makeup. Thus, although the text itself on this page is 24 picas wide, the *overall* width is 33 picas, because it includes sideheads set on a measure of 8 picas, plus one pica separating them from the text. If the running heads were above the text, the overall height would include them. If there is an illustration on the page, it is included in the overall dimensions, even if it bleeds. (Actually, the emage on these pages did *not* include the sideheads and illustrations, for they were pasted and stripped in later, rather than being made up with the text.) The emage in a given area *increases* as the type size *decreases*. (A page of 8 pt. type costs more than a page of 10 pt.) This is because there are more characters per area, therefore more type to set.

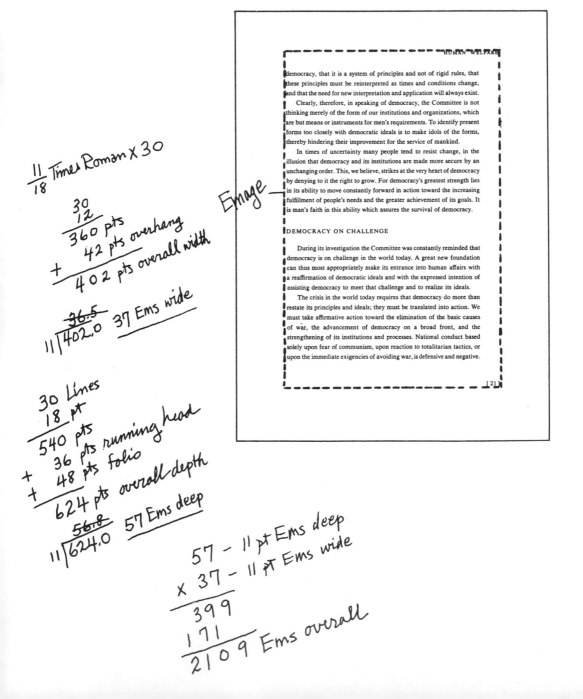

The emage basis is mainly a metal-type practice, since it is based on the area of material used and the amount of labor needed to fill that space. It is used for books in which the pages are mainly straight text. Prices on such material are simple to calculate, as book compositors have certain charges per thousand ems for each size. The rates (for hot-metal composition) are based on normal setting speeds for normal copy and include makeup. There are many variations of these base rates, but they, too, are quite specific—although they vary somewhat according to the practices of each compositor. The main variables are:

■ *Leading*—The rate is based on 2 or more pts. of leading. If less, there is a penalty because there are then more lines on the page. For 1 pt. leading, 5 to 10% is added. For solid lines the penalty is 10 to 20%.

■ *Thin faces*—Some unusually thin faces carry a penalty because the emage rates are based on a normal number of characters per pica. For these faces, the emage is based on one size smaller than that being set (11 is figured as 10, 10 as 9, etc.).

■ *Minimum area*—Pages of less than a certain emage (usually 1000) are charged at the rate for that minimum, because of the extra handling required where there are so many pages for the total emage.

■ *Complicated work*—Usually, there is a separate rate for fiction and nonfiction, assuming that nonfiction will be slower in setting and proofreading because of proper names, unfamiliar terms, and more complicated makeup. The difference is about 10%. An extra penalty is charged when the text is unusually broken up by cuts, tables, formulas, etc. This varies greatly, depending on the kind of typesetting machine used.

■ *Difficult copy*—A penalty, which may go as high as 25%, is charged for setting copy that is difficult to read, as this slows the setting and proofreading. Such copy may be a heavily corrected Ms, a faint copy, negative photostats, extremely small type, copy on index cards, etc.

■ *Foreign language*—The penalty (50 to 75%) charged for setting foreign language copy (including dialect) usually depends on how familiar the language is to the compositor, the availability of typesetters and proofreaders adept at the language, and the number of special characters required. In some cases it is better to take such work to specialized compositors.

■ *Poetry and plays*—Poetry aligned at the left is usually charged at 110% of the base rate, centered poetry at up to 125%. Plays, or play-style material (court testimony, interviews, etc.), are usually 115 to 125% of the base rate. The penalty varies according to how the characters' names are treated.

■ *Mixer*—In Linotype, where there is only an occasional need for type from different magazines on the same line, it probably pays to have the odd type cut in, but where such lines occur frequently in the copy, the entire job is usually set on a Mixer at 1½ times (150%) the base rate for emage. This problem doesn't exist in photosetting.

■ *Double column*—Two-column pages carry a penalty on the makeup time. This varies with the complexity of the work and the kind of machine used.

The trade customs of compositors entitle them to charge extra for almost anything that is not straight text setting—and some do, but others prefer to cover these extra costs in their emage rates.

In general, penalties are charged on only the penalty copy itself, but when this constitutes a major portion of the Ms, the entire job may be billed at the penalty rate. The penalties are also cumulative. For example, a page of double-column, foreign language, centered poetry could be charged at 2 times base rate.

In photocomposition, the emage price includes only typesetting and proofs, with a separate price for makeup.

Bear in mind that each compositor has not only his own base rates, but his own rules for varying emage rates. While the above list is useful as a guide, it is necessary to check individual suppliers. The BMI issues a printed list of Trade Customs which forms the basis for most practices.

While the above charges are based on Linotype composition, to a large extent they reflect the extra time needed to do extra work—so they tend to be applicable to cold composition as well. Whether they do or do not apply to a particular system is a question related to the characteristics of the machine used, so it is necessary to check with the compositor in each case.

TIME CHARGE This is a price based on the time required to do the work at a certain hourly rate. Prices are often based on time charges when the copy is too varied or too little to use the emage basis. The relatively low emage rates are justified only by the efficiency in setting large amounts of fairly straight text. While these rates can be adjusted to cover more complicated work, they are no longer applicable when the amount of straight setting falls below a certain point.

Compositors are reluctant to give estimates of time charges, usually stipulating that such figures are only estimates and not firm prices. Understandably, when firm prices must be given, the estimator adds enough to cover any miscalculation.

Frontmatter [pages preceding the text] and part-title pages (CH. 14) are usually charged at a standard multiple of the text-page price. This is essentially a time charge, based on the average cost of setting and making up such pages, which are sometimes very simple and at other times quite the opposite.

Chapter openings (CH. 18) are usually priced according to the typographic arrangement used. Practices vary from one compositor to another, but there is generally an extra charge if the makeup is unusually complicated.

Usually, no extra charge is made for subheads, captions, or running heads (CH. 18) since they are covered by emage, although additional charges are sometimes applied when machine changes, letterspacing, or complicated makeup are involved.

Because they are based on volume production, the hourly rates of book compositors are much lower than those charged by typographers doing advertising work. The latter can deliver high-quality work on short notice, and offer a large choice of typefaces, but the staff and facilities needed to supply such service (customarily required by ad agencies) call for higher prices.

KEYSTROKE

In all methods of composition using a keyboard—which is really all of them, since even OCR setting (CH. 5) requires that the Ms be specially typed—the volume of work is pretty much the number of times the operator strikes a key, spacebar, etc. In photocomposition this is certainly true, since there is no metal to buy or handle. Thus, many compositors choose to price according to the number of keystrokes required—which is in fact the character count of the Ms. The price per keystroke usually varies according to the difficulty of the copy, as this will affect the time needed for keyboarding and proofreading. Some compositors prefer to *quote* prices per page or per galley, but they almost always use keystrokes as a basis for computing the prices.

The price of composition includes the cost of a certain number of proofs—usually 2 galley, 2 page, and one set of repro proofs—a total of 5. Additional proofs are charged at a price per proof. In photocomposition the cost of proofs varies somewhat depending on the kind of product delivered by the machine (negative or positive film, or paper print).

The composition prices discussed, regardless of the method of pricing, are for the initial setting only, and the original makeup if that is included. Author's alterations (AAs) are charged separately (CH. 5). These are usually charged at so much per line if there are many, and by time if there are few.

Plates

The price of plates of any kind is based on area. In letterpress, the charge is for individual page plates. In offset lithography and gravure, the individual page size is not significant; it is the size of the form that counts. Therefore, elements on the pages within the form need not be close together for economy (CH. 8).

Printing

The price of printing consists of the charge for makeready plus a price per thousand impressions, which is based on the cost of operating the press during the time required, i.e. the pay of the people who operate the press, amortizing the cost of the machine, the rent or taxes on the space it occupies, and general overhead (lights, bookkeeping, maintenance, etc.). Except for parts of the last item, the cost increases with the size of the press.

The ink cost is relatively minor and quite uniform from one job to another, so it is included in the basic price for printing. Occasionally, when an unusual amount of ink is required, a separate charge is made. When more than one color is used on a one-color press—or a color other than black—there is a charge for washing the ink out of the press each time (washup), but this is a negligible amount on a large run and is usually not noted separately.

While all forms of printing are estimated on the basis of make-ready plus impressions, the relative importance of each factor varies from one process to another and according to the specifications of the job. For example, more time is needed to make ready a letterpress type form with pages of inch-thick metal than an offset form consisting of one thin sheet of aluminum; a form of straight text can be made ready and can run faster than one containing color process; a form of 32 pages can be made ready faster than one of 64 pages; the high speed of rotary presses and perfectors reduces the importance of impressions in relation to makeready time; in general, the shorter the run, the larger makeready looms in the price.

Although the printer's cost per thousand impressions is the same for the first thousand (after completion of makeready) and the tenth or hundreth thousand, the price per thousand usually decreases somewhat with larger quantities. The main benefit of long runs, however, is in reduction of the unit cost of makeready.

There is also an advantage in larger forms, up to a point. It doesn't take nearly twice as long to make a 64-page form ready as a 32-page form, so it is usually cheaper to have fewer, larger forms. This is not always true, however, since the time of a larger press is worth more than that of a smaller one. On a very large, fast press and a short run, the much higher cost of makeready time may make it more economical to run more forms on a smaller press, as there is little advantage in the speed.

The price of lithography and gravure printing includes the plates. Usually, they are quoted as a separate item.

Paper See CH. 10.

Binding Estimating binding costs is much more complex than figuring printing prices, as there are many more operations and materials. The price quoted by binders is a unit price (per copy) according to the size of the run, usually without any itemization. There are a great many items involved and not one of them accounts for a major part of the cost. About 20% of the total is materials, and these costs don't vary much per unit in the normal range of quantities used. The cost of operations is, as in printing, divided between makeready, or setting-up, and running, but due to the much slower speeds of binding equipment, the setting-up costs are relatively small compared to running time, even in average editions of 5 or 6000. Consequently, there is not much difference in the unit cost of binding a small edition or a large one. Only in extremely small quantities is there a really appreciable difference. Editions under, say, 2000 become quite expensive because the setting-up cost is spread over so few copies. For example, it might cost 70¢ per copy to bind 5000 copies, 69¢ for 10,000, and 68½¢ for 50,000—a spread of only 1½¢—but the price for 1500 copies would be 78¢.

The only items of material large enough to be worth calculating with a view to saving money are the cover material, which may account for about 10% of the total price, and the endpapers, which may amount to about 5%. For one-piece covers on a 6⅛ × 9¼" (15.56 × 23.5 cm) trim-size book, about 10 covers can be cut out of a running yard (91.44 cm) of material, including spoilage. Thus, using a 70¢ material, the cost per book is about 7¢, a 30¢ material means 3¢ per book, etc. Using this rule of thumb it is quite easy to estimate the effect on unit cost of any change of material. In estimating 3-piece covers, each material is figured separately.

To find the cost of a material used on part of a cover, divide the width of the piece into the width of the roll, then divide the height of the piece into 36" (91.44 cm), multiply the 2 answers and you have the number of pieces that will cut out of a running yard. Divide this number into the price per yard to get the price per piece. Thus, a 5 × 7½" (12.7 × 17.8 cm) trim-size book with a 2½" (6.35 cm)-wide strip of cloth showing on the backbone and sides would require a piece 3" (7.6 cm) wide—to allow each side to overlap ¼" (.635 cm)—and 9" (22.86 cm) high (CH.11). The 3" would cut 14 times out of a 42"(106.7 cm)-wide roll and the 9" cuts 4 times out of a yard of length. This gives 56 pieces (4 × 14) per yard. If the material costs 56¢ per yard, each piece costs 1¢. If the backbone were 1" wide, the side pieces would each be 5" wide × 9" high. If the sides were a paper from a 25"-wide roll, the 5" would cut out 5 times and there would be 4 pieces 9" high out of the yard length. This would provide 20 pieces or 10 books (2 sides per book) out of a running yard. At 30¢ per yard, the sides would cost 3¢ per book. The total cost of cover material is then 4¢.

The cost of a one-piece cover of the same cloth as that used for the backbone in the example above would be 4²/₃¢, i.e. the width of the piece is 12½", which cuts out 3 times from a 38" roll (with ½" waste) and the 9″ height comes 4 times out of the yard, making 12 pieces per yard. Divided into 56¢ this comes to $.0466.

Endpapers are each twice the untrimmed page size. Thus, on a trim-size of 5 × 7½″, each untrimmed page is 5⅛ × 7¾″ , so each endpaper is 10¼ × 7¾″. Endpapers are usually cut from sheets, not rolls. Remembering that the grain should run with the fold (7¾″), this size would cut out of a 26 × 40″, grain-long sheet 10 times (2 times 10¼″ out of 26″ and 5 times 7¾″ out of 40″) with some waste. From here, the cost would be calculated as for any other paper (CH. 10).

The labor costs in binding divide roughly into: (a) sheetwork—folding, gathering, sewing, (b) forwarding—trimming, backing, etc., (c) casemaking, (d) stamping, (e) casing-in, and (f) wrapping. The items vary in amount and proportion of the toal binding cost, according to each book's characteristics and the length of the run. Some of the alternatives are discussed in CHS. 16 and 26, but a general picture of unit costs for an average book might be somewhat as follows:

sheetwork: about 30¢
forwarding: about 5½¢
casemaking: about 6½¢
stamping: about 5¢
casing-in: about 5½¢
wrapping: about 11¢
makeready: about 6¢   (includes all operations)

To the total of 69½¢ for labor would be added about 10½¢ for materials other than the text paper and the cover material. Thus, if the latter were 7¢, the total binding cost would be about 87¢. The prices would vary also according to the individual binder, the kind of equipment used, and when the work is done.

To the above should be added a figure for packing and shipping, as these are customarily in the binder's price. Where packing is on skids and delivery is local in bulk, 2¢ should be enough. For packing in bulk cartons add about 6¢, including the cartons. For individual carton packing, figure at least 6¢ for labor and between 20 and 35¢ each for the cartons, depending on the size of the book, the number of copies, and the design of the carton. Where individual carton labeling is to be done by the binder, there is an additional charge of about 6¢, including delivery in bulk to the post office. There is no charge for skids if they are returned.

CAUTION: See A *Special Note on Prices* on p. xi.

13 | Schedules & records

In making books for publishing, an essential, vital part of the problem is to get the books made not only well and economically, but efficiently. This means getting books finished in time to be published as scheduled. The financial success or failure of a title may hinge as much upon *when* it is published as any other factor.

There are 2 problems in the choice of a publication date: (a) deciding on the time when the book is likely to be best received by reviewers, booksellers, and public and (b) relating publication to the needs of the house for income to cover expenses. The latter is, for all but the smallest publishers, a relatively minor consideration, but once the decision is taken the apparatus of distribution is set in motion—a catalogue is printed, advertising is prepared, salespeople are briefed and begin selling, orders are taken—and any change in schedule means a major upset.

Even if only one title is being produced the problem of keeping a publication date is formidable—but when 50 or 100 are in work simultaneously, nothing short of high efficiency (and a generous helping of luck) will succeed. If the pub date is set before the Ms is completed, as is often the case, there is a good chance that the Ms will be late. The author may become ill, be distracted by pressing personal matters, run into an unexpected difficulty in writing, go abroad on a windfall fellowship, or decide that the Ms is no good and rewrite it. Once he turns it in, it may require considerable editing, checking, or examination for libelous material. When released by the editorial department, the Ms goes to the designer— who may find it a problem because it is not clearly organized, incomplete, or economically impractical. The problems solved and design worked out, the Ms goes out for composition, where it may be delayed by a busy compositor or set in the wrong size by mistake. Once in galleys, it goes back to the author, who may delay its return for one or more of the reasons mentioned. These hazards hold true for paging as well. Before the book gets on press, any one of a number of calamities may strike—loss of proofs in the mail; loss or damage of plates in transit; strikes; late delivery of illustrations, films, or paper; receipt of a new chapter from the author; etc., etc. Delays caused by a busy printer are to be expected, and there could be plate injuries on press or press breakdown. In the bindery, another delay is likely as the binders try to fit the job into *their* schedule; the possibilities for small and large disasters during binding are multiple. These are some of the reasons for missing a publication date even *if* the production department operates efficiently.

Another production obstacle is the concentration of publishing activity in seasons. Everyone in book publishing deplores this, but the problem of distributing books through such a large country makes it difficult to do otherwise. It is more convenient to have one sales conference at which all the salespeople are briefed on the season's list than to brief them individually on a few titles at a time. As they are scattered from Maine to California, it is not feasible to bring them together more than 2 to 3 times a year. These factors, combined with the massive emphasis on the Christmas gift market, tend to perpetuate the practice of producing books in batches.

This throws a heavy strain on all production facilities in the months prior to October, when most fall books are wanted, and a somewhat lighter rush is concentrated in the midwinter months when the spring lists are being prepared. Fortunately, most publishers see the disadvantages of this arrangement and are trying to spread their publications more evenly through the year.

THE TIME REQUIRED   It is desirable for tradebooks to be manufactured in time for delivery about 6 weeks prior to pub date. This gives the publisher time to ship books to all parts of the country, and to send them to reviewers far enough in advance to enable appearance of reviews at or about publication date.

A book of average size with no problems *can* be produced in about 3 weeks—if everyone concerned puts all else aside. The normal time needed is about 5 months. Complicated manuscripts, illustrations, high-quality production, slow proofreading, require still more time. Thus, an average book should go into production not much less than 6 months before the publication date desired, to make allowance for unforseen problems.

A realistic production schedule for an average book (about 320 pages of fairly straight text and few or no illustrations in an edition of 5 to 10,000) printed by offset might run as follows:

analysis, design, & sample pages	2 weeks
composition	3 "
reading galleys	2 "

page makeup	2 weeks
reading pages	1 week
correction & repros	2 weeks
shooting, stripping, & blues	2　"
platemaking & printing	2　"
binding	3　"

total 19 weeks

Although it is possible to make the book in less time, it would be dangerous to allow less unless the manufacturer were to give a firm promise of an earlier completion date—and even then there are too many possibilities for delay (as noted earlier) to depend on the date.

For a book with halftone illustrations, in which all pages must have individual layouts, the following schedule would be normal. The column "elapsed time" takes into account the overlapping of operations that are concurrent, or partially so:

	time required	elapsed time
analysis, design, & sample pages	2 weeks	2 weeks
composition	3　"	3　"
layout	3　"	
reading galleys	2　"	
2 corrections & repros*	4　"	6　"
shooting halftones	3　"	
mechanicals	2　"	2　"
shooting, stripping, & blues**	4　"	4　"
platemaking & printing	2　"	2　"
binding	3　"	3　"
total		22　weeks

　*includes time for reading
　**includes time for checking blues

If color process illustrations are involved, weeks more time could be needed to make separations, proof, and correct. If the color illustrations are included in the layout, this could stretch out the 6 weeks from composition to mechanicals to 10 or 12. If the color work requires little correction, it might be accomplished during the 6 weeks indicated.

Generally, suppliers of services will not give definite schedules PROMISES & PRESSURES
until a job is in hand for production, for they have no way of knowing what work will be in their plant when the job does come in. For a very big or important job they will give a firm date in advance, but this obviously means that some other work will be pushed aside if

necessary. Since you are just as likely (at some time) to be on the receiving as well as the pushing end of this treatment, it is best to avoid asking for such promises. The hard truth remains, however, that with the best of intentions and the most efficient planning, circumstances beyond your control sometimes make a crash program necessary. The object in bookmaking is to insure that such cases are the exception rather than the rule.

With a great many jobs in work at the same time—and conflicting pressures from all sides—suppliers may easily fall behind. While it isn't wise to push too hard too often, a gentle reminder at proper intervals is quite necessary. Knowing just when and how to do this is vital for a production manager. It is best to prod when there is still time to get the job done on schedule even if the supplier has been delinquent. On a long-term job, occasional, well-timed reminders are in order. Written reminders are effective and not as distracting as phone calls.

Records   The number of details involved in producing even one book is astonishing, the problem of keeping track of many in various stages of production is overwhelming, unless systematic records are maintained.

It would be nice to be able to say that a simple chart is sufficient, but it isn't. To be effective, a record system must cover every detail, and this means that a progress chart should provide a place for each item of production. Anything not carried on the chart is very likely to be overlooked at some point.

There are as many ways of arranging production records as there are people keeping them—and any system is good if it works. The basic idea is to provide a space to be filled when a particular operation is completed, so that the blank spaces are reminders of what is not yet done. This would be relatively simple if all operations were successive, but there are many things to be done concurrently, and the problem is to get them all done when they are needed. At one particular moment, for example, all of the following may be in progress on one title:

text in composition,
frontmatter copy coming from author,
foreword being written,
Library of Congress number applied for,
illustration films being made,
a missing illustration being made,
paper for text being made,
paper for illustrations ordered,
binding design out for approval,
bulking dummy being made,
jacket separations being made,
jacket flap copy being written.

This list is not an exaggeration, but a common occurrence. And if ordering something were sufficient to get it done, the problem would be complex enough; but each item must be followed up or it may be late and hold up the entire job.

It is not possible to record the progress of *every* detail of production, yet every detail must be somehow covered. The more records kept, the better for accuracy—but keeping up records takes time too, and a small staff is usually not able to make all the entries desirable. Each office must find its own compromise.

On the following page is a typical record form. Note that spaces are provided for the dates when various items are *due*, as well as the dates they actually (ACT) arrive. A considerable amount of work is needed to maintain such records, but it is better to use a form and fail to keep it perfectly than to use an inadequate form.

In addition to a chart on which the progress of each book is recorded in detail, it is desirable to keep a chart showing the general progress of all books in work. This enables determining at a glance the state of the whole list in terms of the seasonal publication schedule.

Each title should, of course, have its own folder containing a copy of every proof or document relevant to the book's production. Although there is a good chance that the world will collapse under the weight of all the records being accumulated, it is better to keep anything that *might* be useful than to throw it away and need it later. A system of periodic destruction of old files will keep the accumulation from getting out of hand, and microfilming is the answer to permanent filing of important documents.

Most filing systems in production offices are based on letter-size files, but if you are starting a new system, it is not a bad idea to use legal-size files, which are a little larger and very handy where large proofs, sketches, etc. are to be kept.

The most important records in book production, besides those needed to keep schedules, are those concerning expenditures of money. Sometimes an order is given in the course of a conversation, and this may be sufficient for the supplier, but to keep the records straight, a formal order on a numbered order form should be executed. Besides the copy or copies required by the bookkeeping department, at least one copy of all orders should be made for the records of the production office.

There are 2 main reasons for keeping such records. One is to compile figures on production expenditures for the needs of management, the other is to check against any inquiry involving an error in the records of another office. In the latter case, the inquiry may offer the order number, the date, or the name of the job. Your orders may be filed according to any one of these, or 2, or all of them. While maximum efficiency would require 3 kinds of files, there are not likely to be enough inquiries to justify this. If one file

PRODUCTION SCHEDULE

TITLE:	PUB DATE:	BOUND BOOK DATE:
AUTHOR:	TRIM SIZE:	QUANTITY:
EDITOR:	NO. PAGES:	BULK:
COMPOSITOR:	BINDER:	
PRINTER:	JACKET PRINTER:	

	DUE	ACT		DUE	ACT		DUE	ACT
COMPOSITION			PRINTING: TEXT			BINDING		
Ms to design			Dum & ord to ptr			Bdg design IN		
Sample pgs IN			Mechanical to ptr			" " OK		
" " OK			Book blues IN			Dies ord		
Estimate IN			" " OK			" IN		
" OK			On press			Ptd cover: mech IN		
Ms & comp ord OUT			Sheets to bdy			Mech & ord to ptr		
Galleys IN			PRINTING: ILLUSTRATIONS			Blues IN		
" ret			BW Illustr IN			" OK		
Castoff IN			" " to cam			Sheets to finish		
" OK			" " blues IN			" " bdy		
Frontmatter OUT			" " " OK			Sample covers ord		
" pfs IN			Color Illustr IN			" " IN		
" " ret			" " to sep			OK & ord to bdy		
Pg pfs IN			" " pfs IN			Bound books		
" " ret			" " " OK			MISC		
Rev gals/pgs IN			Page blues IN			Imposition req		
Rev pfs ret			" " OK			" to ptr		
Index OUT			Dum & ord to ptr					
" pfs IN			Sheets to bdy					
" " ret			JACKET					
Captions OUT			Jacket design ord					
" IN			" " IN					
Repros			" " OK					
MATERIALS			Flap copy to comp					
Text ppr ord			" " pfs IN					
" " IN			" " " ret					
Insert/endppr ord			Repros IN					
" " IN			Mechanical to ptr					
Jacket ppr ord			Blues IN					
" " IN			" OK					
Bdg material ord			On press					
" " IN			Jackets to bdy					

is kept, it should be according to title, as this is the most generally useful.

Incidentally, it is customary for book manufacturers and printers to file jobs by title, so, even though Mss are referred to by author in publishing houses, confusion is minimized by using the title outside the house. The chances of a publisher having 2 authors of the same name on one list are small, but suppliers deal with perhaps 30 or 40 publishers, and the chance of a duplication of authors' names is considerable. Even when titles are similar, an abbreviated form can be made distinctive.

For a discussion of preparing composition orders see CH.19. Printing orders are covered in CH.25 and binding orders in CH.27.

C

PROCEDURE

14 | Analysis

The process of design has 3 steps:

(1) Analysis of the problem,

(2) Consideration of the possible solutions,

(3) Selection of the best solution.

Essentially, this is the process of problem-solving. Design is the name given to problem-solving in certain fields, of which book-making is one. If the 3-stage process is not carried out, the result cannot be called design.

The application of stock solutions to unexamined problems may produce superficially adequate results at times, due to coincidence, but over a long period there will be many more failures than successes. For that reason, this book offers *guides to procedure*, rather than rules. Rules can be found in stylebooks, but they are primarily to help beginners produce usable work or at least avoid the worst mistakes—they cannot produce excellent design. A few rules are given in this book, but they are related to principles rather than procedure.

With experience, it is possible to shorten the distance between (1) analysis and (3) selection. Repeated encounters with one kind of problem enable a designer to instantly reject some solutions and move swiftly toward others. It may even appear at times that the middle stage of the design process has been omitted entirely, just as it may seem that the transmission process from nerve-ending to brain has been omitted because one shouts in pain immediately upon touching a hot object. In both cases, the speed of the action makes it imperceptible, but the action takes place.

Even intuition can be comprised by the analytic process, since creative intuition will not produce answers of value unless preceded at some time (however far back) by analytical effort. The intuitive process will be discussed in the next chapter; now we are concerned with analysis.

The characteristic of book publishing that makes it perpetually interesting—and confounds the conventional businessman—is its multiple purpose. A single book may be an object of commerce, a work of art, an act of faith, and an article of practical use—or a half dozen other things. The problems of bookmaking reflect this diversity.

Every book presents 3 kinds of problems: (a) mechanical, (b) commercial, and (c) editorial.

■ *The mechanical problem*—Turning the Ms into an efficient and economical book.

■ *The commercial problem*—Producing a book that is suited to its market, aids sales, and can be sold profitably.

■ *The editorial problem*—Creating a book that properly expresses the author's message.

There is some dispute as to the legitimacy of a designer's concern with the editorial content of a Ms. There is a school that would consider the analysis completed once the mechanical and commercial problems have been examined.

Another school holds that the design must do as much as it can for the author—that it must support visually what the author is saying verbally. (See "Schools of design" in CH. 2.) If the latter view is valid, then there *is* an editorial problem in bookmaking. This book proceeds on that assumption. Indeed, the concept of bookmaking on which it is based includes the editorial function as an integral part.

The esthetic element has not been omitted. It is implicit in the 3 factors named, but is subordinate to them. Esthetic success should not be achieved at the expense of any of the basic aspects although, paradoxically, it is doubtful that a book can achieve success mechanically, commercially, or editorially unless it succeeds esthetically.

Mechanical analysis

An analysis of the mechanical problem of a Ms is known variously as a *character count*, *breakdown*, or castoff. Breakdown is probably the most apt term, for there is more involved than just a character count, and castoff is properly applied to the process of counting the number of pages in galley proofs.

A breakdown is a division of the Ms into various kinds of material, with each kind counted by the most suitable method. There are 4 ways of counting: (a) by characters, (b) by lines, (c) by units, and (d) by pages.

CHARACTER COUNTS

Character counts are used to determine the amount of material in continuous prose copy. The text of the Ms itself is usually counted by this method.

Authors and editors use "word counts" in measuring the size of a

Ms, but this is an inaccurate method, even disregarding the fact that there are often kinds of material that must be counted in other ways. Consider first the varying vocabularies used by different writers—or even the same writer dealing with different subjects. A book on sociology, for example, will probably have a higher proportion of long words than will a novel. One writer may average 5.5 characters per word while another may average 6.1. This is a difference of only 10%, but in a 320-page book the difference means 32 pages. There is also a possibility of error when authors make word counts. If they estimate an average of 10 words per line and it is really 9.5, we are off another 5%, or 16 pages. There are other errors inherent in this method, so it would be best for editors to use character counts and encourage authors to do the same.

In a character count, each letter, number, punctuation mark, word-space, and sentence-space is counted as one unit. On a standard typewriter, the widths of all characters and the single space are identical. In type, the widths of characters and spaces do vary, but there are so many in a page that the average for a particular size of a particular face can be assumed to be the same in all cases (some exceptions are taken up later). There are 2 sizes of type on American standard typewriters: *pica* and *elite*. The pica width is 10 characters to the inch and the elite is 12 characters per inch. Justifying typewriters and those having characters of varying width must be treated as typesetting machines for character-count purposes.

|←——— /″ ———→|

Bookmaking:T *(elite)*

Bookmaking *(pica)*

■ *The text*—To make a character count of straight text, first determine the average number of characters per line in the Ms. This is the most crucial estimate in the analysis because it is multiplied thousands of times and any error will carry to the final result in proportion. As we have seen, even a few percentage points of error mean a substantial number of pages in the book. Unfortunately, it is not easy to estimate accurately the average characters per line. In typescript, although the uniform character width makes it simple to determine the number of characters in a line, the varying width of line presents a problem. Assuming that the entire Ms was typed by one person on one machine with the same width of line setting, the problem is fairly small. The usual practice is to draw a line down the right side of the page at what is optically the midpoint between the longest and shortest lines (not including paragraph endings). This line would represent the average width. A more accurate method is to actually measure the number of characters on each line of the page and take a mathematical average. This is not an excessive amount of work in order to arrive at such an important figure. This is best done with several pages.

If, as is more likely, the Ms has been typed by various people and machines, the average characters per line found on the first page can be used only as long as the typescript is similar to that page.

> On just such a night, seven years before, Chrysis had left
> the land of Gennesaret. She remembered it well. They were five men,
> sellers of ivory. The long tails of their horses were adorned with
> parti-colored tufts. They had met the child at the round edge of a well...
>
> Before that there had been the blue lake, the transparent sky, the
> light air of the land of Galilee.
> Her mother's house was surrounded with pink, flax-plants and tamarisks.
> Thorny caper-bushes pricked childish fingers when she went to catch butter-
> flies... She could almost see the wind in the waves of the pine grasses...
> The little girls bathed in a clear brook where there were red shells
> under flowering laurel: and there were flowers upon the water, and flowers
> all over the fields, and great lilies grew upon the mountain, and the line of
> the mountain was that of a young breast....
> Chrysis closed her eyes and smiled a faint smile which suddenly died
> away. The idea of death had just occurred to her. She felt that she would
> be conscious until the last.
> "Ah!" she said, "what have I done? Why did I meet that man? Why did
> he listen to me? Why did I let myself be caught in this trap of my own
> making? Why is it that, even now, I regret nothing?
> "To love or die: that is the choice God gave me. What have I done to
> deserve punishment?"
> Fragments of sacred verses came to her from her childhood. She had not
> thought of them for seven years. They now returned one after the other
> with implacable precision, to define her life and predict her penalty.

A typescript page with a line drawn at the width of the average line.

Wherever a change occurs, a new average figure must be found.

When counting characters in printed copy (anthologies, reprints, etc.), the width of line is uniform, but the number of characters in the lines will vary (up to 10%) because of the justification process (CH. 5). However, if enough lines are counted (there is no easy method, each character and space must be counted), an accurate average can be found. A count of about 20% of the lines on a page can reasonably be projected to that page and all pages set like that one.

When an average character count per line has been determined, multiply this figure by the number of lines of text. To find the latter, multiply the number of lines per page by the number of *full* pages (if they have the same number of lines), and add to this the number of lines on *short* pages—usually chapter openings and endings. If there are spaces in the Ms (around chapters, subheads, etc.) they are subtracted from the line count.

If the Ms has varying numbers of lines per page, either count enough pages to get an average or, better still, count the number of lines on each page and total them. This is not too difficult with the help of an adding machine. On standard typewriters, double-spaced lines measure 3 to the inch (2.54 cm).

The problem is very simple with printed copy because the number of lines per page will be uniform. However, count several pages to be sure you have a normal one. Some pages may be made a line short or long to avoid widows (CH. 5).

Until this point, it has been assumed that the Ms is clean and orderly. Unfortunately, this is not always so. Some handwritten corrections are almost always present, and usually these may be disregarded as they probably cancel out each other, but there *are* Mss with heavy handwritten corrections, pasted-in strips of copy, extensive deletions, etc. About all that can be done is to make a careful, page-by-page guess as to the effect of such irregularities. Don't make a guess for the Ms as a whole; there is too much room for error.

Sometimes it pays to send a very dirty Ms back to the editorial department for retyping. Weigh the compositor's penalty (CH. 12) against the cost of retyping—and the loss of time in slowed setting and proofreading—against the time needed for retyping. Often, the time element means more than the money involved.

A rough character count can be made by determining the number of characters on a typical page and multiplying by the number of pages in the Ms, with the short chapter opening and closing pages subtracted. In a perfectly typed Ms of straight narrative text such a count would be adequate, otherwise it should be used with caution. To make an ideal character count, each line should be counted and the totals kept chapter by chapter.

Any prose part of the Ms which might ultimately be set in a style different from that of the main text should be character-counted separately. If you count everything in with the text, you have no way of knowing how the length of the book would be affected if you should decide to set some part of it in a different size type, a narrower measure, or with different leading. The kinds of copy that usually require a character count are:

- *Extract*—This is quoted material that is not run in with the text.
- *Appendix*—An appendix may be any kind of copy, but when it is prose it should be counted separately.
- *Introductions*—A long introduction is usually set as part of the text, but there is no harm in counting it separately. Short introductions to parts and chapters should always be separated, preferably piece by piece.
- *Notes*—Whether arranged as footnotes or in a group at the end of the book, notes are a separate item.
- *Foreign language*—This may be extract or part of the text, and should be so designated. It is mainly for pricing purposes that foreign language is counted separately (CH. 12).

Any line of copy that will definitely begin a new line on the printed page and will definitely not extend beyond one line may be counted as *line-for-line* copy. Obviously, it is necessary to know how many characters per line the printed page will have in order to make such a count, but an approximation is usually sufficient. Where the copy is clearly less than the probable number there is no problem. Where it is clearly more, but certainly not more than twice the number, 2 lines are counted. In borderline cases, guesses must be made—and these should average out to the right amount.

There are several kinds of line-for-line material and these should be counted separately. This method is used wherever possible, as it is more accurate than a character count. Some of the most frequently encountered line-for-line material is described below:

■ *Conversation*—Short lines of conversation and other lines in text (courtroom testimony, questions and answers, etc.) which will definitely set as one line of type should be counted and the number subtracted from the text line count.

■ *Poetry*—Some poetry has a large number of lines of about one-line width. Take a guess at the possible number of characters per line in the printed book, and make a paper strip of the proper width. All wider lines should be counted as 2. Stanza breaks are counted as one line each.

■ *Tables*—Tables in the text should be counted separately from those in an appendix, as you may want to set them differently. For pricing purposes, tables are usually grouped and counted according to number of columns.

■ *Glossary*—If the definitions are brief, this can be counted line for line, otherwise it is best to make a character count.

■ *Bibliography*—Some bibliographies may have descriptive paragraphs for each title. These should have a separate character count, while the book titles can be counted line for line.

■ *Lists*—If the list is typed double column, the line count should note this. Should you decide later to set the lists in single column, the line count would be doubled.

■ *Subheads in text*—Where the subheads are long enough to average more than one line, a line count should be made in addition to the regular heading count (see below).

Sometimes it is necessary to know only *how many* of a particular kind of material is in the Ms, rather than how many characters or lines there are. This is true mainly of elements of space, or elements surrounded by space. In such cases, the space that can be allocated in the printed book is variable, so it is more important to know the number of elements there are than how much space they occupy in the Ms.

■ *Subdivisions*—Count the *number* of part titles, chapter titles, section titles, and subheads—giving each class of subhead a designating number and a separate count. Do not count lines or characters.

■ *Spacebreaks*—In Ms, these are usually 1 or 2 lines each. They should be counted and the proper number of lines subtracted from the overall line count for the text. Then list only the *number* of spacebreaks.

■ *Units*—The number of occurrences (or units) of each kind of material within the text should be counted. For example it is not enough to know that there are x number of characters of extract, or y number of lines of poetry, you must know *how many times* extract or poetry occur, because you may decide to have some space before and after each quotation and/or poem, and you must be able to compute the amount of space involved (100 lines of extract may be 2 quotations of 50 lines each, or 50 quotations of 2 lines each).

It is necessary to make some estimate of the number of occurrences of footnotes if they are to appear beneath the text, because you will need some space to separate the two. This is difficult to do with any accuracy, because you can't know how the notes will occur in the page makeup. A reasonably good way of figuring this is to count all the footnotes and then, if there are fewer notes than pages of Ms, assume that each footnote will fall on a separate page. If there are more notes than pages, assume that there will be footnotes on every page in the book. You are not likely to be exactly right, but you probably won't be too far wrong.

In the frontmatter, and sometimes in the *backmatter*, there will be material that will obviously fit on one page in the book. The *half-title* [usually the book title set in small type on the first page], the title, the copyright notice, the dedication, a brief acknowledgment, a small contents page, etc., need not be counted for characters and lines. Simply note their existence. The same is true for any such page in the text, such as a full-page table or chart. Make a character or line count only where there is any possibility that the copy will run more than one page.

PAGE-FOR-PAGE COUNTS

If the Ms is a printed book, there is no problem. Simply count the number of lines, making sure that you count the lines in each column, not per page. With a new Ms, you can only guess. As a rule of thumb, allow 1 page of index to every 40 pages of Ms with average copy, 1 to 30 for a Ms with very many names and/or technical terms, 1 to 50 for one with comparatively few. Check your guess with the editor's and use that figure if it differs from yours.

INDEX

This is usually the most difficult part of a mechanical analysis. It is certainly the most difficult to discuss in general terms, because there are so many possible situations.

The first step is to divide the illustrations into: (a) color process,

ILLUSTRATIONS

(b) monochrome halftone, (c) monochrome line, and (d) simple color, halftone, and line—as each kind has its own technical requirements. Then, make a tentative determination of the approximate amount of space to be occupied by each illustration, even if it can be only a rough guess, somewhat as in the following example:

>   (a) color process:
>   8 full page
>   6 half page
>   (b) monochrome halftone:
>   6 full page
>   19 half page
>   23 quarter page
>   (c) line:
>   52 half page
>   67 quarter page

You may be surprised to find how naturally illustrations will fall into such size-groups at a glance. The space might not ultimately work out as you guesssed, but it is very useful to have an estimate such as this from which to start.

TABULATION All information of the mechanical analysis (breakdown) should be tabulated in an orderly and useful form. This tabulation will become a tool in creating the book, so it should be typed for maximum efficiency. Include whatever data may be of some use. There is nothing lost if you don't use a particular figure on your breakdown sheet, but it is very frustrating to need something that isn't there. For convenience, note the Ms page on which each kind of material first occurs.

It is a good idea to type all items to the left, so that the right side of the sheet can be used for inserting the calculated number of pages for each one. If you draw lines across the page under each item there is less danger of overlooking one. On the opposite page is a specimen breakdown sheet. Note that the tabulation is according to parts of the Ms or kinds of material, with the character, line, page, and unit counts for each listed together (c = characters, L = lines, pp = pages). This makes it possible to take all elements into consideration in deciding, for example, how many pages to allow for a bibliography containing material counted in several ways.

Commercial analysis There are many possible considerations, but the main ones are:

>   (a) the size of the first printing and binding (edition),
>   (b) the nature of the intended audience, and
>   (c) the kind of distribution anticipated.

These, and whatever other commercial problems there may be,

TITLE: *Example*   DATE: 12/2/41
Ms pp: 339

FRONTMATTER
  half title__pp, title__pp, cpyrt__pp, ded__pp
  preface 2762 c
  contents 44 L
  introduction 5250 c
TEXT:
  538,050 c
  103 L
EXTRACT: (p.67)
  5892 c
POETRY: (p.29)
  129 L
  14 units
PLAYSTYLE: (p.162)
  1264 c
  10 L
  4 units
TABULAR: (p.212)
  42 L
  12 units
BIBLIOGRAPHY: (p.318)
  4922 c
  53 L
INDEX:
  allow__pp
FOOTNOTES:
  1640 c
  14 units
ILLUSTRATIONS:
  halftone:75
  line:28
SUBDIVISIONS:
  part titles:3
  chapters:8
  A heads:18
  B heads:41
  spacebreaks:19

must be fully considered so that the design and production of the book will contribute to a financially successful publication. The actual sale of the book is not the only commercial consideration. Even with the sale of a large number of copies, a book will not be profitable if it is not well planned in terms of its particular conditions of distribution.

SIZE OF PRINTING & BINDING The publisher's decisions as to how many copies to print and, of these, how many to bind, are based less on the cost of production than on an estimate of the book's sale. One can hold down the unit cost through a large printing, but there will be no profit if most of the books remain unsold.

Most books are printed in relatively small quantities. Yet, it may take the same amount of time to make a job ready to run, the same investment in machinery, the same amount of floor space, the same amount of editorial and administrative work, and the same cost in composition and plates for a run of 5000 as for one of 50,000. Obviously then, the design and production plans for a short run must be quite different from those for a long one.

If the printing is small, more economy in *plant cost* [items not affected by size of edition, i.e. composition, plates, illustrations, etc.] is required. If the printing is large, the expenditures for composition and illustrations are less significant than the cost of materials, hand operations in binding, and other items that remain about the same per unit regardless of the size of the edition. A small edition might make it possible to take advantage of a special lot of paper or cloth at a good price, but a large one will permit you to order a special color, size, or finish without penalty. (Remember that a later printing may be too small for a special order. Have a satisfactory substitute in mind.)

A decision to bind only part of the edition printed has limited effect on design or production planning. Usually, a large majority of the edition is bound, and it is worth ordering materials for all at the same time. Also, it is common practice to carry the sheetwork (CH. 11) through the whole edition and hold back only the remainder of the binding operations until sales justify completion.

Ideally, the bookmaking departments participate in discussions concerning the size of the first printing. In any case, the management's thoughts in this matter should be thoroughly investigated as part of the commercial analysis.

THE NATURE OF THE AUDIENCE Who are the potential buyers and readers of a book? They are not always the same person. The buyers of books read by young children are usually adults, as are the buyers of schoolbooks and most reference books for the young. Books for all kinds of readers are bought by libraries. A large proportion (perhaps half) of the books purchased in bookstores in America are not read by the buyers but

are intended as gifts. In such circumstances, any design considerations based on audience must have 2 aspects: one for the buyer
and one for the reader.

Examine the characteristics of both groups. What are their oc-
cupational backgrounds? What kinds of education have they?
What is their social and economic status? What are their tastes and
prejudices? What are their ages? What physical disabilities might
they have?

These are not impertinent questions. The answers will affect
your decisions. Size and kind of type, shape and weight of the
book, durability, dirt resistance, style of typography, quality of materials, number and kind of colors, number and kind of
illustrations—these and other design factors are subject to
modification according to audience requirements.

For example, take a book on retirement activities for the financially secure. The reader will be past middle age, so the type should
be a bit larger than average (CH.6). Durability is obviously not too
important here, but light weight would be appreciated by the older
readers, particularly those with such ailments as arthritis and palsy
which frequently limit manual powers. Presumably, good quality
materials and attractive but restrained colors would please the
potential readers as well as the younger friends and relatives who
are likely to be buying the book as a gift. The economic status of the
reader suggests a retail price that would make such an approach
feasible.

Most books are sold in several ways. Each method of distribution
has its own needs and these must be known so that they can be met.
Some of them are indicated below.

■ *Bookstore sales*—These usually require attractive jackets and are
helped by illustrations and attractive visual elements in general. In
most cases, it helps to have as large and thick a book as possible,
unpleasant as the thought may be.

■ *Mail-order distribution*—This suggests a lightweight package to
keep down postage, although certain kinds of mail-order books
must be large and lavish to succeed. In any case, weight should be
controlled to avoid going just over a postage weight bracket. Damage in transit is also a factor to consider.

■ *Library sales*—Here, a strong binding is important. The librarians have definite, practical views on binding specifications.

■ *Textbook sales*—Elementary and high school books usually require a lot of color and illustrations. They must meet NASTA
standards of material and manufacture (CH.11).

■ *Gift sales*—Usually made through bookstores, these suggest
large size, extensive use of color and illustration, high quality materials.

Sometimes, the demands of several methods of distribution conflict and have to be reconciled. At other times, the commercial requirements may not be apparent from the Ms alone. For instance, an editor may anticipate subsequent books on the same subject by the author of a new Ms, with the thought that the books might eventually be sold as a set or series. Knowing this, a designer will avoid an arrangement of the title which would not be adaptable to another, will avoid the use of odd lots of material which cannot be obtained for the subsequent volumes, etc. Question the editorial and sales departments to learn what is the commercial problem.

Editorial analysis

Visual support of the author may be mostly practical—taking the form of good organization and a clear presentation of the material. The support may be mostly esthetic—consisting of subtle suggestion of mood and atmosphere. In almost all cases there will be a combination of both. The most practical book, if well designed, will have a functional beauty that grows naturally from its sense of order and fitness—just as in a fine bridge or aircraft. At the other end, even a novel or a book of verse must be made to perform satisfactorily. No amount of atmosphere or graphic beauty is sufficient if the practical problems are unsolved.

In order to make an accurate and effective visual presentation of the text, the designer must become completely familiar with the Ms and must clearly understand the author's intentions. The designer's attitude toward the subject may be different from the author's, but the job is to present the writer's approach—not one's own. Whatever of the designer's personality or viewpoint appears in the result may be only a residual, inadvertent by-product of an effort to express those of the author.

READING TECHNIQUE

It is necessary for a designer to develop techniques for quickly extracting the essence of a Ms, and rapidly learning what he must know about it. No method is perfectly satisfactory if it does not include reading the entire Ms, but this is usually impossible, so a compromise must be made.

In fiction, an effective method is to read the first 18 or 20 pages, then read 2 or 3 pages at intervals of about 30, and then read the last 6 or 8. In this way, one can usually learn the setting and atmosphere of the story, feel the style of the writing, catch the general development of the plot, and discover the ending. With practice, a fairly accurate reading of a 350-page Ms can be made in about an hour. From the standpoint of pleasure, this is a very unsatisfactory way to read, but this is a sacrifice the designer must make. It is important to maintain an alert and flexible approach, however, as some stories are so constructed that a misleading impression might result from a strict adherence to this system.

Nonfiction in narrative form can be read in about the same way. A writer will usually explain the subject and premises in the beginning and state the conclusions at the end. A spot check through the body of the text will give the general drift of the story or argument, as well as the feel of the author's style. If the Ms is composed of several parts by the same or different writers, each piece can be studied in somewhat the same way, reducing the number of pages read in proportion to its length.

Nonfiction of complicated organization or varied content should be examined page by page. The text will have to be read to the extent necessary to understand its organization, intent, and style, and each page must be seen, to insure that every problem has been observed.

There are many kinds of Ms and no one study procedure can be effective for all. In principle, the idea is to sample where a sample is sufficiently revealing, and examine in detail where necessary. Read all prefaces, forewords, and introductions—even if you can't read anything else. For some reason, people are inclined to bypass these, but this is usually a mistake. By its nature, such a piece is a statement considered too important, significant, or special to include in the body of the text. Here, authors often explain their purpose and/or summarize the content of the text. Here, another writer often throws light on the character or background of the authors and their work. These are insights which would usually require a considerable amount of other reading to achieve—here is the equivalent, in many cases, of a chat with the author.

Whatever method is used, enough study and analysis of the Ms must be carried out to determine the exact nature, feeling, and intention of the book. At some point prior to making decisions designers should check their interpretations with the author or the editor. At the very least, they should compare their impressions with the one carried by some advertising or catalogue copy prepared for publication. A briefing of some kind, oral or written, will often have to substitute for a thorough reading of the Ms, because of insufficient time.

It is not a bad idea, particularly when learning, to make a brief written summary of your commercial and editorial analyses. Even in the form of rough notes, such a summary will help clarify your thoughts and fix them in your mind. Remember, *in making an analysis you are not to draw any conclusions about the book you will design*. At this stage you are only to *learn* about your problem. Before you *decide* on anything you must go through a process of consideration, in which all levels of conscious thought and intuition are brought into play.

In conclusion

15 | Creative solutions

The creative problem   In book design, the creative problem is to interpret and indicate the nature of the content. The indication *must* be accurate, it *should be* interesting and pleasing. In an exceptionally successful book the accuracy is such as to create a profound sense of fitness, the design is interesting to the point of being intriguing, and pleasing to the point of being beautiful.

Every Ms has a certain character, and this can be analyzed and interpreted. Whether simple or complicated, the character of the work can be expressed in more or less abstract visual terms. Some books are more easily expressed than others, some appear to be almost impossible to express. Certainly, it is unreasonable to expect that the total aspect of any book can be rendered graphically. Yet, it is probably better to tend deliberately in the right direction than to leave the tendency to chance—with the likelihood that it will go in the wrong direction.

The designer's creative problem is somewhat like that of the abstract painter—to communicate in terms that will reach the subconscious levels of the viewer's mind, where response will be automatic reaction rather than conscious thought. The average reader may be quite unaware of design in books, but cannot escape being affected by elements that establish character and mood. Modern psychology confirms the power of subconscious impressions to modify states of mind, or attitudes. A striking, if rather frightening, demonstration of this principle is the use of subliminal communication to implant ideas. (In the course of a motion picture or television show an unrelated message can be repeatedly flashed on the screen so rapidly that the viewer is not aware of its existence, yet responds to its content.) The designer must exploit the psychological devices that can help to create a receptive atmosphere for the author's work.

Any decision affecting the physical aspect of the book can have expressive value. Every physical attribute contributes to the total effect and helps create the character and atmosphere of the book. It makes a difference whether any part or the whole is delicate or strong, gay or somber, large or small, simple or complex, thick or thin. Even the format can be significant. For example, a different reaction to the sight and feel of a book will result if it is squarish and chunky than if it is tall and slim. The relation of weight to size has a definite effect.

In fact, no element of a book's appearance can fail to have some character and therefore some effect. It is the job of the designer to mobilize all these elements so that their sum, and each one of them, will contribute to a successful solution of the creative problem. At the same time, the creative solution must avoid conflict with the mechanical, commercial, or editorial requirements. Indeed, it should be in complete harmony with them.

To reconcile the sometimes divergent needs of the various aspects of bookmaking, decide first on what *should* be done creatively, then modify these decisions as necessary to accommodate the practical considerations. In other words, plan the ideal first and retain as much of it as you can. This works better than any other procedure because the creative process functions best when it is free of practical considerations. The moment you accept mechanical or economic limitations, your imagination tends to freeze. Not that it merely restricts itself to the practicable—it tends to act as though the limiting walls were made of glass, and it swings in a cramped arc far short of those walls. This is a safe enough procedure, but it precludes any chance of extending the possible. From the experience of civilization we know that even modest advances have usually been the result of expeditions well beyond the practicable. To remain always within the walls leads to stagnation and sterility.

For the best results in conceiving ideal creative solutions, it is necessary to tap the creative forces within us. Merely recalling routine devices and standard arrangements will not produce anything but stock solutions. The processes of rational mental effort will not produce a creative solution unaided. Usually, the automatic mechanisms of the mind will set the creative process in motion, and it will help to some extent—but it is much better to consciously invoke the force and utilize it fully. People who fall into deep water will automatically thrash their arms about in an effort to avoid drowning, and they may succeed, but they are much more likely to succeed if they know how to swim.

After reading and studying the Ms, put it down and relax. Let your mind create associations at random. From these associations, try to recall everything from your experience that is related to the subject—sights, sounds, smells, textures, people, places, pictures, words, colors—anything and everything. Then, if possible, let some time pass while you do other things. A few hours might be

The creative process

enough, but overnight is better. During this time, the conscious thoughts associated with the subject will seep down into the lower layers of consciousness, arriving eventually at the region in which the creative forces originate. The contact of subject matter with creative force produces ideas and imagination. The natural tendency of such impulses is to rise to conscious awareness and, when they do, we speak of "inspiration" and "intuition". Sometimes, these impulses burst into the open despite any obstacle. More often they must be given receptive conditions or they will remain unborn, or arrive in weakened and misshapen form.

The most propitious condition for creativity is an utterly blank mind. Such a state invites ideas just as a blank sheet of paper invites drawing or writing. Far from being a simple matter, achieving a blank mind is quite difficult. Our minds are filled with a lifetime of impressions and thoughts, and these are constantly in motion. The mystics of the East, particularly Taoists, take considerable trouble to develop an ability to wipe their minds clean at will. Some of the greatest works of Asian art are attributed to the creative powers invoked while in such a state. The technique is simply a process of narrowing down the field of mental activity by concentrating on a single point. Eventually, the concentration is complete, and the mind engaged with nothing but a single point of light, a distant mountain peak, or some other isolated focus. From here, the mind goes into a suspended, trancelike state in which even the point of concentration is eliminated. This is, obviously, similar to the process of hypnotism, and indeed it might be termed self-hypnotism. Masters can put themselves instantly into such a trance, even without a concentration point, but this takes years of effort and a lot of will power.

You may think that this is Oriental mumbo-jumbo having nothing to do with you or your work. Not so. For one thing, what the Asians have known for thousands of years is now being "discovered" by modern science. The psychological studies of the past 90 years tend to confirm the understanding of creativity outlined above. Also, unless you intend to exclude creativity from your work (and this is your choice) it is essential to understand and enter into the creative process.

Of course, you can't sit in your office staring for hours at a distant mountain peak or anything else. You would either be fired or carried off in a padded wagon. Nor are you likely to find there the peace and quiet essential to total concentration. The fact is, the conditions of modern business are unsuited to creative activity. Nevertheless, create we must, and there is really no substitute for the creative process, so an effort must be made to utilize that process.

To begin, not every Ms warrants, or can be given, a major creative effort. Also, the creative process is not an either/or matter—it will operate to the degree in which you participate. So if you can't put yourself into a catatonic trance, you can at least shut your eyes and try to concentrate on the darkness for a few minutes. If this fails to produce good enough results, you might get an inspiration in the middle of the night or while dozing on the train. The point is, you must take *positive action* toward freeing your imagination if you want the best results. You simply have to recognize the limitations and work within them. True, not everyone has a fertile imagination and the seeds you plant may not sprout—but the evidence suggests that there is a lot more creativity in most people than is apparent.

The objective of this creative effort is a clear, sharp visualization of the ideal finished book, in all its details. Even though the practical result may not resemble this ideal, the technical facilities available today make anything possible, if not always feasible. But, as time progresses, more and more becomes feasible.

With the desired result visualized, begin to assemble the devices with which to achieve that effect. These devices include all the elements of visual art, used with the insights of psychology as well as the intuition of the artist. The most effective and accessible tools are: (a) *symbolism*, (b) *color*, and (c) *texture*. It is by suggestion that we elicit the reader's subconscious reactions, and these 3 devices are rich in suggestive power. **The creative means**

The use of symbols has vast possibilities, not only for suggestion but for graphic effects. If the symbolism used is visually satisfactory, its effectiveness as symbol is not essential. Therefore, the first principle in the use of symbolism is: it must look good. The symbol will sometimes be obvious, sometimes obscure. If it looks good and is obvious, it will surely be effective to some degree—and it doesn't matter how much. If it looks good and is obscure, the worst that can happen is that it will be ineffective as symbol, but again, it doesn't matter. This is not to imply that it is unimportant whether or not symbolism is effective. The point is that if it fails as symbol it does no harm, provided it is visually satisfactory. In such cases, the symbol is no more than decoration, but it is perfectly justified if it is good decoration. **SYMBOLISM**

Whether the symbol is obscure or obvious, it should be used imaginatively. By treating it in a creative way, you impart the special quality that makes the symbol a meaningful part of the book. The illustrations following are examples of such treatment.

The degree of subtlety required of symbols depends on the nature of the Ms. When the subject of the text is factual and its approach direct, a literal or representational symbolism is appropriate. A book of belles lettres or any text with a romantic quality, shaded meanings, or indirect allusions would call for a more subtly suggestive symbolism. Following are illustrations of symbolism well-related to text in this sense.

The symbols used may represent any aspect of the book. They might be related to the subject, they might be associated with the mood, the atmosphere, a plot, a character, or perhaps the author. Their purpose is to suggest salient features of the Ms, as part of the

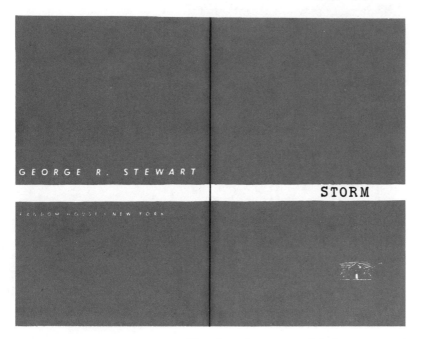

The telegraph tape, a symbol of urgency associated with disaster, is used imaginatively by Ernst Reichl. The background tone was printed in color.

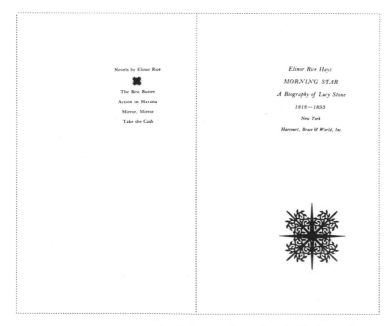

The obvious symbol as handled by Betty Anderson creates a fresh, evocative, and handsome spread.

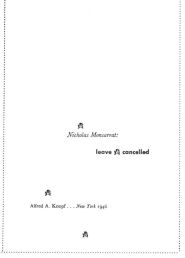

Nicholas Monsarrat:

leave 🌹 cancelled

Alfred A. Knopf . . . *New York 1946*

*Scattered roses are appropriate
symbols for this novel designed
by Paul Rand—*

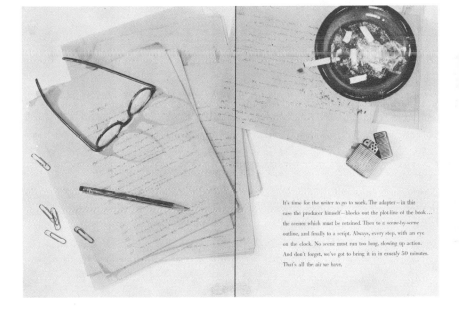

*and the artifacts of conference
are suitable for this factual
account of how a radio program
is made. Design by William
Golden.*

It's time for the writer to go to work. The adapter—in this
case the producer himself—blocks out the plot-line of the book...
the scenes which must be retained. Then to a scene-by-scene
outline, and finally to a script. Always, every step, with an eye
on the clock. No scene must run too long, slowing up action.
And don't forget, we've got to bring it in in *exactly* 50 minutes.
That's all the air we have.

effort to create a book that accurately reflects and reinforces the
author's message.

It is important to keep symbols in balance. If a symbol becomes
dominant in the graphic arrangement, it should be related to the
dominant characteristic of the book. The relationship of symbols
to each other must reflect the relationship of the elements they
represent. The total effect of the symbolism in a design must be a
true indication of the basic character of the book.

The range of possible symbols is virtually unlimited. Symbolism
in graphic form is illustration, and the broad graphic possibilities
are suggested in CH. 7. The symbolic values of color and texture are
discussed later in this chapter. The shape of the book or the pro-

portions of a text page can be symbolic. Even the sequence and placement of illustrations can have meaning. In an edition of Bernal Diaz' *Discovery and Conquest of Mexico* designed by the author, some of the illustrations consist of drawings of Mexican and Spanish weapons of the period. Pages of Mexican weapons occur where the Aztecs were ascendant, Spanish weapons where Cortez triumphed. The weapons are in profusion when the battle waxes and are few when it wanes. The effect is somewhat like the offstage clash of arms in a play.

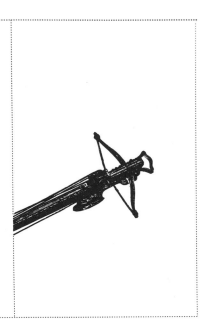

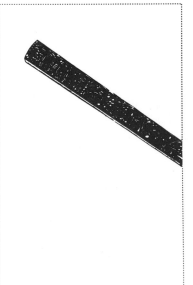

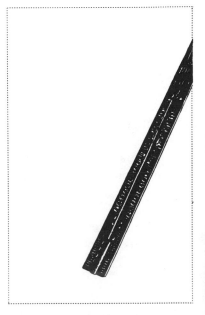

298   THE CONQUEST

many squadrons of Indians were approaching to set fire to his quarters he sallied forth to fight them, and he ordered the cannon to be fired, but it did not go off, and after he had made a charge against the squadrons which were attacking him, and many Indians were bearing down on him, while he was retreating to the fortress and quarters, then, without fire being applied to the cannon, the ball and the small shot was discharged and killed many Indians; and had it not so happened the enemy would have killed Alvarado and all the men who on that occasion carry off two of his soldiers alive.

Another thing Pedro de Alvarado stated, and this was the only thing that was also reported by the other soldiers, for the rest of the stories were told by Alvarado alone, and it is that they had no water to drink, and they dug in the courtyard, and made a well and took out fresh water, all around being salt; in all it amounted to many gifts that our Lord God bestowed on us.

† LXXXVII

When Cortés saw that they had given us no sort of a reception in Texcoco, and had not even given us food, except bad food and with bad grace, and that we found no chieftains with whom to parley, and he saw that all were scared away and ill disposed, and observed the same condition on coming to Mexico, how no market was held and the whole place was in revolt, and he heard from Pedro de Alvarado about the disorderly manner in which he made his attack, and as it appears that on the march Cortés had spoken to the Captains of Narvaez glorifying himself on the great veneration and command that he enjoyed, and how on the road the Indians would turn out to receive him and celebrate the occasion and give him gold, and that in Mexico he ruled as absolutely over the great Montezuma as over all his Captains, and that they would give him presents of gold, as they were used to do, and when everything turned out contrary to his expectations and they did not even give us food to eat, he was greatly irritated, and haughty towards the numerous Spaniards that he was bringing with him, and very sad and fretful. At this moment the great Montezuma sent two of his chieftains to beg our Cortés to go

THE CONQUEST

to the Plaza we placed a cannon and with
..., for the enemy were so numerous that the
..., (which was our greatest danger) deter-
... Plaza, and when the enemy saw this carried
... served the multitude of our allies (although
... of them unless they were in our company)
... allies after them until they were shut up in
... mple, which was enclosed with a masonry

... would be large enough to hold a town of
...s. However, a breach was made and the
... captured it and remained there and on the
... while. When the people of the city saw that
...semen with us they turned again on the
...e them from the towers and courts, and as
...eat danger, for it was worse than a retreat,
... the porticoes of the courts; however, the
...ed them so severely that they abandoned
... to the Plaza whence they were driven out
...were obliged to abandon the cannon which
...ere.

...nable to withstand the onset of the enemy,
...danger and would have suffered great loss
... God that at that moment three horsemen
... entered the Plaza, and when the enemy
...thought that there were more of them and
...he horsemen killed some of them and we
... and enclosure. On the most important and
...h has over a hundred steps to reach the
...ve Indian chieftains had sheltered them-
...five of the Spaniards clambered up, and,
...us fought bravely, they gained the summit

...horsemen had now arrived, and they and
... an ambuscade by which they killed over

...late I got the men together and ordered a
...tired such a host of the enemy fell upon
...een for the horsemen the Spaniards must
... loss. However, as I had had all the bad

The use of type as symbol is discussed to some extent under "Allusion" in CH. 6. This is a particularly difficult area of symbolism because the type has not only its suggestive characteristic, but also communicates thought. It is already a symbol for the words it forms, and no other symbolic association can be free of this effect. On these pages are a few examples of type used symbolically with some success. Typographic symbolism may be valid, but it is easily overworked. Use it with care and moderation.

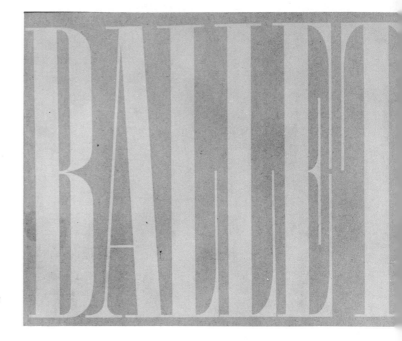

Alexey Brodovitch uses very tall, dramatic letters to suggest a line of graceful dancers and a potpourri of decorative faces to evoke the romantic and diverse world of ballet.

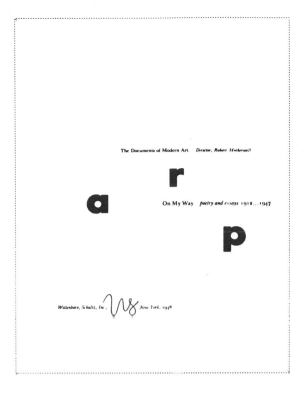

The Documents of Modern Art.   *Director, Robert Motherwell*

a   **r**

On My Way   *poetry and essays 1912...1947*

p

Wittenborn, Schultz, Inc.   NS   *New York, 1948*

The form and feeling of the artist's work is reflected in the choice and arrangement of type for his name. Design by Paul Rand.

TO
Farrar & Rinehart
Simon & Schuster
Coward-McCann
Limited Editions
Harcourt, Brace
Random House
Equinox Press
Smith & Haas
Viking Press
Knopf
Dutton
Harper's
Scribner's
Covici, Friede

S. A. Jacobs uses an ancient typographic technique to raise a cup in dedication.

Search the Ms for symbols used by the author. Sometimes a writer will inadvertently repeat a theme, at other times the motif will be consciously employed. Poets, of course, are entirely at home with visual images, and they are usually known for their favored symbols—W. B. Yeats for his golden birds, towers, trees, etc.; Edith Sitwell for her roses, drums, and so on. Sometimes, the book's subject will be a person with whom some symbol is associated. For example, see the following illustrations showing the use of characteristic symbols for Debussy and Stravinsky. Where no readily apparent symbol is present, the designer must create appropriate symbols from a study of the editorial analysis.

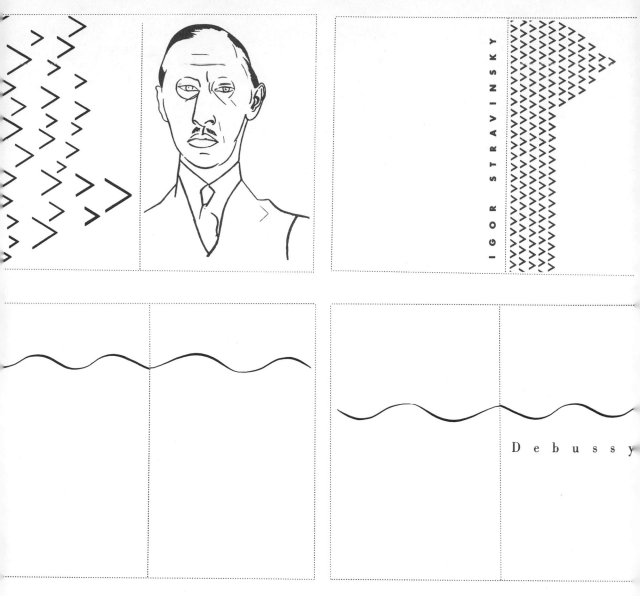

The sharp, staccato symbols of the Stravinsky book and the undulating line in the Debussy volume suggest the characteristics of each man's work. Both designs by Merle Armitage.

COLOR   Of all the graphic elements, color surely has the most powerful psychological effect. Except for some specific associations (discussed below), color is almost entirely without intellectual content and speaks directly to the subconscious. Tests have definitely established a connection between color and emotions. Color is thus one of the most effective tools of communication and should be used in book design far more than it is. A knowledge of the use of color is as important to the book designer as a knowledge of typography.

Because of its psychological powers, color is particularly valuable in creating atmosphere and mood. Sometimes an author will be thinking in terms of a certain color while writing (Flaubert said that he thought of *Madame Bovary* in terms of *puce*, which is the "rich", dark red characteristic of 19th-century French bourgeois interiors) but, in any case, the Ms will have *some* character and this character will suggest a color, kind of color, or combination of colors.

Color has 3 aspects: (a) hue, (b) intensity, and (c) value.

■ *Hue*—This is the "color" of the color (red, blue, yellow, green, orange-red, etc.).

■ *Intensity*—This is the purity of the color (intensity is lowered as the color is grayed or "softened").

■ *Value*—This is the darkness of the color (even in pure primary colors there is variation in value—yellow is lighter than blue, blue is lighter than red, etc.; however, an intense yellow may be darker than a blue whose intensity [and value] has been lowered by the addition of white).

The psychological effect of each color changes as it is modified in hue, value, and intensity. For example, a blue that is slightly tinged with green and is high in intensity may be very happy in effect. A blue on the violet side and lowered in intensity by the addition of black can be quite somber. The same violet-blue grayed with white might be soft and romantic. The variety of colors, considering the modifications possible, is infinite.

Not only is there an infinite number of colors, but these can be used in an infinite number of combinations—each of which has its own psychological properties *entirely independent of the individual colors within it*. For example, 2 colors, both of which are quite mild by themselves may, when combined, create a clash that is anything but mild. Several intense colors can be combined to produce a feeling of subtle harmony, if they are closely related in hue. A dark color of low intensity and a light color of low intensity can be combined to produce a dramatic effect of contrasting values. The ways in which colors can be manipulated in combination is endless—as are the effects that can be created.

Some colors and combinations of colors have very specific associations—school colors, national colors, company colors, club colors, etc. In an appropriate context, these colors convey meaning just as surely as do words. Don't scorn their use because they are obvious. As with graphic symbols, the pertinent questions are: Is it appropriate? Does it look good? If both answers are yes, final judgment will be based on *how* you used the colors, not *why*.

There are other, less specific, associations that can be used symbolically. Certain greens are associated with vegetation and nature in general. Some browns are conventionally connected with masculine matters because of their association with wood and leather.

Some exotic combinations of violets, pinks, and greens have a tropical look, blues are used to suggest water and sky, and so on. These nonspecific color symbols can be used very effectively where they are not required to convey the meaning alone. Again, while subtlety and freshness are very desirable in design, there is no need to avoid the use of an appropriate color just because it is obvious. A slightly odd shade or an interesting combination with other colors can easily save it from banality.

Color has the potentialities of a symphony orchestra, but it is not a simple matter to use color masterfully any more than it is a simple matter to create great music with an orchestra. Much is to be learned, much experience is required—and it helps to have talent.

TEXTURE As a device for communication with the subconscious, texture is as effective as any. It can be apprehended through two senses—sight and touch—which gives it an additional entrance to the area of response.

If texture is particularly effective, it is also relatively limited in its range of expression. However, it is an inevitable element of book design and should be utilized for positive ends.

The textural possibilities in bookmaking are not as meager as one might suppose. Printing papers are made with surfaces ranging from glassy-smooth to pebbly. Endpapers are somewhat more limited in range, but stock cover materials are reasonably varied, and a wide variety of textures can be had on special orders. Vinyl can be obtained with a surface as slick as patent leather and some of the more expensive cloths come as rough-textured as tweed.

The possibilities are greatly enlarged by the use of embossing or blank stamping (CH. 11). Suppliers of binding materials have stock embossings that can be applied as ordered, but these are mostly imitation cloth and leather textures. Far more variety can be achieved by the application of texture in the stamping operation. With etched dies, this is not unduly expensive. For example, on a book about the Florida swamp country, the cover was given a texture of alligator skin by blank-stamping with a die made from an alligator-pattern wrapping paper.

Various subjects and moods suggest particular textures. Obviously, a book about machinery would suggest a smooth texture, while a book on Irish farmers calls for a rough, tweedy feel. The atmosphere of a novel might be slick, soft, or bristly. One book may suggest contrasting textures, another similar ones. At the other extreme, it may be desirable to employ the literal effect of texture by using a ropelike or canvaslike material on a book about sailing, or binding a book about glass in glasslike plastic. These would be rather special and expensive bindings, but a feasible substitute can usually be found.

As in other forms of symbolism, the esthetic and suggestive

functions of texture can be justified independently. Regardless of the psychological use (or nonuse) of texture in the design, it should be well handled for its graphic and tactile values. However, it would be as much a mistake to make a handsome combination of textures that were inappropriate to the feeling of the book as it would be to use the wrong graphic symbol or unsuitable colors.

The most judicious use of symbolism alone is not likely to reveal the nature of the book or establish the atmosphere. Nor is the expert handling of color or texture able to achieve the whole objective by itself. The typography alone can achieve just so much and illustration has its limitations. It may seem impractical to apply so much effort to achieve the relatively minor effect of a good textural scheme or color combination. It would indeed be a waste of time to carefully develop one aspect if the others were neglected. The point to remember is that *each factor contributes something* toward the desired end, and *the combination of them all* is likely to have a positive effect worth the effort.

In conclusion

A perfect orchestration of superbly handled elements will result in a book that greatly enriches the work it conveys. If the result falls somewhat short of this ideal, it will have value in proportion to the success of its parts—and, in design, the whole can't be any better than the poorest of its parts.

16 | The basic decisions

Having analyzed the problem and visualized an ideal solution, you are ready to begin the decision-making process. This includes the second stage of design: consideration of alternatives, and the final stage: making choices. To some extent, you went through these stages in the creative visualization, but no firm decisions were made because only one aspect of the problem was involved. At this point, *all* aspects of the mechanical, commercial, and editorial problems will be brought into consideration, and the decisions made now must be practical and economical, as well as creatively sound.

It may appear that the middle stage is getting little attention in proportion to the first and third. This is because it is necessary to combine the discussion of consideration and choice. Each choice entails examination of the available possibilities, so there is a constant alternation of consideration and decision as the work progresses. Nevertheless, they *are* successive processes, even if they intermingle so closely in operation that it is sometimes difficult to distinguish them as such.

There are 7 basic decisions. These must be made first because they concern the whole book and they affect all others. They relate to: (a) retail price, (b) size of first printing, (c) trim-size, (d) editorial arrangement of illustrations, (e) printing process, (f) paper, and (g) number of pages.

Retail price & first printing
Two decisions, the retail price of the book and the size of the first printing, are usually made by the editorial and sales departments before the Ms is released for design and production. These require estimating what the market will bear for a book of the kind and size. The procedure appears simple enough with a tradebook; it means basing price and quantity on experience with similar books. However, estimating *correctly* is far from simple.

What seemed to have been a similar book sold 10,000 copies 2

years ago, so presumably this one will do about as well. But there
are numerous reasons why this may not work out. In 2 years (or 2
weeks!) the public's interest may have shifted away from the subject, the demand for that kind of book may have been satisfied by
the earlier book and others like it, or, as is often the case, what *seem*
to be similar books in every significant respect may differ subtly,
just enough to make one a popular success and the other a failure.

The price is a somewhat less hazardous decision, but it too has
uncertain elements. A general advance in retail prices may justify
adding $1 to the price of the earlier book for the new one, but a
slightly weaker demand may not tolerate the higher price, or a
general resistance to higher book prices may develop at the time of
publication.

Variations in the cost of manufacture are a likely source of difficulty. Unless the second book was prepared specifically as a duplicate of the first, the chances are that the production costs will
differ. Editors are not usually familiar enough with production to
be able to spot the seemingly small variations that make big differences in cost. Besides, there may have been price increases in
composition, printing, binding, or materials since the other book
was manufactured. Whenever the Ms is complicated or unusual in
any way, one should have production estimates made before the
retail price of the book is decided upon. Such estimates often are
the basis for deciding whether or not the book can be published.

The remaining basic decisions are involved with the bookmaking process, if they are not always part of it.

The page size of the book is generally an arbitrary decision based
primarily on custom. Economy affects the decision, but in most
cases custom has been shaped by economy, so there is little
conflict. Once a press size has been standardized to accommodate
a preferred trim-size, paper is made to fit that size.

In tradebooks, there are 4 sizes in common use (in America):

5⅜ × 8″ (13.65 × 20.32 cm)
5½ × 8¼″ (13.97 × 20.96 cm)
6⅛ × 9¼″ (15.56 × 23.5 cm)
8½ × 11″ (21.59 × 27.94 cm)

By custom, 5⅜ × 8″ is used for fiction and for nonfiction of minor
importance, usually unillustrated. Fiction by major authors (or of
unusual length) and most nonfiction call for 5½ × 8¼″. The 6⅛
× 9¼″ size is used generally for nonfiction of major importance or
for books in which the illustrations suggest a larger page. Picture
books, i.e. books in which pictures are at least as important as text,
are usually made 8½ × 11″. These customs are by no means invar-
iable, but they do prevail in most cases.

The mass-market paperbacks are either 4⅛ × 7″ (10.48 ×

Trim-size
CUSTOMARY SIZES

17.78 cm) or 4⅛ × 6⅜″ (10.48 × 16.19 cm). The (near) stand-ardization here is quite rigid because of the need to fit retailers' racks. A few lines have special racks for their own size. The higher-priced lines are, in many cases, produced in tradebook sizes because they are often printed simultaneously with hardbound edi-tions. These are the "trade paperbacks"—so called because they are sold in bookstores rather than through the mass-distribution outlets where the mass-market lines are sold.

Textbooks in elementary and high school grades vary little in size—ranging from 6¼ × 9¼″ (15.88 × 23.5 cm) to 7 × 10″ (17.78 × 25.4 cm). They are printed almost without exception on web offset presses with 38 to 41″ (96.52 to 104.14 cm) cutoffs and web widths of either 41 or 61″ (104.14 or 154.94 cm). College texts are more often made in common tradebook sizes, as they are sold in stores as tradebooks also. The most used size is 6⅛ × 9¼″.

In children's books, particularly in picture-and-caption books for preschool children (usually called "flats"), page sizes vary con-siderably. Pages of 6⅝ × 10″ (16.83 × 25.4 cm), 8½ × 11″ (21.59 × 27.94 cm) and 9 × 12″ (22.86 × 30.48 cm) are not uncommon. Teenage books are generally made in regular adult tradebook sizes.

CHOICE FACTORS Deviations from the above usages are usually related to the availability of paper. The price of paper being lower on larger quan-tities of one item or one size (CH. 10), publishers tend to buy as few sizes as possible. Consequently, their paper stock may not contain the customary size and the book will be made in a size to fit the paper on hand. Another influence in the use of unconventional size is the desire to make a big "package" to appeal to the gift buyer.

Actually, books could vary in size by using less than the full dimension of standard sheets—for example, by taking 5 × 8¼″ (12.7 × 20.96 cm) instead of 5½ × 8¼″ (13.97 × 20.96 cm) out of 45 × 68″ (114.3 × 172.72cm). This would waste 4″ of the sheet, or about 9%. On larger orders, the paper could be made to size.

Cost is a minor factor in choosing between 5⅜ × 8″ (13.65 × 20.32 cm) and 5½ × 8¼″ (13.97 × 20.9 cm). The only difference is in the amount of paper—about 5%—which usually means less than 2¢ per book. Going up to 6⅛ × 9¼″ (15.56 × 23.5 cm) involves an increase of about 30% in paper, and probably an in-crease in press cost. Either a larger (more expensive) press must be used, or there must be fewer pages per form—and thus more forms. Generally, the larger the page size the more costly the print-ing per page.

STANDARDIZATION Complete, or nearly complete, standardization of book sizes would result in fairly substantial savings in the cost of production. In the 1950s, some printers tried to lower their costs by keeping certain presses set for one size of sheet, plates, and margins. Books that conformed to those specifications were printed at lower prices. Efforts (particularly speeches) in the direction of large-scale standardization have been part of the book industry for decades. These efforts have not been generally successful and are not likely to be, except in mass-market paperback publishing, in which price is the primary element.

A certain amount of *de facto* standardization has resulted from the manufacture of presses to fit the most popular trim-sizes (see above), but there is still some room for varying sizes within the limits of each press. On web presses, the cut-off (CH.9) imposes a definite limit, but it is possible to vary the roll width up to the maximum for the press.

The possible savings in complete standardization are not, however, sufficient to sacrifice flexibility in handling diverse materials, to warrant the considerable extra work necessary to make all books fit one size, or to overcome the competitive urge to do the unusual or the esthetic urge to see variety, rather than uniformity, prevail. Books are not, after all, purely utilitarian objects. They have an esthetic component that justifies some expenditure of money and effort. It would be more economical, also, to make all houses exactly alike, but whenever this is done there is an outcry against "look-alikes". It is true that the houses in many parts of the world were made alike before the industrial era   the thatched stone cottages of western Europe, the tile-roofed stuccoed houses of the Mediterranean regions, the igloos of the Arctic, the buffalo-skin tepees of the Plains Indians—and we admire these structures without deploring their uniformity, but there was an identity of function, material resources, and environment that justified the similarity. In books, almost every problem is unique, so the solutions cannot properly be the same.

The basic decisions concerning illustrations are: Illustrations

(a) where they are to occur in the book, i.e. what physical relationship to the text they will have as a whole,

(b) how and on what they are to be printed, i.e. which printing process and which paper.

These decisions are so closely related they must be treated as one. The same considerations affect both, and each depends on the other. Where the illustrations are a major element in the book, these decisions will have a large part in determining all the specifications for composition, printing, and binding, and will influence the other basic decisions. Variations in treatment of the text are relatively limited, but there are many ways to handle illustrations, and the way chosen will have an important effect on the character of the book.

The decision on illustrations must consider 2 factors (besides time and cost):

(a) editorial requirements for relationship of illustrations to text,

(b) the nature and purpose of the individual illustrations.

EDITORIAL REQUIREMENTS   The question is: must the illustration accompany the relevant text and if so, how closely? Usually, the editor or the author can answer this but sometimes they cannot and it is up to the designer to find the answer.

There is no system for deciding when to place illustrations in close proximity to the text. In principle, the arrangement that is most practical is best, and it is not necessarily better to have picture and text together. Unless there is a need for the reader to see an illustration before proceeding (as in a step-by-step explanation) he might be better served by putting it elsewhere so he may read without interruption. Sometimes an illustration is referred to several times in the text, and it is better placed where it is accessible at any time. This is frequently true of maps, which are more accessible on the endpapers or at the front or back of the text than inside. Some books are written with text and pictures closely integrated, but in many cases the best relationship is not so obvious—and must be carefully considered.

The ideal arrangement of illustrations is not always possible within budget limits. For example, it might have been better to place the illustration of 4-color process printing that is now on the front endpaper of this book opposite the explanation in CH.9. However, an additional cost in paper and binding was saved by putting it on the endpaper, where it is so accessible that inconvenience to the reader is negligible. (Also, this illustration makes an attractive and appropriate endpaper design.)

There are several possible ways of placing illustrations in a book. They may be:

(a) printed on the text paper with the text,

(b) printed on the text paper separately (by a different process),

(c) printed on different paper from the text and bound into the book in one of several ways (CH. 11),

(d) printed on the endpapers, or

(e) printed on the cover (CH. 11).

Any combination of these methods may be used in one book. Where there are many illustrations of various kinds and purposes, the best method or combination should be found for each.

Desirability and cost should be considered simultaneously, but it is quite difficult to do this effectively because of the numerous variables involved. Any change in the plan is likely to affect several other factors. The final cost of an alternative may be higher, even though the alternative itself is cheaper. A printing decision may affect paper and binding, a paper decision may affect printing, which in turn may affect binding, and so on. Where alternate plans are being considered, it is usually necessary to have actual estimates made. Particularly in complex problems, guesses are likely to be off.

Assuming that the book will be printed by offset lithography, there is no extra cost involved in printing any black & white illustrations—line or halftone—in the text, so the decision on their placement can be made entirely on editorial and esthetic grounds. If sales or esthetic considerations call for the use of gravure printed illustrations (CH.9), and if the illustrations may be editorially separated from the text, it is possible to save money by printing them separately. Then the higher cost of printing the illustrations will apply only to the pages on which they appear, rather than the entire book. The same applies to the use of color—and particularly process color—illustrations, although this involves a somewhat different question since the illustrations will also be printed offset. (Even if illustrations are in gravure, the text should be printed offset or letterpress to avoid the rough edges of the gravure screen on the type.)

It is even cheaper to put the color illustrations together and print only part of the book in color and part in black & white, but if the pictures *are* placed in the text, both can be printed at the same time. This is economically feasible when there is a relatively large amount of color illustration in relation to text. If the color illustrations are printed separately, and the highest quality is required, they can be printed on coated paper while the text is printed on much less expensive stock. However, the economic advantage may be lost in the bindery, as the cost of tipping, inserting, and wrapping is high (CHS.11,12,26). That is why publishers tend to compress illustrations into one or 2 sections in the book, even though flexibility of editorial arrangement is sacrificed.

Printing the illustrations separately makes it possible to use the most suitable process and paper for both pictures and text. This factor has economic value in terms of the book's sale and must be weighed with the others in making the basic decisions.

The other primary consideration, the nature and purpose of the illustrations themselves, is discussed in CH.7. There it is explained that illustrations have various uses, and each use has its own requirements. It is these requirements that are taken into account in arriving at the basic decisions.

USE REQUIREMENTS

■ *Informative illustrations*—These must be given maximum size and clarity because their purpose is elucidation. They should not therefore:

(a) be reduced too much,

(b) be printed on too rough a paper (this reduces sharpness),

(c) be bled or cropped if significant details are lost thereby,

(d) be printed in colored inks (black or near-black ink or near-white paper gives optimum clarity),

(e) have too coarse a screen (sharpness in halftones increases as the screen becomes finer, provided the paper and presswork are suitable. See CH. 8).

■ *Suggestive illustrations*—These are concerned with effect rather than accuracy, so any treatment or means of reproduction is acceptable if it achieves the desired end. Unless accuracy happens to be the effect wanted, any amount of reduction, enlargement, cropping, bleeding, silhouetting, etc., is justified. For example, it may be desirable to enlarge the screen of a halftone or gray it down until almost all definition is lost.

■ *Decorative illustration*—This is a distinctly secondary element, so the decisions on printing, paper, and binding should be based on the needs of the text, with the illustrations made suitable for reproduction within the specifications chosen.

■ *Representative illustrations*—These are subject to the same general principles as the informative. All decisions must lead to the most accurate reproduction—with even higher standards required in this group. Nothing should be allowed to prevail over decisions made for the representative purpose. Here, the situation is opposite to that of decorative illustration—if necessary, the text must be treated in less than the best way. For example, if the illustrations call for coated paper it should be used, even though the text may not then be as readable. Or, it may be necessary to print type by gravure (which is unsuitable) if the best reproduction of the pictures requires that process.

Printing process & paper

Many considerations that affect the choice of printing process and paper have been discussed already. Properly, these choices are made to accommodate the copy—text and pictures—with due respect for the commercial aspects of publishing. The sales department will certainly be happy with a book that is handsomely printed on the most suitable paper, but they will be especially anxious to have one that makes a big package. This refers not only to trim-size, but to bulk. More than once has a book been printed on an uncoated or matte-coated rather than a gloss-coated paper to obtain the benefit of larger bulk.

The primary considerations, however, are the requirements of illustrations, the choice of trim-size, and the cost elements in binding. All the basic decisions are interdependent, and each must be made in the light of the others.

Behind an intelligent and perceptive choice of printing processes and papers there must be a knowledge of their characteristics. These are discussed in CHS. 9 and 10, respectively.

The number of possible combinations of copy and circumstances in book problems is infinite, and it is obviously impossible to deal with every one. We will, though, take a hypothetical situation and arrive at printing and paper decisions by the recommended procedure.

Suppose we have a nonfiction tradebook with an extensive text and a fairly large number of illustrations. The retail price will be quite high, and the sales prospects make possible a substantial first printing, so it will not be necessary to find the very cheapest way to produce the book. On the other hand, there is a lot of book to be produced, so the budget does have limits.

The mechanical analysis shows that there are 103 illustrations—of which 75 are photographs that can be called informative, and the other 28 are line drawings having a primarily suggestive purpose. A study of the Ms indicates that the photographs need not appear in a specific place in the book, but they should be fairly close to the relevant text. The line drawings are simply to enhance the atmosphere of the text, so they may be scattered at random.

With these factors to consider, we might decide that to print the text and line cuts together by offset on an antique stock would be the most effective and least expensive method. The color illustrations we would print as 32 pages by offset lithography on gloss-coated paper, to be inserted in the book as four 8-page wraps. The use of gloss-coated stock would give us maximum quality of reproduction. The 4 wraps would spread the pictures fairly widely through the book, permitting us to place them reasonably close to their textual references without excessive cost. Most of the book's pages will be the antique stock, so the bulk will be adequate. The text paper need not be too smooth, as the line drawings do not present any difficult printing problems.

For the book you are now reading, it was decided to print the entire book by offset lithography on an off-white paper with a relatively soft surface. The illustrations should appear with the descriptive text, yet there are relatively few halftones, so it was not considered necessary to print the whole book on coated or heavily calendered paper. The text type is easier to read, the illustrations of book pages and type look better, and the halftone illustrations can be reproduced adequately for their purpose on an off-white stock without excessive smoothness or glare.

Given any Ms, one can make a book of relatively few pages or many. Indeed, an effective demonstration of the role of bookmaking is to place side by side 2 books of radically different appearance, pointing out that the Mss for both were almost identical. The designer has a wide range of possibilities for setting the book, and the choice must be made carefully.

Number of pages

The length of a book is determined to some extent by each of 3 main factors:

(a) the size of the Ms,

(b) the retail price of the book, and

(c) the requirements of paper and presses.

The esthetic considerations of format—whether the book should be thick or thin—may have some influence, but this is rare, and is almost never decisive.

DETERMINANTS: THE MS   In most cases, the size of the Ms is the dominant element in the decision and is modified by the other factors as necessary. A very small Ms is often padded out to justify a retail price, and a very large one is usually held in to reduce the cost, but the number of pages in the printed book is ordinarily related to the amount of material (text and illustrations) in the Ms. In any case, start with the Ms to determine the approximate length of the book as it would be normally set.

There are several methods of approaching this answer, depending upon the nature of the Ms and the nature of the problem, but the principle is always the same—you start with known elements and combine these with a hypothesis or supposition to arrive at tentative answers, which can in turn be used to find other answers. You work from the known to the unknown. The procedure used in each case depends on which elements are known. There are 2 main alternatives: (a) a specific total number of pages is required and the problem is to make the Ms fit, or (b) no specific number is required and the Ms is estimated to determine how many pages it will make.

Suppose you are told that the book should make 352 pages (perhaps because a competing book that sells for a higher price is that size). The problem is to determine if the Ms can be fitted reasonably into 352 pages of the trim-size adopted.

The first step is to make an estimate of the number of pages that would be occupied by all the material *other* than straight text.

■ *Page-for-page material*—In the breakdown (CH. 14) is a list of the frontmatter copy, which can usually be counted in this way. A typical frontmatter sequence might run as follows:

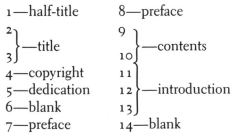

A long introduction may be lumped in with the text for this purpose. A wrong guess of one or 2 pages on the shorter pieces will not be serious at this point. Count other page-for-page material in backmatter, full-page tables, etc. The allowance for part-titles is discussed under "Subdivisions and units".

■ *Character-count material*—At this point, it is desirable to establish a tentative text-page size. On a sheet of tracing paper, rule a rectangle for the trim-size and place within it a rectangle for a text area (not including running heads or folios). The text area may have any size, shape, or position you desire, provided it is far enough from the gutter to avoid the curving of the page—at least ⅝″ (1.58 cm)—and far enough from the outside edges to avoid being cut by the trim. Also, the folding and trimming may not be square so it is a good idea to stay *at least* ⁵/₁₆″ (.79 cm) away from trimmed edges to avoid making irregularities too noticeable. Usually, an allowance should be made at the top or bottom of the text area for running heads and folios, although these may go at the side (as in this book). The most practical distance from the text is about one pica. The width of the text should be measured to an even pica or half-pica. In very large books, it may be desirable to set the text in 2 columns. See CHS. 5 and 6 for discussions of maximum text width.

The purpose of the tentative text-page size is to help determine an approximate number of characters per page for use in estimating the number of pages. A rough rule of thumb is: multiply the width of the text area in picas (exclusive of running heads) by the depth and double this number. For example, if the text page is 23 × 39 picas, the product is 897—so the number of characters per

page would be 1794. While it is possible to have much less or much more on a page of this size, 1794 would be a reasonable starting point.

A still rougher (but even quicker) method is to use 2000 as an average number for medium-sized Mss and 3000 for large ones. While these figures are not likely to be as close to the final result, they are handy for mathematics and they obviate the need for drawing a text area, etc. Since the approximate number of characters per page is only a hypothetical figure which will be corrected anyway, it doesn't really matter how wrong it is, within reasonable limits. With experience, you will be able to guess quite closely how many characters per page there will be in each book.

With an approximate number of characters per page, you can calculate the number of pages to be occupied by any item other than text, if it has been counted by characters (CH. 14). Simply divide the total by your approximate number. If any of this matter should be set smaller than the text, add 20 or 25% to the per-page character number (1794 + 20% = 2152). For footnotes, which are ordinarily set much smaller than the text, add 50%.

■ *Line-for-line material*—To find the number of pages, divide the counts by the text-page depth in picas if the Ms is large, or that number less 3 if the Ms is medium in size. For very small Mss, use that number less 6. In the first instance, we assume that the text will be set on a 12 pt. body, in the second, on a 13 pt. body, and in the third on a 14 pt. body. This assumes also that the text will be about 36 picas deep, so the addition of each point of leading will reduce the number of lines by 3 (1 pica = 12 pts., 1 line = 12 pts., 36 pts. = 3 picas, 3 picas = 3 lines). For example, if there are 363 lines of poetry in a medium-sized Ms, they would take 11 pages if the depth of the page were 36 picas (33 lines of 13 pts.). This method may be used for almost any size page, as the error will not be very large if there are a few picas more or less in depth.

For tabular matter and other line-for-line material which would probably set smaller than the text, *add* 3 or 6 to the number of picas of depth, depending on how many points *less* than a pica the body might be. For example, if the tables were figured for 9 on 11, and the depth of the page is 36 picas, the total number of lines of tabular copy would be divided by 39 (36 picas plus 36 points or 3 picas).

In Linotype composition the *actual* depth of the page will be somewhat more than the theoretical amount. The Linotype system is based on a point slightly larger than the standard (.014 instead of .01384″). In practice, this means a gain of about 1½ points in every 10 picas. Thus, 36 lines of 12 pt. slugs will measure about 36 picas 5½ pts.

In photocomposition, there is theoretically no deviation from the calculated depth. However, careless adjustment of the machine can result in a slight error in the leading. Multiplied by 30 or

40 lines the error can substantially increase the depth of the page.

■ *Subdivisions and units*—The space allowance is figured as follows:

(a) Allow 2½ pages for each part-title—1 page for the title itself, 1 page for the blank backing it, and ½ page for blanks following parts that end on right-hand pages. (As this is likely to happen in 50% of the parts, the allowance is ½ page.)

(b) Allow 1 page for each chapter (½ for chapter sinkage and ½ for the average chapter ending) if it is to begin on a new page. If the chapters are to start on right-hand pages only, allow 1½ pages (there will be preceding blanks as with part-titles). If there are very many chapters and the Ms is large, it may be best to run-in the chapters. In this case, allow part of a page (⅓, ½, etc.) for each one, to account for the space from the end of one chapter to the first line of the next. (This space includes the chapter title, etc.)

(c) Allow a reasonable number of *lines* (text size) of space for each class of subhead—the largest number for the major subheads (perhaps 6), and progressively smaller numbers for the lesser subheads. (This allowance includes the space taken by the head itself, as well as the space above and below it.) Multiply the number of subheads of each class by the number of lines allowed for each. Then divide the product by the number of text lines per page to find how many pages each kind of subhead will occupy. Thus, if there are 150 subheads of a class for which 6 lines each are allowed, they will take 900 lines (150 × 6). If the page has 36 lines, this class of subhead will require 25 pages (900 ÷ 36).

(d) For each occurrence of extract, poetry, tabular, etc., allow some space to separate it from the text. (Make the allowance either ½ line or 1 full line above and below. A full line is best, as the half-line space often creates a problem when the unit starts on one page and ends on another.)

(e) Allow 1 line space for each occurrence of footnotes (CH. 14) to separate it from the text.

(f) Allow 1 line for each spacebreak.

■ *Illustrations*—If there are illustrations that print with the text, a rough space allowance may be made for them as explained in CH. 14. The space allowed should provide for captions also.

■ *Index*—Make allowance as explained in CH. 14.

When everything *except* the actual text has been estimated, subtract the allowed number of pages from the total number required —in this case, 352. The result will be the number of pages to be occupied by the text. Divide this into the text character count to find the number of characters per page required. For example, if everything other than text adds up to 74 pages, there will be 278 pages for the text itself. Suppose that there are 538,050 characters

run-in chapter opening

```
FRONTMATTER
  half title 1 pp, title 2 pp, cpyrt 1 pp, ded 1 pp        6
  preface 2762 c                                            2
  contents 44 L                                             2
  introduction 5250 c                                       4
TEXT:
  538,050 c
  103 L                                                     8
EXTRACT: (p.67)
  5892 c                                                    3
POETRY: (p.29)
  129 L                                                     4
  14 units                                                  1
PLAYSTYLE: (p.162)
  1264 c                                                    1
  10 L                                                      —
  4 units                                                   —
TABULAR: (p.212)
  42 L                                                      1
  12 units                                                  1
BIBLIOGRAPHY: (p.318)
  4922 c                                                    2
  53 L                                                      2
INDEX:
  allow 8 pp                                                8
FOOTNOTES:
  1640 c                                                    1
  14 units                                                  —
ILLUSTRATIONS:
  halftone:75                                               —
  line:28                                                   10
SUBDIVISIONS:
  part titles:3                                             8
  chapters:8                                                8
  A heads:18 @ 6L                                           3
  B heads:41 @ 3L                                           3
  spacebreaks:19 @ 1L                                       1
```

74

```
 352
  74
 ─────
 278

      1935
     ──────
278 │ 538,050
```

*The breakdown with a rough calculation of length. When entering the
figures for each item, leave room for later columns.*

of text. If you divide this by 278 you find that each page of text should have 1935 characters.

If this figure roughly equals the approximate number of characters per page used for your estimate, you may assume that the book will make 352 pages. If the figure varies substantially from your tentative number, you will have to make some changes in your specifications, such as enlarging or reducing the text-page area, changing the space allowance for subheads, modifying the allocation of space for illustrations, etc. If this cannot be done, abandon the idea of making 352 pages and aim for a more realistic figure, either more or less.

When there is no specific total number of pages required, the procedure is somewhat different. First, ideal specifications for text and illustrations are selected, and calculations are made to determine how long the book will run using these specs. The quickest method is to adopt a round number of characters per page as suggested previously and divide this into the character count for text and other character-counted matter, then divide the line-for-line counts by an estimated number of lines per page, and continue to estimate the length of each kind of material as described above. However, a better result is obtained if the number of characters per page is determined by making a page layout, and even selecting type face, size, and leading (CH. 17).

The results of this procedure will represent the "normal" (or ideal) length of the book. This number of pages may be impractical for one reason or another, but you will have, at least, a reasonable figure which can be modified as necessary.

At times, the designer begins with other definite factors which influence the number of pages. The illustrations may be planned for a specific size, the type page may be required to match that of another book, or the type size may be prescribed for editorial reasons. The principle is always: work from the known to the unknown. Use whatever figures or decisions are provided to determine other answers. For example, if you are told that the illustrations must occupy 16 pages, this figure can be subtracted from a total number of pages at the start—or it can be used to arrive at a normal length.

When the second procedure is used, and a normal number of pages is established, a final decision on number of pages is reached by considering the 2 other main factors involved—retail price and the requirements of paper and presses.

Let us say that the normal number estimated from the Ms is 359 pages. Presumably, it is possible to reduce or increase this by about 10% without serious effect. The retail price that seems to be right for the book's potential market is $9.95. In any case, this is what

DETERMINANTS: RETAIL PRICE

has been decided. It is determined that this price won't support a book of more than about 350 pages, considering the illustrations, length of run, etc., but there should be at least that many pages to make the book seem worth the price.

DETERMINANTS: PRESSES
& PAPER

Now we know that the normal length is 359 pages, and the optimum length from the commercial standpoint is 350 pages. What about presses and paper?

The trim-size has been determined as 5½ × 8¼" (13.97 × 20.96 cm). This cuts out of a sheet 45 × 68" (114.3 × 172.72 cm) (CH. 10) which permits printing 64-page forms, so there is obviously an advantage in having a total number of pages that is a multiple of 64. The nearest multiple of 64 to 359 is 384 and to 350 is 320, but these are not very close. If no multiple of 64 comes close to the other figures, a multiple of 32 (a half-form) is almost as satisfactory. (A multiple of 16 can be used, but the printing becomes progressively less economical as the units become smaller [CHS. 9,12].) In this case, five 64s plus one 32, or 352 pages, would seem to be the best number.

In conclusion

The problem has been analyzed and studied in its mechanical, commercial, and editorial aspects. The creative concept of the book is established. The basic decisions have now been made. We know the trim-size, the arrangement of illustrations, the printing processes, the papers, and the number of pages—as well as the retail price and the size of the first run. At this point, it is possible to begin detailed planning of the various parts of the book, in accordance with our overall design.

17 | The text plan

People outside of bookmaking—and some in it—love to say, "A book is to be read", implying that designers are unaware of, or even opposed to, this truism. They seem to assume that the designer is concerned with graphic effects that are unrelated to the process of reading, if not actually obstacles to it. Nothing could (or should) be further from the truth.

The text *is* the book. It is the source of the designers' inspiration and the object of their efforts. Except in some picture-text books, in which the text is hardly more than captions for the illustrations, the text is the primary consideration in all bookmaking decisions. The object is to make it supremely *readable*—which means that it must be extremely legible, inviting, pleasing, and appropriate to its subject (CH.6).

Planning the text is a complex process, despite the often simple appearance of the result. The interaction of esthetic and practical factors must be kept in constant balance during the planning stage, so that conflicts may be resolved without vital damage to either. The demands of readability and economy are dealt with alternately in the following discussion, but they are considered simultaneously in practice.

Copyfitting (I)

In the previous chapter, rough calculations were made to determine the number of pages the book will have. Now refine the calculations to be certain that you do indeed get that number.

The example used gave us 359 pages as the normal number and we decided that we would aim for 352. However, there are several factors that could cause a miss—even though the mathematics may be perfect. The character count might be inaccurate, the author might make changes in galleys, the machine operator might set unusually loose or tight, or there might be an unusual number of bad breaks in chapter endings, subheads, widows, etc. An error of 2% in either direction could easily result from any one of these factors. It would not matter much if we came out 7 or 8 pages short, but it would be quite embarrassing to run 7 pages over. So, instead of aiming directly for 352 pages, we will aim for 344 to get some leeway. This means that we must come down 15 pages from the normal length of 359.

If the space allowances for chapter openings, subheads, etc., were generous, it may be possible to pull in enough pages by reducing these. Usually (not always) chapters can begin on left *or* right rather than right-hand pages, or even run in without seriously hurting the design concept. If it is not possible to reduce these spaces, it is usually possible to save pages by combining frontmatter or reducing illustrations, but it is best to leave such measures for emergencies. Even with the best planning it may be necessary to make a last-minute effort to save space (CH. 20). A sounder policy at this point is to increase the number of characters in the text page—which may not be possible at a later stage.

To find out how much the characters per page must be increased, subtract from 344 the total number of pages of other-than-text (74) as determined in the rough estimate. This will give the number of pages of text you must have (270) which, divided into the text character count, will give the number of characters per page required. Using 538,050 as the text count, the answer is 1992, as compared to the 1935 of our preliminary estimate. Granted that this figure depends on some rough guesses in the calculation of other-than-text matter, it is not likely to be very far off, especially if there is a relatively small amount of other-than-text. However it is subject to further correction after all other calculations are made.

If the alternate method of computing the length was used, i.e. the copy was fitted into a required total number of pages (352), simply reduce the number of text pages (278) by about 2% of the *total* pages (8) and divide the reduced number (270) into the text character count (538,050). This will give the characters per page (1992) needed for 344, the safer objective.

With the basic arithmetic tentatively established, some typographic decisions are in order.

The text   In making choices concerning the text, all the factors of readability should be considered. In CH. 6, these factors are listed and the principles of readability discussed in detail. Since all decisions cannot be made simultaneously, the presently required ones,

    (a) text typeface,
    (b) text type size,
    (c) text measure,
    (d) text leading, and
    (e) number of text lines per page,

must be made in the context of earlier visualizations and general plans. Each subsequent decision is made in the light of the previous ones plus approximations based on the original conception.

Thus, while some of the text-page specifications are not needed until later (CH. 18), some broad plans are necessary now in order to properly develop those required. With the basic decisions (trim-size, paper, etc.) made (CH. 16) and the editorial problem analyzed, what remains is to determine a tentative page pattern comprising the text and whatever other elements occur with it.

The unit used for copyfitting purposes is the single page, but in planning a page pattern, the *double spread* [facing pages] should be considered as a unit. An effective method (but not the only one) of developing the visual arrangement is: (1) on tracing paper, rule the outlines of 2 facing pages in actual size, (2) on separate sheets, rule the outlines of 2 text areas as conceived, (3) move the 2 text areas around under the page outline until the positions seem best, and (4) sketch in a tentative indication of running heads and folios, moving the text areas again if necessary. When the arrrangement is decided, draw all elements on the one sheet. The pattern arrived at in this way is not necessarily final, but it represents thinking that should precede decisions on the text typography.

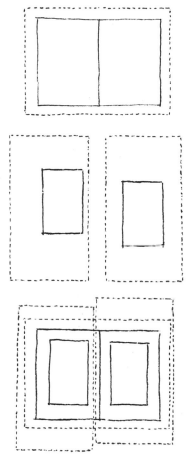

layout of facing text pages

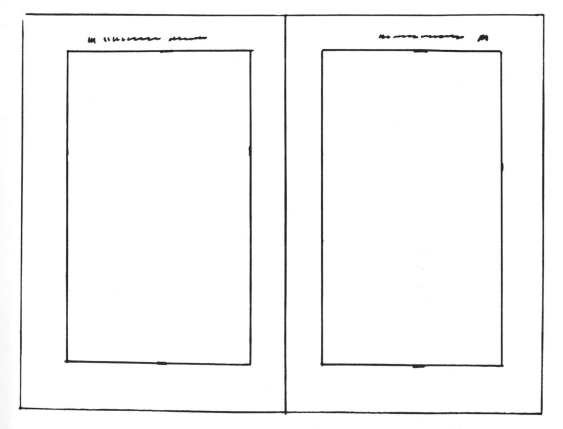

In this book, the pattern was determined by the following rationale: the reader would frequently want to find other parts of the text because there are numerous referrals and the factual and procedural discussions are separated. So, it would be useful to have easy-to-find marginal heads on the outsides of the pages. The ideal width of (10 pt.) text, considering the need to fit in as much as possible, is about 24 picas. To have marginal heads with this measure requires a page at least 6¾" (17.15 cm) wide. Since there would be a large amount of space not occupied by the heads, it was possible to put many small illustrations on the side, thereby saving space in the text. The running heads and folios could also be placed at the outside without using more space, and they would be very accessible for reference. To avoid cramping the pictures, the page was made 7" (17.78 cm) wide. Standard paper and press dimensions suggested a height of 10" (25.4 cm). For economy of space, the text area utilizes as much of this height as is visually and practically desirable.

The text type, Electra, was chosen because it is economical of space due to its narrow width (CH.6), has a clean look suited to the didactic nature of the book, and its tall, narrow shape is harmonious with the shape of the text area. The 11 pt. size is satisfactory for general adult readers, and 2 pts. of leading seems optimum for the length of line.

For the example being used, suppose that all considerations led to a choice of $^{11}/_{13}$ VIP Baskerville $\times$ 23, with 36 lines per page.

Copyfitting (II)

Having made the text-type decisions, it is necessary to calculate their effect on the number of pages. If the result is substantially different from the number needed (270), changes in the specifications must be made. However, these modifications will be final. Note that this concerns the basic text only—refinement of specifications for illustrations and other matter comes later—but in each case the procedure is the same: (1) preliminary calculation is followed by (2) detailed specifications, which are then (3) modified to accord with decisions resulting from the preliminary calculation.

To calculate how many pages of text will result from the specs chosen: (a) find out the characters per pica (CHS. 5, 6,) of the text type and size (11 pt. Baskerville = 2.4), (b) multiply this figure by the measure (23 picas) to get the number of characters per line (2.4 $\times$ 23 = 55.2), (c) multiply that by the number of lines per page to get the number of characters per page (55.2 $\times$ 36 = 1987), and (d) divide that into the total number of characters of text (538,050) to get the number of pages of text (271). This is close enough to the number needed (270) so that no changes in specs are required.

In cases where the number of pages must be changed—unless the difference can be made up by manipulating illustrations or changing one or more of the following:

(a) the typeface (to one that is narrower or wider),
(b) the type size,
(c) the measure, and/or
(d) the number of lines per page.

Changes in lines per page are usually accompanied by an addition or deletion of leading in order to maintain the page depth when more than one or 2 lines are involved. However, if the preliminary calculations of length were done properly, there should be no need to make such extensive corrections. Addition or subtraction of a pica or half-pica in the measure, or a line in the page, should suffice. A change of type face or size is undesirable, if these were carefully chosen for suitability. If a change is made in the dimensions of the text area, its position on the page should be reconsidered. In making *any* adjustments, all of the considerations that went into the original choices should be reexamined.

The various kinds of matter other than text must now be specified in detail so that the amount of each can be calculated. While there are many special problems involved in this material, the same principles of readability that apply to the text are relevant here.

Special matter

There is usually no special treatment of line-for-line matter in text or within extract, appendixes, etc., unless it is one of the separate categories of copy that are counted by lines in their entirety, such as poetry. Sometimes there is miscellaneous line-for-line matter which is neither part of the text nor a separate category, but each such case must be dealt with individually. These items may be telegrams, signs, newspaper headlines, etc.

LINE-FOR-LINE

The most frequently encountered line-for-line matter is poetry. In CH. 28, the treatment of poetry books is covered in detail. Verse appearing in prose text is a somewhat different problem because it is usually in small amounts and is subordinate to the text.

POETRY

As with all brief passages of copy, poetry within text can be set smaller and still be readable. This is good, because it looks best when well differentiated, and it really should be. Poetry in prose usually presents a distinct change in style of expression, especially when quoted from another author. Indeed, it may be set entirely in italic, which has a somewhat more lyrical quality than roman.

It is conventional to center poetry in books having a centered plan, but this rarely works well (CH. 28).

Tables vary greatly in their nature and their relationship to the text, and the ways of setting them vary accordingly. In general, they are

TABULAR

a seed of endless discontent. It is because of men's dissatisfaction with the customs, sanctions and modes of behavior of their age and race that moral progress is possible. New insight begins when satisfaction comes to an end, when all that has been seen or said looks like a distortion to him who sees the world for the first time.

Self-contentment is the brink of the abyss, from which the prophets try to keep us away. Even while the people of Israel were still in the desert, before entering the Promised Land, they were warned to brave the perils of contentment. "When I bring them into the land which I swore to their fathers to give them, a land abounding in milk and honey, and they eat their fill and wax fat, and turn to alien gods, and serve them, despising Me, breaking My covenant . . ." (Deuteronomy 31:20). For this is the way of languid downfall:

> Jeshurun grew fat, and kicked—
> Thou didst grow fat, thick, gorged.
> (Deuteronomy 32:15)

If we should try to portray the soul of a prophet by the emotions that had no place in it, contentment would be mentioned first. The prophets of Israel were like geysers of disgust, disturbing our conscience till this day, urging us to be heartsick for the hurt of others.

> Woe to them that are at ease in Zion,
> And trust in the mountain of Samaria . . .
> That lie upon beds of ivory,
> And stretch themselves upon their couches,
> And eat the lambs out of the flock,
> And the calves out of the midst of the stall;
> That chant to the sound of the viol,
> And invent to themselves instruments of music, like David;

258

---

familiar with as many words chosen from what I aspire to write for all the world!

With the "rhapsody" carefully folded and safe in his pocket, André Chénier met his appointment. It might have been with certain English acquaintances whom he occasionally joined at a club where men of such eminence as Richard Price and William Wilberforce were wont to lead discussions of social problems, or it could have been with a group of artists in Mrs. Cosway's drawing room. But Chénier's inability to converse with ease in the English language would have made him all the more depressed at either a club or at Mrs. Cosway's. So it is more likely that on this day of dejection, when he wanted above all else to forget the "sad circumstance" responsible for his dining in solitude at Hood's Tavern, he had arranged for a rendezvous with a group in whose orgies he participated from time to time, a company of devotees of Bacchus and Venus dominated by Aglaé, Byblis, and other daughters of joy.

> *City of marble colonnades,*
> *Of sculptured images, of trees!*

Late that night, or possibly not until the next morning, he returned to his apartment at the French embassy and filed the "rhapsody" in one of the many portfolios in which he kept his manuscripts. Recently added to the collection, or to be placed in a portfolio within a few days, was an elegy which surpasses the "rhapsody" in showing the depth of the despair in which Chénier found himself at this particular period. The verse pattern he adopted for the piece is that of all his elegies, alexandrines rhyming in couplets.[22]

> *Oh, hard necessity! Oh, heavy slavery!*
> *Oh, destiny! Must I then see, while yet in youth,*
> *My days adrift in this mad flow and counterflow*
> *Of hope and pain—my days, tissues of wants and tears?*
> *Wearied of servitude, of drinking to the lees*
> *This woeful cup called life, of bearing in my heart*
> *The scorn with which the doltish rich burden the poor,*
> *I often summon up an image of the grave.*
> *Desired retreat! I smile at Death, willing and near!*
> *In tears I dare to pray for strength to break my chains.*

Examples of poetry in text; centered and indented.

---

set 2 or 3 sizes smaller than the text. When tables are set on slug machines, the use of horizontal rules usually presents no problems, but vertical rules may be very expensive if it is necessary to cut slugs. In simple tables, each column can be set on its own measure, with vertical rules dropped in between. Complicated tables which require both horizontal and vertical rules can be more economically set by photocomposition. It may be necessary to turn tables the other way of the page (*side turn*) if there are too many columns for the width.

LISTING Lists are usually set in the same size as the text, except where 2 or more columns are required and it becomes necessary to reduce it. Ordinarily, lists can be reduced to 8 or 9 pt. without adversely affecting readability. Under some circumstances (such as a list of ingredients in a recipe) it may be desirable to use a larger size—or even a contrasting face—for emphasis or clarity.

OUTLINE The outline form itself normally provides the distinctions required to clarify this kind of material, so there is no need to make any typographic change. Sometimes, however, the outline is so complex that the customary devices (*indention*, numbered paragraphs, etc.) are not sufficient. In such cases, italics, boldface, or variation of size can help.

SPENCER, D. M. *Disease, Religion and Society in the Fiji Islands.* American Ethnological Society, Monograph 2, New York, 1941.

FIJIAN PHARMACOLOGICAL THERAPY

Plant Drug Employed as Abortifacients		Part of Plant Used and Method of Preparation and Use	Source	Remarks
SCIENTIFIC NAME	FIJI NAME			
Cerbera manglias Linn.	rewa	Inner bark of root is soaked in cold water; drink liquid until desired results are obtained	Field notes	This turns foetus to liquid which is passed out as blood, according to native theory
Hibiscus (Abelmoschus) diversifolius	kalani soni	Juice of leaves used	Seeman [1]	
Hibiscus (Abelmoschus) Abelmoschus	waki waki	Juice of leaves used	" "	

1 Seemann, Berthold. *Flora Vitiensis.* London, 1865–73.

side turn table

Extract is quoted material within, but set apart from, the text, as opposed to that which runs in the text line, preceded and followed by quotation marks. It is important to make clear typographically that such material is from another source, especially if it is by another author. The need for such distinctions becomes greater as speed-reading techniques make it easy to miss a brief attribution preceding an extract.

There are several ways to make distinctions. The use of one may suffice if it is drastic enough, but more likely 2 or more of these devices will be required:

■ *Indention*—The extract may be indented 1, 2, or more ems from right or left, or both.

■ *Size*—The size may be larger or smaller than text, although it is almost always smaller.

■ *Leading*—An increase or decrease of leading is usual, particularly the latter. (It is conventional to type extract single-spaced in double-spaced typescript.)

■ *Face*—Italic, boldface, or even an entirely different classification of type may be used.

■ *Space*—A line or half-line space above and below each item of extract may be used to separate it from the text.

While making extract distinct from text, remember that it also is meant to be read. It can be reduced in size, leading, etc., without serious loss when it occurs in brief passages, but when it is exten-

Two ways of setting extract.

[184] C Y N T H I A

ity Co-ordination, which its chief directed from the thirty-sixth floor of a New York skyscraper.

It is as Cynthia that I knew her and remember her, and it is under that name that she mostly appears in this book, although her baptismal names were Amy Elizabeth and she was known as Betty to her family and friends. Born an American citizen, she twice in her life changed her nationality as well as her surname, first when she took a British husband and later when she married a Frenchman, both of whom were in the diplomatic service of their respective countries.

But whatever we talked about, it would be a great pleasure to see you again. You belong to that happy period that even in wartime exists for those who have a common cause and are especially united where there is a "Quiet Canadian." Long life to him, and to you!

She was brought up and educated in the most conventional, upper-middle-class way, by late-Edwardian standards, with a tiger lurking in her blood, and, unfortunately for her, but fortunately for British intelligence, a cool objective mind. She grew up a passionate, lonely girl, and a far-gone addict of excitement, always set in the most protocol environments. It took a war to stop the war between her two natures. Only as a spy, with a noble cause (essential, with her Edwardian standards) was the pace fast, dangerous and exciting enough to use her total energy and to give her surcease and tranquility. When life was acute, her mind was firm and precise, her aim implacable, her actions swift and exact.

She knew languages, enough about art to enjoy it; she

formed by a network of burlap-covered panels could have had any inkling of the impact that this event would have upon the future of American art. But everyone who wandered about in the din compounded of excited talk, laughter and the strains of Baines 69th Regiment Band ensconsed in the balcony, and loked at the pictures on the walls and the sculptures spotted around the floor, must have felt the electric excitement of that moment. The partitions festooned with greenery, the pine trees, the flags and bunting, the yellow-hued streamers that formed a tent-like cap to the exhibition space, the richly dressed and gay crowd, the bright floodlights and the brassy blare of the band, all helped create a festive air. Congratulations were in order. The AAPS had done the impossible. They had, all on their own, collected and exhibited more than 1200 American and foreign works of art for the edification and education of the American art world and public. The exhibition had been calculated from the beginning as a mental jolt to stir America out of its long esthetic complacency. So it was with an air of exultation that, after a fanfare of trumpets and a few modest words of introduction by the Association's president and the exhibition's guiding genius, Arthur B. Davies, John Quinn formally opened the exhibition.

The members of this association have shown you that American artists—young American artists, that is—do not dread, and have no need to dread, the ideas or the culture of Europe. They believe that in the domain of art only the best should rule. This exhibition will be epoch making in the history of American art. Tonight will be the red letter night in the history not only of American but of all modern art.

It is difficult to be certain whether the Armory Show was the largest exhibition of art held in the last quarter century here or in any other country, and one can pardon Quinn's sweeping assertion, but it was beyond question the most important ever held in the United States to that date and, one might add, to the present. It presented in its over-

184 THE AMORY SHOW

sive, the solution might be to use a different but equally readable type face and size. Note that indention becomes ineffective, unless very pronounced, when the extract occupies full pages, because there is no full-width text for contrast.

Not all playstyle is dramatic script. Any material which is a succession of statements by identified speakers is playstyle. This includes interviews, courtroom examinations, hearing records, etc.

PLAYSTYLE

The problem is mainly how to handle the speakers' names. This is discussed in detail in CH. 28 for the design of plays, but the technique is the same for all playstyle. There is usually no reason to set playstyle within text in another size, unless it has the character of extract, but it is a good idea to separate each passage from the text with a line space before and after—particularly if there is no difference in size.

There are 2 kinds of footnotes: (a) references and (b) explanations. Their treatment depends on their nature.

FOOTNOTES

■ *Reference notes*—These are references to sources and other bibliographical information intended for the scholar and researcher rather than the reader. They constitute a distraction at the bottom of the page and are comparatively difficult to reach at the end of each chapter. The most practical location for them is at the back of the book, where they are most accessible to students and out of the way of the reader. The treatment of reference notes is covered in CH. 23.

■ *Explanatory notes*—These must be read at the appropriate time if they are to be useful at all, and so should appear on the page where the reference occurs. It is an imposition to ask the readers to search for notes at the back of the book (and a felony to make them find them at the end of each chapter). Many, if not most, readers don't bother to read them under these conditions, so the notes are a waste of time and space for part of the audience and a source of irritation for the remainder who do take the trouble to find them.

There is a feeling among publishers, editors, reviewers, and a great many readers that the appearance of footnotes in a book is somehow repellent. The book that is "cluttered" with footnotes is disparaged as a forbidding chore for the reader. This attitude is probably justified, but for the wrong reasons.

After all, if the text is interesting and well written, the addition of useful footnotes should increase, rather than lessen, the pleasure of reading. However, the mingling of bibliographical references with explanatory notes is a real nuisance. At each reference mark readers must go to the bottom of the page to find out whether the note is of interest or not. If not, they must travel back up the page and find their place—probably in the middle of a sentence that must be reread. Where a note *is* pertinent to the text, readers may wonder why it wasn't incorporated in the narrative. (Very often they will be correct in assuming that it was an afterthought which the author found easier to insert as a footnote than to rewrite the text.) Yes, footnotes are to be avoided, but only when they are misplaced or unnecessary. Those that *are* necessary should be placed where they are most useful.

Footnotes may be set in very small sizes, but they must be readable. Very brief notes—a line or two—can be readable in most 8 pt. type with 1 or 2 points of leading. Longer notes should be set larger. In some books, the footnotes are a major part—perhaps 25 or 30%. If these notes are essential, they should be as readable as the text and probably the same size or only one size smaller. They can be distinguished from text by using a contrasting face or a particularly readable italic or oblique.

Footnotes can be separated from the text by a line space when there is a sharp contrast in size. Where sizes are closer, a small typographic device such as a dash, asterisk, colon, or suitable ornament may be set in the space. In some cases, a rule of full measure or nearly so may be required. This must be kept distinct, however, from the full-measure rule ordinarily used above footnote material that has run over from the previous page.

Reference marks may be handled in several ways, and the choice can substantially affect composition costs. The highest expense comes from resetting lines (after page makeup) to insert references that begin a new sequence on each page. This can be avoided by commencing a sequence in each chapter or, if there are not too many notes, continuing one sequence through the entire book.

The reference marks may be symbols, such as asterisks (*), daggers (†), section marks (§), etc., and the doubling and tripling of these. If numbers are used, they may be *superior figures* [small numerals above the x line^2], or the regular text type figures enclosed in parens (2).

The corresponding reference marks in the notes may be either regular or superior figures, although it is preferable to use the same kind as used in the text. In the notes, the use of parens around regular figures is not essential, as these numbers occur only at the beginnings.

The first line of each note may be indented as a paragraph; it may be flush, with the turnovers indented (*hanging indent*); or all lines may be flush. In the latter case, it may be best to separate the notes from each other by some space. Whatever style is used, consider the probability that 2 or more one-line notes will occur successively on the same page.

When there are many short footnotes, it is often possible to set 2 or 3 on each line with a few ems between, rather than waste space by placing one beneath the other.

* This question is discussed on page 273, but in any event *all cop*
be typed in lower case with caps only at the beginning of sentences
and on proper nouns. When setting type, if the specifications call for a

* This question is discussed on page 273, but in any event *all copy s*
be typed in lower case with caps only at the beginning of sentence
and on proper nouns. When setting type, if the specifications call for

* This question is discussed on page 273, but in any event *all copy s*
be typed in lower case with caps only at the beginning of sentences
and on proper nouns. When setting type, if the specifications call for a

Footnotes set in 4 different styles

[7] *Ps.* lxvii, 2.   [8] *Titus* i, 10.   [9] The Manichaeans.   [10] *Ephes.* v,
[11] *Jo.* i, 9.   [12] *Ps.* xxxiii, 6.

It is not necessary to decide on specifications for chapter heads or   SUBDIVISIONS
subheads at this time, as they will be contained within the spaces
allowed for them. Their treatment is covered in the next chapter.

Each kind of special matter can now be calculated for length ac-   Copyfitting (III)
cording to the specifications adopted.

To calculate the number of pages of line-for-line material being
set on lines of the same depth as the text, divide the number of lines
of such matter by the number of lines per page of text. To calculate
copy which will be set on a line of a different depth, first multiply
the number of text lines per page (36) by the size of the text slug (13
pts.) to find the depth of the text page in points (36 × 13 = 468).
Then you can find the number of lines per page for any line depth
by dividing 468 by that depth. So, if poetry is being set 9/11, divide
468 by 11 to get 42 lines. (Drop the odd points left over. These will
be absorbed in the space around each item.) Dividing 42 into the
total number of lines of poetry will give you the number of pages of
poetry.

Prose copy (extract, outline, etc.) should be calculated as
though each kind was the text of a separate book. The only figure
carried over from the text is the depth of the page in points. For
example, suppose the extract is set 10/12 Baskerville and is indented 2½ ems on the left in the 23-pica measure. This gives it a measure of 21 picas (approximately). If 10 pt. Baskerville has 2.6 characters per pica, multiplied by 21 it gives 54.6 characters per line.
Divide 468 by the 12 pt. line depth to get 39 lines per page. A full
page of extract will have 2129 characters (54.6 × 39). Divide this
into the total number of characters of extract to find out how many
pages there will be.

The calculation of footnotes is always inexact, even knowing how they are to be set. It is almost impossible to determine how many pages will have footnotes, which, if any, will run over to another page, or how many short ones can be combined. Nevertheless, the best figures possible must be obtained. The usual procedures in calculating line-for-line and prose copy are followed, with some generous allowances made for combining, frequency of occurrence, runovers, etc.

On the appropriate lines on the breakdown sheet, enter in a column the number of pages calculated for text, each kind of special matter, space allowances, illustrations, page-for-page material, and, if there is one, the index. The total should come close to your objective (344 in the example). If not, carefully examine each item before deciding where to make the changes necessary.

In conclusion In all estimating, it is better to figure a little on the high side than too low. If, after composition, the book should turn out to have fewer pages than estimated, there are usually some easy solutions available. Should the number of pages turn out to be *more* than estimated, there may be serious difficulty. There are several ways of shortening the book, but their use may not be possible in all circumstances (CH. 20).

TITLE: *Example* DATE: 12/2/12
Ms pp: 339

FRONTMATTER
  half title *1* pp, title *2* pp, cpyrt *1* pp, ded *1* pp   6   6
  preface 2762 c   2   2
  contents 44 L   2   2
  introduction 5250 c   4   4
TEXT:
  538,050 c   271
  103 L   3   3
EXTRACT: (p.67)
  5892 c   3   3
POETRY: (p.29)
  129 L   4   4
  14 units   1   1
PLAYSTYLE: (p.162)
  1264 c   1   1
  10 L   —   —
  4 units   —   —
TABULAR: (p.212)
  42 L   1   1
  12 units   1   1
BIBLIOGRAPHY: (p.318)
  4922 c   2   3
  53 L   2   1
INDEX:
  allow *8* pp   8   8
FOOTNOTES:
  1640 c   1   1
  14 units   —   —
ILLUSTRATIONS:
  halftone:75   —   —
  line:28   10   10
SUBDIVISIONS:
  part titles:3   8   8
  chapters:8   8   8
  A heads:18 @ *6L* *4L*   3   2
  B heads:41 @ *3L*   3   3
  spacebreaks:19 @ *1L*   1   1

74 (344) 352

$$\begin{array}{r} 352 \\ 74 \\ \hline 278 \end{array}$$

$$278 \overline{)538{,}050} = 1935$$

$$\begin{array}{r} 344 \\ 74 \\ \hline 270 \end{array}$$

$$270 \overline{)538{,}050} = 1992$$

$$\begin{array}{r} 2.4 \text{ ch/pica} \\ \times 23 \\ \hline 55.2 \text{ ch/line} \\ 36 \\ \hline 1987.2 \text{ ch/page} \end{array}$$

$$1987 \overline{)538{,}050} = 270+$$

The breakdown with final calculations.

18 | Sample pages

With basic decisions and text specifications settled, the design process goes into a largely graphic stage. However, while the details of the book's visual aspect are considered one by one, they are parts of the overall conception visualized earlier, and each choice—no matter how small—should relate to the analysis and must be based on a real consideration of alternatives.

The way to proceed is to have set and printed a sample showing at least one example of each kind of material in the book. This gives everyone, including the designer, a chance to see how the problems have been solved and how the pages will look. Changes made at this stage cost nothing—later on they can be expensive.

For an average book, 2 or 3 sample pages are sufficient. A complex work may require 6 or 8 pages to include all the problems. The object is to make the sample pages as useful as possible in minimizing the number of questions that need to be asked by the printer. This means a careful selection of specimens with typical and extra-difficult problems. You fool no one but yourself by using relatively easy material.

At a minimum, sample pages should show the following (if any exist):

(a) some text—preferably two full facing pages,
(b) an example of each kind of special matter,
(c) running heads and folios on facing pages,
(d) a chapter opening, and
(e) subheads.

It is useful to show a part-title, but this is not absolutely necessary. A careful sketch will usually suffice. To avoid overloading the sample, omit examples of material of which there is very little.

Chapter openings With the text already planned, it would seem logical to design next the running heads and folios, so as to complete the text page. However, the chapter openings set the typographic style of the book, particularly in the choice of display type, and so they should determine how the text page will look, rather than vice versa.

Because the chapter openings are repeated (with variations) throughout the book, their design should be very carefully considered so that *all* of them will look well, not just the one used for the sample. This is sometimes difficult because of wide variations in the copy. There seems to be a conspiracy among authors to make one chapter title so different from all the others as to frustrate any successful design. When most titles have 1 or 2 words, one will almost surely have 12 or 14, or vice versa. So, if small type is chosen to accommodate the very long title, the short ones look weak. If the short titles are set larger, the long one looks enormous.

Chapter openings need to be kept subordinate to the title page and part-titles. They should not reach, or even approach, the limits of emphasis or graphic interest. Remember also that the impact of a single chapter opening in a sample page is one thing, but the effect of, say, 54 of the same may be too much.

The design of chapter openings depends to a considerable extent on 2 factors: (a) the number of chapters in the book and (b) the size of the run. In both cases the consideration is financial. If a chapter opening costs $10 to set and make up, the total cost is not so important if there are only 6 chapters, but it *might* be important if there are 60. The significance of the total amount is relative to the number of books being printed. For example, $600 means 20¢ per copy (about $1 of retail price) in an edition of 3000, but only 2¢ per copy in a run of 30,000.

Before the choice and arrangement of display type is considered, decide on the exact amount of space in which it is to appear. If chapters run-in, this space will have been allocated when the length of the book was calculated (CHS. 16, 17). For chapters beginning on a new page, an allowance of one page was made for each—assuming that the opening would take half. Some change in this is usually possible, so that the space may be more or less than a half page if desired. If there are only a few chapters, the addition or subtraction of some lines of text on opening pages will not ordinarily matter. If the book has very many chapters, variations in the number of lines *may* make a serious difference. To know what, if any, effect such changes will have, it is necessary to calculate the length of each chapter separately (this is fairly simple when the text has no extract, etc., but may be tedious otherwise). You must find out how many lines will be on the last page of each chapter to know which will gain or lose a page when the number of lines at the beginning is changed.

There are several reasons for varying the number of chapter opening lines. You may want to reduce them to make room for

CHAPTER OPENING SPACE

illustrations, or there may be a suggestive purpose in changing the relationship of type and space. Also, don't overlook the fact that this is one of the few opportunities in most books—sometimes the only one—to introduce some space (light and air) into the text.

VII *The Demands of Civilization*

FREUD WAS turning into an adjective and an ism. He who had been disclosing the commonplaces of the home was becoming a household word. Noisily aware and showily advanced circles delighted in finding that they dreamed Freudian dreams and let Freudian lapses slip from their tongues. The sluggard mass before long found themselves buried under mountains of plays, novels, and manuals about child care which reflected someone's view of what Freudianism supposedly was.

Fame shook Freud's balance almost as little as abuse had

the moon is born

When and how the moon was born is one of the great mysteries of science. For more than three hundred years astronomers have studied the moon through telescopes. They have measured the heights of its steepest mountains, finding that many of them stretch higher than the mighty Everest, earth's loftiest peak. They have studied the hundreds upon hundreds of strange circular forms called craters and have given names to many of them—names such as Tycho, Aristarchus, and Herodotus. Every night in nearly every country of the world, men are photographing and making diagrams of small sections of the moon, each hoping that he may discover something new about it. Yet all of their work, which could fill the shelves of a small library, still leaves one of the most tantalizing questions unanswered.

Where did the moon come from?

If you ever ask an astronomer this question, he would most likely say, "We aren't sure. All we can do is guess." But then he would probably tell you about scientists like Sir George Darwin and Von Weizsäcker, who advanced explanations of how the moon was born.

The picture George Darwin (son of the great naturalist, Charles Darwin) painted of the birth of the moon is perhaps the most dramatic

CHAPTER 13

CONQUERORS EAST AND WEST

THE BEGINNING of the new year saw Žižka return from his excursion into politics to his own sphere: the waging of the war. It was one of the unusual features of this new campaign that he began it when the worst of the winter was still imminent. But his peasants were hardly men and by attacking at such time he was most likely to surprise his enemies.

With Chval of Machovice and his friend Peter Zmrzlík as lieutenants, Žižka set out on a long march which took him into the region dominated by the Landfrieden of Pilsen. This powerful alliance of Royalist lords, squires, and towns was the strongest force inside Bohemia with which now, after the armistice with Rosenberg, the country's Hussite forces were still in open warfare.

Žižka attacked the Pilsen region not in its eastern part where his enemies would be most likely to expect him but in the west where he could threaten its connections with Germany.[1] The first gains of the campaign were the fortified monastery and small town of Chotěšov, some twelve miles southwest of the city of Pilsen which he had quietly by-passed on his way. Farther northwest he then took the monastery of Kladruby. Both monasteries had been abandoned in time by their monastic inhabitants. Kladruby was a strong fortress and was now used as such by the Taborite army. As commander of the new garrison Žižka left his friend Zmrzlík. He then tried to go one step further in cutting the main lines of communication between Pilsen and the Empire by investing Stříbro, a town of considerable size and strength, on the main route from Pilsen to Cheb and to German Franconia. At the same time a harrowing war was waged against the outlying possessions of the city of Pilsen.

The people of Pilsen, in a somewhat hypocritical fashion, lodged a written complaint about this treatment. Žižka answered in a letter

[1] Main source for this campaign: Březové, p. 469, Old Annalists, p. 44, Chronicon vetus Collegiati, Höfler, I, 82.

· 199 ·

STYLE & FEELING — The general style of the chapter-opening pages will follow the conception developed in working out the creative solution (CH. 15). If you did not actually visualize the appearance of the chapter openings at that time, you at least conceived of them as being formal or informal, dynamic or placid, masculine or feminine, etc. Now you can interpret these characteristics in terms of the arrangement of the type and illustrations on the chapter openings (CH. 6).

Discussing the characteristics of books in terms of opposites does not mean that there are no gradations or subtle variations. On the contrary, most books will not fall into simple categories. The important thing is to impart to the chapter-opening design the true essence of the book, because this must pervade every aspect large or small, and the chapter opening is the first opportunity to create the proper feeling.

ROUGH LAYOUT — When the chapter-opening space has been decided upon, make an outline of the page (on tracing paper) with the text lines indicated on it, and very roughly sketch in the approximate size and position of the heads, titles, etc. There is no need, at this point, to decide on

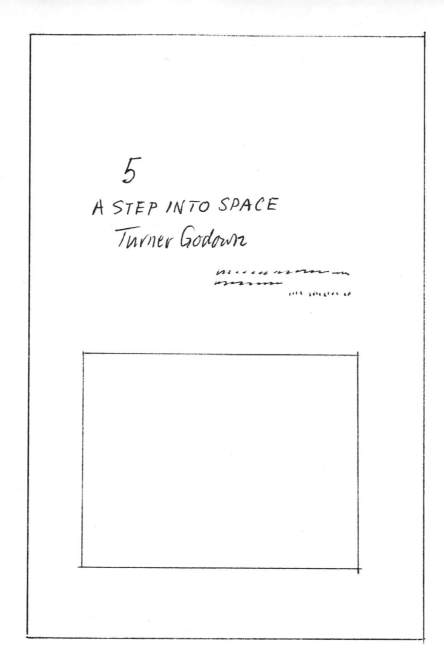

typefaces. The general arrangement should be settled first, with 2 main purposes:

(a) to reflect the relative importance of each element, and
(b) to establish the basic style of the layout.

There are many ways of achieving emphasis (CH. 6), so the designer can maintain a specific order of importance among several elements without sacrificing esthetic or other values. In anthologies and other books in which an author's name and other copy appear on the chapter-opening pages, the problem of creating a proper order of relationships is the same as in designing a title page (CH. 22).

CHAPTER HEADS

Chapter heads [the *number* of the chapter is the head, not the title] are usually the least important elements and are best subordinated unless (a) the numerical sequence has a special significance (as it might in a novel of suspense or a series of lessons) or (b) the head is used as an important graphic element, either because there is no other copy or to emphasize a chapter title by contrast. The word "chapter" usually serves no purpose at all unless it is used as a graphic device, and it is best omitted.

Roman numerals beyond 10 should be avoided in any case where the reader is expected to use them. As the age of the Caesars recedes further into the past, fewer people are able to translate CXLVI or LXIV fast enough for practical use. This archaic form is useful for period flavor or when a decorative purpose is served, otherwise nothing but confusion and irritation result.

CHAPTER TITLES

Very long titles are better set in lower case than caps. Lower case takes less space and is easier to read. (Large amounts of capitals are less readable mainly because we are unaccustomed to them.)

When breaking chapter titles into more than one line, break for sense, i.e. at logical places. Also, avoid excessive breaking. Don't make it too difficult to read the title just to achieve a graphic effect.

Chapter titles are sometimes set like book titles, with all words beginning with a cap except articles, conjunctions, etc. This is impractical, as it deprives the author of the use of capitals for their proper functions—designating proper nouns and the beginnings of sentences. In some books, a lack of distinction between proper

poor sense

SHADOWS IN MODERN
PHOTOGRAPHY

better sense

SHADOWS
IN MODERN PHOTOGRAPHY

nouns and others creates confusion, so it is best to capitalize ac-cording to normal grammatical usage. There are adequate typo-graphic means of indicating the special value of chapter titles without limiting their ability to communicate.

Initials [the decorative first letters of chapters or parts] are usually expensive and rarely serve a practical purpose. They originated as a means of indicating the beginning of new chapters in medieval Mss when there was very little use of punctuation and space was too precious to waste on chapter breaks. This solution is still applicable to very crowded books in which there is little room for space around chapter openings. Initials are useful, too, where there are no chapter titles or heads for display. In most situations they are superfluous.

When initials *are* used, they may be either (a) set into the text (*dropped*) 2, 3, or more lines deep or (b) projected above the text (*stickup*).

DROPPED INITIALS should align with the base of the text line at bottom, and with the top of the x line at the top if the following letters are lower case or small caps, and with the top of the line if followed by caps. The alignment at the top is not vital, but at the bottom, a sloppy appearance results if the initial sinks below the baseline or fails to reach it. Very often it is impossible to find a size of the preferred face that properly fits the desired number of lines. In such cases, the alternatives are to choose a different number of lines or to enlarge or reduce the initial to fit. In any case, be careful of "J"s and "Q"s that descend below the baseline.

STICKUP INITIALS should align with the base of the first text line. They, like the dropped initials, may be followed by lower case, small caps, or full caps for the remainder of the first word, the first phrase, or the whole line. Either kind of initial may be indented or flush.

If no special initial is used, the text may begin in one of several ways: (a) the first word, phrase, or line may be set in small caps or caps with various amounts of letterspacing or (b) it may start with a cap and continue in lower case without any special treatment.

A variant of the display initial idea is to set the first word or phrase in display size, rather than just the first letter. This is effective graphically, but thought must be given to the editorial effect of so much emphasis on these words. There are probably some very special books in which such a device is appropriate, but generally it is unduly distracting.

To some extent, the same thing is true of the use of small caps or caps. In the work of a fine writer, each sentence is carefully designed and the use of capitals where they were not intended does violence to the delicate balance he creates. It can be argued that this affects only a few of the thousands of sentences in the book. It can also be argued that most books are not that well written nor that important. Some writers on book design tend to assume that every book is a classic, but among the thousands of titles published each year, some are fine, some are mediocre, some are hardly more than trash—and each should be designed according to its kind. A classical treatment for a frivolous text is just as wrong as the opposite. However, any typographic device that radically alters the emphasis of words must be carefully weighed.

Indentions of various amounts may be used with any initial style, but it is unwise to indent so far that there is not enough width left to avoid bad breaks. Enough means about 35 characters—and even this may not be sufficient with a particularly awkward combination of words. If the first line consists of letterspaced caps or small caps, the problem is worse.

CHOICE OF TYPE The choice of typefaces for display can now be made. Again, this is a matter of fulfilling a visualization which may or may not have included this detail. In any case, the choices will be based on the considerations discussed in CHS. 6 and 15.

The type size in each case is determined by comparing your rough layout with specimens of the face chosen. It may turn out that there is no size exactly like your sketch. Unless you are prepared to change the face to one that has such a size, the nearest size available will have to be used. Whether it should be smaller or larger than your sketch will depend on the effect of each size on the other elements of the page. *Every time one element is changed, all the relationships in the design must be reconsidered.* If you feel that the type should be exactly the size in the sketch, it should be enlarged or (preferably) reduced from the next nearest size.

THE FINISHED LAYOUT When the type faces and sizes have been selected, the layout can be completed. This means tracing the display type in its exact position and indicating the position and general characteristics of the text sizes. The finished layout should be as much like a printed page as you can make it, within reason. It is much cheaper and faster to make changes on the layout than in type, so, the more accurate the layout, the better you will be able to visualize what the proof will look like.

There are 2 faults that commonly spoil layouts: (a) the presence of guidelines and (b) failure to catch the true character and weight of the typefaces.

■ *Guidelines*—These are necessary to insure the straightness and squareness of lines of type, but they need not show on the finished sketch. Draw them on the *back* of the tracing paper, then they can be erased easily after the tracing is finished. Also, there is no need to draw guidelines on both top and bottom when type is being traced. The bottom line is sufficient. No guidelines or outlines, except the outline of the trim-size, should show on the finished layout. Since no such lines will appear on the printed page, they would be misleading.

■ *Tracing type*—Doing this well requires some practice and a bit of a knack. Laborious effort will help to some extent, but it is not enough. Each typeface has certain features that give it its special look, and you must be familiar with these in order to capture the right feeling. This cannot be done, ordinarily, by tracing the outlines of the letter and filling them in. Try to rough in the *masses* of the lines in their proper weight, and observe the essential forms and details. If the transition from thick to thin is abrupt, be sure you make it so; if gradual, make it so. If the serifs have no brackets, make none; if the ends are square, make them square. Not every detail need be drawn fully and perfectly, but draw enough to convey the feeling of the face. You must learn to put down a minimum of rapid strokes that accurately catch the salient features—not to produce a masterpiece worthy of the Louvre but in order to properly evaluate the effect of the type as it will look on a proof.

Doubt

poor

Doubt

good

For convenience, we have spoken in terms of making all your type selections first, and then completing the layout. In practice, it is better to make the choice of each face and size after having traced the one before. Thus you can *see* what the effect of a particular line of type will be, rather than just visualizing it. Actually, the process of visualization, consideration, and choice are usually intermingled and will vary in relationship according to the particular problem and the individual designer.

Indicating illustrations is discussed in CH. 21.

Choice of tools is as important here as it is in any craft. A certain amount of personal preference is involved, but the necessities largely decide the matter. The drawing tool must be capable of making very fine and very heavy lines. It must be suitable for making straight lines and curves, large forms and very small ones. It must make a reasonably dark mark that is erasable, but should not smear easily. It must move smoothly and be suited to the surface of tracing paper. All these requirements add up to a graphite pencil of medium hardness. An HB or H is about right.

LAYOUT TOOLS

Besides a drawing tool, you need a ruler for pica, inch, and metric measurement, and a right-angle triangle. A T-square is essential for finished mechanicals, but is not needed for making layouts. It is handier to have a printed grid (with lines ruled every ⅛", pica, or millimeter) to put under the tracing paper when drawing rectangles or parallel lines. Grids of this kind on 8 × 10″ plastic sheets are available in art supply stores. If you make mistakes, buy a kneaded eraser. They make no crumbs.

Subheads

Subheads are like chapter openings on a lower scale of value, so problems of design are basically the same: (a) How much space shall each be allocated? (b) How is the first line of text to be treated? (c) What type face and size? (d) What shall be the position? In each case, the decision should be related to the chapter opening, with a descending order of emphasis (chapter title, first order of subhead, second order, and so on).

■ *Space*—The allocation of space was decided in determining the length of the book (CH. 17). If a closer examination of the problem suggests a change in this allocation, some compensating change must be made so as to retain the same total number of pages.

■ *First line*—The first line of text following subheads usually calls for some special treatment, but unless the subdivision is of major importance, beginning flush or setting the first word in small caps is the maximum distinction appropriate. For lesser subheads, the regular paragraph indent is sufficient. In no case should the treatment of a subhead be more distinctive than that of a superior subhead or a chapter opening, as the primary purpose is to clarify the book's organization by indicating the relative value of headings.

■ *Type face and size*—The typographic treatment of the headings themselves should reflect their relationship to each other. A number 2 subhead does not merely *follow* a number 1 head, it is a subdivision of it, and this should be made clear. Remember, though, the average reader is not as sensitive to typographic distinctions as you are, so the differences among classes of headings must be quite pronounced or they may be overlooked.

For economy, it is best to use variations of the text font for subheadings—caps, small caps, caps and small caps, or italics. However, in a complex book it may not be possible to get enough contrast and variety from these alone. The cost of a change of type face or size varies according to the typesetting method and the billing practices of the individual compositor, but it is not a large enough amount (CH. 12) to deter such a change if it is needed.

One of the values of subheads is the graphic interest they add. Many subheads are inserted in books simply to break up the large blocks of text that seem to discourage some readers, especially children and those who do not ordinarily read books. But even where the subheads have a real textual function, they offer opportunities to add variety and visual interest. Contrast with the text is useful not only to enliven the page, but to help the reader find the subheads. The amount of contrast should be adjusted to the importance of the subhead and the frequency of its occurrence. A degree of visual excitement which is desirable in a few places can be irritating when repeated too often.

■ *Position*—The arrangement of subheads within the spaces allowed should be consistent with the style established for the chapter opening. (From here on, the need for consistency must be considered in connection with every choice or decision.) Consistency in this sense does not mean necessarily *the same in form*, but it does mean *the same in spirit*. Achieving a finished book that has real unity—the total visual integration that conveys a sense of "rightness"—is much more difficult than it may seem. It is possible to have the outward forms entirely consistent but the total will not hang together or have the inner harmony that is essential. It is somewhat like trying to make a man by putting all the right parts together in the right way. You will get the form, but you won't get a living thing unless there is something more than that.

Subheads may be centered, set flush left or right, indented from left or right, or centered on some point other than the center of measure. They may be set on a separate line or run-in on the first text line. In a book with several classes of subheads, a combination of these positions will probably be necessary. Be sure to provide for those occasions where 2 or more classes of subhead occur together. The combination of centered and off-centered arrangements should be avoided as much as possible (CH.6) but the needs of editorial sense must be met, even at the expense of harmonious design.

Run-in subheads should contrast sufficiently with the text type to stand out. The use of italics is usually inadequate, although the addition of a substantial space (at least one em) after the subhead may make enough difference. Attention can be drawn to a run-in subhead by using a strong typographic device at the beginning, such as a paragraph mark, bullet, star, etc.

The style and position of subheads must be considered in relation to the running heads as well as to the text. Any subhead may break just beneath a running head, so they should not be too similar. If possible, no subheads should be set in the same size and face as any running head, unless one is italic and the other roman, or one is in small caps and the other italic, etc. Where running heads and subheads are only slightly dissimilar, it helps to set one flush left and the other flush right. Subheads that are numbered, or contain numbers, should be considered in relation to folios. Usually, the subheads take precedence over running heads where there is a conflict. Especially in complex books, it is easier to change the running heads.

The subheads in this book, being outside the text, did not require size or weight to stand out. They are set in small size because of the narrow measure and are in a contrasting class of typeface

(CH. 6) to make them distinct from the text and the running heads.

Running heads may serve as practical guides, as in reference books, textbooks, etc., or they may have a purely decorative function. In books with no part or chapter titles, the book title may be used as a running head, not only to add graphic interest to the spread, but to heighten a psychological effect. (An example might be a book entitled *Pressure*, about tunneling under a river. Repetition of the word "pressure" would give an appropriately insistent quality to an ever-present menace in the text.) On the other hand, repetition of a title of no evocative value is pointless and irritating unless it can be justified typographically. There is almost never any excuse for repeating the book title twice on one spread (i.e. once on each page).

Conventional practice is to use the left-hand page for a book or part-title and the right for the next smaller subdivision (left, book; right, part—left, part; right, chapter—left, chapter; right, subhead, etc.). However, the arrangement should be based on the usefulness of the various heads.

Sometimes book, part, and chapter titles are very similar in wording. It is particularly important in those cases, but useful in all books, to make a typographic distinction between the left- and right-hand running heads if they are different titles. This helps clarify the book's organization, permits distinctions in emphasis, and provides graphic interest. The typographic difference should be sufficiently pronounced to avoid vagueness, and thus confusion. A frequently used combination is small caps on one side and italics on the other. Entirely different typefaces can be used, but this may involve extra expense.

If the titles being used for copy are very long, don't specify widely spaced caps or deep indentions. Sometimes, the titles are so long that cutting is unavoidable, but don't pick a style that will just miss fitting in short or medium-length titles.

The simplest and cheapest way to set running heads is to use the book title only and set it in the text type and size (CH. 5). In general, as composition and makeup increase in complexity, the cost goes up (CH. 12), so the fewer changes of running-head wording there are, the less the cost. If the book title is used, it is set only once (presuming it is set by machine) and sufficient duplicates are made. If subheads are used, there may be dozens (or even hundreds) of changes. This can be quite significant, especially if letter-spacing is used.

Folios vary in importance, as do running heads. In some reference books they are vital and should be prominent in style and position. Other reference books, particularly those with alphabetical-order running heads (directories, etc.), need no folios at all. In any book with an index, the folios should be very accessible. In fiction, folios are helpful to some readers, but most use the jacket flap or a library card to mark their place. (We can ignore those who turn down the corner of the page.)

The most effective position for folios is the upper outside corner of the right-hand page, the closer to the edge the better. The lower outside corner is only a little less practical. The folio becomes less readily found as it moves further in toward the gutter. For books in which the folio has no practical value to the reader, the inside corner, top or bottom, is a satisfactory position.

There is some difference of opinion as to the need for folios on chapter opening pages. They have no value in locating the chapter, because the opening page is identified by the title once it is seen. Indexes do refer to page numbers, but there is usually a folioed page facing the chapter opening. If chapter opening folios *are* used, it is probably best to place them in the same position as on the other pages. If this is not possible, they should still be treated as a respectable part of the page. Too often, these numbers are simply tacked on to the bottom of the page in reduced size without regard for their appearance.

From the reader's standpoint, a good case can be made for the elimination of left-hand folios on many books and the omission of all page numbers on some. Certainly, it should be sufficient in most cases to number the spread rather than each half of it. However, folios are helpful to the compositor, printer, and binder, and it is worth retaining them just to prevent a mixup of pages that might tell us whodunit in the middle of the story.

RELATING RUNNING HEADS & FOLIOS

The relationship of folios to running heads is not too significant, except where having them together enables the reader to use either one for reference. Otherwise, they may be: (a) on the same line, either close together or at opposite ends, (b) on separate lines, one above the other, or (c) on separate lines with one at the top of the page and the other at the bottom. If they are on the same line, it is usually desirable to have at least a pica space between, or some typographic device to separate them.

Bear in mind that each folio means an individually set line. Even if the running heads are simple, if they are to be set on the same line as the folio, they become individual lines rather than duplicates. The additional charges involved in setting difficult running head lines can be substantial, so it is best to check the cost.

POSITION & LAYOUT

If the price of composition is based on emage (CH. 12) there is an advantage in having the running head and folio on one line rather than 2. However, if the book is being stretched out to a larger number of pages by using a small text area, placing one at top and the other at bottom tends to fill the page more.

"It is a portion of a stag's antler. It was, when still fresh, exposed to fire and it was worked with a crude stone implement, probably not a flint; some sort of primitive chopping tool."

"But that's impossible. It comes from Choukoutien."

"I don't care where it comes from; it was fashioned by a man and by a man who knew the use of fire."

The bit of horn came, in fact, from a site in the Western Hills, some thirty-five miles southwest of Peking where had been found, during the preceding three years, portions of the skulls and other bones of a sort of Man that had not been quite satisfactorily classified, but who obviously lived a very long time ago. It was, in fact, some 400,000 years ago. No one in 1930 suspected that this "Peking Man" had used fire. Man's mastery of fire was thought to have been achieved much later on in our history. Indeed, until comparatively recently, some held that fire did not enter into men's lives—at least as a servant—until the time of pots and pans, earthenware; that is to say, in New Stone Age or neolithic cultures which even in the Near East did not begin until some 10,000 years ago at the most, and not until very much later (about 2500 B.C.) in Britain.

A fortunate meeting, then, between two priests in Paris, led to one of them radically changing our ideas about Man's past. Although it was known by some in 1930 that the Neanderthaloids used fire maybe a hundred centuries ago, no one had supposed that the much more primitive "Peking Man" had been a fire maker. Since learning to control fire was the first great step towards Man's mastery of his surroundings—for such control enabled him to see in the darkness and to penetrate into new areas—obviously men, a very long time ago, were more advanced in com-

ing to terms with their environment than had been thought probable. This identification of the Choukoutien implement as having been fired was but one of the many discoveries we owe to the Abbé Henri Breuil who, during his long lifetime, was to revolutionize prehistory—that is to say, mankind's history before the invention of writing—and consequently our views of Man's past.

On the matter of the Choukoutien bone, he was proved to be absolutely right. His deduction of a great fact from a tiny bit of bone was indeed one of his more spectacular achievements. For the proof he gave that hominids (a less question-begging term than "men") hundreds of thousands of years ago used fire gave us new concepts of the life of our remote ancestors and threw light on one of the most puzzling problems in our whole history.

There is evidence that men occupied caves from very early on in their careers. Yet it is fairly clear that man could not occupy caves until he knew the use of fire and could light a blaze to keep off prowling beasts attracted by those rattling grunts he makes while he sleeps (further proof of our kinship with gorillas, chimpanzees and orangutans). The great apes and ourselves are the only mammals to snore, emitting a buzz-saw noise while sleeping.

In Europe, in fact, there is little evidence that our ancestors used caves as homes before possibly 150,000 years ago, during the last Interglacial, or warm, Period between two Ice Ages. But then, until the last Ice Age (or Würm, beginning some 70,000 years ago) men probably did not live in Europe at all during the great cold.

However, in other parts of the earth, sparks from flint chipping, lightning, volcanic eruptions, all offered Man flames very early on in his story. Maybe men played with

has contributed so much to the vocabulary and syntax of other modern western languages, particularly English, that it is almost impossible to gain an intelligent control of any of those languages without it. Greek, on the other hand, supplies major portions of our scientific and technical vocabulary. Often scientific terms which are puzzling in their English form become crystal-clear when they are analyzed into their Greek components. ("Microscope," for example, is "small-see," while "telescope" is "distance-see.") This situation is not at all peculiar to English but applies to all western languages. So widespread is Latin and Greek participation in the terminology of the more scientific, literary, and intellectual segment of European vocabularies that many people think this Graeco-Latin complex will form the nucleus of the international language of the future.

The Latin-Greek role in the formation of modern languages is not, however, merely a matter of vocabulary contributions. The civilization of the Greeks and Romans forms the basis of our common western culture. Views of life and habits of thought that Westerners today hold in common have been inherited from Greece and Rome, having been blended with a new religious element stemming from the Hebraic culture of the Jews and early Christians. Our philosophy of religion, government, human relations, science, and progress rests firmly upon this classical foundation, which has a continuous history extending from antiquity to our own day.

During the Middle Ages and the Renaissance, Latin was the common language of scholarship and international intercourse in western Europe, while Greek performed a similar function in the Balkans and Asia Minor. With the fall of Constantinople to the Turks in 1453, Greek was

reintroduced by refugee scholars to western Europe, and the two languages were used side by side until the final emergence of the modern tongues as languages of written and official as well as spoken communication relegated them to the position of cultural tongues.

Today, Latin is fully available in the American educational system, and it is the language selected by many as their first choice when they venture outside the field of their native English. Greek, once widespread, is now less generally available. The study of Hebrew, once the pursuit of Biblical scholars, has a new vogue in connection with the rebirth of a national Jewish state in Israel.

From the point of view of the individual seeking to expand his knowledge of languages, the claims of the classical tongues deserve serious consideration.

The practical, spoken-language use of Hebrew is limited to the relatively small population of Israel, which is less than two million. The classical Greek taught in the schools has strong points of contact with the modern Greek used by about eight million inhabitants of Greece, and a transfer from the one to the other is not too difficult. Latin, outside of its use in the Catholic Church, has no immediate speaking population.

There is, however, a powerful transfer value that attaches to each of these tongues. Hebrew unlocks the gates to the Semitic languages, and one who knows Hebrew finds Arabic relatively easy. A good foundation in Latin acts as a key to the entire Romance group of modern languages and gives us a sharper understanding of English. Both Latin and Greek give an insight into the basic structure and vocabulary of the entire Indo-European language family (see page 254), of which they are typical. Since some of the languages of the family, notably Russian and the other

Text pages with running heads at top and at bottom.

Except where the demands of easy reference dictate a particular position, there is no reason why the running head or folio must be at top or bottom. The conventional position for running heads is at the top of the text area, but they might just as well be at the bottom or the sides. When they are not being used for reference, they are actually less obtrusive at the bottom left corner than anywhere else. A running head that is flush left at the top has a tendency to read as the first line of the page, particularly if it is similar to the text type and when the space underneath is not much more than the text leading. Compositors are inclined to place running heads close to the text for economy, but there should be enough distance between to avoid difficulty for the reader. An optical space (CH. 5) of about a pica is the minimum needed with normal text sizes and leading. This space should be increased if there is more than 2 pts. of leading in the text.

When the running heads and folios have been designed they should be carefully sketched on the sample-page layouts. With experience, it is possible to visualize these elements well enough to dispense with tracing the type, but it is better at first—and where there is any doubt as to the visual effect—to treat running heads and folios as you would display type.

In this book, it was decided to use the chapter title at right, where it is most easily found when going through the book from front to back (as one would do after using the contents page), and place the chapter number on the left—where it is most accessible to a reader referring *back* from one of the many chapter references in the text. Both running heads and folios are in the upper outside corners for maximum convenience. The line underneath prevents any confusion resulting from the occurrence of a subhead directly underneath.

Margins

It is true that the designer should think rather of relating graphic elements on a page (page pattern) than in terms of margins (CH.6), but, having done so, one must specify margin dimensions in order to indicate the position of the type area on the paper for printing purposes (CHS.9,25).

With the sample page layouts completed, the basic text margins are determined by measuring the distance from the top edge of the (paper) page down to the topmost element of the type area *(head margin)*, and measuring the distance from the gutter to the nearest element of the type area *(inside margin)*. No other margins should be given. The width and height of both text area and paper page are fixed, so that establishment of the head and inside margins automatically determines the other two.

Be sure to allow for the requirements of perfect binding, side stitching, and mechanical binding when planning inside margins of books to be bound by such methods (CH. 11).

Margins are given in inches, because they relate to paper dimensions which are measured in inches. Measurements *within* the text area are given in picas and points, because they relate to type—which is measured that way (CH. 5).

Specifications

The requirements of type specification are described in CH. 5. The sample page layouts should contain such specifications in full in addition to the title of the book, the trim-size, and the text margins. The trim-size and margins are not composition instructions but are necessary for printing the sample pages.

If the text type has both lining and old style figures, indicate which are to be used. The choice is purely esthetic. Old style figures look well in text because they have more space around them, but for some kinds of tables they can be confusing.

19 | Ordering composition

Estimates

The sample pages usually contain enough information to enable an estimate of the cost of composition to be made and, with a few additional specifications, an estimate of the printing and binding costs. In most cases, such estimates are required before production of the book may begin.

It is good practice to have a printed form on which the essential specifications can be tabulated for the estimator's use. This form provides a record of the specifications and enables the estimator to work while the layouts are being used for composition of the sample pages. It also serves as a check list. On the following page is a typical specification form. (With a few modifications, the composition order form may be used for this purpose.) When the sample pages are unusually complex, the estimator may need the layouts, or a copy of them, in addition to the specifications.

For a discussion of cost estimating, see CH. 12.

Copyediting & keying

When the sample pages have been approved by all concerned, the Ms is, presumably, ready for composition. It is *not* ready for composition if it has not been completely *copy edited* to correct errors of fact, grammar, and spelling. Such corrections are just as easy to make in the Ms as in proof, and are expensive if made after the type is set (CHS. 5, 12, 40).

The copy editor should also *key* the Ms to the sample pages where this is necessary. The sample will indicate *how* a number 2 subhead is to be set, but it cannot tell the compositor *which* heads are number 2, which are number 1, etc. Sometimes the Ms is typed so well that these distinctions are perfectly clear, but this is rare. The best practice is to have every subhead keyed with a number (or letter) in a circle. Extract should be indicated by a vertical line in the margin, and any other special material should be identified in the margin by some clearly understood symbol. All

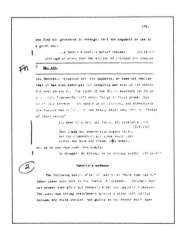

SPECIFICATIONS FOR ESTIMATING

title _____ date _____

publisher _____ designed for _____ pages by _____

type face _____

text page ____ x ____ picas overall _____ lines ____ picas rh ____ picas folio

s i z e s   o f   t y p e   d i s p l a y

text _____   part number _____

extract _____   part title _____

poetry _____   chapter number _____

outline _____   chapter title _____

playstyle _____   initial _____

tabular _____   subheads (1) _____ (2) _____

bibliography _____   (3) _____ (4) _____

appendix _____   running head left _____

index ____ d.c. ____ pages   running head right _____

footnotes _____   folio _____

spacebreaks _____   chapters start: left or right ____ run-in ____ lines ____ right

_____ pages of front matter   _____

illustrations: ____ line @ ____ page each ____ halftone @ ____ page each ____

p r e s s w o r k

quantity _____ trim size ____ x ____ edges _____

text: ____ type ____ offset   illustrations: offset ____ gravure ____ margins: ____ head ____ inside

b i n d i n g

quantity _____   cover material _____

insert _____   back _____ ext. ____ in. on side

headbands ____ stain ____   sides _____

back ____ board _____   stamping ____ imp. ____ foil ____ sq. in.

ends _____   imp. ____ ink _____

jacket _____   sewn ____ adhesive ____

such markings should be made with a colored pencil. When the copy is very complex, several colors may be used.

No matter how complete the sample-page specifications, no matter how well edited and keyed the Ms, a written and signed composition order is essential. One reason is that compositors are entitled to a formal set of instructions to use as a basis for *their* instructions to the plant, and to use in the event there is any misunderstanding—although a misunderstanding is far less likely to occur when there *is* a formal order. Also, neither the sample-page specifications nor the estimate form answers all the questions.

The composition order will vary according to the process by which the text is to be printed, as well as the method of setting. If the printing is to be letterpress, the order must indicate whether or not plates will be made, and if so, what kind of plates, as there are differences in the composition and makeup (CH. 9). If offset lithography or gravure printing is involved, this must be indicated so that the type and makeup will be suitable for reproduction proofs—unless the type is to be set by photocomposition, in which reproduction copy or film is the normal product. In this case, the kind of product wanted should be specified (after checking with the printer).

Proof requirements, at least for galley proofs, should be noted on the composition order (CHS. 5, 20). It should name the authority to be consulted on questions of style, grammar, and spelling—usually one of the major dictionaries (CH. 36)—although a properly edited Ms will not raise any questions other than the manner of breaking words at the end of a line. The proper instruction for punctuation, spelling, and other matters of style should be: Follow copy.

All the other information required should appear in the specifications set with the sample pages. There are certain questions of choice in connection with page makeup which are not included in the composition order, because they are subject to change *after* the galleys are cast off (CH. 5). These are discussed in CHS. 20 and 24.

In most Mss, particularly nonfiction, there are minor problems of composition which are not covered by the sample pages, nor is it practicable to give such detailed instructions in the composition order. Also, some points may escape an inexperienced designer on initial examination. Therefore, the designer should go through the Ms thoroughly before sending it for setting, to find and dispose of any typographic problems not covered by the sample page or general instructions. Each instance should be marked for style where it occurs. Even where the general style has been established and shown in the sample—say, for tables—there may be unique headings or other material within some of the tables and these must be marked. No detail may be omitted, because *some* style must be used, and there may be a delay if you have not made a decision before composition begins. Unfortunately, the rapid pace of most modern book publishing provides too little time for such careful attention, but the best effort must be made.

Below is a typical composition order form.

COMPOSITION ORDER

To _____ Date _____

Title _____

Author _____ Order number _____

Trim size _____ Overall type page _____ x _____ picas

Type face _____ point _____ on _____ point body

Cast off from galleys at _____ lines per page   overall length wanted _____ pages

Running heads _____

Folios _____ Lining _____ Old Style

Chapt. nos. _____ sink _____ picas

Chapt. titles _____ sink _____ picas

Initials _____

_____ lines of text on chapter opening pages

Heads   ( ) _____ _____ pts. above, _____ pts. below
         ( ) _____ _____ pts. above, _____ pts. below
         ( ) _____ _____ pts. above, _____ pts. below
         ( ) _____ _____ pts. above, _____ pts. below
         ( ) _____ _____ pts. above, _____ pts. below
         ( ) _____ _____ pts. above, _____ pts. below

Tables _____

Back matter _____

Extracts _____ space above and below

Footnotes _____

Index _____

Illustrations _____

Captions _____

Galley proof _____ plus _____ B O M bound,

Page proof _____   Plate proof

Reproduction proofs, 3 sets _____ Film _____

Send forms to   your pressroom
                 prints from slugs   cast plastic plates
                                      ship plates to _____

With this order is copy for   sample pages
                               manuscript   complete
                               to come   front matter   index
                               "   "   _____

Remarks _____
_____
                                    By _____

MARGINS: _____ gutter
         _____ head after trim

20 | Galley proofs & castoff

Procedure at this point varies with the kind of book, the schedule, and circumstances. It is certainly most desirable to design the entire book together and have the maximum opportunity to achieve unity—which means planning the title page, frontmatter, backmatter, binding, etc. at the same time as the sample pages. However, this is not always practically possible. Very often the title is not yet definite or some part of the copy is incomplete. Pressures from several directions may require turning attention to other urgent work. Also, where there are many illustrations in text it is often better to first determine the exact length of the text—because this will strongly affect the treatment of illustrations and perhaps front and backmatter as well. This requires waiting until complete galley proofs (CH. 5) are delivered so that corrections and a castoff can be made. (When the design *must* be interrupted for any reason, the value of a strong and complete initial visualization becomes apparent.)

Usually, a minimum of 3 sets of galleys are pulled: the Master Proof, one set for the editor, and one (retained by the compositor) for the castoff. If a dummy is to be made (CH. 21), an extra set should be pulled. In addition to these, other sets are usually required for promotion purposes. These may range in number from just a few BOM sets (CH. 5) to dozens for advance reading by prospective endorsers of the book.

Galley proof corrections

The methods and practices of proofreading are covered in CH. 37. Here we are concerned with design rather than editorial corrections and changes.

Design corrections in galleys (other than changes needed to adjust length) should involve no more than minor adjustments of space, improvements in letterspacing of display lines, and occasional refinement of layout. The cost of *re*setting type is much higher than original composition, so any major changes should have been made in sample pages. In one sense, the opposite is true in computerized setting, where the type face or size or almost any feature of the typography can be changed after the Ms has been keyboarded, simply by changing the codes on the tape (CH. 5). However, there is a considerable cost in running out all new proofs, so such drastic changes are not to be taken lightly, even though the cost is only a small fraction of what the same changes would cost in metal typesetting. Indeed, one of the marks of a competent designer is the ability to achieve the objective in one try. Extensive and/or numerous changes in proof indicate that the designer is unable to visualize clearly or is unable to translate the visualization into effective specifications. The economics of book publishing are not suited to such deficiencies. It is true that first-rate work usually requires more care and effort than the ordinary product, and truly great work often needs to be fussed over and refined repeatedly, but few of the books that are published can support this kind of treatment. Generally, the designer must utilize the available time and energy to develop a conception of the book and improve its preparation. Once production is under way it must continue without major change, or the book will suffer serious, perhaps fatal, consequences in cost and schedule.

It is a good idea for the designer to go through the galleys to check on the appearance of unique items of special matter that were not shown on the sample. Designers' corrections should be made on the Master Proof, in a color different from any other markings.

The castoff

With the galleys, it is possible to determine within a page or two (usually) the actual length of the text, and therefore to make the adjustments required, if any, to reach the number of pages desired. To accomplish this, it is necessary to make a castoff—which involves measuring-off the number of pages in the galleys.

HOW TO MAKE ONE

To make a castoff, cut a strip of tough paper about 1″ (2.54 cm) wide and a little deeper than the full text page. Lay it down on a galley proof or sample page and make a mark along one edge at the base of each text line, for the number of lines on the text page as estimated. Number each mark consecutively, from 1 at the top. (It is useful to make a special mark indicating the number of lines on chapter opening pages or any other frequently used measurement.) Using this scale, measure off the number of lines on each page, making a mark on the galley where each page ends. At the end of each galley, simply note how many lines remain from the end of the last full page and carry this number over to the next galley. When finished, go back to the first galley and number the pages straight through to the end. (Recheck this numbering carefully, it is the most frequent cause of castoff error.)

go back to the first galley and number the pages straight through to the end. (Recheck this numbering carefully, it is the most frequent cause of castoff error.)

Casting-off a book of straight narrative text is fairly simple. Making an accurate castoff of a book containing many subheads, special matter, and illustrations is not very different in procedure, but requires a great deal of care and good judgment. The simple job may left to a reasonably intelligent clerk, but a difficult one is best e by the designer, as many decisions are involved which affect layout of pages and other significant matters. With a particu- y complicated book, it may be necessary to make a dummy 21) since a castoff would be too difficult.

re are 2 kinds of castoff: justified and unjustified.

njustified castoff—This is simply a linear measurement without vance for alignment of short or long pages due to widows 5) or other makeup problems. However, an unlucky sequence idows can throw a chapter over to another page by adding al lines and, if there are part-titles or chapters beginning on -hand pages, this can materially affect the overall length. For reason, an unjustified castoff has limited value.

stified castoff—To make a justified castoff, use revised galley fs if possible. Unrevised proofs may be used if the corrections inor and the Author's Proofs are at hand, so that the effect of hanges can be taken into account. A difference of a line or two ome cases a word or two!) may have a serious effect when the ber of pages is very close to the limit.

a justified castoff, the pages should come out exactly as in cup, which means that all problems must be solved in detail. e include: (a) final determination of the space to be used for rations, (b) disposition of odd amounts of space resulting from er set in lines of various depths, (c) provisions for widows s), and (d) disposition of the various problems caused by run- eaks that fall at the ends of pages.

treatment of spacebreaks, run-in chapter titles, and subheads fall at the bottoms of pages is a major problem of the castoff. osing, for example, that a number 1 subhead is normally in a space, but the preceding text ends only 4 lines from the m of the page. There are 2 alternatives: either the space d the subhead is reduced so that it, and a minimum number t lines below it, will fit, or the page will be kept short (like nd of a chapter) and the subhead will go at the top of the page. This choice requires policy decisions as to:

How many lines of space may be "stolen" from around the (The space may be reduced to the minimum acceptable visu- ut not less than that of an inferior class of head.)

What is the minimum acceptable number of text lines be- e head? (For most subheads, 2 lines are sufficient, for major ads or chapter openings 3 or 4 may be appropriate.)

If the head goes to the next page, how many lines of space be left above it? (This is measured in *lines of text*, exclusive running head.)

same procedure is followed whether the break is a minor d or a run-in chapter. In all cases, the relative value of the must be preserved.

One-line spacebreaks present a special problem when they fall at the bottom or top of the page. Some people prefer simply to omit the space. This solution does eliminate the graphic problem, but it is editorially unsound. The author puts in the line space because he *wants* a break in the text—inferior to a chapter or subhead to be sure, but presumably of some editorial value—and it should be maintained in all cases.

None of the alternate solutions is ideal, and each should be considered in relation to the running heads, if any. The simplest practice is to retain the 1-line space at bottom or top as it falls, but

Casting-off a book of straight narrative text is fairly simple. Making an accurate castoff of a book containing many subheads, special matter, and illustrations is not very different in procedure, but requires a great deal of care and good judgment. The simple job may be left to a reasonably intelligent clerk, but a difficult one is best done by the designer, as many decisions are involved which affect the layout of pages and other significant matters. With a particularly complicated book, it may be necessary to make a dummy (CH. 21) since a castoff would be too difficult.

KINDS OF CASTOFFS There are 2 kinds of castoffs: justified and unjustified.

■ *Unjustified castoff*—This is simply a linear measurement without allowance for alignment of short or long pages due to widows (CH. 5) or other makeup problems. However, an unlucky sequence of widows can throw a chapter over to another page by adding several lines and, if there are part-titles or chapters beginning on right-hand pages, this can materially affect the overall length. For this reason, an unjustified castoff has limited value.

■ *Justified castoff*—To make a justified castoff, use revised galley proofs if possible. Unrevised proofs may be used if the corrections are minor and the Master Proofs are at hand, so that the effect of the text changes can be taken into account. A difference of a line or two (in some cases a word or two!) may have a serious effect when the number of pages is very close to the limit.

In a justified castoff, the pages should come out exactly as in makeup, which means that all problems must be solved in detail. These include: (a) final determination of the space to be used for illustrations, (b) disposition of odd amounts of space resulting from matter set in lines of various depths, (c) provisions for widows (CH. 5), and (d) disposition of the various problems caused by run-in breaks that fall at the ends of pages.

CASTOFF PROBLEMS The treatment of spacebreaks, run-in chapter titles, and subheads that fall at the bottoms of pages are major problems of the castoff. Supposing, for example, that a number one subhead is normally in a 5-line space, but the preceding text ends only 4 lines from the bottom of the page. There are 2 alternatives: either the space around the subhead is reduced so that it, with a minimum number of text lines below it, will fit, or the page will be kept short (like the end of the chapter) and the subhead will go at the top of the next page. This choice requires policy decisions as to:

(a) How many lines of space may be "stolen" from around the head? (The space may be reduced to the minimum acceptable visually, but not less than that of an inferior class of head.)

(b) What is the minimum acceptable number of text lines below the head? (For most subheads, 2 lines are sufficient, for major subheads or chapter openings 3 or 4 may be appropriate.)

(c) If the head goes to the next page, how many lines of space should be left above it? (This is measured in *lines of text*, exclusive of the running head.)

The same procedure is followed whether the break is a minor subhead or a run-in chapter. In all cases, the relative value of the heads must be preserved.

One-line spacebreaks present a special problem when they fall at the bottom or top of the page. Some people prefer simply to omit the space. This solution does eliminate the graphic problem, but it is editorially unsound. The author puts in the line space because a break in the text is *wanted*—inferior to a chapter or subhead to be sure, but presumably of some editorial value—and it should be maintained in all cases.

None of the alternate solutions is ideal, and each should be considered in relation to the running heads, if any. The simplest practice is to retain the one-line space at bottom or top as it falls, but this creates an ambiguous effect. The reader is usually less aware of a line space than that the text is not aligned on the facing pages. When the space falls at the top, it is apparent enough only when there is a substantial running head on both pages. A 2-line space may be used at the top, but when there is no running head even this is not really enough, particularly if the folding is inaccurate. One solution is to make top or bottom breaks more definite by introducing into the line space some unobtrusive typographic device such as an asterisk, colon, dash, or elipse. Although this makes these breaks a little more prominent than the others, it is probably better to emphasize them somewhat than to omit them entirely. It might be even better to use a device in *all* spacebreaks, and thus eliminate the problem.

Where illustrations in the text are involved, the allowance of space must include the picture itself, the caption (if any), the space between picture and caption, and the space separating the illustration from the text.

Adjustments for length

When the castoff is completed, you will know whether there are too few pages, too many, or—with luck—exactly the right number. There are many possible ways of coping with the problems.

■ *Too few pages*—If circumstances permit, pages can be added by stretching out the front and/or backmatter, by starting chapters on right-hand pages if they were left or right, or by making full page titles (backed blank or not) of the chapter breaks. (The latter means upgrading the chapter break value, and should have the editor's approval.) None of these measures requires a new castoff. Simply renumber the pages.

When none of the foregoing solutions is feasible, it may be possible to: (a) reduce the number of lines on the text page, (b) increase the amount of space around heads, illustrations, etc., or (c) if no films have yet been made, increase the size of the illustrations themselves. In such cases, a new castoff should be made.

If only a few pages are left over, there is no harm in having a blank leaf or two at the front and/or back of the book. Where the number of blanks is large—say 8 or more—it is usually better to *cancel* them [cut them off the sheet].

■ *Too many pages*—The reverse of most of the above measures may be applied. In some cases, frontmatter can be telescoped by combining copyright notice and dedication, starting a foreword on the back of the contents instead of on the next right-hand page, etc. If chapters begin on right-hand pages, save the preceding blank pages (CH. 16) by making all chapters begin left or right. Blanks backing part-titles can be saved by beginning the text on those pages. The entire 2 pages for each part-title can be saved by putting the part-title on the opening of the first chapter. Again, no new castoff is needed.

If these measures are not sufficient or practicable, it may be necessary to: (a) *add* one or more lines to the text page (if space permits), (b) *decrease* the space around heads (or even run-in the chapters), or (c) decrease the size of illustrations. In most cases, it would be desirable to make a new castoff.

If all the available measures are used and there are still too many pages, it may be necessary to print an additional 4, 8, or 16 pages—a rather expensive matter, to be avoided if at all possible.

21 | Layout of illustrations

In CH.7, illustrations were discussed from the standpoint of their origin, nature, and function. The relationship of illustrations to text, printing press, paper, and binding were covered in CH.16 in connection with the basic decisions. From the standpoint of layout, there are 3 basic kinds of situation, with several variations and combinations possible. The illustrations are:

  (a) scattered through the text,
  (b) accompanied by some text, and/or
  (c) printed separately without text.

The sizes of the illustrations were determined roughly in calculating the length of the book.

In making the castoff, the space allowances were further refined and perhaps, where there are relatively few illustrations scattered through the text, a specific page was assigned to each one. In books containing a very high percentage of illustrations, the castoff generally determines only the total space to be allotted to them, modifying the rough calculation as necessary. Where the illustrations are printed separately, the castoff has no bearing. In all cases, there is no need to use the sizes originally chosen, but there should be compensatory changes whenever a size is radically changed.

In crowded books, there is a tendency to make all the illustrations medium in size to save space. A better solution, in most cases, is to make some large and some small. This has the editorial virtue of reflecting the relative importance of the pictures (they are rarely of equal interest), it gives the designer an opportunity to cope with variations in quality of copy, and it introduces contrast and variety into the layout.

The sizes of pictures are related primarily to their importance and purpose, but their shape is largely an esthetic matter, provided their

General principles
SIZE

SHAPE

content is not sacrificed. Make an effort to create interesting and varied shapes. A book full of similar rectangles can be very dull. Most photographs can stand much more cropping than is done, so it is usually possible to vary the golden rectangles with some narrow ones and some squares. A sprinkling of silhouettes helps greatly.

CONTRAST & VARIETY In general, contrast is preferable to insufficient variety. While a majestic effect can be achieved by skillful repetition of identical elements, a profusion of similar elements is likely to become boring, unless broken occasionally by a sharp change. Contrast is accentuated variety; it can be used to enliven the page and create a distinct rhythm.

There are many ways to achieve variety and contrast in illustration layout—not only in size and shape, but in value, pattern, style, scale, subject, period, atmosphere, etc. The problem is rather to orchestrate the complex elements into a unified whole than to find means of achieving effects.

Some of the (obvious) ways of producing variety and contrast are to use:

(a) large pictures with small ones,
(b) square pictures with silhouettes,
(c) long oblongs with squarish oblongs,
(d) photographs with line drawings or engravings,
(e) dark pictures with light ones,
(f) close-ups with panoramas,
(g) curving subjects with angular subjects,
(h) crowded areas with blank areas,
(i) old subjects with new subjects,
(j) quiet pictures with active ones,
(k) color with monochrome, and
(l) formal with informal arrangements.

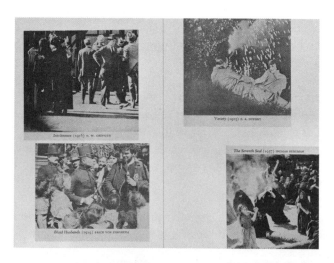

Pages with uninteresting shapes.

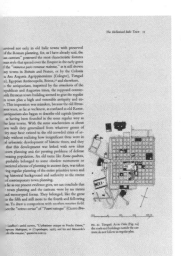

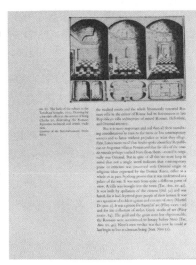

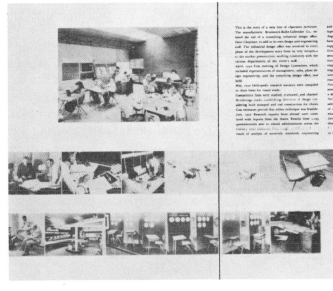

In creating dynamic layouts, it is necessary not only to maintain a sense of unity and order, but to be consistent with the nature of the text. It is quite possible to have a beautiful and very dramatic illustration layout that is wrong because the text is low in key or vice versa. The intensity of contrast and the extent of variety must accord with the book's character.

CONSISTENCY

Regardless of how simple an illustration layout may be, it should be considered as a double spread. It will be *seen* as a spread, so it should be planned as one. There must be an effective balance of all

PROCEDURE

elements on the facing pages—text, illustrations, captions, space, and, if any, running heads and folios.

Layouts should be made the actual size of the book. It is difficult enough to visualize the final effect without confusing matters by using a different size. Thumbnail sketches are useful for preliminary planning, but the effect of small layouts is quite misleading. The best practice is to make a dummy, whether a small signature or an entire book is involved. In this way, the layouts can be related to each other and to the whole. In general, the closer you can approximate the end result in your planning, the less you have to imagine.

Illustrations scattered through text

Four kinds of development in sequence.

In books that have occasional illustrations appearing in the text, it is necessary to determine:

(a) their size and shape,

(b) their vertical position—whether they are to be placed at the top, bottom, or middle of the page,

(c) their horizontal position—centered, indented, flush left or right,

(d) how much space will separate them from the text, and

(e) the style and position of captions.

Thought must be given to the *sequence* of illustration position and size, as well as to the layout of each spread. Variety, rhythm, and order should be planned in terms of the whole book—which has a consecutive order more like a motion picture than a series of separate frames. For example, illustrations might be placed alternately at top and bottom, or they might repeat a sequence of bottom, middle, top, etc. Sizes and shapes should develop in an interesting pattern from first page to last. A haphazard sequence will result in confusion and lack of unity. This is one of the more subtle aspects of book design, but it is real. The book exists in time as well as space—which is one of the features that distinguishes it from other graphic forms.

Runarounds [narrow illustrations with text alongside] are to be avoided for both practical and esthetic reasons: (a) they are costly and inefficient because the text around them must be reset when the pages are made up, and (b) when the lines alongside are short, they usually look poor because of the awkwardness of word-spacing and breaking in a narrow column.

If the book has just a *few* small pictures, it is better to place them in the full width of the text and avoid runarounds. When there are a great many, they may be combined so that 2, 3, or more fit on one page, or it may be possible to place them in the margins (as in this book). The latter solution depends on editorial requirements and relative costs (CHS. 16, 17).

Pictures that occur at the tops of pages or occupy a full page may or may not have running heads and folios. If there are a great many such pictures, the advisability of omitting that many folios is involved. Otherwise, it is simply an esthetic matter. Usually, illustrations look better without running heads at the top.

The space occupied by text can be adjusted with considerable accuracy and little trouble. When only a few illustrations are involved, a miscalculation of the space they will take is not likely to cause a serious error. But, where the proportion of pictures and text is heavily weighted toward pictures, the problem is more complicated, particularly if there is to be a close relationship of illustration and relevant text. Not only is it more difficult to achieve a specific number of pages, but very often the size of pictures must be changed in order to keep them on the same spread as the text to which they refer.

First, the text is set according to the text plan (CH. 17). A castoff (CH. 20) will show whether or not the space allowed for illustrations should be changed. If a drastic change is called for, the illustrations should be reviewed and re-sized accordingly. Small variations can be managed in the course of making the final layout. For books of this kind, a dummy is essential.

Λ blank dummy is made, and the pages numbered. The most practical dummy is a Smyth-sewed, unbacked, uncovered book of about 70 lb. plain vellum paper. This will open flat, yet stay together, and the paper is tough enough to take a lot of handling.

An allowance is made for the estimated number of pages of frontmatter and backmatter, and those pages are clipped together. The text and illustrations must fit into the pages remaining. The galleys (a duplicate set) are cut into pieces of the proper number of lines and taped down. The illustrations are sketched in to complete the layout.

Exactly how the layout is made depends on the nature of the book. If it is editorially sufficient that the illustrations appear within a few pages of the text reference, the problem is fairly simple. Examining a galley or two at a time, the designer can see how many of what size pictures will be needed, and the layouts may be made according to the general scheme visualized at the beginning. It is better to have pictures occur *after* the reference rather than before it but, except for this requirement, it should be possible to make each illustration about the size allocated.

Rather than cut up all the galleys in advance, first mark them off with the appropriate page numbers written in the margin. In this way you can go through the entire dummy, indicating the amount of text and roughly sketching in the size, shape, and position of each illustration. If at the end you find that you have pages left over, or not enough pages, it may be possible to change the front

Illustrations accompanied by text

DUMMY

mortals have the power to destroy much of mankind. We may be used to the fear, but it does not go away. We may shrink from thinking about the unthinkable, but there is no topic that requires better thought. To make us think about it is the purpose of many novelists whose books would like implausible tall stories if they did not dramatize possibilities tha be probable. One specialist in 1

Peter

runaround showing bad word-spacing.

and/or backmatter specs enough but, if not, you can make changes in the text more easily than if the galleys had been cut up.

It is useful to check your calculations at intervals (every 2 or 3 chapters) to see if text and illustrations are being used in correct proportion to the number of pages laid out. This practice reveals tendencies before they go too far and when adjustments are less painful.

The same procedure may be used when the illustrations and references must appear on the same spread, but only if there are not too many pictures in proportion to text. When there are 3 or 4 illustrations for each page, the problem of layout becomes so complex, it is just about necessary to proceed spread by spread—working out each one in considerable detail. In some books (particularly textbooks) where this situation prevails, there is no anticipation of a definite total number of pages. The layout is completed as editorially required, and the front and backmatter are adjusted (sometimes by adding or deleting copy) to make an even form—even if it is a small one.

There are several ways of proceeding with a dummy once the preliminary layout is made. With the galley proofs pasted in: (a) the pictures may be sketched in, (b) photostats may be made to the proposed size and pasted in position, or (c) the illustrations may be sized, negatives made by the printer, and blueprints pasted in (CHS. 5, 8).

These methods involve an increasing degree of commitment from first to third, so the choice will depend mainly on your confidence and skill, although there is not as much difference in cost between positive stats and blueprints as one might suppose (especially when you consider that the blueprints are not wasted, except for the few that may be changed, while the stats are entirely an extra expense). Comprehensive sketches take time to make, and are not nearly as close to the final result as either stats or prints, although they can be changed without any cost (except your time). So, unless it is necessary to obtain approval in the sketch stage, it is just as well to go from rough sketches to blues.

Making good sketches of illustrations is a special technique requiring some ability and practice. The first problem is to define the function of the sketches. Generally, they must give a reasonably accurate impression of the distribution of light and dark masses, dynamic lines, details, and other prominent features. Also, they are usually expected to be clear enough for identification of the picture.

To achieve the necessary effects quickly, it is worth spending a few seconds studying each picture before beginning to sketch, in order to fix the salient points in your mind. Then sketch rapidly with a soft pencil, and the main features will tend to come through automatically. Don't begin in one corner and work your way across,

but make broad strokes fairly lightly all over. This produces a basic pattern which can be refined as needed. Then use the side of the pencil point to lay in the heavier masses of dark tones. Finish by using the point to make a few outlines and details to provide definition and identification. One or two minutes should be sufficient for a half-page illustration. If the proportions and relationships are correct, there is little need for time-consuming details or refinements.

When pasting in galley proofs, wait, if possible, until the corrected galleys have been returned by the author. If the corrections are extensive, have revised proofs pulled. The need for revised proofs will depend on how complex is the problem of fitting pictures to text. In some books, a change of a few lines will be serious, in others, not.

Be sure that each piece of galley proof has the galley number written on it. An unidentified strip of proof might mean searching through a hundred galleys to find 3 or 4 lines of type. The safest practice is to write or stamp the galley number 6 or 8 times on each galley *before* it is cut apart. Even then, watch for strips cut out between the numbers.

The proofs, blueprints, etc. may be pasted in the dummy with rubber cement but it is quicker to use "magic mending" tape—the clear plastic tape which is easy to tear off and has a matte finish that will accept pencil or ink. Changes are easier and there is less mess.

The *principles* of layout for picture-text books are not different from those for books with only occasional illustrations, but the *practice* is more complex. Pictures are more flexible to arrange than lines of type, but they require more imagination and ability to organize. Thus, the possibility of making a stunning layout with pictures is greater, but so is the possibility of making a botch. Not

LAYOUT

only must each spread be appropriate, interesting, and handsome, but it must remain an integral part of the whole book, having a well-balanced relationship to the other spreads and to the basic pattern and spirit of the design.

A sense of order and continuity can sometimes be created amid a profusion of varied layouts by repeated use of a prominent element (such as a running head or folio) that recurs in the same position on all or most spreads. Another effective measure is to repeat the layout pattern of a particular spread. When any of these devices are employed, they should be pronounced enough to impinge themselves on the reader's awareness.

If the demands of the picture-text relationship are not too confining, try to vary the amount of text on each page. This adds variety and provides another way to create an orderly pattern.

Illustrations separate from text

When illustrations are to be printed separately and inserted as a tip, wrap, insert, or signature in the text, the problems of layout are somewhat simpler, although (again) the principles remain the same. Everything said about illustration layout applies here, excepting comments on the relationship of pictures to text on the page.

Of course, the first and last pages of such inserts will face pages of text or blanks, or perhaps the endpapers, and these too must be treated as parts of spreads. Sometimes it is impossible to know what the facing page will be like, but an attempt must be made to find out as soon as possible, and the illustration page should be adjusted accordingly.

While the absence of text (except for captions) on such pages relieves the designer of the problem of editorial accommodation, it creates the responsibility for making a sensible, as well as an esthetically satisfactory, arrangement of pictures. The sequence of pictures is usually decided by the editorial department, but there is often considerable variation in the way they may be combined and arranged. The designer must plan each spread so that it makes sense and must arrange the sequence of spreads so that the whole section tells a coherent story.

Sometimes the editor (or author) has no idea in mind other than to include all the illustrations provided; sometimes a sequence is suggested which can be changed to a more effective order. Even when the editor's sequence is followed strictly, there is need for intelligent thought in layout. For example, if pictures 6, 7, 8, and 9 are related in subject, while 10 and 11 belong to another category, it would be more reasonable to place the first four on two facing pages and the other two on the next page together, than to put 6, 7, and 8 on one spread and 9 on the next page with 10. This seems obvious enough when put this way, but designers sometimes neglect consideration of the subject altogether.

The problem is further complicated by the various *kinds* of subject relationship that could be the basis for an arrangement. The same group of pictures might be arranged chronologically, geographically, or by subject development in a number of different ways. A perfectly good arrangement could be made on each basis, but one may be better than the others.

■ *Captions*—These are elements of the page design just as much as pictures or text. If they consist of just a line or two, they may be used to contrast with a large block of text or a picture. When they are extensive, they become blocks of type to be given graphic consideration of the same kind as the text.

Captions must be readable but must contrast with the text sufficiently to avoid confusion. They are usually brief, so they may be set 1, 2, or even 3 sizes smaller than text and still be readable. It helps to set them in italics or in another face. In crowded layouts, there is often a need to set captions in narrow measures, but there is a limit to how short the line can become without the usual trouble in word-spacing (CH. 6).

When placing captions above and below illustrations, particularly square halftones, remember that there are usually more ascenders and caps than descenders. This means that there is optically more space below a line than above, so it is necessary to specify a little more space (perhaps 2 pts.) between pictures and captions placed below than those placed above. The closer the captions to the illustrations and the larger the type, the more significant this factor becomes.

■ *Credit lines*—Especially where the acknowledgment is to an institution, it suffices if credits are legible. This satisfies any requirement that the source of a picture be identified. There is no reason why obtaining this information should be made especially easy or pleasant. In most cases, the credit line is an advertisement for the supplier of the picture and is disproportionate to the picture's contribution to the book—particularly when a fee has been paid. For such pictures, the credit should be made as inconspicuous as feasible; 4 or 5 pt. type is sufficient. Any position that is visible, clearly associated with the relevant picture, and graphically useful is valid.

Where an individual artist or photographer is credited for a substantial contribution, it is customary to include the credit in the frontmatter. In many books, the photo credits are printed in the backmatter as a list or paragraph.

Illustration proofs
BLUEPRINTS

When a photomechanical plate is made (CH.9), it is possible to have a blueprint or one of its variants (CH. 5).

Prints of this kind are no certain indication of the quality of a film and should not be taken as such. The appearance of a spot or other unwanted mark on a blueprint should be brought to the attention of the printer, as the defect *might* be in the film, but such marks are usually in the print only. And remember that most such prints shrink irregularly.

On *square* [rectangular] *halftones*, the first things to check are size and squareness. On silhouettes, check silhouetting to be sure that it follows the edges of the subject exactly, and that the edges are soft and natural. Watch out for inside silhouetting (such as the space between legs) where the background should be dropped out.

Printers charge extra for the blueprints, so their usefulness must be weighed against their cost. *Loose blues* [blueprints of individual illustrations] are usually ordered for dummying. Page blueprints are standard for checking makeup (CHS. 8, 24, 41).

There *are* prints that are good enough to use for checking the quality of the film, and many offset printers will supply these (under various trade names) for prices considerably higher than those for blueprints. However, even these do not give an entirely reliable indication of the final result, as the plates can affect the quality of halftones (see below).

PRESS PROOFS

In offset, it is not common for press proofs to be made of black & white pages because the cost is usually prohibitive. Unless the proofs are printed on the production press—in which case the press cost is high—the plates used for proofing must be discarded. Not only is this expensive but the value of the procedure is debatable, since the results with the production plates may be quite different. However, where excellent halftone quality is required, press proofs are worthwhile.

In proofs, look for a good range of tones. There should be definition of form in the lights and shadows, and a nice spread of middle values between. Watch out for either a flat, lifeless proof of *all* middle tones or an excessively contrasty one with washed-out highlights, solid shadows, and *no* middle tones.

Remember that the halftone reproduction cannot (normally) be expected to be better than the original, and don't assume that it will be as good. The percentage of failures and mistakes by even the best camera operator is high enough to warrant a close examination of *all* proofs.

For a discussion of checking and correcting color proofs, see CH.9.

The separator furnishes 2 sets of progressives, and one of them must go to the printer. Six proofs should be provided; one complete proof goes in the file and another may be used for a dummy.

For jackets, covers, illustrations, etc., there is often a demand for additional proofs for promotion. There is an extra charge for each proof in addition to the regular number.

22 | Title page & part-titles

The frontmatter is the entrance to the book and so it should be revealing and interesting. It should invite readers and give them confidence that the book will be esthetically and practically satisfying. The front pages should be at least as excellent in every way as any part of the book. In books that have no illustrations or chapter display type, the frontmatter will be the only place to provide interest and variety. This opportunity should not be lost.

Title page The dominant feature of the frontmatter is the title page. To express its relationship to the book we might compare a book to the human body, and say that the text is the torso, the frontmatter the head, and the title page the face.

It is best to design the title page before the rest of the frontmatter. There should be perfect harmony among all the front pages, and it is better to coordinate the other pages with the title than to compromise the design of this key element to fit them.

However, *the title page must be in complete harmony with the text that is already designed*. The title page provides an outstanding opportunity to express the book's character and make an effective display, but it must never fail to be an integral part of the whole book—no matter how excellent it may be as an individual unit. It is sad to see a well-designed text and a superb title page that don't go together. Although the parts are good, the total is a failure.

The tendency to produce unrelated title pages is very common. Designers frequently become engrossed in these attractive creations and begin moving things about without regard for what already exists. To avoid this, it is a good idea to work on the title page with a sample page in full view—to fill the eye with the spirit and character of the text.

POSITION The title page is conventionally thought of as a right-hand page but, as elsewhere, both sides of the spread are visible and thus both

Pavel Eisner : *Franz Kafka* and PRAGUE

Golden Griffin Books [*Arts, Inc.*]

A title spread with all type on 1 side.

are part of the title-page design. This does not mean that type or illustration must appear on both sides. It does mean that the design must reckon with the whole spread—even if there is nothing but space on half of it. Space is as much part of a design as the type and illustrations that form and divide it (CH. 6).

There is no question but that the right side of the spread is the more prominent one. Where a conventional arrangement is in order, and there is no special consideration to indicate otherwise, the title-page type is just as well placed on the right-hand page—and so it is in most books. However, once the type or illustration reaches across the spread it may be assumed that the reader will perceive all of it. The title page is not a poster that must catch the eye of a passing shopper—that is the role of the jacket or cover—it is for the use of one who is already aware of the title and is interested enough in it to have opened the book.

It has been customary, also, to confine the title-page type to the text-page area. This practice tends, as does any uniformity, toward simplicity and unity—2 highly desirable attributes—but there is no reason to be limited to it if your design objective can be realized in other ways. From an economic standpoint there is a slight advantage in keeping the title page within the type-page area in letterpress—in litho or gravure, none at all.

Indeed, not only need the title not be confined to the text area or the right-hand page, it does not necessarily have to appear entirely on one spread. If the problem calls for such treatment, the copy and illustrations may be extended over 4, 6, or more pages. Just as in a movie—which exists through successive frames as the book exists through successive pages—the title and credits may appear in sequence rather than at once. Used inappropriately or ineptly this device could be extremely irritating. Well-handled, it can serve several useful purposes: (a) it may be used to build suspense,

PETER DE MENDELSSOHN

THE AGE
OF CHURCHILL

❈

Heritage and Adventure

1874-1911

New York: Alfred · A · Knopf
1961

A successful use of 6 pages for the title, by Merle Armitage.

(b) it can be an effective way to deal with complicated and/or extensive copy, (c) it can be a means of creating atmosphere, and (d) it can help fill out a short book, provided that the device is justified by a valid editorial purpose.

ELEMENTS The title page may contain all or some of the following elements:

(a) title
(b) author
(c) subtitle
(d) credits (translator, editor, illustrator, author of introduction)
(e) *imprint* [the publisher's name]
(f) *colophon* [the publisher's trademark]
(g) date
(h) copyright notice
(i) quotation
(j) illustration
(k) *ad card* [a list of other books by the author]

The designer's first obligation is to establish and maintain the proper relationship of emphasis among these elements. Ordinarily, the order of importance would be roughly as listed above, but circumstances might suggest an entirely different one. A well-known author's name might be more important than the title. Where the title is "literary" and the subtitle descriptive, it might be best to emphasize the latter. In books that are extensively illustrated it may be appropriate to give the illustrator billing equal to the author's, and so on. The editor will have views on this matter so it might be best to discuss the problem before making a design.

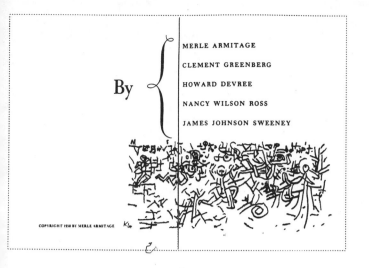

If illustration is desirable at all, some should appear on the title page, where it is likely to be most effective. Especially in books with titles that neglect to reveal the nature of the text, illustration can serve an important function in suggesting the subject matter. It is almost always possible to manage *something*, even on a very small budget (CH. 7).

ILLUSTRATION

Sometimes a "*frontispiece*" is supplied with the Ms. The term is misleading because it implies that this picture is something separate from the rest of the book, and in practice it is often so treated.

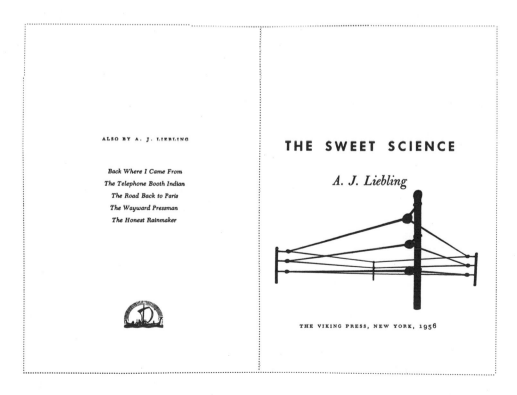

The title page of a book on boxing, with an illuminating illustration by the designer.

But the "frontispiece" is actually an illustration meant to appear on the title-page spread, and it should be treated as an element of the title page. This is true even if the illustration is printed on different paper from the text—as in the familiar case of a halftone on coated stock tipped into a book printed on antique paper. The variation in paper then becomes an element in the design and should be used to good effect.

The popular concept of a "frontispiece" is that of a picture alone on the left-hand page (perhaps with a caption) and all type on the right. Regarding it as a title-page illustration, don't hesitate to move it to the right side of the spread, or to place some of the type on the left with the picture. It is most important to integrate the picture into the spread. To this end, it is sometimes useful to silhouette the picture or, if possible, to separate it into parts and distribute them over the spread.

Two spreads in which a "frontispiece" (not an illustration made for the title page) becomes an integral part of the design. The one at left is by Alvin Lustig, the one below is by Albert Cetta.

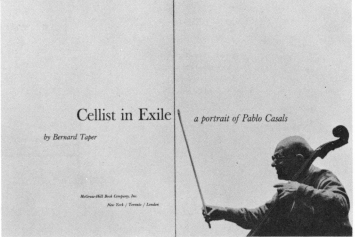

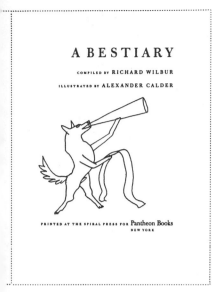
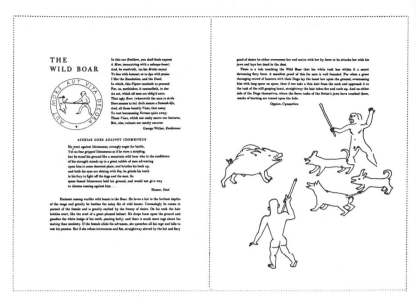

A title page in complete harmony with the text. Design by Joseph Blumenthal.

The title-page arrangement—whether it is symmetrical or asymmetrical—should be consistent with the design of the text (CH. 17). Not that blind consistency is necessary, but the Ms characteristics that suggested the chapter-opening arrangement would also indicate how to handle the title page. In both (and all) cases, the nature of the text is the key.

Nor is it necessary that the same type be used for the title page as for the other parts of the book. What *is* essential is unity and harmony. It does not matter whether these are achieved by using a close match or strong contrast. Sometimes a combination of both is most effective. Quite often, a good result is achieved by setting everything on the title page in the same face as the other type, except for the title itself—which may be set in a distinctly contrasting face. The same principles apply to the other aspects of typography (CH. 6).

Where type runs across the spread, it is important to recognize that the gutter does exist and is a substantial obstacle. Not only does it create a physical break in which a certain space is lost, it is a psychological barrier. Further, unless the title spread is in the middle of a signature, irregular folding may cause a misalignment of the two sides (CH. 11).

To avoid the worst effects of crossing the gutter, use a fairly large size of type. The gutter in a Smyth-sewed book requires that about 2½ picas of space be kept clear, to be sure that nothing gets caught in the fold. In order that this space does not make too noticeable a break in the line of type, it should be not very much greater than the normal space between words or letters—whichever falls at the gutter. For example, if the normal word-spacing is 1½ picas, a space of 2½ picas between words at the gutter will not be too disturbing, because almost 1 pica will disappear into the fold, so the optical space will be just about 1½ picas. However, a word-space of 1½ picas would be normal for quite a large size of type—perhaps 36 pt.—or for a letterspaced line of somewhat smaller type. Since the space needed at the gutter is constant, it is obvious that the smaller the type, the more excessive that space will seem. Also, if the pages don't align, the fault is less noticeable when the type is larger.

In both examples the space between BOOK and MAKING is the same. In both, also, the pages are ⅛" out of alignment (in original size).

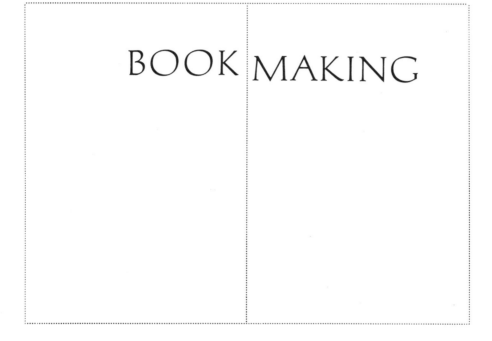

In a perfect-bound book, add 1½ picas (before trim) to the gutter space, and in side-stitched books, add 3 picas. In both cases, the optical space remaining will be about 1½ picas, as in Smyth-sewed books (CH. 11).

When a second color is used on a title page, it should be used as part of the design. Rather than merely adding an element of gaud to the page, it should serve an editorial and graphic purpose (CH. 15).   COLOR

Color can be used to establish emphasis, to create atmosphere, or to make graphic distinctions not otherwise possible. The conventional use of a second color is to print the title or a small illustration, but there are many other possibilities. Graphic elements in color may overprint the type successfully if they are light enough. Print a pattern or a solid panel with some or all elements dropped out. Color borders have always been used, but there are certainly new ways to use them. When appropriate, a ghost effect may be obtained.

When using color on the title page, consider using it also on other pages on the same side of the sheet, as virtually no additional cost is involved. Be sure, though, that the color makes sense wherever used. It is better not to use it at all than to throw it in simply because it is available.

The effect of a second color may be lost to a large degree if it is too dark. Particularly where it appears in small areas, the color is affected by its contrast in value with the paper. When this contrast is almost as great as that of the black, the color (hue) itself becomes relatively unnoticeable. Second colors that are not more than 50% of the value of the black ink are most effective. The intensity of the color has some effect here, but not as much as the value, except in extreme cases.

In choosing a swatch of color to be matched, remember that color looks lighter in value and more intense in large areas than in small ones. This is especially significant when the color will be used for type or fairly narrow lines, where the printed color will look considerably darker than on the swatch, even if the ink is an exact match (also due to the effect of contrast with the white background). To avoid this difficulty, choose a swatch somewhat lighter than you want the color to look. And remember that type printed in color will not look as heavy as when black. It may be necessary to compensate by using a larger or heavier face.

Part-titles fall between chapter opening and title page in emphasis. As there is this order of interest and value among these elements of the book, it is important to keep all of them in mind while working on each one. You may find it more satisfactory to design the part-titles before the title page, but don't make them so much more   Part-titles dramatic than the chapter openings that there is no room for a still more important treatment of the title. If the title page is done first, it should be enough stronger than the chapters to allow for the part-titles to fall in between.

The part-titles may include echoes or reiterations of a title-page motif. This tends to unify the design and enhance the effect of the title page.

When appropriate, part-titles may vary considerably to reflect the nature of differing parts. For example, if the parts each deal with a different era, the titles might be designed in the styles of each period. With such an arrangement, although the part-titles are entirely unlike each other, they must nevertheless preserve the unity and identity of the book. (This sounds like a tall order, but it is possible.)

Don't overlook the value of part-titles as opportunities to inject space into a book. When the text is crowded and there is not much space around chapter openings and subheads, it may be best to hold down the size of part-title type to get the relief of white space.

There are usually few practical demands on part-title pages, so there is a great opportunity to use imagination in their treatment. In general, the considerations of typography, layout, illustration, etc. that apply to title pages are valid for part-titles as well.

This design by John Begg carries the title page feeling through the book by using the same typeface and size for the title and part-titles, varying only the position on the page.

23 | Frontmatter & backmatter

The treatment of frontmatter pages is determined mainly by the design of the rest of the book, where a pattern of layout, typography, and feeling has been established. The problem is to design the frontmatter pages so that each will be entirely suited to its purpose and yet fit into the established patterns. Each page must be given careful consideration, no matter how unimportant it may seem to be.

Generally, the display type and layout on frontmatter pages is the same as that of chapter openings, but not always. Items of lesser importance may be given subordinate headings, which may or may not appear elsewhere in the book, or it may even be desirable to use entirely different display type.

The sequence of frontmatter is a subject of some dispute. There are various arrangements suggested by different authorities, and a good case can be made for an order different from any of those. Below is a sequence widely accepted as proper:

  (1) half-title
  (2) ad card
  (3) title
  (4) copyright
  (5) dedication
  (6) acknowledgments
  (7) preface (or foreword)
  (8) contents
  (9) list of illustrations
 (10) introduction
 (11) second half-title (or first part-title)

These elements will be discussed in the order given above.

The half-title before the title is a superfluous anachronism. It HALF-TITLE originated when books were stored and sold without covers, to be

The	•
Tables	•
Of	•
The	•
Law	•

Although Paul Rand used the half-title, it is incorporated in a strongly suggestive design element.

bound individually for the purchaser. For protection, the title page was printed on p. 3, so p. 1 needed the title for outer identification of the volume. This requirement has not existed on any large scale for generations, but the practice hangs on.

The first half-title may be eliminated entirely and the page left blank, or the page may be used for some other purpose. Much can be said for placing the dedication there. An inscription and/or autograph by the author is ordinarily written on this page (or the flyleaf of the endpaper), so it seems reasonable that the dedication should appear at the very beginning of the book rather than several pages back.

Page 1 may be used for a symbol or other element that sets the tone of the book or that builds up to the title page. This might be a quotation supplied by the author, it might be an illustration suggestive of the whole book, it might be an element of the title page (such as a subtitle or a series title), or it could be the author's initials. This is a wonderful opportunity to set the stage or play an overture.

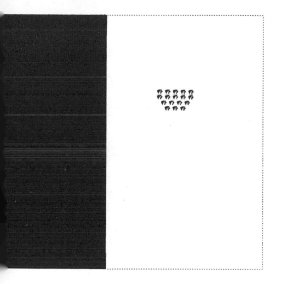

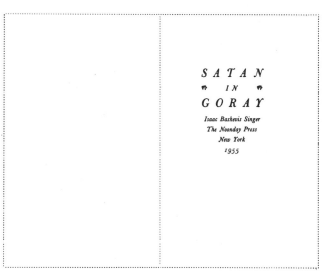

In this book designed by the author, a pattern of type ornaments is used on page 1 to introduce the title page.

One possibility is to use p. 1 for a blurb about the book. This is a logical substitute for the jacket flap copy when there is to be no jacket (CH. 26).

If the title *must* be repeated here, it should be made as inconspicuous as possible. Bear in mind that it appears on the jacket, binding, title page, and (sometimes) the second half-title as well. The repetition is particularly irritating if there is little frontmatter, when the title page is preceded and followed by half-titles in rapid succession.

In designing p. 1, remember that it is part of a spread, of which the other part is the endpaper. Also, consider what will happen to p. 2 when the material on p. 1 shows through, especially when 2 is part of the title spread. Try to back up all elements, particularly in books using lightweight paper.

The ad card is generally on the title page, but it is just as effective on another except, perhaps, where it is desirable to call attention to a successful previous work by a little-known author. In this case, the older form of ad is sometimes used, i.e. "author of . . ." is placed beneath the author's name. Usually, there is a separate

AD CARD

heading ("other books by . . .", etc.) under which the titles are listed. Wherever it appears, this type may be quite small.

When it is not on the title spread, the ad card is usually placed ahead of it—which requires at least 2 additional pages. The usual practice is to put the ad on p. 3, making the title spread 4 and 5.

TITLE PAGE See CH. 22.

COPYRIGHT NOTICE The copyright notice customarily appears on the page backing the right side of the title spread or, occasionally, on the title page itself.*

Other material than the notice usually appears with it. The Library of Congress catalogue card number is almost always on the copyright page, where it is usually incorporated with the CIP (Cataloging in Publication) data (a reproduction of the reference card used by libraries) that many publishers print in their books to facilitate cataloging. The CIP card is one of the rare designs that is both functional and homely. Perhaps it is convenient for librarians to have it on the copyright page, but it is a typographic blight and is probably just as useful at the back of the book where it will not offend. Another reference aid is the ISBN (International Standard Book Number), which provides a unique identification for every title to which such a number is assigned. This is a valuable tool for book distribution.

The country in which the book was printed is almost always indicated on the copyright page, particularly if it is the United States of America. Under both the old and new (1978) copyright laws, the copyright of a work by a U.S. citizen is affected by the place of printing (CHS. 7, 35). In many countries, this information is required by the customs service. The printer's name frequently is added, as well as a credit for the designer. Acknowledgments that involve copyrights (as in anthologies) should appear on the copyright page. If there are too many to fit on this page, they should begin on it and run over to the next page. (There is a divergence of legal opinion in this matter.)

The copyright notice is not meant for the reader and may be set very small. As in credits on pictures, legibility is all that is required. Occasionally, more important credits are included, and they are set larger.

Although the copyright-page content is usually of little interest, the type on it is a graphic element of the book no less important than any other. (In design, there are no unimportant parts. Everything must be on the same level of quality or the whole loses its wholeness.) The copyright notice may be greatly subordinated in *emphasis*, but it must be entirely consistent in *style* with the rest of

---

*The 1978 copyright law requires only that the notice be put in a "reasonable" place.

the book. It is necessary to stress this point because it is so common to see copyright pages that are badly at odds with the general scheme. Even in many otherwise well-designed books, one sees the copyright notice set as though it had not been given a thought. The most frequent fault is the use of a centered arrangement in a book that has an asymmetrical pattern, or vice versa. The effect is jarring.

The copyright page is part of a spread that includes the facing page, and should be designed as such. However, try to back up

A spread with copyright notice poorly related.

COPYRIGHT, 1946, BY JAMES M. CAIN

All rights reserved. No part of this book may be reproduced in any form without permission in writing from the publisher, except by a reviewer who may quote brief passages in a review to be printed in a magazine or newspaper.

FIRST PRINTING, MAY, 1949
SECOND PRINTING, NOVEMBER, 1949
THIRD PRINTING, DECEMBER, 1949
FOURTH PRINTING, MAY, 1955

Preface

THIS STORY goes back to 1922, when I was much under the spell of the Big Sandy country and anxious to make it the locale of a novel that would deal with its mine wars and utilize its "beautiful bleak ugliness," as I called it at the time, as setting. I went down there, worked in its mines, studied, trudged, and crammed, but when I came back was unequal to the novel; indeed, it was another ten years before it entered my mind again that I might be able to write a novel, for I had at least learned it is no easy trick, despite a large body of opinion to the contrary. But then I did write a novel, and the earlier idea began recurring to me—not the part about labor, for reflection had long since convinced me that this theme, though it constantly attracts a certain type of intellectual, is really dead seed for a novelist—but the rocky, wooded countryside itself, together with the clear, cool creeks that purl through it, and its gentle, charming inhabitants, whose little hamlets quite often look as they must have looked in the time of Daniel Boone. And then one day, in California, I encountered a family from Kentucky, running a roadside sandwich place. Certain reticences about a charming little boy they had led me to suspect he was the reason for the hegira from Harlan County, and the idea for a story began to take shape in my mind

v

A well-designed spread.

Library of Congress Catalog No. 63–13496
Copyright © The Joseph H. Hirshhorn Foundation

All rights reserved. No part of this book may be reproduced in any form without permission in writing from The Joseph H. Hirshhorn Foundation, except by a reviewer who may quote brief passages in a review to be printed in a magazine or newspaper.

Distributed simultaneously in Canada by McClelland and Stewart, Ltd.
Manufactured in the United States of America by H. Wolff, New York

The pine tree, used on flags during the American Revolution, was the official emblem of the Armory Show. The lettering used for the title on the title-page and the initials at the beginning of each chapter is adapted from the cover of the March, 1913 issue of Arts and Decoration that featured the original Armory Show.

To
The members of the
Association of American Painters and Sculptors,
in memory.

elements of the title page with copyright-page copy, to avoid the latter showing through in open areas. To accomplish this, the copy may be set in any reasonable and suitable arrangement—line for line, centered, flush left or right, run-in in a block, all together, or in 2 or more parts.

DEDICATION

If there is a dedication, it usually appears on the page facing the copyright, although the first page seems a more logical position. When frontmatter is being compressed to save pages, the dedication is sometimes placed on the copyright page itself.

The dedication should dominate the spread, but it should not be too large. Text type size is about right under most circumstances. Names can be given added importance by setting them in small caps with letterspacing.

Authors frequently type their dedications in quite definite patterns (usually centered) but the arrangement should be made to follow sense and the typographic style of the book. After copyright notices, dedications are the most commonly incongruous elements.

ACKNOWLEDGMENTS

How acknowledgments are set will depend on their nature and importance. Some are routine (such as the anthology credits mentioned in connection with copyrights) and some are virtually recognition of co-authorship. In many cases, the acknowledgments are not so important to the book as they are to the author, who may use them to gain good will or repay obligations. At other times, an acknowledgment may be so sincerely felt as to constitute almost a dedication. The typographic treatment may range from the 8 or 9 pt. of the copyright notice to text size. One size smaller than text is usually appropriate. On extensive acknowledgments, the heading may be set in chapter-opening style; on brief copy, a subhead style will do. When only a few lines are involved, the heading may be omitted.

PREFACE & FOREWORD

There is some confusion about what is a preface, a foreword, and an introduction. The terms are often interchanged without any apparent reason. To some degree, the confusion is justified, because most dictionaries give about the same definition for all 3. The only useful distinction is that a preface is about the book as a whole, while an introduction discusses the text itself. A preface is most often either a background note by the author about the writing of the book or a comment on the book and/or the author by another person. An introduction may contain such matter, but it is primarily a preparation for, or explanation of, the content. These would seem to be editorial questions, but they are of concern to the designer in that they affect the placement of the copy in the frontmatter. (Foreword is properly interchangeable with preface.)

It is logical to put prefaces *before* the contents because they are not part of the text. (Also, when the preface is written by a prominent person, commerical considerations indicate a position up front.) An exception is made, sometimes, when the preface is so long that it pushes the contents page too far into the book.

In most cases, prefaces are set in text size, with the heading treated as a chapter opening. Occasionally, an exception is made when a brief but very important preface is set more prominently than the text, or one is set in another size in order to adjust the length of the book. However, the readability of a preface should not be reduced excessively unless there is an editorial reason.

CONTENTS

The contents page has been the least satisfactorily solved problem in book design from the beginning. The early printers got off on the wrong foot and stayed there. In this matter, convention is of no help and is best disregarded. Logic and instinct must be the guides.

Especially in a complex book, the contents page is a major problem in typographic design. A good one is an efficient tool, but it must also be closely integrated with the typographic scheme of the book. In addition, the contents page has a role in selling the book, and this must be played well too.

Primarily, the contents is an aid in using the book. Its function is to simplify finding material and to clarify the organization.

☞ CONTENTS

Ideas About Ideas

In Business

The Ideas

A. MAKING & SELLING

A complicated contents

When the contents will not fit on one page but will fit on 2, it is better to run it on facing pages rather than on a right-hand page and its back-up. This eliminates the inconvenience of turning the page, and enables both reader and buyer to see all of it in a glance. (There is always the danger that a browser will think the book contains only what is shown on the first page of contents.)

Contents

Since the main purpose of a contents is to show where each item may be found, the most practical place for the page numbers (folios) is *directly following* the item titles. It is sufficient to separate title and folio with an em space in most cases, although a punctuation mark or ornament may be preferable when the items are crowded or, as sometimes happens, the titles end with figures (for instance, dates). The folios may be placed *before* (to the left of) the titles if there are no chapter numerals, and they will function well enough placed immediately *below* the titles in a centered arrangement with not too many items. The important point is that the folios should be *adjacent* to the titles.

In the past, it was customary to place the titles flush left and the folios flush right, and a row of periods (*leaders*) joining one to the other. Not so many years ago, it was recognized that leaders look awful, so, instead of eliminating the need for them by moving the folios close to the titles, the leaders were eliminated, thus making it more difficult to find the page numbers. In some books with a wide text page and short chapter titles, it is almost impossible to tell which folio belongs to each title without using a ruler to align them. This arrangement is still used in some books, although it would appear to have no advantage except in making it convenient to add up the folios, if anyone should care to do so. The practice

CONTENTS

CONTENTS.

CONTENTS

Left, *a contents page with leaders*; right, *folios aligned but close.*

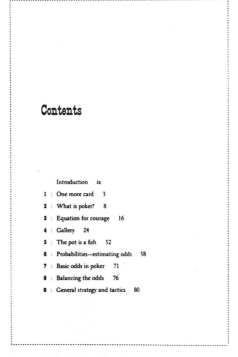

Contents

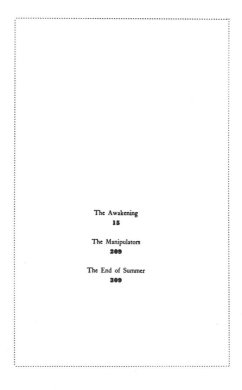

Left, *folios adjacent to titles*; right, *folios centered under titles.*

can be used successfully if the titles are all of about the same length, and the line of folios is moved so it is no more than about an em to the right of the longest title.

The contents should be extremely legible—which requires careful spacing as well as proper choice of type face and size. A judicious use of leading and indentions can set off a line of quite small type so that it is clearly visible, whereas a crowded page of larger type may be more difficult to read. In a complicated contents, a variety of sizes, italics, caps, small caps, boldface, and even other faces should be used as necessary to make a clear and practical page. Economy should not be maintained at the expense of usefulness in a contents page.

Normally, there is no need to set the word "chapter" above the chapter numbers, or to set the word "page" above a column of folios, if there is one. It is perfectly obvious what these numbers are. Also, there is usually no value in putting running heads and folios on contents pages, as these only add to the problem of simplifying and clarifying. Occasionally, a contents running head is desirable in a book that contains much material similar to a contents in appearance, and folios might be called for on a long contents that is preceded by a long, folioed preface.

It can be assumed that the book will be read from front to back, so there is no need to make reference on the contents page to items that precede it. If, however, there is a preface by a prominent person, it may be commerically desirable to list it, with the author's name.

The functional problem of a list of illustrations is about the same as that of a contents. The titles should be legible and the folios should be adjacent to them.

LIST OF ILLUSTRATIONS

One problem is how to refer to illustrations on unfolioed inserts and wraps. A practical solution is to use the term "facing page . . ." for single pages, and "following page . . ." where a group of such pages occurs together. Readers are thus directed to the group of illustration pages containing the picture they want to find, and they find the picture itself by using the sequence in the list.

An introduction is almost always set like the text and has an opening in the style of the chapters. When it is considered part of the frontmatter, it may be set differently from the text in order to adjust the length of the book. When it is part of the text, it would be rather awkward to set it differently, but this may be done in some circumstances. For example, if the introduction is by a different writer than the text (as in anthologies) it may be desirable to set it in another style to emphasize this fact.

INTRODUCTION

A question of style arises when the introduction (or preface) is signed by its author. If it is by the author of the text, no signature is really needed, but it is not uncommon to use initials at the end, often with a dateline. The latter is usually set on the left, in a small size. If the introduction is not by the author of the text, the name of the writer should probably be placed at the beginning, particularly if it is a prominent person whose name adds stature to the book. More often, however, the name appears at the end.

In this connection, it is worth mentioning an odd and unexplained phenomenon. Almost invariably, and even though there may not be another style indication anywhere in the Ms, the signature on the preface or introduction will be marked for cap and small cap. It is never marked for even small caps, all caps, or italics, and it is rarely unmarked. The mystery is double—what fascination causes this particular item to be singled out for marking? and what universal force impels every author and/or editor to choose this particular style? The answer would be simple if we had one school in which all editors were trained uniformly, but alas, this is not so—and the mystery remains.

SECOND HALF-TITLE The second half-title has, unlike the first, a real function—to mark the end of the frontmatter and the beginning of the text. It is usually called p.1, being considered part of the text. Ordinarily, the pages that precede it are numbered in a sequence of Roman numerals (i, ii, iii, etc.). This enables the text to be made up into pages independently of the frontmatter, which is more subject to last-minute changes in copy and length. Many books, especially brief ones, are folioed all through in arabic numerals.

If a first half-title was set, the second may be an exact repetition of it. Otherwise, the book title may be set, or some other material may be used on this page such as was suggested for the first page.

When the book is divided into parts, it is not necessary to have a second half-title, as its function is performed by the first part-title. However, when the introduction is considered part of the text, it is preceded by a second half-title and is folioed in the sequence of arabic numerals. The first part-title, if any, follows.

Backmatter The backmatter, though not part of the text, continues in the sequence of arabic folios, as changes in it will not affect the text pagination.

Whether or not there are part-titles in the text, they are generally used to divide the various parts of the backmatter, provided these are reasonably long—say, 6 pages or more. Such part-titles may be omitted to save space, but then it is desirable to begin each part of the backmatter on a right-hand page.

Backmatter may contain almost any kind of material, but it can all be encompassed under the following headings, listed in the order usually followed:

(1) appendix
(2) notes
(3) bibliography
(4) glossary
(5) index
(6) colophon

The sequence is not especially important. In general, it is best to put material to which the reader may want to refer at the end, where it is most accessible. Thus, if there is an index, it is invariably the last item (except for the colophon which, if it appears at all, takes only one page). Sometimes a glossary or list of abbreviations should be used while reading. If these cannot be placed at the end, it may be possible to print them on the endpapers.

Some publishers include a brief note about the author at the very end of the book. It is rarely more than one page.

The appendix is really a catchall for any material that neither is part of the text nor falls under one of the other backmatter headings. Appendixes (or appendices, take your choice) may be letters, lists, tables, documents, charts, forms, speeches, etc.; anything that supplements or supports the text. The nature of the copy may vary from straight text to very complicated tabular material, so there is no way to indicate how it should be set. APPENDIX

The design of appendixes must, however, be based on their use. Don't set them very small just because they are not very important. If they are expected to be read, make them reasonably readable.

Notes in the backmatter are likely to be references of interest to the scholar and researcher rather than to the reader. Even if they are extensive, they are not meant for continuous reading so they may be set very small (usually 8 pt.). If they are explanatory in nature, they should be set larger and made quite readable. NOTES

Reference notes should be made easy to use, so the subheads and running heads on these pages should be treated as they would be in reference books (CHS. 18,28).

There are some variations in bibliography style, but generally the author comes first, followed by the book title, publisher's address (city), publisher's name, year of publication. Often, one or more of the last 3 items is omitted. BIBLIOGRAPHY

There is not much need for rapid reference in a bibliography so it isn't very important to use a distinctive way of setting the authors' names. They may be set in small caps, with a deep indent (usually 3 ems) for turnovers, or simply in roman upper and lower case with the book titles in italics. Bibliographies may be set quite small if necessary, but if the list of books is very brief, it is just as well set in text size, or any other size that is being used elsewhere in the backmatter. Sometimes there is a paragraph of description for each title, and these are usually set in a smaller size. In bibliographies divided by subject it is usual to put the book title first.

GLOSSARY   A glossary is essentially a dictionary. The items should be set so as to stand out from the definitions, especially if the latter are lengthy. Caps work well, but if the definitions do not turn over, the caps may look too crowded one under the other. Small caps work better in this case; they are just as distinctive, but have more space around them. Boldface upper and lower case is also satisfactory. Most italics do not make sufficient contrast unles the definitions are long, in which case the turnovers may be indented (*hanging indent*) so that the items stand out. Use a generous indent—at least 2 ems. A colon or dash after the items helps set them off.

There is no reason to capitalize the items unless they would ordinarily begin with a capital. To cap *all* the words eliminates the distinction between proper nouns and others.

abhyāntara vṛitti—that variety of *prāṇāyāma* in which the inhaled breath is held at maximal or near maximal lung capacity for as long as possible.

Aham Brahmāsmi—one of the great Vedic utterances used by a meditator as an aid in reaching the supreme state. It means "I am *Brahman*."

ahamkāra—universal ego, of which the individual sense of "I-ness" is a manifestation.

ahiṃsā—noninjury by body, speech, and mind, and the general attitude of welfare for the entire world. It is one of the yamas.

ājñā cakra(m)—the sixth of the seven *cakras*. It is located in the midbrain and is represented by the thalamus, which is the center of individual consciousness.

INDEX   The index is a unique typographic problem because the copy does not arrive until after pages have been made up (except when the book is being reset from another edition). Its length must be a guess (CH. 16) unless, after makeup, you calculate how many lines will fit in the space available and tell the editor how many items can be used.

To do this, allow for sinkage on the first page and make a liberal allowance for turnovers (25% should be enough). Thus, if you have 8 pages, and there is room for 50 lines per column, with 2 columns per page you will have 100 lines per page or a total of 800 lines, less whatever is used for sinkage. If this is 70 lines (actually 35 lines × 2 columns), there will be 730 lines available. To leave some room for error, drop half of the last page (50 lines), leaving

680. If 25% of the lines (170) are turnovers, there will be room for 510 items. This might work.

The index does not have to be set large, but the more legible it is the better. If necessary, however, the type size may go down to 7 or even 6 pt., with no leading. If the trim-size is large enough to take 3 columns of 9 or 10 picas in width, plus about 9 pts. between columns, this may be a better solution for a long index. If the index is too short, it may be padded out by using a type almost as large as the text size, with 2 or 3 pts. of leading. Another method is to insert space between the alphabetical breaks. This may be justified somewhat by using large initial letters in the spaces. Rather than making a ridiculously inflated index, it might be better to add a part-title, or find another means of using the extra pages (CH. 20).

The organization of index copy is quite standardized, as there is not much choice. The problem is to indicate the relative value of sub-items, sub-sub-items, etc. by indention, without getting them confused with turnover lines. In a simple index having only one class of sub-items, the main items are flush, the sub-items are indented one em, and the turnovers of both are indented 2 ems. When there are 3 or 4 classes of sub-items, each with turnovers, matters become more difficult. However, the problem is purely mechanical and will submit to a little thought aided by some rough diagrams.

There is a matter of choice in the use of "continued" lines. When sub-items or turnovers fall at the top of a column, some prefer to reset the main item, followed by (continued) or (cont.), above the first line. This is done mainly when the break comes at the top of the first column on a left-hand page, less often where the break is from a left-hand to a right-hand page (facing pages). The use of "continued" lines is not vital, and may be decided on the basis of available space.

COLOPHON

In the early days of printing, the colophon was the printer-publisher's signature, usually consisting of a trademark and some information—his name, address, patron, date, etc. This material became separated when the functions of printer and publisher divided. Today, the publisher's name and address are called the imprint, the trademark is often called the colophon, and sometimes a paragraph of information about the book's design and manufacture is called a colophon also. The imprint and trademark now appear on the title page, while the descriptive colophon—which contains the name of the designer, printer, etc.—is usually put on the last page, although it sometimes appears on the copyright page. In most books, there is no descriptive colophon at all. In some, it appears as a rather precious survival. There is, however, a proper place for a straightforward colophon in books of such quality as to justify pride on the part of all concerned with their making.

The colophon in Fust and Schoeffer's Psalter of 1457.

24 | Page makeup & proofs

Page makeup (CH. 5) follows the castoff (CH. 20) to whatever degree is appropriate. If the castoff was unjustified, an attempt is made to arrive at the same total number of pages, but there may be variations within the total. A justified castoff can be followed exactly. The danger here is that an error in its paging will throw off the entire makeup.

Most problems are solved in a justified castoff, but there is one matter remaining—the handling of running heads. The questions are: (a) Should running heads appear on pages that have run-in chapters or subheads at the top? (b) What copy shall be used for running heads? (c) How shall the copy be cut if it will not fit in the space and style provided?

■ *Run-in heads at top of page*—This question is largely esthetic. An important factor is the amount of contrast between the running head and the title. If they are at all similar in style they are less acceptable together than if they are very different. Usually, the running head, if not the folio, is omitted over chapter titles and retained over subheads. A practical consideration is the copy involved. When the running head repeats the title immediately beneath it, the repetition seems needless.

■ *Running-head copy*—The sample pages establish a general pattern, but many books have elements that to do not conform. The scheme may call for part-title left and chapter title right, but what if there should be an untitled introduction after a part-title, or an epilogue after the last part, or some other such problem? There is no stock answer. In each case, the answer must fit the circumstances. Sometimes, the solution may be elimination of one running head; at other times, repetition of the same head on both sides. If the latter is chosen, and the left- and right-hand running heads are set in different styles, which style will be used?

■ *Cutting running-head copy*—This is an editorial function, of concern to the designer mainly in that the necessity for such cutting should be minimized. If titles *must* be cut, give the editor the maximum number of characters.

Where a dummy has been made, makeup is a routine matter of following instructions (CH. 5)—presuming that the dummy has been properly marked (CH. 21).

If the book is set in metal type to be printed by letterpress from type or duplicate plates (CHS. 5, 9), no further choice is necessary. When photomechanical plates are to be made, the page makeup may be accomplished by (a) making a mechanical, (b) stripping up film, (c) a combination of these, or (d) a combination of metal type makeup and one or both of the other methods. The considerations are both technical and economic (CHS. 5, 8, 9, 12).

Page proofs

Because of the high cost of making corrections in pages, the checking of page proofs should involve no changes in layout except, perhaps, when an exceptionally complicated page fails to work out properly. (Even this will not occur where a dummy has been made.) Otherwise, it should be enough to make certain that the makeup instructions were followed properly. Where the makeup follows an unjustified castoff, some unfortunate breaks may occur, but these are probably unavoidable and cannot be corrected without major changes.

In books consisting mainly of text, there will be little to check in page proofs other than running heads, the handling of run-in breaks, folios, and the makeup of chapter-opening pages. The latter can be a problem when uniform sinkage is desired. The number of text lines on the opening pages may increase or decrease because of run-in breaks or widows. It is important that instructions be given to provide for the disposition of space in such cases. It is usually best to maintain the sinkage and the space between items of display, letting the space between the display and text vary as necessary. However, where chapters begin on right-hand pages only, it is possible to maintain all of the spacing, letting the foot margin vary. This will not usually be noticed since there is no facing full page.

When the pages consist of many illustrations and only some or no text, page proofs are crucial and must be examined carefully, especially where bleeds are involved. The checking of *all* spaces and dimensions would be excessively tedious, and it is usually sufficient to compare the page proofs visually with the dummy, measuring only those spaces that appear to be incorrect. It is helpful to draw the outlines of the trim-size on tracing paper or acetate and lay this over the proof. Litho and gravure printers supply page proofs in the form of folded and trimmed blueprints, which greatly facilitates checking (CH. 5).

Unless letterpress page proofs (instead of galleys) are being used for book club submission or reviews (which sometimes occurs with illustrated books) the only copies pulled, usually, are the author's set and two duplicates, one of which is kept by the compositor. Lithographers charge separately for page blueprints and normally only one set is ordered. The customs of the cold-composition houses (CH. 5) vary according to the kind of product and proof involved.

25 | Ordering printing

The book is ready to go to press when (a) all proofs have been finally corrected and approved, (b) the plates, if any, have been made and checked for quality, errors, and damage, (c) the paper is on hand, and (d) the printer is in possession of complete instructions and a written, signed order to proceed. In order to arrive at this point, it is necessary to select a printer.

Selecting a printer   In choosing a plumber or shoemaker, the only considerations are their competence, reliability, and prices, plus your personal convenience and preference. Presumably, any of them can do what you require. When selecting a printer, all of the same considerations are involved, but in addition you must find a printer who is equipped with the plant and experience to match the specific job in question. Printers vary tremendously in the kind of work they can do—and do well.

A man with a platen job press is a printer, and so is one with a dozen 4-color web-offset presses with synchronized folders. If you need 300 letterheads, the first man is the best printer for you. Should you want 100,000 copies of a book illustrated with full-color photography, it is strongly suggested that you select the second man. The economical printing of *any* job requires selection of a printer specializing in that kind of work. The job-press man *could* print your book, and the man with the web-fed press *could* print your letterheads—but in both cases the cost would be astronomically higher.

Until you have had enough experience to find the right printer yourself, it is best to ask the advice of an expert. A direct approach to a printer may be successful—if that one happens to be the right one or sends you to a suitable shop. However, there is always the chance that the printer may take on the job even though not a good choice for it. Your choice may need the work badly or may not know enough to realize that another printer could do the job better.

There are many considerations involved in matching printer to job, but the main ones are:

(a) the *kind* of presses (letterpress, offset lithography, gravure),
(b) the *size* of presses,
(c) the *number* of presses (this relates to capacity to produce),
(d) the kind of work done,
(e) the quality of work,
(f) the quality of the plant and equipment,
(g) the schedule, and
(h) the prices.

The printing order

All the information needed by the printer should appear on the printing order except details relating to individual pages, and at least a reference to those details should be included. For example, if it is necessary to provide a dummy giving individual margins for each page, the printing order should have a note indicating that such a dummy is being supplied. This insures that no directions will be overlooked because they are separate from the order.

The printing order should constitute both the official instructions and the official authorization for doing the job. The latter requires only (a) a statement to the effect that the job is to be done according to the instructions thereon, (b) the number of copies to be printed, (c) the place to which the sheets are to be delivered, and (d) the buyer's signature with the date.

The instructions should be complete, and it is best to use a printed form—if only to be sure that nothing is overlooked. On the next page is a sample form which could be used for any kind of printing. Bear in mind that the printing order is a purchasing order; it should have a number and be treated in the same manner as other financial records.

DIFFERENT KINDS OF PRINTING

There are basic differences between ordering (a) letterpress and (b) offset lithography or gravure. (a) When ordering letterpress, the job is ordinarily ready to go on press, using type or plates produced in another shop (or another department). (b) In lithography or gravure, the plates will be made by the printer (CH.9), although the plate preparation (camera and stripping) may be done by a separate company.

(a) In letterpress, it is necessary to arrange for delivery of type or plates to the pressroom, and to inform the printer of those arrangements (unless the composition was done by or was ordered by the printer). (b) For lithography or gravure, completed mechanicals (CH.8), a dummy with marked copy (CH.21), or a combination of both must be delivered.

INFORMATION REQUIRED

Regardless of the method of printing, the dimensions of the job must be clearly indicated. The trim-size, basic margins, total

Print Order

NO. _____

DATE _____

TO: _____

TITLE _____

AUTHOR _____

TEXT

QUANTITY _____ TRIM SIZE _____

_____ PAGES, TO PRINT AS _____, CANCEL _____ PAGES.

PRINT FROM _____ YOU WILL RECEIVE FROM _____

MARGINS: _____ IN GUTTER; _____ IN HEAD AFTER TRIM.

GET FOLDING IMPOSITION FROM _____

IMPOSE FOR _____

PAPER _____

_____ FROM _____

ILLUSTRATIONS

QUANTITY _____ PAGES, AS _____

COLOR(S): _____ PRINTED ONE SIDE.
PRINTED TWO SIDES.

PAPER _____

_____ FROM _____

LAYOUT

_____

_____

_____

_____

_____

_____

_____

_____

_____

_____

_____

_____

_____

_____

_____

_____

_____

_____

_____

_____

_____

DELIVER SHEETS TO _____

_____

TO BE AT DESTINATION BY _____

_____

PRODUCTION DEPARTMENT

number of pages, and layout are the essential facts, and to these should be added any pertinent information about binding that would affect the imposition. The placement of all wraps and inserts should be indicated so that the printer will be aware of the need for any unusual arrangement of signatures. Although the printer will get the imposition from the binder, providing the primary information is extra insurance against error.

Not only the name, size, weight, and quantity of the paper, but its source should be on the printing order. This enables the printer to make direct contact with the supplier in case any trouble with the stock should arise while on press. The paper for sheet-fed printing is ordered in terms of weight and number of sheets (CH. 10) but the printer's records are usually kept in *reams*, so it is best to indicate the quantity in that measure. Parts of reams are expressed in fractions, using twentieths as the unit (1 ream = 500 sheets, 200 sheets = 8/20 ream).

In offset printing, the order should specify the kind of plate wanted—surface, deep-etch, etc.—and your requirements for blueprints (CHS. 5,8).

If possible, the printing of separate sections of illustrations should be done after the text is off press. This enables the printer to adjust the illustration run to the actual net number of text sheets—which may be somewhat more or less than the quantity ordered.

■ *Lithographic or gravure printing*—It is necessary to supply either (a) a dummy indicating the exact position of every element on every page in the book, (b) mechanicals on which everything is pasted in correct position, or (c) a combination of these. Often, a mechanical is supplied with some of the elements (usually the text, running heads, and folios), while the other material (usually illustrations and captions) is supplied separately with a dummy to indicate their position or with directions written on the mechanical. If the makeup is simple, the type elements may be supplied as loose page repros, with the illustrations again separate. As there would then be no mechanicals, a dummy must be provided. No dummy is needed for the text pages of books in which all have the same head and inside margins.

DUMMIES REQUIRED

■ *Letterpress*—Even when the margins vary there is usually no need for a dummy if all pages are made up to the same size, and the plates, if any, are all the same size. The head margin is then measured to the top of the *page or plate*, so no distinction need be made between pages on which something appears at the top and those in which the highest element is further down the page. Even when the page layouts are quite irregular, it is necessary to indicate only 2 margins on each page in the final proof, as all the elements are already positioned in relation to each other.

It is good practice to provide for *any* printer a dummy showing the frontmatter and the first 3 pages of text, with margins indicated. This has several virtues: (a) the dummy enables the designer (and others) to see how the book will appear when printed—at least with respect to the positions of frontmatter and text pages in relation to the trim-size and, sequentially, in relation to each other, (b) the exact position of each item of frontmatter can be indicated, and (c) there is less chance of an error in pagination.

In ordering the printing of jackets, a dummy should be provided on which the positions of *flap copy* [the type printed on the flaps] and *back ad* [the advertising copy on the back of the jacket], as well as the front and spine, are indicated (CH. 26).

COLOR SWATCHES & PROOFS

On printing orders, specify the color of ink to be used and, if there is to be a color other than black, provide a substantial swatch or specify a standard ink that can be ordered by the manufacturer's number. Swatches should be at least 2 square inches and solid in tone. Watercolor or pencil swatches that vary in color may be difficult to match. The ink should be specified as transparent or opaque, and the sequence of colors should be indicated where any question exists (CH. 9).

26 | Binding design

The binding design as such has not been mentioned so far, although some binding factors have been considered in connection with the illustration arrangement (CH. 17). In practice, the binding design is ordinarily dealt with while the rest of the work is in progress, but it has been bypassed until now to avoid interrupting the discussions of text and illustration.

The first attention given to binding is in the creative visualization (CH. 15). Then it is customary to provide some specifications on which to base a cost estimate, probably at the time of making the basic decisions (CH. 16). Ideally, the actual binding design is made immediately after the sample pages, title page, etc. are designed, so that the entire book will be planned in one period without interruption or lapse of time. Unfortunately, it is rarely possible to work this way, but the main benefit of the procedure—a unity of concept—can be realized through the initial visualization. In any case, the general outlines of the binding design should be established by this stage.

To understand the problem of binding design (which refers to all features of the book other than the planning and printing of its pages) it is necessary to realize that a book's binding has several functions.

Originally, the only purposes of a binding were to hold the pages together and protect them. The sheets were sewed together along the folded edge and wooden or leather boards were put at the beginning and end of the book, to be held in place by leather thongs joined to the threads or cords holding the pages together. Later, leather or vellum covered the boards and extended around the spine, concealing the threads and cords.

Books were precious objects at that time (about the 9th century A.D. in the Middle East and parts of Europe), so they were decorated—usually with gold tooling, sometimes with inlays of

The functions

semiprecious stones. Except for the possible sales value in the marketing of a particularly handsome volume to a prince or merchant, it is unlikely that the decoration served any but an esthetic or devotional purpose. To a large extent, the books produced then were religious in nature, and the binding designs, as well as the illuminated pages, were acts of glorification. (If they were incidentally acts of vanity we should not object, because the results are so wonderful.) But, if binding decoration was not at first of practical value, the techniques developed were useful when they became needed a thousand years later.

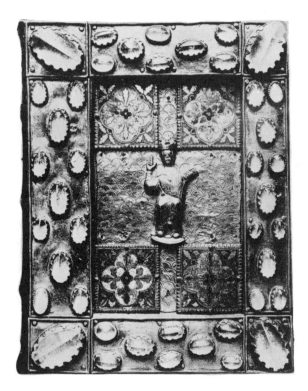

Until printing spread through Europe, books were so few in number that it was unnecessary to have titles on their covers for identification. With a few exceptions, libraries of manuscripts were small, and their contents well known to their proud owners or custodians. When books became numerous, the binding acquired an additional function—identification of the content.

In the 19th century, competition among publishers resulted in the decoration of book bindings to attract buyers. At this point then, the binding had 4 distinct purposes:

(a) construction,
(b) protection,
(c) identification, and
(d) attraction.

To these is now added a 5th function. The binding must also be
expressive of the content. With the technical facilities that have
become available in the past 40 years, it has become possible to
create virtually any graphic effect on a book binding. Now the
binding design may be integrated with the design of the text to
produce an expressively unified entity. It is now possible to raise
book design to a level of expression comparable to the other ancil-
lary arts, such as architecture, stage design, or theatre music.

The functions of binding apply not only to the casebound book,
but to paperbacks and mechanical binding, although not in exactly
the same way. To these variations must be added the problem of the
jacket.

■ *Jackets*—The introduction of book jackets has complicated development of binding design in particular and book design in general. To a large extent, the jacket is a superfluous cover, performing
some of the functions which should—and now could—be performed by the real cover of the book.

Having begun life as a plain paper wrapper meant to prevent
soiling, the jacket was given a sales role when the marketing of
books became more aggressive (in the 1890s). When publishers
wanted to apply the new techniques of advertising design to their
books, it was not possible to achieve the desired effects on book

jacket of 1897

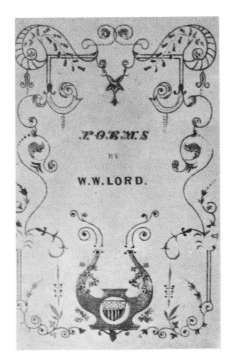

book jacket of 1845

covers, nor were there many artists capable of such design then working in the book field. The solution was to use the wrappers as posters, and call in advertising artists to design them.

Today, the wrapper is not needed for its original purpose of protection. The application of plastics to binding can provide much better resistance to soiling and abrasion. The jacket's role in identification and attraction, as well as its ability to be expressive, are now well within the possibilities of the book cover, due to modern printing and binding techniques.

In cost, the conventional binding plus a jacket is not less—and may be more—than the kind of cover that needs no jacket. In fact, a book with a jacket actually has 2 covers.

That this is unnecessary is demonstrated by the millions of paperbacks in existence—particularly the trade paperbacks. These lines, one of the most successful parts of book publishing today, have no jackets, sell to a considerable extent on the attractiveness of their cover designs, and provide less protection for their pages than any unjacketed hard-bound book. A place in them is found for advertising copy, even though there are no "flaps"—and book buyers seem to find and read this copy.

Why do jackets continue to be used? Well, for one thing, by the time they became unnecessary they were a "tradition"—and traditions die very hard in the book business. More important is the legitimate doubt that covers can succeed in serving the poster requirements of a jacket and also maintain a pleasing aspect in keeping with the restrained character of some books. Certainly it is easier to design a jacket or a paper cover if there is no need to integrate it with the design of the text, which means that there is no compromise in the quest for maximum display effect. This fact, combined with a few relatively minor advantages, such as their value in library display and their usefulness in showing favorable comments, etc., will probably keep jackets in use for a long time to come, despite their anomalous role and economic impracticality.

■ *Paperbacks*—For a paperback binding, somewhat lower standards of construction and protection generally prevail. In the other 3 respects—identification, attraction, and expression—the paperback covers, can, and often do, perform superlatively, although here, as on jackets, the expressive function is sometimes slighted in favor of the poster needs.

■ *Mechanical binding*—The mechanical binding is used in lieu of either case or paperback binding when its particular structural features are required, and these are quite unique. As far as identification, attraction, and expression are concerned, it functions as any external cover (mechanical bindings rarely have jackets).

Functional factors in binding design

Each decision in binding design must take into account all the functional factors. Consideration of the functions is not separated in practice because almost all decisions involve more than one, but it is useful here to think of the binding design elements in terms of the individual functional problems for which they are the solutions.

The manufacturing processes and materials are described in CH. 11. Binding costs in general are discussed in CH. 12. Here we deal only with the influence of these factors on binding design decisions.

For visual purposes, the design of jackets, paper covers, and hard covers will be considered varying aspects of one problem—cover design. A distinction will be made only when a point peculiar to one aspect is discussed. However, bear in mind that cover design is only one of the visual factors in binding.

CONSTRUCTION

The aspects of construction that most affect binding design are: (a) the method of holding the pages together and (b) the endpapers.

■ *Method of holding pages*—The choice of method (sewing, stapling, gluing, or mechanical binding) depends on the nature of the book and the costs.

The advantages of perfect-binding are obvious. No sewing or utilitarian considerations prevent folding larger (and thus fewer) signatures. Single leaves may be inserted without concern for the weakness or cost of tipping, and the book is ready to be joined to its cover with several fewer operations than is a sewed book.

It is not price but function that indicates the use of a mechanical binding. With some of these, a book can be made not only to lie perfectly flat when open, but to stand up like an easel or to fold back on itself so that it is no larger when open than closed. Others enable pages to be removed, inserted, or changed around. When such attributes are wanted, a mechanical binding of some kind is required.

The spiral wire or plastic comb kinds are relatively inexpensive, while the loose-leaf ring or post bindings can run into large sums. Generally, mechanical bindings cost more than the standard case binding.

The cost of materials in a mechanical binding is more significant than in other binding methods. This cost varies not only with the trim-size of the book and the kind of apparatus used, but with the book's thickness. As the bulk increases, the strength—and therefore the weight—of the wire or plastic used must increase also. In fact, it is not generally feasible to use a spiral or plastic binding on books over about 1″ (2.54 cm) in bulk.

Because of the way mechanical bindings are made, this is a practical method to use when only a few copies are needed. There is little of the high cost of setting up automatic machines, so the unit cost for a few hundred copies (or one copy!) is not very much more than for several thousand.

If sewing is used, the choice between Smyth and side stitching will probably be made for you. Side stitching holds the pages together so well that it is quite difficult to keep the book open, so it is used only where utility and appearance must be sacrificed to strength. This method is now required for almost all school uses below the college level, and is almost essential for library sales of children's books.

Saddle-wire stitching is used mainly for pamphlets, where there is only one signature and a paper cover. Side-wire stitching is probably the strongest and cheapest method of holding pages together, but it is more objectionable than side sewing with thread.

The kind of text and illustration paper used has a bearing on the choice of binding method. This is discussed in CHS. 10 and 11.

■ *Endpapers*—A book with many pages of heavy coated paper needs a stronger endpaper than another of the same trim-size but printed on a bulking antique. Two books of identical specifications call for different endpapers if one has an ephemeral subject and the other is a reference book. The heavy book needs a paper of good edge and tensile strength, while the reference book needs a stock with good folding or flexing strength. In general, the choice of endpaper from the structural standpoint depends on the book's characteristics.

These varied considerations could cause confusion, except for the practice of making all paper sold specifically for endleaves strong enough to meet the NASTA standards for textbooks. Very few books require stronger paper; and most of the 80 lb. (118 gr) text papers, and even some of the 70 lb. (104 gr) weights, are perfectly safe for tradebooks of average size where no strenuous use is involved.

The least expensive endpaper is the regular white stocked by the binder. Although it is about the same quality as the colored endpapers available, its price is slightly lower. On an average-sized book, however, the difference comes to only about 2¢ per copy. If one of the finer text papers is used, the difference may be around 3½¢ (unless the paper cuts out badly for the trim-size, in which case it may be almost twice as much).

Self-lining is a relatively weak construction, suitable for small- to average-sized books of which repeated use is unlikely. The advantages are (a) a saving of about 6¢ and (b) the opportunity to print on all parts of the endleaves at no cost, these being part of the text sheets themselves.

PROTECTION To protect a book effectively, the binding must be resistant to numerous hazards such as flexing, abrasion, soiling, tearing, impact, etc. The burden of providing such protection is shared by various features of the book: (a) cover material, (b) board, (c) headbands, (d) edge stain, and (e) the jacket.

■ *Cover material*—The most important protective features of the case-binding cover material are resistance to flexing and tearing. In both cases, the strength is needed at the joint or hinge.

Flexing is involved in the opening and closing of the book. Since the cover material bends each time this occurs, it is necessary to use one that can stand the probable number of flexings required by the particular book. Certainly a reference book will receive more flexings in its life than a topical work, so the former will require a stronger hinge; but the question of use is somewhat complicated by library practices. A title which might be expected to get no more than one or 2 readings (say, a novel), may get many times that number in a library—but some libraries will rebind the book upon purchase and others may not.

NASTA specifications settle the question for textbooks. Children's books meant for library use are usually given special bindings by the publisher. They are not only side stitched but are bound in a cloth usually up to NASTA specs or better. The problem of hinge strength is given consideration also for reference books, manuals, etc., but for most general books the cover material is selected on the theory that it will be strong enough for normal use, and that libraries will rebind.

The problem of tearing at the hinge concerns generally the same kinds of books (particularly elementary textbooks) that can expect much flexing. The choice of material is not affected when NASTA standards are required, but there may be a question when using some papers and plastics. Many of these materials are likely to have relatively better flexing qualities than tearing strength.

Abrasion and soiling are hazards to which all books are subjected in varying degrees. Again, school and library books are most vulnerable and the materials required for them are made to take considerable abuse. Abrasion is usually more of a problem on the bottom edges of the cover than anywhere else, although reference books can expect exceptionally heavy wear on the sides. Any material used for cases should either be dyed-through, to avoid having another color show as the material wears thin, or be heavily coated, or both. Soiling is an important consideration in cookbooks and other manuals whose users may have dirty hands (CH. 28). To prevent soiling, materials should be coated or impregnated with a resistant compound such as pyroxylin.

Since (a) the strains of flexing and tearing are only at the hinge and (b) there are relatively inexpensive materials that provide adequate protection for the sides of most tradebooks, it is a common practice to use 3-piece covers on such books. A strong, flexible material—usually cloth or a non-woven plastic—is used for the spine and hinges and a weaker but more abrasion-resistant material—usually paper—is used on the sides. A soil-resistant paper can be used at a little higher cost.

When a 3-piece cover is made on an end-feed, web-fed case-maker in one operation—provided the edition is large enough to absorb the longer setting-up time (5000 is about the minimum) and there are no special running problems—the cost is about the same as making a one-piece cover. If, for example, a 70¢ per yard cloth is used for the spine and hinge and extends the minimum amount onto the side boards (about ⅜"), the cost of the cloth will be about 1½¢ on a book of average size. A 30¢ per yard material on the sides will add about 3¢, for a total of 4½¢. Using 70¢ material all over would cost about 7¢ per book.

If the run is too short to warrant setting up a web-fed machine, the cover can be made in 2 operations and may still be somewhat cheaper than the one-piece cover, but the cost difference will probably be so small that the loss of time and efficiency might not be justified.

The protective aspects of mechanical-binding cover materials involve only the resistance to abrasion and soiling needed for sides, as the flexing and tearing hazards are borne mainly by the mechanical device. The same considerations apply to the cover material here as in case-bound book sides.

In general, the qualities of book-covering material can be determined by reference to the grade or price range. The decision to use a particular quality for a book should be taken in consultation with the binder or another experienced person.

For *paperback covers* almost any stock may be used, provided it has sufficient folding strength, tear strength, rigidity, and abrasion resistance. How much is sufficient? This depends on what is expected of the book. If *maximum* protection is required, a hard cover is the answer. If maximum protection *for the price* is the object, the answer is the regular 10 pt. coated stock usually used.

As paperbacks become more generally accepted, and are purchased even by libraries and schools, there is greater demand for cover durability. This demand, combined with a search for economy in hard binding, has created a trend toward a midpoint at which the distinction between softbound and hard bound virtually disappears. Certainly, where the trade paperback is concerned, such a disappearance is conceivable, as the differences in production and distribution between these books and their hardbound counterparts is minor.

■ *Boards*—Damage from impact—usually in dropping the book (or in using it as a missile in school)—is borne mainly by the boards. If a good and heavy-enough board is used, the book will not ordinarily suffer too badly, but a light board may crumple and the book will probably be ruined. Remember that the heavier the book the harder it falls, so a heavier, tougher board is needed. No material short of textbook specifications is likely to fare well under the stress of severe impact, but few books used outside the elementary schools are likely to receive such blows.

■ *Headbands*—Headbands have no structural value, but they do provide a bit of protection for the spine. In pulling a book off a full shelf, the common practice is to apply pressure at the top of the book near the spine and pull down and out. The headband takes some of this strain, which might otherwise rip the spine.

■ *Edge stain*—The protective function of the edge stain is real—it protects the edges from a soiled appearance caused by handling or the accumulation of dust and soot. This concerns the top edge mostly, and it is the top that is generally stained. The other edges *can* be stained, but this would be for esthetic reasons only. An interesting effect is obtained by staining the top and the fore-edge different colors, but it is a relatively expensive operation. Another possibility is to color only the fore-edge, but this also costs more than staining the top.

■ *Jacket*—The protective factor in choosing jacket material is important because jackets do get relatively hard use. Of course, if the cover is sturdy enough, one has a right to assume that the jacket will not be needed by the reader and is justified in using material adequate only for distribution purposes. But the jackets *are* used by readers (and libraries), so the tendency has been to provide materials that will stand considerable handling.

For most tradebooks, a 70 lb. (104 gr) text stock is sufficient, although 80 lb. (118 gr) is better. In coated papers, 80 lb. is the minimum. Heavier books and those that get exceptionally hard use, such as dictionaries, cookbooks, etc., usually get 100 lb. (148 gr) coated stock. Often a plastic lamination is added for its glossy appearance, but this also adds considerably to the jacket's resistance to tearing, soiling, and wrinkling. Even more tearstrength can be added by folding over an extra 2 or 3 inches of paper at the top and bottom.

Actually, protection of the book has 2 aspects: (a) keeping the book intact during use and (b) preservation of the book's bindery-fresh appearance in the bookstore and warehouse. The jacket is not adequate for the former but it is of great help in the latter—and its material should be chosen with that function in mind.

The acetate jacket provides good protection and gives a luxurious, glossy finish to a book, like the cellophane wrapping on a package of cigarettes, but it is not inexpensive. The cost is usually more than that of a 4-color process jacket for an average-size book. The cost goes higher as the size gets larger, but goes down for larger quantities. Wrapping books with acetate jackets is somewhat slower than with paper jackets, which adds to the cost. Acetate has a tendency to become cloudy from the abrasion of normal use and sometimes cracks or tears. Despite these drawbacks, the acetate jacket is effective packaging, usually worth its cost for books expected to sell on visual appeal—given a really good cover design.

The strongest visual necessity in cover design is identification. The title, author's name (last name, at least), and publisher's imprint should appear on the spine in any case. (An exception might be a new edition of a classic so well-known that the author's name can be omitted without loss of identification.) Inclusion of the author's first name is preferred by some publishers.

The title's position on the spine is the subject of considerable disagreement. Some insist that the title read horizontally on all but the narrowest spines. Others insist that it read from top to bottom when it must be vertical. In England, they prefer the title running from bottom to top. The choice in each case is presumably concerned with legibility, but there are several factors affecting the legibility of titles on spines, so that no one position is best in all circumstances.

All other things being equal, a horizontal line is certainly easiest to read. However, a word which can be made no larger than 14 pt. across the spine would be much more legible set vertically in 48 pt. type. This is true of thick books as well as thin ones.

Legibility is affected by the contrast and clarity of the type also. A poorly chosen color combination or typeface can kill the legibility of *any* arrangement. Conversely, a change in color can make an otherwise unsatisfactory arrangement work quite well.

Whatever may be said about the relative merits of bottom-to-top vs. top-to-bottom titles, it is a fact that italics and cursives are much more easily read from bottom to top. This position is actually less of a departure from the normal horizontal arrangement for them than it is for roman type, the latter being perpendicular to the normal angle, whereas italics are turned considerably less than 90°. When italics run down the spine, they are much *more* than 90° from the usual axis and require a twist of the neck to be read. Whether this disadvantage is worse than the inconvenience of reading one title up on a shelf of down titles is a matter of personal choice. It is probably best to avoid the problem by not using italics on spines at all.

The need for having the title and author's name on the front cover varies with circumstances. They are of prime importance when the book is to be displayed and sold in stores—but this applies only to jackets, paperback covers, and hard covers of books having no printed jackets. When the book has a printed jacket, there is usually no reason to put the title on the front of the cover, unless it is expected to be used as a schoolbook also, in which case the jacket will not be used. The title is considered essential on the front cover of textbooks, not for the ultimate user, but for sales purposes at conventions and other places where such books are displayed for buyers.

For display purposes, the cover design problem is to attract atten-

tion and hold it long enough for the title and author to be read.
There is much room for variation in method.

It is not absolutely necessary that the title be the attracting element. A striking illustration or even a particularly effective abstract
pattern may be used to catch the eye, while the title itself may be
quite small and/or restrained. In such cases, the design must be
sufficiently intriguing to lure the shopper close enough to read the
title. Occasionally, the latter has been omitted entirely, with a very
familiar illustration (usually a well-known personality) carrying
the entire burden of identification. This practice is not being recommended, but it does demonstrate that use of the title as the
primary element of display is not essential, and it emphasizes the
value of a highly relevant illustration.

The competition for attention in bookstores today is terrifying
—and getting worse. Not simply because the number of titles published is enormous, or because there are so many other things di-
verting the public's attention, but because the proportion of effective design on books is increasing. Before the 1960s, an outstanding jacket design stood out easily in a desert of mediocrity. Today, it
is less noticed. This is really a good thing. The pleasure of browsing
is heightened, and the quality of publishers' output is constantly
under pressure to improve.

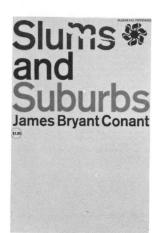

All this points to 2 principles. First, the effectiveness of a design is relative to its background—"effectiveness" meaning, primarily, the ability to be noticed, which in turn implies being different from the others. Thus, no practice is more effective than another under all conditions. A red cover may be successful if no others are red, but probably not if surrounded by red ones. A photographic design may stand out on a shelf of typographic jackets, but might become lost in a display with all photographic designs. This is not to say that the designer should strive to be "different" at all costs, but design trends should be taken into account, if only to avoid repeating the current fads.

The second principle is in some ways a contradiction of what has gone before—now it must be said that use of the title as the attracting device is probably best. The title is *the* identifying element—not just graphically, but aurally and psychologically. The title usually has overtones of meaning and association more specific than any illustration or pattern can have. Particularly when it is brief and descriptive ("Horses", "Play Ball!", etc.) it offers graphic opportunities which, combined with its literal values, make a powerful effect possible. The poster value of the title diminishes as it becomes longer and less descriptive (unless it is sufficiently odd).

On the other hand, when the book is by a very popular author it may be best to emphasize his or her name, and give the title a secondary or equal place. This choice must be made with care. Consult with the sales and editorial departments before proceeding along this line.

EXPRESSION For some books, putting the title on the cover is sufficient for sales purposes. Titles like "Algebra for Beginners" or "Operating a Drill Press" reveal enough for prospective buyers to decide if they should look into the book. On the other hand, a title such as "Out of the Blue" may concern aviation, meteorology, psychology, music, fishing, an unexpected visit, romance, or fortune, retirement from the Navy, an invasion from another planet, or any number of other subjects, so it becomes necessary for the binding design to indicate what the book is about.

The binding, as well as the rest of the book, must indicate the content also because the design should be a reflection of the text. The degree of literalness or subtlety appropriate is discussed in CH. 15, but it is obvious that the binding—if it has a sales role—is the place for a rather direct expression. If it has *no* poster requirement, the principles of expression are the same as for the book as a whole. The elements of a binding design that concern expression are: (a) subject, (b) illustration, (c) typography, (d) material, and (e) color.

■ *Subject*—Even when the cover is used for display, it must not hold the viewer's attention too long. If one becomes too intrigued

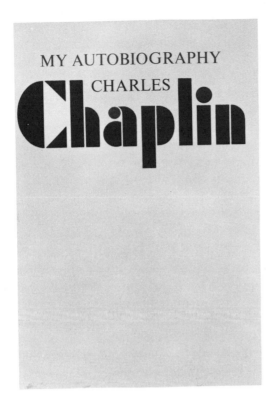

with an intricate or detailed cover design, the time spent in this examination will be taken from the precious few seconds allottable to the book—seconds which could otherwise be spent reading the flap copy or perusing the content. The cover design should attract attention and arouse interest in the content, not satisfy the curiosity it stimulates.

Designs should be general as to the content of the book, but very specific and individual about the subject. For example, a book about exploration of the Pacific Northwest is not just about exploration, or about exploration of a wilderness in America, but about an expedition by a *particular group of people* to an area with *specific characteristics* in a *certain period of American history*. All of these and other salient features should be evident in the design because they give the book its unique character. On the other hand, it is not especially desirable to illustrate an actual incident from the text. To do so would not reveal any more about the nature of the book, and it might divert attention from further examination. Sometimes, of course, an incident in the book is so graphically dramatic that it can be illustrated on the cover with good effect, but even then it should be a simple occurrence that can be grasped in an instant.

■ *Illustration*—Illustration for covers may be taken from inside the book or elsewhere. In any case, their use follows the principles discussed in CHS. 7, 15, 16, and 21. On covers, the purpose is likely to be entirely suggestive, although it may be considered partly reproductive in the case of art books. Here there is also the display consideration—which may affect their treatment. Indeed, the distortion of values required by the poster needs of cover design tends to separate the (display) cover esthetically from the rest of the book, making it difficult to maintain a feeling of unity.

■ *Typography*—Unity is a problem also in the choice of lettering or typography. A single spirit should prevail, yet the needs of display may indicate a quite different kind, weight, or size of letter from that inside the book. However, remember that not only harmony but contrast can create unity (CH. 6).

■ *Material*—The cover and the endpaper materials will be chosen partly on the basis of technical and economic considerations discussed earlier. The visual factors follow the principles indicated in CH. 15 and the conception visualized at that stage. Color and texture are the esthetic components of this choice, and these may be selected tentatively for their suitability, but the final decisions must take the practical factors into account.

■ *Color*—On paperbacks and hardcover books which will have no printed jacket, color choice is entirely open if there is no color in the text. Where there *is* color in the text, cover colors should be effectively related to those already used. Otherwise, any suitable colors can be chosen.

When a book has 2 covers, i.e. a case binding and a printed jacket, a controversial situation arises. One view has it that the jacket is merely a promotion piece wrapped temporarily around the book, so there is no need to consider its colors in designing the book itself. Another school holds that this is unrealistic because in fact the jacket almost invariably remains on the book, so a harmonious relationship between them is as essential as it is between any 2 of the book's parts.

It can be argued thus: (a) On paperback books and unjacketed hardbound books the design of the cover and pages *must* be integrated, even though a permanent cover performs the sales function. (b) The only difference between these and jacketed books is that a jacket *can* be discarded, but (c) if it is not, and usually it is not, then there is really *no* difference, and the jacket should be treated as though it is a permanent part of the book. It would be another matter if, by making the jacket clash with the book, the purchaser would be induced to discard it, but this doesn't seem to work that way. The ideal solution would be to make the jacket conform to the book's design, but this might involve a limitation of sales, which is not likely to be accepted at all.

Besides the cover, there are 4 other binding elements that involve color: endpapers, ink or leaf, edge color, and headbands. These may be used to bridge over a poorly related jacket and binding color combination, but in any case, they provide an opportunity to use a considerable range of color in the service of both attraction and expression.

Whereas the production of jackets and paper covers requires no special techniques, making designs on cloth and the other binding materials involves some unique problems.

Printing on cloth, plastic, or non-woven materials is almost always done by offset lithography, so the material must have a surface suitable for lithographic printing. The printing must usually be locked in by a transparent finish to protect it from abrasion.

The cost of printing on binding materials is generally more than printing on paper. Except where very long runs make coordinated web-printing and web-casemaking feasible, the high cost of pre-printing covers is made higher by the necessity of making the cases on a sheet-fed machine. However, no stamping is needed and, if *no jacket* is needed, the cost becomes comparable to that of a stamped cover with a printed jacket.

Preprinted covers are relatively more economical for short-run titles which would require sheet-fed casemaking anyway. The ideal situation might be an edition of less than 3000 of a fairly small book of minor importance—say, a routine mystery or western story. This would probably go on a sheet-fed casemaker anyway, and the saving in stamping dies would be relatively high per unit. The size and nature of the book would permit the use of paper cover material, thus simplifying the printing (CH.9). If a soft-finish paper were used, no coating would be required.

It may be even more practical in some instances to preprint the covers by silk screen (CH.9). The process is suited to short runs and can produce excellent results if suitable copy is used. Although nothing comparable to halftone printing by lithography is possible, the silk screen technique is now capable of printing quite detailed subjects. Also, the ink used is resistant enough so that no other finish is necessary, and the process can be used on the roughest materials.

What is described above is, in effect, a paperback with hard cover. The cost of a jacket is saved, and the saving in stamping would about equal the cost of printing the cover—depending, of course, on the kind of stamping and printing involved. This is not only the most economical way to bind a hardbound book (of these characteristics), it is very little more expensive than a paperback binding. The economic advantages diminish as the quantity increases enough to make web-fed casemaking feasible.

A variation of the preprinted cover is a 3-piece binding on which a cloth spine is stamped and the sides are a preprinted material. There is no economic advantage in this arrangement unless the design permits elimination of a printed jacket. However, if the sides can be printed in rolls and run with the cloth backstrip in a single casemaking operation, this is not likely to be more expensive than a one-piece preprinted cover made on a sheet-fed machine.

STAMPED COVERS The stamping processes are described in CH. 11. The cost of stamping depends on the combination of labor and materials used. With several factors to juggle, it is possible to spend a little for a lot, or vice versa.

The labor cost of stamping is relatively uniform at about 5¢ per impression. Price differences are in the kind and size of die, and the amount of ink or leaf used. Ink is a negligible cost factor unless an unusually large amount is used. Leaf varies somewhat according to color, but the main difference is between the cost of pigment or metallic leaf (about ¾¢ per square inch) and genuine gold (about 8¢ per square inch).

Labor costs can be held down by reducing the number of impressions required. This can be done by utilizing the stamping presses' ability to run more than one roll of leaf at a time. There is room for considerable ingenuity in this area, but there are also mechanical limitations (CH. 11). Before planning this kind of operation, check with the bindery for their requirements and practices.

Economies in the amount of leaf used can be realized by careful placement of the elements to be stamped. For example, if 2 small elements in the same color are placed far enough apart so that the leaf can be "jumped" between them, you will pay for only the amount of leaf they use. If they are a little too close, you may have to pay for the leaf covering all the space between—even though it is not used. This could easily be twice as much as the amount actually used. In fact, if you stamp a border of leaf around the edge of the cover, you must expect to pay for all the leaf in the middle. Again, until you are experienced enough, check with the bindery.

Don't overlook the value of blind stamping. There is no cost at all for materials, and some very handsome effects are possible. True embossing requires expensive dies, but the effect of embossing can be obtained by the use of reverse (negative image) dies (CH. 11). This requires a design that includes the necessary background in a logical way. For example, see the colophon stamped on the spine of this book.

In planning designs with leaf, remember that colors are not entirely dependable from one run to another, nor are paper or cloth colors. For this reason, it is not wise to use color combinations of such subtlety that a small color variation will spoil them.

Sketches There are 2 reasons why it is important to make very comprehensive sketches for hardcover binding designs. First, these arrangements involve very distinctive textures and colors which are

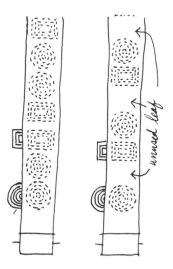

unused leaf

usually not subject to adjustment. That is, having decided on a
particular cloth, leaf, etc., the designer can rarely make small corrections of color and texture in the proof stage, as there are relatively few choices in these lines. Therefore, it is desirable to see in the sketch exactly how the end result will look. Second, once a sketch has been approved, the commitment of time and money necessary to see a proof is usually so large that a major change due to dissatisfaction with the proof may be impossible, and will almost certainly be awkward.

The same principles apply to the preparation of sketches for jackets, paper covers, preprinted covers, etc., but with a lesser degree of necessity. The materials are rarely as significant in color or texture as cloth, and it is possible to modify colors or even plates without too much difficulty. However, changes are not desirable, and the best practice is to make all sketches as near as possible to the finished appearance.

■ *Material*—Hardcover sketches should be made same-size on the actual material being proposed. The suppliers will be pleased to provide sample sheets for this purpose. It is not necessary to make a cover with boards, etc., as you will probably have sample covers made later. It is sufficient to trim the material to the size of the front cover plus the spine (see "Camera copy preparation" below). Bear in mind that it is not feasible to stamp in the ¼" (.64 cm) alongside the spine, since this is the hinge and there is no board there.

■ *Layout*—The arrangement of the type, illustration, etc. to be stamped should be carefully drawn on tracing paper. Particularly on the spine, care must be taken to trace the type to make certain that it will fit. (By this time, the bulk of the book should have been definitely established.) Presumably, if the sketch is approved, the copy for dies and plates will follow the arrangement exactly, so it is important to place everything properly.

■ *Transferring the design*—The means of transferring the pencil layout to the material will depend on whether leaf or ink is to be used. For ink stampings, rub the back of the layout with a pencil or chalk similar in color to that desired, tape the layout in position on the material, and go over the letters or illustration with firm pressure of a fairly hard pencil. This will transfer a reasonably accurate facsimile, which may be refined as necessary by using colored pencil or a brush with opaque water colors (tempera). Note that wax-base pencils or crayons will not transfer.

Whereas the ink color can be made to match your sketch, the leaf you specify cannot be modified, so it is best to use the actual leaf in making the sketch. To transfer gold leaf, simply use the pressure-sensitive leaf sold in stationery stores. Place the sheet of gold face down underneath the layout and apply fairly hard pressure with a very hard pencil or stylus. This is genuine gold and is

quite expensive but it is very simple and quick to use, and can be applied with great accuracy. To apply pigment leaf, or other metallic leaf, heat is required. For this, obtain a tool sold in art supply and hobby shops for burning designs in wood and leather. This is an electric pencil-like device. Place a piece of the leaf face down under the layout and, when the tool has heated to the proper degree, apply light pressure with the point. Until the point is hot enough, it won't release the pigment; when it is too hot, it will burn through the tracing paper. It takes a bit of practice to use this instrument well, but anyone can do it. This may sound like a lot of trouble, but don't forget that there is only one tracing involved. Once the leaf is transferred there is no need to go over it as with the other method—and the color is exact. Samples of leaf may be obtained from the suppliers. Warning: the point of that tool gets *very* hot, so don't leave it plugged in or forget where you put it.

Blind stamping can be indicated by tracing the design with the burner without any leaf. For larger areas this is not too satisfactory, and sometimes a better effect is obtained by using a leaf slightly darker than the material.

To make blank or colored panels or large areas it is easiest to find a piece of cloth or paper of the proper color, cut it, and glue it down.

■ *Endpapers*—When colored endpapers are being suggested, get a sheet of the actual paper, fold it, trim it to the trim-size, and glue it to the inside of the cover sketch. This will leave the ⅛" (.3175 cm) borders (*squares*) around the edges of the glued-down half, and will leave the other half free, as it would be in the book.

■ *Edge stain*—Edge stain can be indicated by cutting a piece of colored paper the proper size (width of trim-size x paper bulk) and taping it on the back to the back of the free leaf of endpaper. One edge of the "topstain" will then be hinged to the top of the endsheet, so it can be bent over at right angles to it.

When the spine of the cover is folded back at the hinge, a 3-sided box will be formed, showing the parts of the binding design in their correct relationship to each other. (The design is actually 3-dimensional and should not be judged in only 2 dimensions.) A length of headband cut to the paper bulk may be taped to the back edge of the "topstain" to complete the sketch.

For the preparation of copy for dies and plates see CH.8.

Camera copy preparation

PREPRINTED HARD COVERS

The only difference in copy preparation between preprinted hard covers and other kinds of printing is in positioning the copy on the material. For the dimensions of cover material see CH.11. Of the ⅝" (1.587 cm) allowed for turn-in, about ⅛" (.3175 cm) goes around the thickness of the board and the rest is on the inside of the cover. Copy that is meant to bleed at the edge of the cover should extend to ¼" (.635 cm) (or less) from the edge of the sheet. This will mean that about ⅛" of the copy will be covered by the endpaper.

PAPERBACK COVERS

In width, the trimmed cover for a flush-trimmed paperback (CH.11) is the trim-size of the book, doubled, with the paper bulk and the thickness of the covers added. Some people add ¹/₁₆" (.1588 cm) to this to allow for some loss in going around the corners at the back. The trimmed cover height is the same as the trimmed page size. The *un*trimmed cover has ⅛" (.3175 cm) more on all 4 sides because it is put on the book before the pages are trimmed. If there are any bleeds, an additional ⅛" must be added to the copy on that side. Be sure that the proper placement of the cover on the book is made clear to the bindery, if the design does not do so itself.

JACKETS

Copy for jackets needs ⅛" (.3175 cm) more on top and bottom than paperback covers, because of the overhang of the boards. On the front edge, bleeds should extend at least ¼" (.635 cm) past the edge, as the bleed should go around the thickness of the cover so that no white paper shows if the jacket is not accurately wrapped on the book. Copy that bleeds on the back edge of the spine should extend ⅛" past the spine onto the back cover for the same reason. Jacket dimensions for a book of 7 × 10" (17.78 × 25.40 cm) trim-size, ⅞" (2.2225 cm) paper bulk, and round back would be as

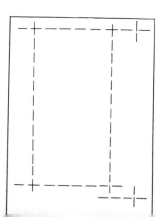

shown alongside. See also discussion of cover dimensions under "casemaking" in CH.11.

The position of flap and back-cover copy is given relative to the front cover and spine. Again, if the position of the spine on the book is not perfectly obvious, have a proper indication printed on the jacket.

Dies & stamping

Making stamping dies is a photomechanical process, so the procedures for preparing camera copy apply. Since dies can be etched to various depths, it is sometimes necessary to indicate the depth desired.

Layouts for cover stamping are much the same as mechanicals for jacket printing, except that only the front cover and spine are (usually) shown, and the layout is not camera copy but an indication of position. Proofs of the dies are positioned in a layout showing the edges of the front cover and spine, including any division of cover material (CH.11). The dimensions are as indicated for pre-printed covers, except that there are no turn-ins here. Remember that there is a space of ¼" (.635 cm) between the spine and the front and back cover boards (the joints), in which no stamping can be done.

The position of each die is indicated by measurement in inches from an outer edge of the cover and/or an edge of the spine. Where there is more than one impression, overlays should be used as in multicolor printing. Dies should be kept at least ¹/₁₆" (.1588 cm), and preferably more, from the edges of the spine. The stamping operation is not as accurate as printing, and the inaccuracies of casemaking sometimes add to the error. The stamping layout for this book is shown.

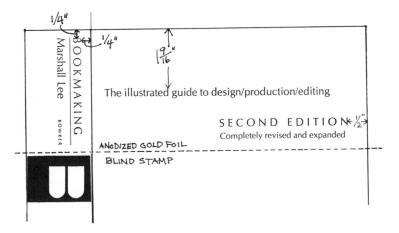

Sample covers

When the binding design has been approved, it is desirable to make *sample covers*—which are the equivalent of proofs.

Sample covers are made by hand, using the actual materials specified, and are stamped with the dies to be used for the edition. Besides providing a final opportunity to approve or modify the design, they reveal any problems in stamping and materials. If a particular leaf or ink doesn't show up or will not take well on the cover material, it is better to find out on sample covers than when the edition is being run. However, sample covers are rather costly to make and they may be omitted when the design is very simple. For example, if the dies are being stamped in gold foil on a black cloth, there can be no surprises when the job is run, so there is no need for sample covers.

It is comforting to see the completed cover in advance, and sometimes alternate colors of leaf or material may be tried, but in general, all of the design decisions should have been made in the sketch stage. Trial and error is uneconomical and, except in unusual circumstances, unprofessional.

Besides its value for the publisher, the sample cover is a useful guide for the binder, who uses it as a model for stamping. An OK'd cover with any corrections noted serves as the binder's "Master Proof". It should be returned to him with the binding order or earlier.

27 | Ordering binding

Schedule
The binding order may have to be delayed for some reason that does not affect the cover materials or stamping—perhaps because of some uncertainty regarding the jacket or illustrations. Where the schedule is tight (as it usually is by binding time), it may be best to return the approved sample cover to the binder with instructions to order the necessary materials and leaf. If these orders are delayed until the binding order is ready, it may turn out that an item is not in stock and there is not time enough to wait for it.

The binding order
As is true of composition and printing orders, the binding order is both instruction and authorization. The latter frequently indicates that only part of the edition printed is to be bound, and should specify what is to be done with the sheets being held. Most binders prefer to hold sheets in the form of folded, gathered, and sewed books, partly because it is much more economical to process the whole edition together, and partly because it is more convenient to store the unbound books that way than as *flat sheets*.

The order should contain, also, instructions for the disposition of the bound copies—how they are to be packed, whether they are to be held at the bindery or shipped, and if so, to where—and an authorized signature with a date. Here, too, a printed binding order form saves time and reduces the likelihood of important omissions. A typical order form appears on the following page.

Space is usually a problem in a bindery and it is very awkward if a partly finished job cannot be shipped out because something is missing. For this reason, few binders will schedule a job unless everything—text sheets, illustrations, dies, cover materials, and jackets—is on hand.

To prevent a mix-up, indicate on the binding order where the printed sheets and jackets or covers are coming from. This also enables the binder to act directly when there is a delay or discrepancy in shipment.

The items listed on the specimen order form are generally self-explanatory, but there are a few points worth mentioning:

(a) Where illustration inserts, wraps, and tips are not clearly identified by captions or folios, it is best to order a set of folded and gathered sheets for checking their position.

(b) Presumably, your dies and jacket or cover were made to fit a bulk calculated from the paper bulking tables or derived from a dummy. As there is a considerable amount of leeway in smashing antique book papers, it is a good idea to specify on the binding order the bulk you used, so the smash can be adjusted accordingly.

(c) Provide a good color swatch to match for the edge stain if any.

(d) Attach a printed copy of the jacket indicating how it is to be placed on the book. This is best done by marking the point at which the front joint is to come.

Date_____

Binding Order

Title_____
Author_____

PLEASE BIND _____
Quantity

FROM _____PRINTING OF _____HOLD BALANCE OF SHEETS_____

SHEET SIZE _____ FROM

TRIMMED SIZE _____wide_____high   FULL TRIM ☐   SMOOTH TOP, ROUGH SIDE & FOOT ☐

MARGINS FOR TEXT: Gutter_____Head_____TOTAL PAGES _____

PRINT AS_____ FOLD AS_____SEWING _____ ADHESIVE _____

BULK _____ ENDPAPERS:

LINING: super & paper ☐   other _____ STAIN _____

HEADBANDS_____ REINFORCEMENTS_____

INSERTS/ILLUSTRATIONS:____ pp. TO BIND AS _____

BACK: ROUND ☐   other_____ BOARDS _____

COVERS _____

STAMPING: Spine_____ FRONT _____

Verso _____ DIES FROM _____

JACKETS FROM _____

SPECIAL INSTRUCTIONS:

PACKING_____

BOUND STOCK READY_____   Signed-------------------------

28 | Special design problems

Except in a few instances, the discussions of design in this book have been general in nature. It has not been feasible to elaborate each point in terms of the many different kinds of books there are. But there are categories of books with specific and unique problems which need to be discussed. Some of the most common of these are dealt with in this chapter.

Cookbooks
A large number of cookbooks are published each year, and they vary considerably in their content. A few are narrative in form and present no special problem. We are concerned here with the recipe book, which has design problems unlike any other.

The use of a cookbook is basically the same as other "how to" books that deal with manual operations, but there are few that require such intimate involvement with such messy work. Most manuals give instructions which are referred to less and less as the worker gains experience. In cooking, each receipe is a unique operation to be followed step by step. It is this feature that makes cookbooks a special problem in design.

As a workshop guide, the cookbook requires: (a) a high degree of legibility, (b) an arrangement that minimizes the amount of handling needed, (c) resistance to soiling, and (d) a format and construction suitable to its use.

Legibility here means a size of type large enough to make reading possible while the book lies on a table or counter and the cook stands. This requires 12 or even 14 pt. type in most faces. The leading should be at least 2 pts. and preferably 3 or more. This ideal usually conflicts with a desire to keep down the number of pages, but it remains the ideal.

A large type size suggests a large page size also. In theory, a large book is less practical where work space is limited, but it is probably better in practice to sacrifice a small amount of space than to require the bending, squinting, and handling caused by small type.

The necessity for handling a cookbook in use can be reduced by placing the complete instructions for each recipe on a single spread. (If, in the middle of a crucial sentence, the cook must turn the page with greasy or floury little fingers or else suffer a culinary disaster, the book is not doing a good job.) The difficulties of achieving such an arrangement are great, especially if the text is crowded. It is almost impossible to manage without shifting recipes around. Such shifts are much easier to make in Ms than in galleys, so the ideal situation is a page-for-page arrangement by the author that provides the most practical breaks. Even this may not succeed, as shifting recipes in sequence is impossible when they are in alphabetical order, and sometimes extremely awkward when they are arranged by subject. Also, with such an arrangement, it is usually difficult to avoid wide variations in spacing to achieve pages of uniform depth. However, there is really no reason why the pages *must* be uniform in depth, so this is not a problem.

To avoid having to flatten the pages while the book is lying open on a table, the text should be kept well out of the gutter. A gutter margin of ⅞" (2.2225 cm) is the minimum, and more is better. A mechanical binding enables the book to lie perfectly flat, which eliminates this problem. If the book can also be folded back all the way, this saves space too.

The text paper for cookbooks should be as dark as possible, consistent with readability, to minimize the effects of soiling. The standard buff or tan available in many lines is satisfactory, although any other color of suitable value and intensity (low) may be used. When using tinted stock, remember that the type must be chosen with consideration for the lower contrast between ink and paper. Lighter colors, even the regular off-whites, are satisfactory if the paper is waterproof or water resistant so that it can be cleaned. Truly washable paper is too expensive for most cookbooks, but some water resistance is found in all plain papers, even the least expensive (CH. 10).

Materials used on the covers of cookbooks should and can be washable (most washable materials are relatively soil resistant anyway, which is good, as few people take the trouble to wash them). The cost of plastic- or resin-impregnated materials is often not significantly greater than others, and pure vinyl, which is totally impervious to water and most other liquids (CH. 11), is in the medium range of binding material prices. Lacquer coating and plastic lamination—both liquid and sheet—are useful on preprinted covers, although they are not always entirely satisfactory (CH. 11).

There are other important special factors in the design of cookbooks, such as the need for structural strength, ease of reference, etc., but they are not peculiar to cookbooks, being common to all books of this nature.

Generally, the problem is to present the pictures in the best possible way without sacrificing too much in the layout and typography. In some books, however, the text is primary and the illustrations are merely adjuncts, as in many histories of art. These illustrations are informative rather than representative (CH. 7), and it is probably not correct to call such books art books at all.

Where the purpose of the illustration is clearly representative, the closer to actual-size (of the original picture) the reproduction can be made, the better—so, the larger the book the better. However, there *is* a point of diminishing returns in relation to both reading convenience (and shelf space) and to manufacturing economy. This limit is about 10 × 13″ (25.4 × 33.02 cm). Art books can be, and are, made larger, but the disadvantages of such size must be outweighed by some vital consideration to warrant it. Usually, the consideration is a desire to make a big splash. This is a good enough reason if (a) the retail price can stand the much higher manufacturing cost (in large sizes, many bindery operations no longer fit on machines and must be done by hand) and (b) the book consists almost entirely of reproductions, so that reading inconvenience is a minor factor. (There are skeptics who doubt that the texts in art books are read at all.)

The large size of even an average art book page creates typographic difficulties. A 36-pica line of 11 or 12 pt. type has about 85 characters—which is more than enough (CH. 6). On the other hand, 36 picas is not much on a page of, say, 9″ (22.86 cm) width. Esthetically it can be made to work, especially if the arrangement is asymmetric, but it may not provide enough text on the page. One alternative is double (or triple) column makeup. If it is not necessary to have much text on the page, another solution is to set the type in a large size, say, 16 or 18 pt., on a wide measure.

Books in which full-page pictures are faced by a descriptive text present a problem when the amount of text varies considerably. If most units of text are short but some are long, the typography must accommodate the large units and will look awkward with the small ones. Rather than using very small type to get the large units on one page, it might be better to run long sections over at the back of the book (as in magazines) or to the following page. The latter will work only when the text unit will make an odd number of pages. Another possible solution is to continue the runover text at the bottom (or top) of the new text that follows. This can be done only where the next unit of text is short enough to fit on the page *with* the runover material. Otherwise, the new text will have to run over, etc., etc.

Putting all the text in one section and all the pictures in another has 2 advantages: (a) each section may be printed with the process and paper most suited to it and (b) the pictures may be arranged without the complication of fitting them to a text. From an editorial standpoint, this arrangement is usually unsatisfactory, as the reader cannot conveniently see the pictures while reading the relevant text. However, this is very economical for co-productions (CH. 29).

A basic creative problem in art books is the relationship of the style of design to the style of art in the book. There are 3 alternatives: the design may be (a) unrelated to the art, (b) related to the period of the art, or (c) related to the spirit of the art.

The use of period design is probably the least valid, except where the subject *is* a period or style of art. In books on the work of a particular artist or school, it is more reasonable to reflect the spirit and character *of the work* than the time in which the work was done. A dynamic and radical artist who lived during a conventional era would be badly served by a period treatment, as would an academic artist living today be misrepresented by a radical design. Something can be said for using a moderate contemporary style for all art books, thereby avoiding the hazards of choosing an appropriate expression in each case. Such a solution is definitely indicated in omnibus works (such as a museum collection) in which there is no single style or character.

Poetry

The problem of style in the design of poetry books is very much the same as for art books—only more so. Again, unless the book is an anthology of no single style, the significant feature to which the design should relate is *the essence* of the poet's work. The need for harmony between the design and that which is characteristic in the content is more vital here because the poems are an attempt at direct communication between author and reader, and the designer must not produce a false note that might break the spell. An entirely neutral design is virtually impossible, as *some* character will become evident in any work in which so many choices are made. It is better to try to make appropriate choices, and fail somewhat, than to try to be neutral and arrive accidentally at something unsuitable. Here too, it is the nature of the work that is important, not so much the period in which the work was done. This does not mean that national or period style elements should not be used, it means simply that such features are secondary to the central one—which is the spirit of the individual work.

As a practical typographic problem, poetry is unique but has several variations, depending on the form of the poems and the organization of the book. The latter is largely a question of whether the poems run in or begin on new pages—usually a matter of space. If there are so many poems that they must run in, the only associated problem is how to break stanzas at the end of a page. It is best not to break them at all, and full use of the available space is warranted to avoid such breaks. If this fails, keep a minimum of 2 lines on both pages. Beyond this point, breaking is a matter of judgment in individual cases. Each poem is a unique thing—especially the less formal modern poetry. But, formal or not, a poem is a most delicately balanced expression, and its physical arrangement is very important.

When the poems begin on new pages, breaking can be controlled somewhat. Make and tabulate a line count of each poem, allowing for turnovers as accurately as possible (CH. 17). In deciding on a maximum number of lines per page, avoid a figure that would result in frequent breaks 2 or 3 lines from the ends of poems. For example, if most poems have less than 36 lines, only a few have between 37 and 40, and the remainder are well over 40 lines, then a 36-line page will leave very few problems. On the other hand, a page of 34 or 35 lines might be extremely awkward.

A similar procedure is useful in avoiding turnovers on the width. Ideally, all lines in poetry should be printed exactly as written, with no turnovers due to accident of page size. This is not always possible, but it should be attempted by making the text page the maximum feasible width. There is no justification for using a measure too narrow to accommodate the longest lines of poetry until margins have been reduced to the limit. This limit will depend partly on the nature of the poems. Where they consist mainly of long lines, the right-hand margin should be somewhat larger than is necessary for poems with only occasional long lines. The latter require no more than about ¼" (.635 cm) on right-hand pages and about 9/16" (1.4288 cm) on left-hand pages. For poems with mostly short lines, a small outside margin and a fairly large inside margin on right-hand pages are necessary to bring the main body of type out of the gutter toward the middle of the page. On left-hand pages there is no such problem, as the short lines will fall naturally on the outer part.

To determine the best measure, calculate the width of the longest lines and the shorter long lines to arrive at the number of characters in the *average* long line. If possible, the measure should accommodate the average long lines, leaving only the longest to turn over. If *all* lines will fit, so much the better, but try to avoid a measure that will result in frequent one-word turnovers.

Poetry is by nature aligned at the left, so it does not lend itself to centering. The only way it can be centered is optically, which is very awkward if there are any long lines. Such a situation presents 2 alternatives: (a) breaking the long lines, which is not justified merely to achieve centering, or (b) moving the type mass to the left to accommodate the long lines, which is no longer centering. It is better design to respect the essential form of the material than to force it into an unnatural arrangement. For most poetry, this means alignment at the left. Optical centering is feasible only for poems of formal construction with uniformly short lines. Actual

I had read and thrown.
Oh, but not to boast,
Ever since Nag's Head
Had my heart been great,
Not to claim elate,
With a need the gale
Filled me with to shout
Summary riposte
To the dreary wail
There's no knowing what
Love is all about.
Poets know a lot.
Never did I fail
Of an answer back
To the zodiac
When in heartless chorus
Aries and Taurus,
Gemini and Cancer
Mocked me for an answer.
It was on my tongue
To have up and sung
The initial flight
I can see now might —
Should have been my own —
Into the unknown,
Into the sublime
Off these sands of Time
Time had seen amass
From his hourglass.

42

IO

THE QUESTIONER

WHEN EVENING bows its head so does the farmer,
I have seen him do it, haggard with sweat and fatigue
As he limps his way home to the daily chores,
I have been the man myself.

I have come to the lane that leads off toward the barns
And leaves the fields, and the streams of growing,
If one can think of earth as a moving tide
Where the flow is vertical.

I have stopped at the gates where maples lean on my shoulder
As confidential friends with nothing to say,
Staying to keep me company while the sunset
Squats on a burning hill.

Is this really the way it looks or is it seeming,
A distortion of the eye to fool the heart,
Collector of imitations, but still believing
It does not beat for nothing?

This is what I ask myself, is there a ledger
That adds this work and sweat to my account?
I know I do not fill my barns with dreaming,
But what's the accounting for?

centering is meaningless (unless all lines are short) as it is not apparent.

Some poets, particularly of our era, use typography to convey meaning. In typescripts, it is important to watch for indentions, groupings, or other arrangements that are meant to be followed exactly in setting and makeup. These are often indistinguishable from vagaries due to irregular typing, so it is a good idea to check with the editor where special requirements are suspected. In some cases, the words may be arranged to take curved forms, etc. (this has been done by Apollinaire, e.e. cummings, Norman Mailer, and others). A practical procedure is to have the type set without regard for position, then paste up repro proofs in the desired arrangement.

A basic problem in books of verse that do not run in is to achieve a sense of order and continuity, as the type area varies in shape, width, and depth on each page. For this reason, it is desirable to establish some constant relationships. Aligning the poems flush left helps by creating a uniform left-hand margin. Placement of poem titles and folios in a fixed relationship to the beginning of the

96

LITTLE OLD LETTER

It was yesterday morning
I looked in my box for mail.
The letter that I found there
Made me turn right pale.

Just a little old letter,
Wasn't even one page long—
But it made me wish
I was in my grave and gone.

I turned it over,
Not a word writ on the back.
I never felt so lonesome
Since I was born black.

Just a pencil and paper,
You don't need no gun nor knife—
A little old letter
Can take a person's life.

97

CURIOUS

I can see your house, babe,
But I can't see you.
I can see your house,
But I can't see you.
When you're in your house, baby
Tell me, what do you do?

poems is effective. By setting these units flush left or slightly indented from the left, a structural order is created in the upper left corner of each page. The poems then become variations on this order, rather than a chaotic succession of unrelated forms. Order can be achieved also by the use of recurring devices, such as rules, ornaments, etc., and it helps to use strongly positive typography—large or bold titles and/or numbers.

Plays   The question of style in designing plays, as in poetry and art books, is better resolved in favor of the spirit and essence of the work than the period. The use of this approach in stage productions is an interesting parallel. Some of these have been notably successful, but there have also been some misuses of the approach, such as modern-dress productions of old plays that *belong* to their period. The indiscriminate use of contemporary style and dynamics is just as bad as blind application of period trappings according to date of composition.

Typographic considerations in play composition begin with the question: For what use is the volume intended primarily—for reading or for performance?

Where the book is to be used by actors, the text should have a higher degree of legibility than is otherwise necessary. The performers should be freed as much as possible from the need for close attention to the type, so they can use their minds and bodies for acting. For example, consider the type used in television prompting. If half the size were used, the effort required to read it would distract the performers and diminish their effectiveness. The same principle holds for a performing copy of a play. True, the book is not used during a public performance, but it *is* used for tryouts and other occasions during which the actors should be at their best.

Not only must the text be more legible in a performing edition, but there should be more emphasis on the names of the characters, as it is important that the actors quickly recognize their own lines. This means that the names of speakers should stand out clearly, with both typographic style and position contributing.

It makes little difference whether the speaker's name is abbreviated or spelled out. The performers identify their parts with whatever is used, once they have seen it. Indeed, it is possible that a single abstract symbol for each character might be less distracting and more readily recognized than a name. Particularly on a first reading, actors might have an easier time if they knew that their lines were preceded by a triangle or a circle rather than an unfamiliar name.

Where the conventional identification is used, there are several alternatives. If all the speeches are long, centering the speakers' names may work. However, if there are some short (less than half a line) speeches, centered names are very awkward—practically, because the eye must shift repeatedly from center to left and back again; visually, because the centered names frequently will hang out in space with no type directly under them. Also, where the speeches are brief, the lines occupied by the speakers' names become a very large percentage of the total, and add substantially to the length of the book. This is true even when the names are flush or slightly indented from the left on separate lines. The most satisfactory solution then is to place the names at the beginning of each speech.

With the name on the first line of the speech, it is important to make it visually distinctive. The usual method is to use caps, small caps, or caps and small caps. Boldface is effective also, but may involve expense. In performing editions, it is best to further set off the speakers' names by adding a colon, a dash, or a space at the end. In reading editions, a period is sufficient. Italics are not a good choice, as there is often italic within speeches (sometimes at the beginning). Then too, italics are generally used for stage directions. It is helpful to indent turnover lines, but this device cannot do the whole job because it is not available where a succession of single-line speeches occurs.

Sometimes a distinction must be made between (a) stage directions for the actors (*enters left, laughs, etc.*) and (b) information for the reader (setting, time, background of action, etc.) The relative emphasis will depend on whether the edition is for performance or reading.

Anthologies

The special problem in anthology design is the sometimes very diverse material to be set in a single typographic style. The text matter rarely presents difficulties, but it is often quite difficult to devise an arrangement for headings that will encompass all the selections. The style chosen must provide unity, yet it must be flexible.

A .practical procedure is to set a sample page using the most complicated selection heading, and then let the editor mark up the Ms, keying each element to one of those in the sample. In extreme cases, it may be necessary to make an individual layout for each selection heading.

Reference books

To a certain extent, all books are tools—but a reference book is *entirely* a practical instrument and its design is concerned with the problem of use almost to the exclusion of anything else. This does not mean that reference books cannot be handsome. On the contrary, a particularly well-thought-out reference work is likely to have a distinct functional beauty, even if no conscious effort is made toward this end.

There are basically 2 kinds of reference books: (a) those that give *facts* and (b) those that give *instructions*.

■ *Fact books*—The main consideration here is convenience in locating items, so the running heads and/or folios are of primary importance (CH. 18). Subheads and alphabetical indicators should be made prominent also, as they are the guides followed by readers who are not inclined to use running heads or folios.

In directories, encyclopedias, and other reference books in which the user will be reading brief passages, the text type may be quite small, particularly where 2- or 3-column composition results in a narrow measure (CH. 6).

■ *Instruction books*—These are essentially the how-to books. In design, they follow most of the principles applicable to cookbooks, combined with those indicated above for other reference works.

Learning usually requires considerable effort, which most people naturally resist, so the instructional book should be designed to *appear* simple in organization even if it is not. This is not always easy to accomplish, but when it *is* managed, it is a distinct contribution to the value of the book. The designer should study the Ms until its organization is *thoroughly* understood. Only then is it likely that it can be made understandable to the reader.

One particularly useful device is to give the various classes of headings and subheads quite contrasting treatment. The more nearly similar they are, the more confusion arises. A distinctly different treatment in type face, size, space, position, and/or weight tends to establish an order that reassures the prospective user. Space around subheads, charts, etc. reduces the forbidding aspect of a page of difficult text. There is an unfortunate tendency to set professional-level technical books without consideration for the readers' comfort—mainly on the theory that they *must* read the book so why bother—but this is unfair and, in the long run, impractical. One may be technically talented and lazy at the same time, so the unreadable text might scare away some potentially great discoverers.

Although textbooks are one of the major subdivisions of book publishing, they are not really a separate category of book design. They are unique in the *method* by which they are created—usually being a collaboration of author, editor, designer, and illustrator—but even in this respect they differ from other books only in that they, textbooks, are produced as books *should* be, whereas most books are created by authors, editors, designers, and illustrators who never see or speak to each other.

It is also true that schoolbooks sometimes have features not often found in other books, such as tests, summaries, foot glosses, etc., but these are typographically little different from similar material used elsewhere, and represent no fundamental departure. Essentially, textbooks fall into the functional category of reference books and their problems may be approached accordingly.

The schoolbooks with the most special character are those for elementary grades, especially the earlier ones. The design problems in these books are not so much *different* from instructional material for adults as they are more *acute*. A greater effort must be made to simplify matters and present them effectively. To this end, illustration, color, particularly legible typography, and careful layout are required. These devices are just as useful in adult books of instruction, but they are rarely used because they are thought to be unnecessary, and they involve extra expense. The principles, in any case, are the same. All graphic devices must be brought together to achieve maximum clarity and arouse maximum interest. The latter is thought to be more important in books for children, because motivation is weaker, but this is true only in the sense that school children are *required* to learn what is in their books, whereas the only adults who use instructional material are those who have decided that they want to learn the subject. However, learning is a chore at any age and at any level of motivation. Textbooks (and all books) should always be made as interesting as possible.

The specific design problems of mathematics texts, literature, social studies, etc. cannot be covered in detail here. In many respects, the material will be similar to the various kinds discussed in CHS. 17 and 18, but some situations will be so special that their solution must be devised without the aid of anything but previous experience with the same or similar matter. In general, the basic principles of design apply—analyze the problem, consider possible solutions, select the best one.

29 | Co-productions

A *co-production* is a book produced at one time for 2 or more publishers. The participating publishers may be of the same country—e.g. a trade publisher and a book club—or of different countries. Their purpose is to save money by sharing costs and enjoying the economies of large quantities.

The economics
There are 2 kinds of costs in book production: (a) plant costs— one-time expenses that are not affected by the size of the run, and (b) manufacturing costs—the costs of labor and materials that vary according to the number of copies printed and bound. The main economies in co-productions are found in sharing plant costs. Some books with high plant costs are prohibitively expensive in the quantities that one publisher can sell, and the *only* way they can be economically published is by arranging a co-production. For example, a book with a large number of color process illustrations (CH. 8) might have a plant cost of $40,000; for an edition of 5000 copies this means $8 per copy. By the normal economics of publishing (CH. 2) this would account for about $40 in the projected retail price—with more needed to cover the cost of manufacturing. At a retail price of, say, $50, the project would probably be priced out of its market. However, if publishers in 3 other countries were each able to sell 5000 copies, the total edition would be 20,000 copies and the plant cost would come down to $2 per book—only about $10 of the retail price. This would enable a retail price under $20, a practical amount for the book.

There are also some fixed costs in the manufacturing processes that can be divided among participants in a co-production. These are the setting-up or makeready costs in printing and binding (CHS. 9, 11,12). Again, for a short run the makeready costs loom large; divided among a large number of copies they can be negligible.

Another possible saving in the manufacturing costs of a co-production is in lower prices for larger quantities of materials.

Book cloth and paper are sold by the yard and pound at prices that decrease as the size of the order increases. These decreases are not graduated but occur at widely spread breaks in quantity. In paper, for example, the pound price in the United States is the same from 5000 lbs. (2268 kg) to 10,000 lbs. (4536 kg) (CH. 10) and then drops substantially. Thus, the unit cost of paper for an edition of 5000 that requires 7500 lbs. (3402 kg) would be lowered if another edition of only 2000 copies—requiring 3000 lbs. (1361 kg) of paper—were added to the run. There would also be a reduction in the *amount* of paper used per copy, since the spoilage in makeready would be the same for 5000 copies as for 7000, and the cost of the spoiled paper would be shared.

It is customary for foreign-language participants in a co-production to translate the text, have the type set, and supply the originating publisher with films of the text at their own expense. They also pay for the cost of their text plates, changing the text plates during the press run, and, usually, shipping their books. In compensation for these extra costs, they generally are charged a smaller royalty than English-language publishers.

Note that co-productions with book clubs usually do not involve sharing plant costs, and sometimes not even the makeready costs. When a book club is sold books at the run-on price, the only possible saving is in materials—and in some cases even this does not occur.

Procedures

PREPARATION

The preparation for printing involves several processes (CH.8): typesetting, mechanicals, color separation, black & white photography, and stripping. All of these costs are shared equally between English-language publishers, except for a very minor additional cost to all but one of them for stripping in their changes on the title page and copyright page. This cost is usually borne by the publisher(s) other than the originating one, e.g. if the book originates with the U.S. publisher, then the cost of changing is paid by the British and/or Australian participants.

When a foreign-language publisher is involved, the cost of composition is shared only by the English-language publishers, since the text must be set again in the foreign language—which is done at the expense of the foreign publisher. In scheduling, it is important to leave enough time for the translation, typesetting, proofreading, and preparation of films for the text. The most common and difficult problem in co-productions is getting the foreign-language text films in time to keep the press schedule.

It is necessary to make a complete set of black plates for each foreign-language publisher, and this means stripping their text films on a set of flats (CHS.8,9). The most practical procedure is to have the foreign publisher send the text with one complete page on each piece of film—with register marks to enable the printer to position the pages properly in relation to all the other elements.

Rather than combine the black flats of the illustrations with the text flats, it is better to leave them separate, so that a single set of illustration film may be used for making the black plates for all languages. (When this is done, the illustration flat and the text flats are exposed [burned] onto the plate separately to make a single plate that includes everything black.) If, on the other hand, the foreign-language texts are stripped up with duplicates of the black illustration flats, there is not only the additional cost of the duplicate film, but the danger of enlarging or reducing the dots in the duplication process—which could result in color imbalance (in well-made duplicates this should not happen).

PRINTING   The largest economy in co-productions is in preparation, but the worst complications are in printing. As noted above, the main difficulty is coordination.

It is not acceptable to delay delivery to the other participants because of the failure of one or two publishers to send films as promised, so it is desirable to plan an alternative procedure. This usually means making a set of black plates without text so that the color printing can be done in one run, even if the text for late participants must be printed separately later. Since the cost of color makeready is much higher than that for black only, the late publishers get most, if not all, of the benefit of the combined printing.

Another complication is the problem of getting the right quantities for each participant. When only one edition is being printed at a time, there is only one makeready for each form, and the paper allocation can usually be worked out fairly well. With several editions being printed, there are several changes of black plates with a makeready for each, and paper is spoiled each time. Under these conditions it is more difficult to come out with the proper quantity for each publisher—especially the last one, who may come up short if spoilage runs higher than expected.

There is also the problem of quality control. This is in the hands of the originating publisher, and there should be no trouble if the results are excellent. It is true, however, that publishers in each country tend to have a national sense of color. Some like color more intense, others prefer softer effects. Some lean toward reddish color, others like yellower tints. It is a good idea to check these preferences with the participants before printing.

It shouldn't happen, but it is not unknown for a printer to mix up the plates and/or the quantities in co-productions. Sometimes the plate with the British copyright is put on press to back up the U.S. title page or vice versa. Sometimes the quantity for the French edition is run for the German and vice versa. If you are at the press you should be able to catch such gaffes before they go too far. If not, the results can be disastrous.

It makes little difference where the preparation work is done, since proofs, film, etc., can be easily and economically sent by air. When it comes to printing, the cost and time involved in getting the printed sheets or bound books to the participating publishers is an important element in deciding where to print. The cost of transporting a book of, say, 7 × 10″ (17.8 × 25.4 cm) across an ocean might be 20 to 25¢, depending on its thickness and the number shipped, so it is usually best to print on the continent where most of the books will be delivered. But there are other elements to consider: (a) the relative cost of printing (costs vary with currency fluctuations and inflation, but in general there are not now, in 1979, great differences in the prices of equivalent work among the major industrialized countries—lower prices are available in the technologically less advanced areas, but quality and delivery schedules may not be as reliable; however, these conditions are subject to change and should be checked in each case); (b) convenience of access (watching the printing when the press is 3000 miles away from home is a lot more time-consuming and expensive than when it is nearby); (c) language differences; and (d) transportation time. All of these considerations, plus the relative merits of individual printers, must be weighed carefully. And remember that the work will be done perhaps 6, 8, or more months in the future, when conditions may be different.

The stripping and plate change problems are about the same for jackets as for the text. However, it is desirable to design jackets for co-productions so that the minimum number of colors will be affected by plate changes. The ideal design has all type in black, so that only the black plate need be changed.

PAPER

The paper for a co-production is ordered just as though there was to be only one edition printed, except that an allowance must be made for the additional spoilage resulting from the black plate changes. The printer should calculate these quantities. In web-fed printing, paper spoilage is relatively high at best, and the spoilage for these plate changes can be considerable. If expensive paper is being used, the extra spoilage can wipe out the printing economy, so it is wise to get estimates for sheet-fed printing as well. This becomes an especially important consideration in reprinting, when the quantities are likely to be smaller than those of the first run.

If a co-production is to be printed abroad, it is important to see samples of the paper the printer intends to use. Paper in each country does not necessarily match the grades made in other countries.

In times of paper shortage there can be long waits for deliveries, so it may be necessary to get quantity commitments from participating publishers well in advance of printing so that the paper can be ordered in good time.

There are few special problems in binding co-productions. Makeready is a relatively small item, so the cost savings are minor. All binding operations except stamping can be run with a single makeready for all editions, since the language differences do not affect these procedures. In stamping, or in preprinting covers, there is a change of imprint for the English-language publishers and a complete change of dies for the foreign-language participants. The number of plate changes in preprinting covers depends on the design, as was indicated previously for jackets.

Keeping the various editions separated—and making certain that the Italian covers are not put on the Spanish books or the French jackets put on the Italian books, etc.—is not a difficult matter for a well-run bindery, but mistakes do happen. The binder should be alerted to these problems just before the work begins.

Packing for overseas shipment is different from the normal practice—waterproof cartons are used and skids are usually shrink-wrapped—unless the books are being shipped in containers. The latter are huge, metal, watertight boxes 20 to 40′ (6.15 to 12.3 m) long that are loaded at the warehouse or bindery, sealed shut, and loaded onto ships. They provide the best protection in transit and normal packing is sufficient. Nevertheless, all of the publishers should be asked to provide packing and shipping instructions, since they usually have a definite preference about the handling of their books.

Conclusion

The present discussion of co-productions may or may not make this operation seem terribly difficult. In case there is any doubt, it *is*. The difficulty multiplies when there are 5 or 6 participants—but it is bad enough with only 3. Getting all parties to agree to a plan and schedule is hard, but the big trouble comes when one or more publishers fail to keep their schedules, send the wrong material, or make changes at the last minute. Inevitably, some of these things *always* happen. The advantages of co-productions are real, and can be decisive for a publishing project—but any decision to do one must be taken in the full knowledge that they are not easy to do well, and a lot of good luck is necessary.

PART II Editing

A

THE PROFESSION

30 | Background

In the sense that editing means selection and discrimination it can be said to have existed almost from the beginning of man's civilized life. Even before there was writing, editorial judgment shaped the oral literature. Each successive teller of a story related it a little differently, perhaps omitting the duller parts and rephrasing others to make the whole more effective. No doubt there were some embellishments and probably some substantial additions from time to time. Once writing began, it can be safely assumed that some persons other than the writers decided what writings would be cut into clay or stone and accepted into the official record. Further, it is reasonable to suppose that someone with authority asked for or made changes in the work submitted. The point is that in all such cases the "published" work was the product of not only its originator but also of another person whose judgment affected either the work itself or its publication—or both. Although such persons would not have been called "editors", they performed editorial functions.

It is probable that some professional editing was done on the ancient Greek plays by their producers and it is known that people were hired to assist in producing the vast amounts of Roman literature. These antecedents of the modern editor were followed by the scribes who made the medieval manuscripts. They applied not only selection and discrimination but a certain amount of the corrective work that we call "copy editing". Certainly there was "proofreading" in the sense that the work was not considered finished until it had been read and the errors corrected. If this editorial work was not up to the standards we set for ourselves today, neither was there the authority of an established dictionary to consult. Without accepted rules of grammar and spelling, the "editors" were left to make their own choices—but choose they did and languages developed through this process. Presumably, the works that showed better clarity, consistency, and logic were admired and imitated—leading to the eventual adoption of their style by the lexicographers to come.

Once printing began, the editing of books became institutionalized in the sense that it was then done as a professional routine. In the first decades after Gutenberg, printer-publishers generally did their own editing, although proofreading was given to an employee or family member. As printing-publishing houses grew larger, scholars were engaged to evaluate and sometimes correct or modify projected works in their discipline. Many printers were themselves considerable scholars, and several, like Aldus Manutius and Christopher Plantin, were honored as much for the editorial distinction of their books as for the quality of their typography.

By the 18th century, the full-time editorial employee was an established feature of publishing houses—which by that time were often separate from the printing offices where they began. Even then, the main editorial judgments were probably made by the head of the house and the editorial employees were primarily proofreaders. It was not until well into the 19th century that the size of publishing houses exceeded the capacity of the owners to handle all the editorial decision making. They still made the primary decisions to publish or not, but even these were delegated in part to editors when the companies grew very large and began to departmentalize.

The professional editor as a qualified specialist has existed for not much more than one century. Since World War II, the profession has been dividing into specialties that form a chain linking management to the various departments of publishing. Where our image of an editor before 1950 was the Maxwell Perkins type who worked with authors and manuscripts from concept to printed book, we now sometimes have as many as 4 editors involved with a single book, each concerned with a different part of the process. As book-publishing companies become larger and their domination by professional managers increases, this tendency toward fragmentation and specialization of the editorial function will probably continue.

31 | Function

The editorial function is the same thing whether performed by one person or 4: (a) book projects must be brought to the house (whether through the initiative of author, agent, editor, or publisher), (b) there must be an editorial hand in the development of manuscripts that fit the needs of author and publisher, (c) the manuscripts must be editorially corrected and styled to prepare them for the printer, and (d) the editorial work must be organized.

In the course of (a) there must be negotiation of the contract between author and publisher. While this work has traditionally been handled by the editor, the complexities of many contracts today require the attention of specialists familiar with the problems of movie, television, reprint, foreign, and other rights. Nevertheless, this function remains in the editorial sphere.

Where the functions are divided—and there is almost always some overlap—we speak today of (a) an acquiring or sponsoring editor, (b) a working or manuscript editor, (c) a copy editor, and (d) a managing editor. There is another category called "production editor" which refers to one who functions as a link between the editorial and production departments, sometimes overlapping (b) and (c). (Production editors are found mainly in textbook houses.) The preparation of contracts is often done by a "contracts manager" who is usually in the editorial department. However, the negotiation of contract terms is a function of the acquisitions editor.

Relationships

EDITORIAL TO MANAGEMENT

The acquiring (or acquisitions) editor has the power to reject books, but does not usually have the authority to accept a book. However, in many cases where the editor is very senior in the company, or has a strong reputation, this authority is actually or practically in his or her hands. Under these circumstances, the editor is, in effect, part of management, since the decision concerning what is to be published is a business function as well as an editorial one.

In some cases, editors are given autonomy, financial backing, and their own *imprint* within the company. The 1970s saw a trend in this direction. In cases where the final decision is made by management—i.e. the publisher as distinguished from an editor, an editor-in-chief, or editorial director—the editorial department has the role of professional advisor.

Editorial advice is usually accepted by management when it is given with enthusiasm, supporting facts (such as market research or the author's previous successes), and the concurrence of the sales department. In the case of complex or illustrated books, the management's decision may be affected by cost factors that outweigh editorial judgment.

Most publishing houses have policies or guidelines concerning the kinds of books they want to publish. The editor must observe these rules in general, but occasionally a book comes along that is so attractive a proposition that it is accepted by management even though it does not fit into the current program. Editors with their own imprints generally set their own policies—in consultation with the house management.

In all respects, the editor acts as the link between author and publisher, protecting the interests of both. However, the editor is primarily the publisher's representative and in contract negotiations must try to make the best terms possible in the company's favor.

EDITORIAL TO
DESIGN & PRODUCTION

See CH. 2.

EDITORIAL TO SALES

This chapter refers to "sales", "advertising and promotion", and *subsidiary rights* as separate departments, and so they are, but it should be noted that in the larger houses it is usual to have a marketing director who coordinates and controls the activities of these departments and any other activities related to the marketing of the books. In some companies, however, "sub-rights" is the responsibility of the editor-in-chief.

A discussion of the economics of publishing and the factors that influence sales of a book is included in CH. 2 under "Design and production to sales". This material is equally relevant to editors and should be read.

The first point at which editorial and sales intersect is when a project is first presented to the house for consideration. The decision to publish or not is based on 2 considerations: the intrinsic quality of the book and its profit potential. Sometimes one aspect greatly outweighs the other and a mediocre book is taken because it is expected to sell very well, or a superb book is accepted even though it is not expected to make money, but generally it is necessary for both factors to be positive.

When both the editorial and sales departments are immediately enthusiastic about a project there is no problem—except where an expensive production makes publication impractical because the retail price would have to be too high. (In such a case, possibilities are explored by the editorial, design, and production departments early in the discussions initiated by the editor.) There may, however, be conflict between editor and sales department over the question of market. Generally, the sales department is accepted as the authority on the sales prospects of a book, since it is staffed by those having the most experience in selling. Sometimes, though, the author, the editor, or both, have special knowledge of the audience for a particular book (for example, the author may know of a strong collector interest in beer cans, but lacking that knowledge the sales manager can be expected to consider a book on the subject unpublishable, to say the least) and the editor must press for acceptance against the reluctance of sales.

Just as the special qualifications of the sales people are respected in matters of sales, the judgment of the editor is usually accepted in considering the merits of the book. But such judgments are subjective to some extent and differences of opinion sometimes occur. The sales manager will probably defer to the editor's judgment, but editors, and publishers, are usually wary about publishing a book that does not have the wholehearted support of the sales department. Most companies publish more books than can be effectively sold anyway, and only those that are most actively promoted have much chance of success.

Once a book has been accepted, editorial and sales join again in considering jacket and cover designs submitted by the art director. The editor is concerned that the jacket properly represents the book, and both editor and sales manager are anxious that the jacket be effective in sales. The most common disagreement is when the sales department prefers a design that the editor feels misrepresents the book. In most houses, the editorial department has the last word, but in some the sales department is given the power to decide. In deadlocks, the publisher usually settles the question.

The sales department is usually not concerned with the design of the book, but there is sometimes an exchange of ideas with the design and editorial departments on large illustrated books.

After publication, editorial keeps in touch with sales to make decisions on revised editions, reprints, etc.

While the main responsibility for subsidiary rights sales—book clubs, translations, motion pictures, television, radio, condensations, etc.—rests with the sub-rights manager, the editor is interested in promoting such sales because they add to the success of the book, and therefore of the editorial department. There is no objection to an editor's contribution in making useful contacts or in speaking up for the book at the right time, but friction can result

EDITORIAL TO
SUBSIDIARY RIGHTS

if the editor acts independently and fails to coordinate with the sub-rights department.

Terms for the author's share of the sub-rights sales are specified in the contract, but sometimes deals are made that are not covered by the contract or that require author approval and the editor must see that the author (or the agent) is properly brought into the negotiations. However, the sub-rights department usually has the responsibility for arranging terms between the house and the buyer of rights. The editor is notified of the terms but rarely consulted on them unless a very substantial deal is involved.

EDITORIAL TO ADVERTISING/PROMOTION

Editors almost always want more advertising and promotion for their books than is planned, but the controlling factor is the budget. The amount allocated for each book in the budget is determined by the sales prospects of the book (a book that does not have exceptionally good prospects is, alas, not likely to get *any* advertising budget at all) and to some extent its audience (which might be reached fully through ads in a single publication). This means that the sales manager has an important voice in the decision. In most houses the editorial department has some power in the budgeting of advertising and promotion money, but in some the decision is entirely up to marketing management. (The advertising and promotion people who spend the money rarely have much to say about how much is to be spent on each book.) Strong editorial support for a book can sometimes boost the initial advertising budget, but once the book is published its sales performance determines how much advertising is done. It is generally believed that advertising alone cannot make a tradebook sell, it can only boost the sales of a book that is already selling. (This publishing axiom is never accepted by authors, who are usually certain that their books would sell very well if well advertised.)

Approaches to editing

The layperson's vision of publishing features an editor reading manuscripts sent in by hopeful writers, selecting a promising one, and calling in the ecstatic author to sign a contract. The editor then asks the author to make a few changes—which is done more or less willingly—and the manuscript is sent off to the printer.

This picture is representative of only a tiny percentage of publishing today. It was never *generally* accurate, but was much more the case two generations ago. Now, many publishers will not even look at unsolicited manuscripts from writers. The only projects they consider are: (a) those offered by agents or by the few established authors who have no agent, (b) those conceived by editors inside the house, (c) those offered by someone known to a person in the firm, and (d) those offered by outside packagers who develop book projects that are sold to publishers as completed or partially produced books. Other publishers, however, do have procedures for screening unsolicited manuscripts, although it is rare that one is accepted. Publishers also buy rights to books originally published by foreign publishers, and sometimes enter into agreements to simultaneously co-publish a book with a group or consortium of foreign publishers. (This may involve a co-production, whereby the several editions are manufactured together for economy—see CH. 29.)

The new situation tends to enhance the publisher's chances of making a profit on each book, but it has been criticized for its possible exclusion of valuable work written by the as-yet-unpublished who have no contact with agents. As the flood of unsolicited manuscripts gets turned away by publishers, it finds its way to the agents—who are even more inclined to react in the same way as the publishers, since they have even more limited resources. However, most publishers and agents are sensitive to the cultural problem and make conscientious efforts to deal with it—always, of course, in the hope that a literary masterpiece (and potential best seller) will be discovered.

Under the circumstances, there is obviously a premium on good contacts with agents and authors, and some successful editors function mainly as conduits to these sources of "product", systematically meeting with them and talking about projects. While any editor worthy of the name is able to, and does, assist authors in developing their books, an editor who does no more than bring in an important writer is considered—and is—a valuable asset to the house.

The contribution of an editor can be anything from conceptual to mechanical, and all contributions are necessary and valid. Some editors are concerned only with seeing that the main outline of a book is right and will leave the detailed give-and-take with the author to another. Some insist on seeing the work through to the final product themselves. In any case, there is always a going-over by a copy editor (CHS. 36,41,43) before the manuscript goes to the printer.

A surprisingly large percentage of books published are not "accepted" at all, but rather are originated by in-house editors who either hire or contract with writers to carry out an idea. This process is discussed under "Concept" in CH. 38.

32 | Requirements

Talent
The innate abilities required by an editor depend on the kind of editor being considered. Acquiring or sponsoring editors need a natural rapport with the kind of person who produces the kind of books desired. If the editor is interested in how-to books, the people involved are likely to be relatively down-to-earth but enthusiastic amateurs or no-nonsense professionals. Pursuing the best sellers means being comfortable with the high-powered agents and lawyers who handle the big-name writers. In both cases, the editor must have an instinct for sensing the real thing—the idea that is *really* sound, the book that will *really* get written, the agent who is *really* serious about getting together, the movie that will *really* get made. Acquiring editors must also have good business heads as they are primarily responsible for the terms made with the author. Finally, there must be a natural sense of quality—not so much the ability to discern high art as the ability to recognize what is excellent of its kind. Presumably, an editor with the personal qualities needed to inveigle writers and agents into the company fold will be good at persuading the company to accept what is brought in, although this is not always true.

The manuscript editor should also have an effective way of dealing with people. Working closely with writers, particularly creative ones, is often a trying experience because writers have a strong emotional commitment to their books and no matter how mild-tempered they may normally be, they tend to guard their work with a passion ranging from intense to ferocious. Even professional hacks can be difficult if their personalities don't jibe with the editor's or if they feel that their work is being maltreated. Indeed, diplomatic talent is even more necessary to a working editor than to an acquiring one because the strain is usually sustained much longer and the matters dealt with are more emotionally charged.

Working with a manuscript *also* requires a sense of what is good and true, but there must be in addition an ability to know what will correct deficiencies. Sometimes it is enough to be able to point out a flaw and the author will correct it—but often it is necessary to show the author what can be done to correct it. Theoretically, an editor need not be a good writer—but in fact every working editor does a considerable amount of writing in the course of making manuscripts work, and the success of the editor depends to a large extent on how good this writing is. Even some very fine writers are inclined to let stand a sentence well rewritten by a respected editor.

The role of the copy editor varies from house to house. In some, copy editors are actually the manuscript editors and work directly with the authors. In most, they have very little latitude in changing the text and rarely deal with the author directly. Thus, such a person does not need the personality traits of the acquiring or manuscript editors, but does require the ability to spot and correct awkward or badly constructed sentences. Beyond this, the copy editor should have a natural inclination to be precise and meticulous and have the patience to examine very closely sizable amounts of material that may not be personally interesting. The worst fault of a copy editor is a tendency toward lapses of close attention. A good copy editor has the ability to sustain intense concentration over long periods, even when dealing with boring material, and can avoid becoming so involved in interesting material as to lose sight of the details. Proofreading requires much the same group of talents as copy editing, but writing ability is not necessary.

A managing editor needs to have the same kind of qualities as a production manager, being at the more-or-less calm center of a swirling storm of complex activity. This job requires: (a) a talent for judging people, since it usually involves hiring the administrative personnel of the department and, sometimes, the freelancers; (b) a natural organizing ability that enables handling the traffic of editorial work efficiently (it is no small matter to control the comings and goings of dozens of manuscripts and proofs to a large number of authors, editors, artists, designers, sales people, promotion people, production people, sub-rights people, and others); and (c) a non-abrasive personality that keeps relations between the editorial and other departments smooth and effective. In some companies, the managing editor is responsible for the preparation of the department budget, so a mathematical talent is desirable. In sum, this job calls for a good administrator. In small companies, the managing editor often does some copy editing and manuscript editing as well.

The *ideal* background for any editor is to have (a) an MA in English or comparative literature from a first-class university, with many courses in languages, psychology, and business administration, (b) been an insatiable reader since childhood of everything from newspapers and magazines to literary classics, as well as to have

Background & training

been a movie and TV fan, (c) had a two-year postgraduate course in publishing—including editing, design, production, sales, and management, (d) spent at least one year working in bookstores and another year in typesetting, printing, and binding plants, (e) put in a few months' apprenticeship in every department in a publishing house, and (f) spent at least a year as a *traveller* [a salesperson on the road servicing bookstores, wholesalers, libraries, and schools]. It wouldn't hurt at all to have (g) spent a few months as a librarian. To be the child of a major publisher or editor and know personally a large number of important agents and writers would also be useful.

Few can afford to prepare themselves as fully as described above—or be so fortunate in their birth—but a considerable part of this education and experience is quite possible, and a substantial part of it is really essential to a well-trained editor. Indeed, there are publishers heading large houses who have had practically all of this ideal background. Many companies are willing to give promising young people the apprenticeship opportunities referred to above, and to finance some professional training as well.

At the end of CH. 3 there is a discussion of professional courses available.

33 | Opportunities

Although editors function in different ways, these distinctions are not as structured as the different functions in design and production. To a great extent, an editor is hired as an editor without any other designation than, perhaps, "junior", "senior", or "associate". Generally, the way an editor operates tends to define the position more clearly than does a title.

An exception to this rule is the copy editor, who is almost always hired as such and is limited to the specific functions of a copy editor in that house. As discussed above, however, the definition of the copy editor's functions varies from one company to another, and in some houses copy editors are also manuscript editors.

Another exception is the production editor, who is also given specific functions and a specific designation. There is some variation in the duties of production editors, but they rarely extend into manuscript editing or even copy editing.

Of course, the managing editor has a very definite job which does not, except perhaps in the smaller companies, overlap the other editorial functions. Indeed, the managing editor does not ordinarily edit. The work could actually be done by an administrator with no editorial ability.

The contract-writing function is either included in the duties of the editors or is the work of specially qualified people who are designated "contract managers" rather than editors.

Many publishers now hire people specifically as acquiring or sponsoring editors, but others simply hire editors who acquire projects and work on manuscripts to the extent that suits their interests and the needs of the company.

The general category "editor" is subject to the same hierarchical structure as other professions, with an editor-in-chief at the top, a managing editor below and a little to the side, then senior editor, editor, junior editor, associate editor, assistant editor, editional assistant. The actual meanings of these titles in terms of responsibilities are far from exact. They represent levels of pay and perquisites, but the work each does depends on the house. In one company, an assistant editor may be doing little more than secretarial work, in another, manuscript editing. The titles tend to proliferate in the larger companies and drop away in the smaller ones. This is because in the latter each editor is likely to do a wide range of work so that the distinctions between the editors are very small.

At the bottom of the pyramid—but not to be ignored—are the editorial secretaries. While they often do the same work as others with more exalted titles and feel undervalued, the important fact is that they are *in* the editorial department. This is the first rung of the ladder, and it leads to the second just as the second leads to the third and so on.

The number of staff editors that a publishing company employs usually varies in proportion to the size of the house; the number can range from one or 2 in the smallest to dozens in the largest, where they are usually organized in separate departments. Textbook publishers are likely to employ more editors than trade houses, but these are mostly copy editors and production editors, whereas the tradebook publishers will have a large proportion of acquiring editors.

An editor-in-chief usually does some acquisition, but the job is essentially one for an executive, whose primary concern and responsibility is the success of the firm's list. In very small houses, the title "editor-in-chief" may exist without the function, as the publisher personally supervises the work of the editors. The larger packaging houses also have staff editors, but relatively few compared with large publishing companies.

Here a word about proofreading is in order. Proofreading is as much a part of the editorial function as anything else, but it is not normally treated as a separate function in publishing houses. Sometimes proofreading is done in the house within the copy editing department, but more often it is given out to freelancers (most of whom also do copy editing). Proofreading is also done in typesetting houses (CH. 5), and, in fact, was once left entirely to the printer, except for that done by the author. In some countries, that is still the practice. Today, in the United States, most publishers have all proofs read at least once (in addition to the printer's and author's readings), and many have their nonfiction proofread by two readers (CH. 37).

Because proofreading, copy editing, and manuscript editing require days or weeks of uninterrupted work, they lend themselves well to freelancing. A large percentage of the proofreading, a somewhat smaller percentage of the copy editing, and a still smaller, but substantial, part of the manuscript editing done for publishers goes to freelancers.

Ambition to succeed in editing can mean 3 different things, depending on one's interests:

(a) For those with a taste for high-living and an appetite for glamour, excitement, and recognition, the goal might be senior acquisitions editor in a successful trade house, buying million-dollar properties by big-name authors, making newsworthy movie and paperback deals, and using an unlimited expense account to entertain important agents and writers. This possibility is real enough in today's publishing arena to be attainable for someone with the right kind of ability. An editor with a few top-money authors under contract can almost always name a salary and get it. The route to such positions could be a step-by-step climb from editorial assistant ($9,000 to $12,000) to junior editor ($11,000 to $16,000) to senior editor ($15,000 to $40,000) or, for the exceptionally gifted, a jump from assistant to the top without stopping at the intermediate rungs. In this game it is only the results that count, and they can be readily seen and counted.

(b) For those who crave position and executive authority, editor-in-chief in a major firm is the goal. Pay for such a job can range upward from $25,000 to $45,000 or more. Smaller houses usually pay about the same rate to an editor-in-chief as to senior editors—with the title as compensation in lieu of more money. The advancement to editorships-in-chief is likely to be step-by-step, but a strong show of talent can result in a jump to the top in some cases. Very often, a stint as managing editor (perhaps $12,000 to $25,000) leads to the top executive post.

(c) If you are more interested in making books than making deals, and have no love for administration, you would strive to become a senior editor in a good "literary" house (one that shows an interest in serious, substantial books and is less avid for the hot commercial property than most, but where profit is high enough to pay good salaries). You would probably end up near the lower end of the salary scale for senior editors, but you would enjoy the pleasure of doing what you like to do. Here the route to the top is most likely to begin at the editorial assistant level and proceed in fairly slow steps through the intermediate positions.

Copy editing is a specialty that is its own reward for those who enjoy the nitty-gritty of manuscript work and are not personally interested in acquisition. Sometimes people move from copy editing to acquisition, but most regard it as a profession that calls for the best they can give, and derive satisfaction from doing it well. Salaries range from $10,000 to $20,000. Freelance copy editing is paid for by the hour at rates from $6 to $9. While acquiring and manuscript editors *rarely* get credit lines in their books, copy editors almost *never* do.

Proofreaders can make $180 to $250 per week on salary, and $4.50 to $6.50 for freelance work. These rates, as well as those for copy editors, are for normal work. Prices for exceptionally difficult or specialized books can be higher.

How to get a job

As noted in ᴄʜ.4, jobs in book publishing have often gone to someone who happens to be around rather than to a qualified person from outside. This is not as true as it was, but to the extent that it is, it is probably more true of editorial jobs than any other, despite the fact that this field is the most sought-after in publishing. Other industries systematically recruit for their more attractive entry positions from the top graduates of the best schools in the country; publishers have often given these jobs to someone's friend or relative, an ambitious employee from the lower ranks, or someone who replies to a want ad and seems better than the other applicants.

There are some fairly good reasons for this state of affairs, but the most significant factor is probably the difficulty of knowing who will turn out to be a successful editor. A publisher who picks a bright English major from a top college knows that intelligence and some knowledge of literature will be brought to the job, but whether this person will have the ability to produce profitable books cannot be predicted.

It would, of course, make a big difference if publishers could recruit from a publishing school as a chemical company recruits from MIT, but unfortunately no such place exists in America. Under the circumstances, the accidental, hit-or-miss approach has been inevitable. There are now a considerable number of excellent publishing courses being offered (ᴄʜ. 3), and this is all to the good, but they are not a substitute for a 4-year curriculum—where a student can demonstrate ability as well as learn. There is, however, a growing trend toward hiring the graduates of the better courses.

How then does the aspiring editor get a job in the field? There is no way to show competence in the necessary skills except to submit writing that is skillful and gives evidence of a knowledge of grammar, structure, and style. The character of the presentation will suggest personal qualities such as neatness, taste, and perhaps flair. Any publication experience—even the editorship of a high school newspaper—can indicate talent, knowledge, and competence, if good examples are shown. A good academic record is helpful and recommendations by school authorities or former employers are positive elements—and every little bit helps. Certainly a good personal appearance indicative of cleanliness, orderliness, and taste are essential (although none of these characteristics are actually needed to provide the house with money-making properties).

Suppose you have all that is described above; how do you reach a person who can give you an editorial job? There are 7 routes: (a) take a good course in publishing and/or editing and make your desires known to the instructors, who are often asked for recom-

desires known to the instructors, who are often asked for recommendations, (b) sign up with a personnel agency specializing in publishing jobs, (c) get a letter of recommendation to an editor or publisher from a mutual friend or associate, (d) send a very well written, interesting, exceptionally well typed letter with a resume to many editors and publishers, (e) reply to want ads in *Publishers Weekly* and the major newspapers, (f) leave your resume and appropriate forms with the personnel departments of many publishers, (g) go to bars, restaurants, resorts, and publishing festivities where editors go, and try to meet them.

For your first job you will be competing against the people who are already visible and known to the hiring editor—a secretary in the department, a freelance copy editor, a cousin who has the same background as you. However, there is not always a suitable applicant nearby, so the outsider has a chance. As more editors become aware of the increasing number of editing courses available, they are more inclined to choose people who have taken them rather than others with no professional education at all. If you take all 7 routes listed above, or even some of them, you have a good chance of getting a job in a reasonable time.

Obviously, being known to editors makes it unnecessary to take *any* of the 7 steps (although courses should be taken for their own value), so the best thing to do is to get a job inside a publishing house in *any* capacity, if you can. All other things being equal, you have a much better chance for the first editorial opening if you are on the spot. Being on the spot can also mean working in an agent's office, where you have frequent contact with editors. Increasingly, editors hire people with agency experience, because agents today perform many editorial functions.

See CH.4 for some comments on the merits of freelancing. In editorial work, the relatively routine jobs of copy editing and proofreading are given to freelancers as a matter of course in most publishing houses, as previously discussed. At the other end of the scale, it is likely that the exceptionally complicated and/or difficult editorial tasks will go to freelancers also, but for different reasons. It is simply impractical to tie up a staff editor for long periods of time on one book, and, except in specialized publishing companies, there is usually no one in the house who is as qualified to do certain jobs as the freelance specialists available.

Freelancing

Just as it is convenient for publishers to give editorial work to freelancers, it is comfortable for editors to work on a freelance basis. There is relatively little running back and forth, no equipment is needed, and the work can (usually) be done alone. The pay is not high considering the amounts that are paid for less demanding work, but it is adequate—if there is a steady flow of work. The key question is: Can you expect to find enough work to keep you busy? There can be no certain answer, but you may be willing to take the chance in order to enjoy the freedom of freelancing.

Along with the risk involved in keeping busy, you will also have the problem of cash flow. A freelance professional is, in effect, running a business, and this means making sure that the money you earn comes in quickly and steadily enough to enable you to pay your bills (in this case, living costs) on time. The terms of your agreement to work for a publisher should include an understanding on the schedule of payment—and large companies can be just as slow in making payments as small ones.

B

BASIC KNOWLEDGE

34 | Agent and author relations

The value of an editor can be measured essentially in the quality of imagination, instinct, and taste brought to the finding, guiding, and launching of good books—and "good" in the publishing sense inevitably means profitable as well as excellent. But even with these qualities the success of an editor is very dependent upon interpersonal relations. To acquire a book for the house on terms that are advantageous requires having a positive relationship with the agent; to work with the manuscript constructively and effectively requires having a strong professional and personal rapport with the author.

Agents began to be a significant factor in publishing in the 1920s, but they were usually resented by publishers as unnecessary intruders in the happy union between publishers and authors. It was felt that they could bring nothing but complications and difficulties to the process of publishing—and, undoubtedly, some publishers worried that their commanding position in contract negotiations would be weakened if they had to face an experienced and aggressive advocate instead of an (usually) eager, perhaps timid, author with little business knowledge. In those days, there were no big book club and paperback sales to make writers financially independent; they were totally in the hands of the publishers.

Agents

The concern of the publishers was to some extent justified in the beginning. Authors were as vulnerable to the blandishments of agents as to publishers, and some turned up at contract meetings with agents who brought sharp and aggressive tactics but little knowledge or understanding. The role of advocate is a very delicate and dangerous one; it requires only that the best terms be gotten for the client but puts no constraints of reasonableness, fairness, or even honesty on the advocate. It is very easy for a zealous lawyer, statesman, labor leader, or agent to become convinced that such constraints are harmful to the interests of the client and jettison them at the take-off. We have all (including the advocates) suffered from the results of such advocacy. The aggravation and frustration endured by those who have had to deal with such advocates is extreme, and has led to many an unwanted result—closed businesses, dropped deals, ended marriages, wars—when these seemed the only way to turn. It is hardly necessay to point out that in such cases the advocate made the worst possible deal for the client—who would have been better off without an advocate.

Such is the negative aspect of the agent's role. If this was prevalent in the early days it had largely (though not entirely) disappeared by the 1950ˢ. This was due, perhaps, to the fact that author-publisher contracts have become much more complex than they were and now demand—and bring—a higher level of professionalism. While it is still possible for an author to choose a negotiator without experience, it soon becomes apparent to all concerned that the person does not know enough to handle the matter effectively and it is likely that a professional will be brought in to take over. (Such a logical outcome is less likely if a *lawyer* inexperienced in publishing is the agent. Lawyers are accustomed to dealing in subjects about which they have little knowledge, since those who know the subject usually don't know the law. However, there is rarely a question of law in publishing contracts—except tax law, and that is secondary—but there are usually many questions that even the best lawyer can't handle without a lot of publishing experience. There are, of course, lawyers who regularly represent authors and know publishing well.)

Another bar to obdurate agents is the size and activity of publishing today. The sheer number of authors, publishers, books, and opportunities, gives both sides enough alternatives to discourage intolerable behavior (by either party).

Indeed, publishers now welcome the agent as a knowledgeable, experienced business person who is usually a more reasonable and efficient negotiator than an author who knows little about the business of publishing and is often so emotionally involved with the book as to be unable to deal objectively with publishing arrangements. Authors also read about large advances and often have unrealistic ideas about their rights and responsibilities. This is not to say that difficult and incompetent agents no longer exist, but only that they are now the exception rather than the rule. An author (or editor) in search of a respected agent can easily find one by enquiring at the Society of Authors' Representatives in New York or by asking any experienced editor or writer. Agents are listed in *Literary Market Place* (Bowker) and writers' magazines.

Just as there are different kinds of editors, there are agents who emphasize different aspects of their business. Some are mainly concerned with signing up profitable writers, others are specialists at making complicated deals and tie-ins, others like to work with authors in developing their books. As with editors, all agents must do all of these things to some extent, but some concentrate on one or two. In the larger agencies, it is possible for an agent to get specialized help in areas such as movie contracts, translation rights, etc.

The social aspects of dealing with agents are not different from any other such business practices. Suffice it to say that even the most professional of agents are more inclined to do business with those with whom they are friendly than with others. While it is doubtful that many agents will consciously take a book to the wrong editor because of entertainment or gifts enjoyed, all other things being equal some well-handled wining and dining can certainly swing things your way. In the end, however, it is probably simple liking and respect that will bring two parties together—provided, of course, that the business conditions are right. What all this means is that maximum social contact with agents is desirable.

The means of establishing such contacts are virtually unlimited, but the usual practices are: taking selected agents to lunch, frequenting bars and resorts favored by agents, attending parties and other functions where agents are likely to appear. Usually, editors find agents who are particularly sympathetic and develop these relationships in depth. Bear in mind that agents are also anxious to establish good relationships with editors, since most manuscripts are not so easily sold. However, an agent is the sole means of access to certain writers, while the agent has a wide choice of editors.

Entering contract negotiations with agents requires appraisal of the nature and knowledge of the agent. You may face an agent who is relatively inexperienced and tries to hide behind bluster and intransigence, or one who knows more about the intricacies of movie, serialization, and *co-edition* [publishers in 2 or more countries share the editorial costs of a book] deals than you do. How you approach an agent should be determined by who that particular person is—and that can vary considerably. Remember that the agent is sizing *you* up also and will act accordingly. Contract negotiations usually involve a little formal dance at the beginning but then settle down to a point-by-point bargaining (CH. 35) that quickly reveals the qualities of each party.

An excellent survey of the subject is available in the booklet *Literary Agents* obtainable from Poets and Writers, Inc., 201 West 54 Street, New York, N.Y. 10019.

Authors

The history and function of agents were discussed at length because agents are the editor's point of contact with the world of writers and books-to-be. Far from being a handicap, this situation is a boon to the editor. Instead of having to wade through countless unpublishable manuscripts sent by untalented writers and passed through by readers unsure of their own judgment, the editor now need consider only projects offered by qualified agents who have not only screened them to eliminate those that are unlikely to be sold, but have worked with the writers in many cases to improve the books before they are presented. This funneling of the writer's work to the publishers makes life easier for the editor in some ways, but it also makes editors, as well as writers, dependent on a comparatively few agents, for whose favor they must compete. From the writer's standpoint, there is also the very real danger that this system will result in screening out excellent books that are not so interesting financially to agents. (This is not too likely to happen in an economy that encourages the publishing of more and more books, but is a definite possibility whenever publishers find it necessary to cut or restrict their output.) Indeed, many agents, like many publishers, will not read unsolicited manuscripts.

Since editors generally obtain their manuscripts from agents, there is comparatively little to say about editor-author relations in the acquisition stage. There are, however, some exceptions to the rule: (a) editors do come into contact with writers through friends, social meetings, etc.; (b) some writers with published books prefer to deal directly with editors and seek them out; (c) editors will often go directly to a writer who might be able to execute their ideas; and (d) editors sometimes approach promising writers whose work they have read in a book or periodical. In many of these cases, after an initial contact an agent is called in, but sometimes the contract is arranged by the editor directly with the author. This is much less frequent with fiction than with nonfiction.

There are some writers who have had a lot of experience with contracts and know as much as any agent, but this is quite rare. Most writers have little knowledge of the publishing business, and many have very strongly-held misconceptions. It is not that writers are ignorant and prejudiced as a class—on the contrary, they are probably the best minds in any society—but book publishing is a subtle business full of contradictions which are not easily accepted by writers affected by emotional concern for their work and a natural suspicion of the entrepreneur—a suspicion justified too often in fields other than book publishing and occasionally in this business as well.

There is no best way to negotiate with an author. Much depends on the way the personalities of author and editor combine. The only general advice that can be given an editor faced with an especially difficult author is to suggest that an agent be engaged. Reluctance to give an agent the standard 10% commission can be fairly met with the opinion that an agent is likely to gain much more for the author than 10% of what the author would get without an agent. This is not always true, but it is true often enough to justify the statement. If the author comes into negotiations with a lawyer or friend inexperienced in publishing you can only do your best and hope that reason will prevail.

Working with an author in the editing of a book that originated with the author takes the true measure of an editor. There are at least 4 elements involved: (a) the personality of the author, (b) the personality of the editor, (c) the editor's conceptual and literary ability, and (d) the author's understanding of publishing.

If the personalities clash badly, there is little hope of a happy outcome; assuming there is no final break, the resultant book is likely to be less good than it could have been. If the author's personality is difficult but there is nevertheless strong respect for the editor's ability—as demonstrated by work on the author's book—there is an excellent chance of a good manuscript, and even a good relationship. If the author doesn't understand publishing and therefore doesn't give proper value to a good editor's work, the prospects are very poor; a very tolerant author will give the editor the benefit of any doubt and accept enough to keep the relationship going, but authors who are both ignorant of publishing and difficult personalties usually break off the relationship or make life hell for the editor. Bad advice from inexperienced friends combined with ignorance can also cause a break.

An impressive display of editorial talent and skill, while not foolproof, is probably the best single guarantor of a successful author-editor relationship. In a really good match of author and editor the work can reach heights that could probably not be attained by the author alone. The editor's satisfaction in such a result can be worth whatever agony is suffered along the way.

The assumption so far has been that the author is the proprietor and creator of the work. There is also the increasingly ubiquitous "ghost"—the writer who is hired to write for an "author" unable or unwilling to write the book satisfactorily. Ghosts are professionals who are usually, but not always, easy to work with.

Packagers

A word is needed here to cover situations in which the editor acquires a book from a *packager*. The packager is an individual or company that, for the purposes of this discussion, combines the functions of agent and author—being the proprietor (author) of the work *and* the party (agent) with whom the business arrangements are made. An author who negotiates a contract is also acting as agent, but an agent is never also the author; so, the editor relates to the packager as to an author, but an author with the experience of an agent.

The aspect in which a packager differs from an author is that a packager also produces and sells the books, or at least part of the production, to the publisher. While the two aspects, authorship and production, are generally tied together, they are actually separate functions and can be handled separately. Indeed, packagers usually deal with both an editor and the production manager once the contract is made. There are even some editorial packagers who deliver only a manuscript. The essence of the package deal is that the publisher gets whatever is delivered complete and ready for the next step—whether that is design, printing, or distribution.

In sum, the editor should think of a packager as an agent in the sense of being a source of projects, and as an agent-headed author in contract negotiations. Once a contract is made, the editor should have nothing to do with the actual writer—who is under contract to the packager—but should be given the opportunity to examine and approve the manuscript, illustrations, layout, and proofs. However, if the editor spends substantial time doing manuscript-development work that the packager is supposed to have done, the financial value of the package deal is not fully realized by the publisher.

Business dealings with packagers are usually comparatively easy, since the packager is—or should be—a highly experienced professional who not only knows the publishing business very well, but has a proprietary interest in the deal—and will not kill it by being unreasonable. Trouble with packagers usually comes, if at all, not in the contract stage, but in the delivery phase, when results fail to match promises. Delivery problems can, and do, result from failures beyond the packager's control—just as they happen due to matters beyond the publisher's control in the production of house books—but the best way to avoid disastrous failures due to the incompetence or unrealistic promises of packagers is to deal only with those who are known to be experienced and reliable.

35 | Contracts

Most publishers have printed contracts known as "boilerplate". These, like insurance policies and real estate leases, used to be printed in very small type to discourage careful reading. Some are still, but most houses have, for one reason or another, reset their contracts in readable type—often with subheads and marginal notes to facilitate use and understanding.

Like leases, publishers' contracts contain terms that are as favorable to the house as can be reasonably expected to be accepted. This practice has considerable psychological force. By printing these terms, the other party is led to believe that they are customary, and is more likely to accept them. Actually, the terms in publishers' contracts usually *are* customary. If ever they were not, the pressure of agents and competition have brought them into line. However, what is customary in one situation may not be in another, so it is often necessary to modify the printed terms to fit an individual deal.

The editor is expected to try for terms at least as good for the house as those in the printed contract, and cannot very well ask for more. Thus, any initiative to change the terms is likely to come from the author or agent. (Since most contracts are negotiated by agents, for brevity this discussion will refer only to the agent.)

Publishers hope that the standard form will be usable for all contracts, so it contains provision for almost every kind of circumstance—but there are usually some inapplicable clauses in each case. Following are brief comments on the various parts of a typical contract:

(a) *Preamble*: This legally identifies the parties to the contract and the work involved.

(b) *Specifications*: Defines the nature and extent of the work to be delivered; number of words and illustrations, bibliographies, indexes, other material to be included, etc.

(c) *Warranty:* The authors give legal assurance that the delivered work will be their own property, will not contain libelous or obscene material, and will not violate the rights of others. Most contract forms include a provision that the author will fully indemnify the publisher for all costs in connection with any lawsuit. Agents and authors' lawyers usually put up a strong fight against this clause. Editors can avoid a confrontation by referring the question to the company's legal department. The outcome is a fairly accurate indication of the relative strength of publisher and author in a particular deal.

(d) *Territory:* This defines the geographical area in which the publishers will have publication and distribution rights. American publishers ordinarily get the United States, Canada, the Philipines, and U.S. territories at least, sometimes world English-language rights, and less often the world rights. Even in the first instance, the U.S. publisher usually gets open market English-language rights—which means that both the U.S. and British publisher have the right to sell their books outside of the exclusive territories assigned to each. Agents usually (and packagers almost always) retain foreign-language rights, especially if a co-production is involved (CH. 29).

(e) *Delivery:* Specifies the dates on which the work is to be delivered. There is usually a grace period after which a penalty is sometimes levied. However, any experienced publisher knows that creative work cannot be turned out on order, like sausages, so this clause is enforced only when there is evidence of bad faith or some extraordinary circumstance.

(f) *Approval:* This provides that the publisher can reject the work if it is not judged publishable. There is often a provision for return of part, or all, of the author's advance [see (h) below] if the work is later sold to another publisher. The judgment of unpublishability is too subjective to be easily foisted on an author who has worked a year or more on a manuscript (and spent the advance) so this is probably the most controversial clause in the contract when it is put into effect.

(g) *Publishing:* The publisher warrants that the book will be published within a limited time (usually 1 to 2 years) after (and if) the manuscript is approved. The publisher's penalty for failure to meet this schedule may be forfeit of the advance and dissolution of the contract. The author agrees that the publisher has the sole right to make all publishing decisions, such as price, format, timing, advertising, etc.

(h) *Royalty:* There is usually a sliding scale, depending on the quantity sold, starting at 10% of the list price, going to 12½% and finally 15%. The quantities at which these breaks come is a matter for negotiation, since the sales prospects of individual titles vary greatly. An *advance* on royalties is generally paid, ranging from a modest to very large sum—usually about two-thirds of the royalty on the first printing. It is not uncommon for important authors to get advances amounting to the royalties on a quantity that is unlikely to be sold, in the publisher's hope that subsidiary sales income will justify the payment. However, since it is understood that advances are not expected to be returned (except as noted under (f) above) even if unearned by sales (although this is rarely written in contracts), such large grants are extremely hazardous and are usually made only under the pressure of competition from other publishers. The risk is sometimes reduced, or even eliminated, by prior indication of book club and/or paperback purchases. Very little or no royalties are paid on books remaindered [see (m) below] at cost or below.

(i) *Subsidiary sales:* Defines the various kinds of subsidiary rights and other sales that are possible, and assigns the share that author and publisher will get from each sale. Most form contracts used to provide for a 50/50 share of the net proceeds of all sales of rights and for 5% royalties on mail-order sales and cheap reprint editions sold by the publisher. Some of the 50/50 provisions have come under strong pressure from agents, so the author's share of movie and some other rights often rises to 90%, and even 100% in some cases. Here it is author clout and agent know-how that make the difference. Where top authors are involved, these negotiations can mean large sums of money and should be handled only by an experienced person on both sides. Bear in mind that it is the income from subsidiary sales that in most cases provides the profit in trade publishing (CH. 2).

(j) *Payment:* The advance payment on royalties is sometimes paid in full on signing the contract, but more often it is paid in installments—usually half on signing and the remainder on acceptance of the manuscript or part of it. Sometimes the advance is divided into 3 parts, with one payable on signing, one on delivery of part of the manuscript, and the last on final acceptance. The terms of payment, like the size of the advance, vary greatly and are subject to bargaining. This clause will also provide the schedule of royalty payments—usually paid semi-annually.

(k) *Reversion:* A provision is often made for the rights to be returned to the author if all editions of the book have remained out of print for a certain period—usually between 6 and 18 months— and the publisher refuses to reprint.

(l) *Copyright:* The publisher agrees to take out copyright in the name of the author.

(m) *Remaindering:* Some contracts provide that the publisher will not *remainder* [sell books at cost for resale at a reduced retail price] the book within a certain time after publication, but many publishers insist that this is a publishing decision reserved by them.

(n) *Free copies:* The publisher agrees to give the author a certain number of free copies—usually 6 to 10—and to sell the author additional copies at a discount ranging from 40% to 50%.

(o) *Continuity*: Both parties agree that the terms of the contract will be binding on their heirs and assigns, i.e. on anyone who acquires their property.

(p) *Bankruptcy*: This provides that the rights will automatically pass to the author if the publisher declares bankruptcy.

(q) *Option*: The author grants the publisher an option to publish the author's next book, which the publisher must exercise within a certain time (usually a month or so) after submission of the manuscript. Options are granted less and less by agents as publishing becomes more competitive.

The foregoing comments touch on only the main points in the average contract. Many details are omitted and some contracts contain other provisions and lack some of those included above. Many have little legal paragraphs that limit liability, fix responsibility, define jurisdiction, or otherwise try to nail down the possible hazards in such agreements. The Authors League has a model contract that is used extensively by agents. It is a good effort, but is inclined to represent the author's interests as much as publishers' boilerplate represents theirs. Experience shows that it is hopeless to try to cover in a contract every possible contingency, and any serious attempt to do so results in endless leapfrogging that does nothing but make work for lawyers. In the end, the best insurance against trouble is to make contracts only with people you feel are honest and reliable—and make the contracts simple and clear. Generally, a contract that only a lawyer can understand is a bad one.

Ghost writers sometimes have agreements with the author that give them a share of royalties. In such cases they are, in effect, co-authors and are often included in the author's contract with the publisher. In other cases, there is a separate agreement between ghost and author that provides for the ghost's compensation—a share of the author's income, a flat fee, or both.

Contracts with packagers vary considerably from the provisions discussed above. In clause (b), the specifications of the book as well as the content are given. If only part of the book is to be delivered by the packager, the part is defined and described. Clause (e) provides dates for delivery of the books as well as the manuscript and illustrations. The royalty clause (h) is sometimes omitted, as a package deal may involve a single price that includes both the book and the royalty. When a royalty is provided separately, it is often less than 10% for illustrated books—sometimes going down to 5%. The publisher's rationale is often that the combined cost of the books and royalty should not exceed 50% of the *net* [wholesale] *price* (usually 53 to 54% of the retail price—see CH. 2) if the publisher is to make a profit, so the higher the book cost, the less there is for royalty. Obviously, the royalty could be maintained at 10% by increasing the retail price, but this might price the book too high for its market. However, the whole matter is largely a question of how the publisher's overhead is calculated. This is discussed under "Acquisition" in CH. 38. In package contracts, payment terms (j) are based on production of the book, with a series of payments made on the approximate dates the packager will pay the bills for editing, design, and manufacturing. The royalty amounts are usually included in these payments. They are paid on the number of books delivered to, rather than sold by, the publisher.

Package contracts also contain a clause specifying the number of copies ordered by the publisher. There is always a provision for overruns or underruns of 5% to 10% or more, depending on the quantity. The smaller the quantity the more difficult it is to produce the exact number ordered, so the allowance is larger. The packager usually agrees to provide about 10% more jackets than books (to provide for replacement of damaged jackets and for promotional use). Sometimes a package contract provides for books to be supplied for book clubs at the *run-on price* [the cost of manufacturing without plant or makeready costs (CHS. 12, 29)] to enable them to sell at a price lower than the list price.

Contracts for college textbooks, reference books, and technical books usually have a clause giving the publisher the right to decide if a revised edition is needed, and to have one written by someone other than the author if the author is unwilling or unable to do the revision. This is a potentially controversial clause, since some such books represent a personal approach to the subject by an author who is understandably reluctant to have someone else revise the work. At the same time, the publisher usually has a considerable investment in the work and is not happy to see its sales stop for lack of needed revision. It is best for this point to be settled in the early stages of negotiation, as neither party may be willing to yield.

Elementary and high school (*el-hi*) textbooks are often written neither by their authors—who may be expert teachers or scholars but not writers—nor by ghosts, but by editors working for the publisher. The authors provide a master plan and guidance for editors who are proficient and experienced in the highly specialized technique of writing team-produced textbooks. The contracts with authors in such cases provide for this special circumstance. They also sometimes provide for the production of other works based on the material used in the book—tapes, workbooks, audio-visual presentations, etc.

36 | Copy editing & style

Copy editing   As remarked in CH. 31, the nature and extent of copy-editing is somewhat indefinite, but for the purposes of this chapter it will be considered to be the finishing of a manuscript—i.e. after the author and editor have done all they want to do, the copy editor will do whatever else is needed to make the manuscript ready for production.

Finishing a manuscript involves 5 functions:

(a) correcting errors of typing,
(b) correcting errors of fact,
(c) correcting errors of grammar,
(d) improving awkward sentences and paragraphs, and
(e) styling and marking.

Copy editors often go well beyond these limits and revise the structure and even the sequence of chapters, rewrite large passages, and generally perform the function of editor. There is nothing wrong with this provided that the author and editor are willing, and the copy editor is competent. However, when such extensive work is done, it cannot properly be called copy editing. This chaper will deal only with the 5 functions listed above.

CORRECTING ERRORS OF TYPING   This is self-explanatory.

CORRECTING ERRORS OF FACT   The problem here is deciding how far to go in finding errors. Obvious errors (Napoleon died in 1914) are not the problem. It is errors that *seem* correct that cause trouble. If the text says "Napoleon died in 1813", the copy editor will properly check and correct the date if it seems wrong, but should it be checked if it seems reasonable? Such checking might be feasible in a book containing few such facts, but in a text full of facts, checking is no longer copy editing but a separate function that is properly the author's responsibility.

The question here also is how far to go. In a work of fiction, or even nonfiction, there is the author's style to consider. "Cleaning up" the grammar could mean stripping the book of its character or altering its tone. The rule should be *hands-off* unless a clear understanding is reached with the author or editor. Also, the copy editor must be careful to distinguish between clear, undisputed errors of grammar and the optional usages that define style in the grammatical sense. The considerations involved in the latter are discussed below under "Style".

This is the most dangerous area, bordering as it does on the author's prerogative. If hands-off is the rule for grammatical corrections that could damage the author's style, then the rule here should be *stay away*. However, not every author is a stylist and many times the structure of a sentence or paragraph is unintentionally awkward. In a book where such bad locutions are few, they will be obvious and cry out for correction. In books where they are numerous, or the rule, it is probably best for the copy editor to consult with the editor before undertaking any large-scale revision. In those cases, the problem is usually that the author writes badly, and if the editor does not want to rewrite, then it falls to the copy editor to do so.

The copy editor frequently finds problems that only the author can solve, and often has opinions about the writing that should not be imposed on the book without the author's approval. In such cases, it is customary to write queries to the author or editor. These questions, which are properly written on slips of colored paper (*flags*) pasted or clipped to the Ms page affected, should be phrased carefully to avoid causing irritation. Sarcasm, condescension, or peevishness are unprofessional and have no place in these communications.

■ *Styling*—This term is not to be confused with the word "style" as used in connection with a writer's manner of expression nor with that elusive quality of sophistication we call style, and certainly not with style as fashion. Here we are concerned with the ordering of a text in 2 ways: grammatical and typographical. In styling, the copy editor imposes a consistent system of grammatical usage on the manuscript, and a consistent, logical arrangement of the editorial components of the text—headings, subheads, *extracts*, listings, etc.—to clarify the organization of the book for the reader and to identify it for the designer.

If every writer and editor knew, and consistently used, a universally accepted body of grammatical rules, styling in the sense of establishing a pattern of usage (or style) would not be needed. But style exists as a problem because there is substantial disagreement on certain points. The copy editor's job is to resolve these differences in each manuscript and make the usage uniform throughout. How the differences are resolved for a particular book depends on an agreement reached after the preferences of the author, the editor, and the copy editor have been reconciled. Some publishers have a definite house style that must be followed; others allow the editor and/or the author to use their own. Occasionally, the matter is left to the copy editor's, or even the typesetter's, judgment (CH. 5). The various considerations involved in style are discussed below under "Style".

■ *Marking*—Marking the manuscript is the process of identifying the components of the text after it has been styled in the sense of arranging its parts in a logical order. The first step is to clarify the structure and organization of the book by putting its subdivisions in order. There should be a clear hierarchy of headings from part-titles descending in importance through chapter titles and the various subheads, if any. The heads should accurately reflect the importance of the subdivisions they precede. Once the order is established, the heads should be identified according to category, writing the code letters alongside them in colored pencil, as A, B, C, etc.

Any material in the manuscript other than straight text should be similarly marked after being identified and checked for consistency. For example, if there are many listings, be sure that the same style is used for all; if each item in the list is preceded by a lower-case letter in one place, be sure that capitals are not used in another. Or, if there are many quotations, see that they are *either* run in with the text with quotation marks *or* set off as extract below. If you want short quotations to be within the text and only the longer ones set as extract, fine, but establish a rule and make it consistent. Mark each occurrence of each kind of material to identify it as such. A vertical line in colored pencil alongside extract, listings, poetry, etc. will bring these to the designer's attention. Write either "extract", "poetry", etc. as appropriate, or a code letter in the margin to identify the material. In complicated manuscripts it is helpful to use different colors to make distinctions (*color coding*).

When the designer receives the Ms, your markings will be the basis for doing the *breakdown* (CH. 14). Once a typographic style for each kind of head and special material has been specified by the designer (CH. 17), your markings will tell the typesetter which copy is to be set in each style. Note that there is a clear division of function here—do not confuse matters by making typographic markings on the manuscript, i.e. do not write "center", "flush", or other positional instructions, and do not underscore words for italics, caps, small caps, or boldface unless the author has done so for emphasis within the text. Particularly, do not mark the author's name at the end of the introduction for caps and small caps—a practice that is unaccountably almost universal among editors. In other words, the copy editor provides clearly identified copy; the designer specifies its typographic style.

Everyone who marks a manuscript, for whatever purpose, should be considerate of those who must read their markings. Write legibly in reasonable size with a pointed pencil or pen that will not smudge. Copy editors should bear in mind that both the designer and the typesetter will need space for *their* markings. Corrections in manuscript are made on the line or between lines. Only in proofs are corrections made in the margins.

Style

Style, in the editorial sense, has no meaning unless it is consistent, but consistency is not its purpose. Style is the guardian of 3 values: (a) clarity, (b) grace, and (c) structure. It has no independent value.

The relationship of style to tradition is specific but subtle. The mere perpetuation of usage is not valid, but style-as-rule is justified if it preserves usages that are clear and logical, protecting them from debasement through error. This does not mean that language should not be enriched by the infusion of new words and expressions, or enhanced by the dumping of outworn forms. What style *should* prevent is the blurring, through repeated error, of a language's ability to express thought clearly, precisely, and subtly.

The criterion of correct usage must be the logic of its function as determined historically, not its current treatment. If the reason behind a usage has been lost in time, it should be restored, because the function of language is to serve expression, and it can work only if it is efficient. A word or form that is ambiguous is inefficient.

Efficiency of a language is vital to both the expository and the creative writer. For both, the ability to make fine distinctions is essential—and one cannot make fine distinctions with words and usages that have no clear, universally understood meaning. In this sense, the protection of English from erosion through sloppy use is just as important to the poet as to any other writer.

Nevertheless, the virtue of consistently-applied style rules for explanatory or descriptive writing is equaled only by the necessity to avoid their use in creative writing. The work of a novelist or literary stylist stands or falls on the choice of words and how these are arranged. The arrangement may appear to be bad but it cannot be judged wrong by any criteria of style; it is actually bad only if it fails of its purpose. It is as misguided to force a work of literary art (no matter how low its level) into a straitjacket of style as it is to use deliberate distortions of language by a fine writer to support the acceptance of error. If a Faulkner or a Hemingway uses an incorrect word or form or spelling for literary purposes, that does not mean that he thinks the usage is correct—merely that it is appropriate where it is used. (Of course, there is always the possibility that the author was mistaken, and the editor failed to point out the error.)

If it makes sense to have rules to protect the integrity of the language—and guide the copy editor—then it is necessary to have a rulebook to which the writer or editor can look for authority and guidance. Unfortunately, there is none, in the sense that there are so many which differ that no one is universally accepted.

Matters of style are covered by 2 kinds of authorities: (a) the stylebook and (b) the dictionary. If there was only one of each there would be virtually no question of style, but this is not the case.

■ *Stylebooks*—There are a dozen reference books that give style rules, but only 3 that are generally used: *The University of Chicago Manual of Style*, *The New York Times Manual of Style*, and the *U.S. Government Printing Office Style Manual*. The latter is useful in many ways, particularly for its foreign-language material, but it is primarily for government publications and is limited in value for other books. The other two are the main references for style questions, although each of them is somewhat specialized; the Chicago Manual was planned for a university press and the *Times* Manual for a newspaper. However, both are excellent and sufficient. If they were identical—which they should be—there would be no need for both, but they do not agree in every respect. Most editors use the Chicago Manual, and, failing publication of a better one, it would be best if everyone would adopt it so that some uniformity could be brought to the treatment of the more formal features of style, such as punctuation, abbreviation, capitalization, hyphenation, etc.

■ *Dictionaries*—For many years *Webster's New International Dictionary of the English Language* (Unabridged; Merriam, 1934) was almost universally accepted. But new terms and meanings were coming into use in great numbers, and in 1961 the same firm issued *Webster's Third New International Dictionary* (quickly known as W3, while the 1934 work came to be dubbed W2). This unabridged volume presented thousands of new words and definitions, but it contained fewer entries in all and, more important, was assailed by literary authorities for being only a compendium of usage with too little guidance as to standard, nonstandard, substandard, slang, erroneous, or other kinds of usage. Indeed, many common errors are labeled "acceptable" or "alternate" meanings. Furthermore, W3, amazingly, failed to capitalize proper names. For these and other reasons, W2, though out of print, is still in demand and is consulted by careful editors, along with the admittedly indispensable W3.

In 1966 a smaller unabridged volume, *The Random House Dictionary*, with helpful notes concerning usage, was published. *The Random House College Dictionary* followed (revised edition, 1975), providing much up-to-date terminology. In 1969 American Heritage and Houghton Mifflin introduced *The American Heri-*

tage Dictionary (New College Edition, 1976); it emphasizes expert guidance on usage and grammar.

Webster's New Collegiate Dictionary, 1973 (new edition, 1976) from G. & C. Merriam is based on W3. It gives even less information on differing levels of usage, but it does capitalize proper names. In any case, it is considered authoritative by some and is probably the most widely used general dictionary in the United States. The Collins+World *Webster's New World Dictionary*, 1970, and its companion *Second College Edition*, 1976, are also heavily used and are also considered authorities. (For a detailed analysis, see Kenneth Kister's *Dictionary Buying Guide* (Bowker, 1977).

Obviously, if there are several "authorities" that differ there is *no* authority, but this is the situation until some publisher comes along with a dictionary as good as W2 that is up to date and achieves universal acceptance. When that happens the work should be made part of the nation's constitution.

QUESTIONS OF STYLE

Most matters of editorial style are generally accepted in one form: cat is spelled C-A-T, the first word of a sentence is capitalized, affirmative or declarative sentences end with periods, and so on. But there are many areas in which there is no agreement, and options must be decided.

To a great extent, the question of style divides into 2 schools, generally designated "British (or English) style" and "American style". While the latter is generally accepted in the United States, many American experts are inclined toward some of the British procedures, which are usually more logical.

Below.are some of the principal points of style concerning which choices must be made. Where the alternative given is British style, (B) follows. The American style is followed by (A). (A common problem in the United States and England is the styling of copy originally set and printed in the other country. If a change of style is required, the changes must usually be made in the copy, as compositors are reluctant to accept blanket instructions to "follow American [or British] style".) Omitted from the following list are questions ordinarily left to the designer, such as the choice between *old style* or *lining figures.*

■ *Capitalization*—In chapter and subheadings are all words except articles and prepositions to be capitalized as in book titles, or only the first word and proper nouns?*

■ *Division of words*—Are words at the ends of lines to be divided

* This question is discussed in CH. 18 under "Chapter titles", but in any event *all copy* should be typed in lower case with caps only at the beginning of sentences or titles and on proper nouns. When setting type, if the specifications call for all words to be capitalized it is easy to *add* caps, but changing from caps to lower case involves editorial choices and the copy must go back to the editor for marking. Awkward delays can be avoided by proper typing of copy.

according to pronunciation as in democ-racy (A), or according to etymological derivation as in demo-cracy (B)?

- *Compound words*—Which words are to be hyphenated (as in "self-control") and which combined (as in "everything")?
- *Numbers*—Which are to be spelled out and which set as figures?
- *Names*—Which names are to be italicized and which not? (The question arises usually in the case of minor publications, aircraft, television shows, etc.)
- *Punctuation*—When is italic punctuation to be used? Are dashes to be 1 em (A) or 2 em (B)? Are double quotes to be used first and single to be used for quotes within quoted matter (A) or vice versa (B)? Is punctuation not belonging to quoted matter to be placed inside the quotes (A) or outside (B)?
- *Reference marks*—Are figures or symbols to be used for reference?
- *Spelling*—Presuming that American spelling is to be used rather than British ("-or" not "-our", "-er" not "-re", etc.), which dictionary is to be followed in doubtful cases?
- *Continued lines*—In an index and similar copy, when breaking an entry from one page to another, is the heading to be repeated at the top of the new page with the word "continued" after it?

There are many other minor questions involved, as well as variations of those listed above. See "Read this first" on page vii for a discussion of the style used in this book, and "Style" in CH. 5.

When decisions have been made on all the optional questions, the editor or copy editor prepares a *style sheet* on which these decisions are listed. This is vital as a reference and checklist for both the copy editor and the proofreaders.

37 | Proofreading

In CH.5 you can read a discussion of proofreading customs and marking proofs as they relate to design and production people. But proofs are the point of contact between those people and the editorial department, so anything on the subject important for them to know is equally relevant to editors. This chapter continues those discussions with details related to the editorial function.

Proofreading is not generally considered highly skilled work, and in small publishing houses it is often given to secretaries or other office workers to do. Many tasks, such as writing, designing, and editing, that don't require manual skill, are often undertaken by unqualified people in the belief that such work can be done by *anyone*, adequately if not excellently. This is not true. Anyone *can* write, design, edit, or read proofs—but not necessarily well enough to be considered "adequate".

    Good proofreading means accurate proofreading and requires experience, knowledge, and skill. Readers must not only find and correct errors, they must be able to understand copy editors' markings and mark corrections properly. Besides having a sharp eye and good powers of concentration, they must have enough knowledge of style (and, if possible, fact) to be able to spot errors that escaped the copy editor. The latter is not a proofreader's responsibility, but many a whopper has been discovered by proofreaders, and editors are wise to look to readers' findings as another chance to perfect the text. In any book there are a great many errors possible, and few books have been published without some of them getting into print. No means of detecting and exposing errors should be overlooked.

    For a serious text, experienced professional proofreaders should be employed. There is no harm having an amateur read also, but do not depend on such readers. For books that have reference or instructional value, it is best to have the proofs read twice—by two

Reading technique

professional proofreaders. It is practically certain that each will find errors not found by the other.

The best way to catch errors is to have one person (the copyholder) read the manuscript aloud while simultaneously another (the reader) reads the proofs. This gives the reader a check of the copy without having to turn away from the proof. Besides that technical advantage, this procedure enables the reader to pick up errors that are so reasonable they might be overlooked if there was no such check. Obviously, this kind of reading is more expensive than having just one person read, so the practice is becoming increasingly rare. (However, in books that have a large number of proper names, technical terms, and/or foreign words, it can be a slower and more expensive process to have a single reader check the Ms for the spelling of each of these names and words than it would be if the copy-holder spelled them out.)

When there is a single reader, the practice is sometimes to read the proof with the manuscript at hand to check whatever seems to be wrong. The weakness here, of course, is that errors that do not *seem* wrong won't be checked and corrected. Since "errors" in proofreading terms are simply disparities between proof and copy, the proofreader using this method must be alert to the author's and copy editor's preferences in optional questions of style. (For example, the lack of a serial comma in the proof is an error if it is the editor's style to use serial commas, but is not otherwise.) The more careful proofreaders read the manuscript and the proof alternately line by line or sentence by sentence—or even phrase by phrase or, when very complicated, word by word. Perhaps the best practice is to put the manuscript page on top of the proof, covering everything above the line being read, then follow the Ms copy with a finger of one hand while following the proof with a pencil in the other. It is essential that the editor provide proofreaders with the style sheet used by the copy editor (see "Style" above).

A growing practice is for a single reader to act as copy-holder and read the Ms into a tape recorder, and then read the proof while listening to the tape. This seems like an ideal solution, but it has certain weaknesses—it cannot compensate for the tendency of people to overlook their "blind spots" (certain errors that they will not see under any circumstances), and the method cannot provide visual confirmation that what they verbalized is what was actually written in the Ms. In addition, unless the reader is an exceptional speller, chances are that hearing a word over the recorder will not call attention to a subtle misspelling in the proof.

Marking proofs Unlike the approach to style, the standard proofreaders' marks are universally accepted (they differ for each language, however). The problem here is not lack of a commonly understood system, but the failure of some authors, and even editors, to learn and use the system correctly.

As previously noted, corrections in proofs are made in the margins (with a mark in the line to indicate where the correction goes) rather than on or between the lines as in manuscript. This is mainly because the compositor must be able to find the corrections easily, but also because there is normally not enough room in typeset text to write most corrections. In manuscript, on the other hand, the compositor is reading the corrections in the course of setting, and has less trouble if they are in their proper place. There is ordinarily enough room in double-spaced typescript for the amount of correction needed in the copy-editing stage.

In CH. 5 the principles of marking proofs are discussed. Following is a chart showing the standard proofreaders' marks, with demonstrations of their use. Every person working in the editorial, design, or production part of publishing should study and learn these marks and use them correctly.

PROOFREADERS' MARKS

Marginal sign	Mark in text	Meaning	Corrected text
ℰ	Proofreading/	Delete, take out letter or word	Proofreading
ℰ	Legibil/ity is	Delete and close up	Legibility is
first	the‿requirement	Insert marginal addition	the first requirement
◠	of a proof reader's marks.	Close up entirely	of a proofreader's marks.
◡	Symbols should be	Less space	Symbols should be
⊥	made‖neatly and	Push space down to avoid printing	made neatly and
#	in‸line with	Add space	in line with
eq.#	the‿text‿to‿which	Space evenly	the text to which
¶	they refer.⌋Place	New paragraph	they refer.
	marks carefully.⌐	No new paragraph	Place marks
no¶	⌐Paragraphs may be		carefully. Paragraphs may be
☐	☐ indented one em	Indent one em	indented one em
☐☐	☐☐ two ems or (rarely)	Indent two ems	two ems or (rarely)
☐☐☐	☐☐☐ three ems. Head-	Indent three ems	three ems.
⊏	⊏ings are flush left	Move to the left	Headings are flush left
⊐	or flush right▭	Move to the right	or flush right
⊐⊏	⊐ or centered ⊏	Center	or centered
⊔	Mar‾gin‾al marks	Lower to proper position	Marginal marks
⊓	are ‾sep‾arated·	Raise to proper position	are separated

Marginal sign	Mark in text	Meaning	Corrected text
x	by ver_t_ical	Replace defective letter	by vertical
ꞓ	lines. The first correction	Invert this letter	lines. The first correction
w.f.	in a line of type	Wrong font; change to proper face	in a line of type
tr.	is beside noted the	Transpose	is noted beside the
?	nearest bend of the line.	Is this correct?	nearest end of the line
Sp.	and the (2nd) next.	Spell out	and the second, next.
	(in this way) both margins are used	Transfer to position shown by arrow.	both margins are used in this way
b.f.	English Finish	Change to boldface type	**English Finish**
b.f. ital	English Finish	Change to boldface italics	***English Finish***
rom.	*galley* proof	Set in roman type	galley proof
ital.	is laid paper	Set in italics	is *laid* paper
u.c.	Book of type	Set in upper case, or capital	Book of Type
Caps	Book Papers	Set in large capitals	BOOK PAPERS
s.c.	BOOK PAPERS	Change to small capitals	BOOK PAPERS
c.s.c.	Book Papers	Initial large capitals; other letters, small capitals	Book Papers
l.c.	the first Type	Change to lower case or small letter	the first type
x	bas-t-ball player	Broken type	baseball player
Stet	to ~~the~~ editors	Retain crossed out word	to the editors
₂	Water, H₂O	Insert inferior figure	Water, H_2O
²	$X^2 \div Y^2 = Z$	Insert superior figure	$X^2 \div Y^2 = Z^2$
≡	pri_n_ted	Straighten line	printed
‖	The paper / The ink / The type	Align type	The paper / The ink / The type
ld	prepare copy and submit it	Insert lead between lines	prepare copy and submit it
hr. #	P/A/P/E/R	Hair space between letters	P A P E R
⊙	to the printer	Insert period	to the printer.
⌄	the proof but	Insert comma	the proof, but
; or ;/	excellent it is	Insert semicolon	excellent; it is
: or ⊙	to the following	Insert colon	to the following:
ᵛ	authors notes	Insert apostrophe	author's notes
ᶜᵛ/ᵛᵛ	called caps	Insert quotation marks	called "caps"
-/or =	half tone	Insert hyphen	half-tone
em	Robert Henderson	Insert em dash	—Robert Henderson
en	1939 1940	Insert en dash	1939–1940
?	"Where" she asked.	Insert question mark	"Where?" she asked.
!	"Stop" he cried.	Insert exclamation mark	"Stop!" he cried.
(/)	author see page 2	Insert parentheses	author (see page 2)
[/]	To be continued	Insert brackets	[To be continued]

C

PROCEDURE

38 | Concept & acquisition

The title of this chapter recognizes the 2 basic sources of book properties: (a) the house-conceived project and (b) the project or manuscript brought in from outside. The proportion of published titles resulting from each of these sources varies greatly from company to company. In some trade houses, perhaps half the list originates inside; in others, usually the more "literary" publishers, few books are done in this way. In elementary and high school textbook publishing almost all titles are planned in the house to meet competition or a need reported by educators. Proposals for college texts generally come from professors or from college travellers, i.e. salespersons who sell to college bookstores.

House-conceived books tend to be scorned by some editors and publishers for being commercial concoctions. They usually are just that and that is indeed usually the intention. Sometimes an editor will plan a book to fulfill an intellectual or cultural need, but most house books are conceived as objects of desire, with a definite market in mind. Either the editor recognizes a widespread interest in a particular subject and develops a book intended to satisfy that interest or a book is created out of a particularly intriguing idea that is expected to arouse the buying interest of a part of the public. For the editor, this is not the same as being the instrument by which a writer-artist reaches an appreciative audience, but it is a valid part of publishing—and is probably the part that makes it economically possible to also be an instrument of literature and art.

Concept

Editors in publishing offices are not the only ones who conceive book ideas. These come in various states of development from agents, writers, illustrators, photographers, freelance editors, and packagers. The last named come to publishers with fully planned projects which are acquired in the same way as manuscripts from agents or authors (CH. 34), but the others usually approach editors with projects that are in the form of written proposals, outlines, or simply proposed in conversation. If the idea is sufficiently developed to be practicable, the originator is usually asked to proceed with its realization, or at least to carry it to a further state and submit a detailed outline, some sample text and perhaps a dummy for visualization. In other cases, the editor takes the raw idea and develops it within the house—hiring writers and illustrators as necessary.

The question of compensation for ideas is one of the most difficult an editor faces. There is no copyright protection for ideas that do not have a tangible form, so an idea itself has no legal standing. This is an upsetting concept to people who are creative and have good ideas that they cannot execute themselves, but it is rooted in the understandable difficulty of establishing value in the absence of a concrete work. If the creator of an idea had a copyright and failed to produce or publish, this would prevent anyone else who got the same idea from producing it, and the idea would be lost to the world. This would be contrary to the purpose of copyright laws, which is to encourage bringing creative works to the public.

At the same time, ideas can have enormous commercial value, and the use of them should be compensated accordingly. The problem is to determine what percentage of the profit from a product is due to the idea, the realization, and the marketing. The proportion varies in every case, and even a Solomon would lack enough wisdom to make an accurate judgment. In the end, the various contributors must negotiate and arrive at a division that reflects their actual strength. Unfortunately, the person with the idea is usually in the weakest position and often gets less than is deserved.

In fairness, it must be said that many people who have ideas undervalue the realization and marketing contributions. They see their idea as the unique element that causes sales, and the others as replaceable mechanics. They often fail to appreciate that given the idea, it could succeed or fail according to the skill and imagination with which it is produced and sold. There is also a tendency to underestimate the element of risk in publishing, and the compensation deserved for the risk.

When an editor has an idea for a book, the next step is usually to write: a proposal comprising a description of the project; a statement of the sales prospects in terms of potential audience, propitious circumstances (if any), previous successes in the same field (if any), and the competition (if any); a note about the proposed author and illustrator (if any); a suggested format, retail price, and publication date. The proposal is generally accompanied by cost estimates obtained from the production department—particularly if the project involves color illustrations or other costly production.

Assuming that the editor needs the approval of higher authority to undertake the project, the proposal is submitted to the editor-in-chief for consideration. The approval of the head of the editorial department may be sufficient, but in some companies the policy is to submit all proposals to an editorial board consisting of the heads of editing and marketing, one or two officers of the company, and sometimes the senior editors. In some houses a majority vote decides, in others the votes are advisory and the publisher makes the final decision.

In most cases, the editor has discussed the idea with a writer in the proposal stage. But, if the project is approved and no author is already involved, the editor will either try to interest a particular writer or writers—directly or through their agents—or ask one or more agents to suggest writers they represent.

The terms in such cases may be a flat fee, or a fee plus a small royalty, for the writer, particularly when the writer makes a relatively small creative contribution and does not have a selling name. If the writer's name is likely to bring in large sales and/or if the text is sizable and there is little or no illustration, the full royalty may be paid, even though the idea is the editor's. Should negotiations with the writer break off, it is understood by custom that the idea remains with the house and cannot be used by the writer for a book for another publisher.

If the project requires illustration, the editor will consult with the art director or designer. (A full discussion of illustration planning and acquisition is contained in CH.7.) If existing pictures are used, the terms of the owners prevail—usually the payment of a reproduction fee. If new illustrations are to be made, the terms usually correspond to the magnitude and sales value of the work; as with the author, a fee with or without a small royalty if the contribution is relatively minor, a substantial royalty if the illustrations constitute a major part of the book and/or the illustrator's name can be expected to attract buyers. For a book in which both author and illustrator are major contributors—as in a juvenile *flat* [a large format picture-and-text book of 32 to 64 pages for preschool children]—they may share the royalty equally. (See CH.35 for a discussion of contracts.)

Acquisition

Here the project is orginated outside the house and submitted by an author, agent, or packager.

In the case of a packager, the submission will be in the form of a proposal such as described above, but including, usually, a specific author and illustrations, with a dummy showing some of the pages as they will appear in the finished book, and a jacket or cover design. These will be, in most cases, accompanied by complete specifications for the production of the book, and a proposed price. Sometimes, only a price for mechanicals or films (CH.8) is given and a royalty proposed (CH.35).

The acquisition of packaged books is very advantageous for a publishing company, as such deals result in the delivery of products ready to be sold; not only does the house staff expend only a negligible amount of effort, but very often the books provided are of a nature which the staff would be technically unable to produce. Packaged books are also financially attractive for the publisher if, as is usually the case, they can be bought for the packager's cost plus a small royalty. This allows the publisher to charge to these books the same overhead as house books without the actual expenditure of editorial, design, and production overhead. Since the packager gets paid the royalty on all books delivered, whether sold by the publisher or not, the publisher's risk factor is higher than usual (although author's advances are frequently equal or nearly equal to the royalty on the first printing), but this is offset by the relatively small royalty and also by the fact that the packager has the financial risk of the production; a mistake in specifications or the failure of a supplier can cost more than the whole royalty is worth. For this reason, some packagers prefer to deliver only mechanicals or films and let the publisher print and bind the books.

Because packaged books are usually illustrated and thus higher in cost than most books, and since the cost of the book is included in the price, their acquisition involves large sums, the expenditure of which usually requires approval of managment. For the editor, no further work is needed once the contract is signed (CH. 35), except to approve the materials submitted by the packager (CHS. 34, 35).

When a book is proposed by an author or agent, the project may be in any state of completion ranging from an idea to a finished manuscript with a dummy. The more successful the writer, the less sample work is likely to be shown before contract. Top-selling writers can get a contract for their next book without their even knowing what it will be about. At the other end of the scale, a first book is usually submitted in the form of a completed—or nearly completed—manuscript. For authors of neither of those extremes, it is not uncommon for an agent to get a contract on the basis of an outline and sample chapter.

Until fairly recently, submitting a manuscript simultaneously to more than one publisher (*multiple submission*) was thought to be very bad form, and few publishers would consider a book they knew was being read by others. Today, the practice is so widespread that any publisher who resists it is at a severe competitive disadvantage. It is still considered important, however, for agents to inform editors that others, and how many others, are reading the manuscript.

In the normal order of things, each editor informs the agent of the house's interest or noninterest in the proposal. The agent then begins negotiations with whichever editors did indicate interest or, if none of the first lot did, sends the proposal out again to another group of publishers. If more than one publisher was interested, the agent either chooses one on the basis of preference and/or judgment, or takes the one that offers the best terms. Sometimes early low bidders are given the opportunity to top the highest offer and an auction ensues.

In the case of an extraordinarily desirable project, it is likely that the agent will go directly into an auction, sending the proposal simultaneously to 5 or 6 publishers with a list of minimum acceptable (*floor*) terms and a date and hour by which offers are to be received. The period allowed may range from 48 hours to a few weeks, depending on the nature of the material submitted. Provision may be made for 2 or more rounds of bidding to give low bidders a chance to increase their offers.

Publishers often allow purchases under a certain amount of money to be made by the editors alone and require management approval only of bigger deals. Auctions generally involve the larger sums, so it is necessary for acquiring editors to go to higher authority if they want to make a bid—both for approval of the project and determination of the amount to be offered. Bids may include various details of the terms, such as *escalator clauses* [increases in the royalty rate as sales increase], subsidiary income splits, or advertising guarantees, but the basic element is the royalty guarantee (advance)—which may exceed the estimated royalty earnings for the hardcover edition if the publisher can count on large subsidiary rights income (book clubs, paperbacks, film, or television). (Indeed, as hardcover trade publishing becomes more marginal there is more insistence on sub-rights possibilities in accepting a manuscript for publication.)

Proposals and manuscripts accepted for consideration by an editor and then rejected should be returned within a reasonable time. The nature of the material and other circumstances (holidays, etc.) determine the time required for consideration, but the agent or author should be given some word within about a month. In the case of specialized nonfiction it is quite normal for an acquiring editor to send the manuscript to experts for appraisal, and this takes a length of time that is determined by the readers, not the editor. An agent will understand this if kept informed.

Manuscripts that come into the house should be logged in with a careful record of the time and date of arrival and the means of delivery. The wrapping should be kept if there is a postmark or messenger service label on it. The main purpose of this is to avoid loss of the manuscript, but these records are also useful in disputes about the period of time a manuscript is held, particularly if it is rejected. A record should be kept of the movement of each manuscript from person to person, and signed receipts obtained. In all cases, the author should be told that it is expected that a duplicate manuscript exists. Similar, but even more detailed, records should be made of the arrival and movements of artwork and photos received with manuscripts. In many cases there can be no duplicates of these and their loss—or claimed loss—can result in high-cost lawsuits.

An acquiring editor cannot read every manuscript submitted, even when unsolicited ones are excluded, so some screening is necessary. A small percentage of manuscripts sent by agents or authors whose judgment is highly respected will be read immediately by the editor, but otherwise at least one prior reading is done and a report submitted to the editor with a recommendation. At one point, the larger houses all had staff readers and some still do, but now that unsolicited manuscripts are rarely being accepted, this practice is declining, particularly since agent-submitted manuscripts are already screened by the agent. Now, reading is done mostly by freelancers or by the junior members of the editorial department. In borderline cases, a Ms may go from the first reader to a second, more experienced one, whose recommendation will enable the editor to decide to read it or not. Ordinarily, a Ms will be sent out to an expert for reading only after the editor has made a tentative judgment that the book would be publishable if it were factually sound.

After the preliminary readings are done and the editor has decided that the book should be published, the procedure is the same as when an editor has a house project. A proposal is prepared for consideration by the editor-in-chief and/or the editorial board, or the publisher in a small house. In the larger houses, where the editorial board has many members, it is common practice for acquiring editors to do some lobbying in favor of a project to influence votes days before the next regular board meeting.

When the decision has been made to accept the book, unless an auction is involved, the process of negotiating a contract (CH. 35) begins.

The acquisition of existing books from foreign publishers is similar in procedure to acquiring a manuscript, if the book is in English. If the text is in a language that the editor does not read, then it must be screened through a reader in the original language and a judgment made on the basis of a summary in English and a report. Such books most often come through agents or scouts abroad who are paid a fee to find suitable properties. The terms for foreign books usually include a royalty that takes into account the U.S. publisher's cost of translation, if any.

If the foreign book has not been produced yet, the terms may be based on a co-edition, whereby all the participating publishers share the editorial costs. This is most practical with large projects such as encyclopedias, sets, etc., where the editorial cost is very high. If the project involves much color illustration, then the several publishers may enter into a co-production, whereby the plant costs are shared as well (CH. 29).

Some publishers offer proposals for projects that are not economically feasible *unless* a co-edition and/or co-production is arranged. Such arrangements are usually initiated at international book fairs, such as the one in Frankfurt that is held each year in the fall. Many purchases of rights to foreign books also are made at book fairs, usually by the principals of small firms and/or the top editors of large ones.

39 | Working with marketing

Publishing is a business and the object of a business is to reap profit. Occasionally, when it is felt that the book is outstandingly important and should be published, a company will publish a book that is expected to lose money. This does not happen often in trade publishing because such books can more easily find a home at a university press where this kind of publishing is more common. Even when a publisher takes in a book that is sure to lose money but bring prestige to the house, there is a long-range commercial purpose behind the decision. Prestige attracts good writers and good writers can bring profits. Some books with poor commercial prospects are published because a publisher believes that the author will produce profitable books later and it is important to maintain the relationship. Almost without exception, the decision to publish is based on an expectation of—or at least a hope for—profit.

Yet, book publishing is one of a few industries that are intermediaries between the public and its culture, so there is an implicit responsibility to act in the public interest. Like art dealers, concert managers, and theatrical producers, publishers, more than other businessmen, are inclined to allow considerations of quality to influence their decisions. While these considerations will rarely persuade a publisher to issue a book that is a sure loser, they often cause the rejection of a potentially profitable book that is deemed substandard. Borderline commercial decisions are sometimes nudged into the affirmative column by the exceptional quality of a project.

Thus, the decision to publish has 2 components: (a) the sales potential of the book and (b) its quality. The meaning of this for the discussion of *marketing* [the sum of all the activities that advance the sales of a book—sales (the apparatus of selling), promotion, advertising] is that the editor should have sales in mind when planning the publication of a book, but must also be guardian of the book's intellectual and artistic integrity. Some of this respect for the work should be, and usually is, present in sales and promotion people, but their specific responsibility is in selling the book and their zeal sometimes obscures concern for its cultural values. This is most frequently expressed in small but important—if unconscious—misrepresentations of the nature of the book. This distortion may be found in the advertising, the jacket design, the *flap copy,* or the salespeople's presentations—or all of these. It is the editor's duty to defend the book against inaccurate representation, if the occasion arises.

See CH. 28 ("Commercial analysis") for discussions of the marketing considerations in design and production, including background information about the marketing of books.

The editor starts working with marketing when a project is first proposed—whether from within the house or outside. As indicated above, the commercial prospect is paramount, so, whatever the editor thinks of a project, it must have the support of marketing as evidence that it is commercially interesting. The first question that an editor should ask when confronted with a proposal is: Will it sell? If the editor believes that the answer is yes, then the next question—which should be asked in the same breath—is: Is it good enough? If that, too, is answered affirmatively, a third question, less important but nevertheless significant, is raised: Is it consistent with our publishing program? If the editor's answer to all 3 questions is yes, then the editor can go to the marketing or sales department for an opinion on the first one: Will it sell?

If the editor is negative on the first point but very positive on the other two, a check with marketing is still in order. If marketing also is dubious of the sales prospects, the editor will drop the project unless there is a very compelling consideration besides profit—such as prestige or author relations. However, to go ahead with a project for such policy reasons would be a decision for management rather than the editorial department.

Although the editor looks for a yes or no opinion from marketing at this stage, the marketing people are likely to do some specific thinking about *how* to market the book in the course of forming their opinion of its salability. It is usual for the editor to become involved in such thinking, partly to persuade but mainly to give marketing the benefit of the editor's knowledge of the project and its presumed audience. So, although these discussions are unlikely to extend very far, since it has not yet been decided to publish, the planning of the book's marketing has begun.

Once a contract has been signed, in the case of a project acquired from outside, or the decision has been made to go ahead with a house project, the editor meets with the marketing people to consider the marketing approach that will be taken, and the scope of the marketing effort that will be made. These decisions will, in turn, often affect the way in which the editor develops the project.

Sales concepts

The editor must understand how the selling of the book will be approached, but before an approach can be formulated, the marketing people must listen to the editor carefully to learn exactly what the book will be, i.e. what they will be selling. A misunderstanding at this point is likely to lead to a mistaken approach to selling, and the project will suffer.

For a "literary" book—a work of art or scholarship written and published on what might be called an as-is basis—there is no way that the book can be modified for sales purposes so a simple exchange of information between editor and marketing is sufficient. The editor must be careful to make clear the exact nature, content, and quality of the book, and tell as much as is known about the audience the author is trying to reach and has reached with previous books—including their sales histories. Marketing tells the editor what the sales possibilities appear to be, and gives some indication of the advertising and promotion program that is planned; at this point, it must be decided how much, if any, advertising will be done, and whether or not a promotion tour by the author is feasible. Some thoughts about the advertising approach (if there is to be any—which is not likely unless the book either has big sales potential or begins to sell well after publication) will probably be conveyed to the editor in this meeting. There will also be a discussion of the general approach to the jacket design. If the editor disagrees strongly with marketing's plan—either its extent or nature—an argument will develop that may have to be resolved by management. (It is reasonable to expect management to back the editor, whose proposal was management-approved.) Otherwise, the editor begins working with the author to ready the manuscript for production, and marketing begins to develop a program.

In some companies, a request to the art director for a jacket or cover (in the case of a paperback) design is initiated by the editor, in others it comes from the marketing department. In either case, all three discuss the approach to be taken, with the object of achieving a result that will be a good synthesis of editorial, marketing, and design ideas.

When the project is conceptual—that is, can be shaped by the publisher's staff and/or the author to produce a desired result—the meeting of editor and marketing is more in the nature of a creative thinking session than an exchange of information. The editor presents the idea with the hope that marketing will come through with a sales concept which will add something of value to the project—perhaps causing the editor to revise it, the better to fit the ideas of marketing. A give and take between a creative editor and creative marketing people can and does often improve the original concept of a project. The editor's role here is not to defend the project but to be open to constructive criticism and ideas. This is not to say that the editor should abandon the original concept to the opinions of marketing, but there can be more flexibility in such projects than in those in which a work of art or scholarship is involved. In the course of such a meeting, marketing will not only get a clear and full picture of the project, but will probably form some thoughts about a suitable marketing approach. At this point, the procedure is similar to what happens in the case of a "literary" work once the editor and marketing people have formulated their own ideas and shared them with the others.

The jacket design ("jacket" in this context is to be taken to mean "cover" when a paperback is involved), like the design of the book itself, is determined partly by editorial and partly by sales considerations. Neither concern should be served at the expense of the other in either case, but the jacket is primarily a selling device so the sales considerations are dominant. (See CH. 26 for a full discussion of the various aspects of jacket design from the designer's standpoint.) This, however, is where the editor must be alert to any failure to represent the nature of the book accurately. Because the sales function is primary in jackets there is a tendency on the part of the art director and designer to be more concerned with sales-effectiveness than with editorial accuracy, and the marketing department is not inclined to complain if a small distortion of the book's character is present in a strong selling design.

This is not to suggest that a deliberate distortion would be made or encouraged. It is simply that zeal to produce a sales-effective design sometimes overwhelms concern about the correctness of the representation. Also, under the pressure of deadlines, designers sometimes don't have time to read enough to get a true picture of the book, or they get a mistaken impression of it from the information they are given. While it is the art director's job to get a correct understanding of the book and pass this accurately to the designer, it is ultimately the editor's responsibility to see that the jacket does properly present the essential nature of the book.

Thus, the editor must initially convey a clear idea of the book to the art director. This can be done either directly with a verbal and/or written presentation or through the marketing department, if that is the practice of the house. Then, the editor must check the design submitted to see that it does accurately reflect the book.

This is the point at which conflict between editor, art director, and marketing manager often occurs. Conflict can be minimized if the editor takes a stand only on the element of editorial integrity and leaves it to the art director and marketing manager to battle over the question of effectiveness. The only sense in which the editor is properly concerned with the esthetics of the design is when its style may be at odds with the style of the book. In any case, the art director is hired as an expert in esthetics, so the editor should not try to impose a judgment of taste on the design except as it relates to the matter of appropriateness. The editor usually has final responsibility for approval of the jacket, and it is important that this decision be made on the basis of specialized professional judgments rather than personal taste.

BOOK DESIGN Roughly the same procedure as for jacket design is followed in the design of the book. (See "Editorial analysis" in CH. 14, and all of CHS. 15, 16, and 17 to understand how a designer approaches the editorial considerations in book design.) However, in most cases the emphasis is more on editorial than sales aspects—not because sales is a less important concern but because, as is true of the text also, the way to help sales is to make the best book possible.

The extent to which the editor becomes involved in the book's design depends on the nature of the book. Where there are no illustrations or other visual elements, the editor meets with the art director and/or designer primarily to convey a clear picture of the text. At this meeting, the designer may suggest a design approach and ask the editor's opinion. Again, this would not be for esthetic reasons so much as to check the correctness of the designer's interpretation.

When a design is conceived, the design department will present it to the editor in the form of layouts and sketches or a printed sample. As in reacting to the design of a jacket, the editor must here, too, balance editorial and sales considerations; but here the editorial side will carry more weight. Nevertheless, the design is expected to be a help in selling the book (CH. 2), so the editor must give appropriate reign to this aspect.

If the book is extensively illustrated and the visual element is an important part of its interest, the editor becomes more deeply involved in the design. In some houses, the marketing people will also participate in the planning stage of design.

With books of this kind the editor and designer should join in developing a design concept that will most effectively and accurately convey the content of the book to the reader. In such efforts, the designer should control the results, but the editor should contribute understanding of the author's intentions and needs, ideas for expressing these intentions, and constructive reactions to the designer's proposals. The design result should be the sum of what both editor and designer can bring to the problem. If marketing can suggest directions that will be effective in reaching or arousing interest in the audience, so much the better.

It is tempting for editors to take command of the design of their books (and the jackets) and order changes to suit their ideas. In one sense, this would be appropriate, as editors are the only ones whose roles correspond to that of the director of a play or movie (CH. 2), and it seems logical for them to control all of the elements to bring unity and a high level of quality to every aspect of the work. Unfortunately, editors do not ordinarily bring the necessary talents or background to their jobs, and are not expected to be competent in any but editorial functions—although they are expected to have good taste, i.e. a sense of fitness. Similarly, designers are supposed to be talented and trained specialists in their area. The reality is that editors exercise the coordination and executive functions of a director in the absence of such a person, but it is wise for them to exercise a restraint appropriate to their limitations and to the professional qualifications of the designers. There are occasional situations in which an editor has, in fact, better taste, imagination, and design sense than the designer, but this is an anomaly that the editor must handle with utmost subtlety in order to achieve the maximum input while preserving the illusion of role integrity. The danger, of course, is that many editors are likely to *believe* they have superior design abilities whether they do or not. The principle should be to respect the professional standing of the others.

Editors should read *all* of the text in Part I of this book to gain as full a knowledge and understanding of the design and production of books as they can, with the object of exercising the directorial power they have with the maximum wisdom and judgment.

Advertising & promotion

Marketing departments are interested in getting as much knowledge of the book as possible from the editor in order to write correct advertising and promotion copy, and are obliged to respect the editor's definition of the book's nature. The extent to which the obligation is observed varies from house to house, depending on the position and personality of the marketing manager and the editor.

Properly, the editor should supply marketing (and design) with an information sheet describing the book in detail, giving a biographical note about the author, and presenting whatever is known or believed by author or editor about the prospective audience. On the basis of this, and a verbal presentation by the editor (made, usually, at a regular editorial meeting), the jacket flap copy and the ads (if any) are prepared.

In most companies, the flap copy is written by someone in the editorial department—sometimes an assistant to the editor of the book or even the editor—and then sent to marketing for review. In others, the advertising department prepares the copy and sends it to the editor for review. The question of who has the final word depends upon the policy of the house—which is usually based on the relative strength of the editorial and marketing chiefs. Again, it is the editor's responsibility to fight, if necessary, for a true representation of the book. Again, too, the special skills of the marketing people should be respected by the editor in situations involving questions of the sales approach and appeal to the book's audience.

The preparation of ads is initiated by the marketing people and the results are shown to the editor and, ordinarily, to management. Sometimes everyone is pleased by the first layouts and there is no problem. More often, someone disagrees with the approach, layout, or copy and a more or less polite battle develops. Unfortunately, the outcome of the battle depends on power. Certainly management can get what it wants (although in extreme cases it may lose an advertising manager in the process) and in some companies the more senior editors can prevail. Usually, a compromise is reached.

Advertising of books divides into 2 categories: (a) trade (primarily aiming to reach booksellers and librarians—mostly through *Library Journal* and *Publishers Weekly*)—and (b) consumer (leveled at the general public and special interest markets). There are differences in approach and content, but these are of little concern to the editor. The trade ads are about the same as the others, but include reference to the success of related books and offer special deals (one free with 10 ordered, etc.) to the bookseller.

The editor's main concern with ads is, as always, that the book (and the author) be properly represented. A certain amount of hyperbole is tolerable, but too much is embarrassing and improper. A serious work of history shouldn't be promoted as a now-it-can-be-told exposé. The more sensational aspects of a biography or a novel can be mentioned but the ad should not give the impression that the whole book is like that. A reasonably sophisticated public reads between the lines of advertising copy and discounts much of the excess, but the editor must speak up when the book is presented as something substantially different from what it is. This is true also if the ad writers happen to make less of the book than is actually present.

A close watch should be kept by the editor on all promotional and publicity copy. The latter is particularly a problem, since it usually gets rewritten by newspaper and magazine writers who generally make some mistakes and distortions in their haste and relative ignorance of the book. The editor has no control over such rewrites, but at least the copy sent out should be accurate.

If the book has good retail sales potential and the author is an attractive and articulate person, the promotion department might want to arrange a tour of cities where TV or radio appearances could be booked. In this event, the editor is asked by the promotion people if the author would be willing to make such a tour (at the publisher's expense). If the author is willing—and few are not— then the editor brings author and promotion manager together and from there on the editor is not involved, except to comfort outraged authors who complain (as almost all do—with justification) of: no books in the stores of a city where a smashing TV appearance aroused great demand, failure to be met at one or more airports, expenses beyond the amount paid by the publisher, no customers at a bookshop autographing party due to lack of publicity, etc. The editor must do the best that can be done to protest faults and make amends to the author. However, the problems mentioned, and others, are endemic to the promotion tour business, and there is little hope for relief. Large sales will, in most cases, have a soothing effect.

Author tours, incidentally, are arranged mostly for nonfiction books. Such tours are done with fiction only in exceptional circumstances—usually when the author is well known or the book has a timely interest.

In el-hi textbook publishing, the editor's relation to marketing is somewhat different than in tradebooks. The purchaser of the books is not the public but usually a professional buyer with a committee of educators and bureaucrats to convince, so the selling material is a factual prospectus that makes the book sound as good as possible, but is without the amorphous hype used for tradebook jacket flaps and newspaper ads. In all textbook marketing there is a complex web of academic purchasers, administrators, and influential teachers to reach and persuade. This is done in many ways and often involves the use of personal contacts by the editor.

40 | Working with manuscripts

There are, theoretically, times when an author delivers a manuscript that is ready to be turned over to production with nothing needed but a transmittal memo. In real life this does not happen. All manuscripts need *some* editorial work.

The work needed to make a manuscript ready for typesetting is divided into 2 categories: (a) *manuscript editing*—substantive revision of the text, and (b) *copy editing*—finishing the manuscript as described in CH. 36 and marking it for composition.

No manuscript, no matter how well written, is sent to production without copy editing. The copy editing might produce very little change, but it is necessary, if only to find out that the text is perfect without it. However, it is doubtful that any book-length manuscript has been delivered by an author free of the kind of errors and inconsistencies that copy editing is meant to correct. In any case, the manuscript must be marked with coded instructions that enable the designer and typesetter to do their work.

While copy editing is unavoidable, manuscript editing may or may not be required. It is extremely unlikely that none will be needed, but it is not uncommon to get a manuscript that requires very little revision. In most cases, substantial revision is needed, and in some, the revision is extensive.

The obvious question is: Who says that extensive revision is needed? The answer is: The editor. Next question: Does the author agree with this judgment? Sometimes yes, sometimes no— usually, yes and no. Indeed, this is the most critical point in the relationship of author and publisher. If the author has confidence in the judgment of the editor, matters can go quite well (CH. 34). If the author does not accept the call for revision, matters will go poorly or not at all, i.e. the editor will refuse to accept the Ms; the author will ask to be released from the contract or to have another editor (rarely done). None of these alternatives is pleasant, and in practice, this point is usually raised before a contract is signed, if a complete Ms has been submitted. If there is no agreement then, it is easy to break off before a contract is made. The real trouble arises if the manuscript is delivered *after* there is a contract in effect and the author and editor disagree.

Considering the strong attachment that writers normally, and quite naturally, have for their works, it is really surprising that so much author revision is done at the request of editors. After all, it seems quite unlikely that an author—who may have had a string of successful books—after spending perhaps two years writing and polishing a text will gladly accept a request to substantially, possibly drastically, change it, particularly if the request comes from a person with no author's credits or other visible evidence of superior perception. Yet, such changes are frequently made under such circumstances. The answer probably lies in the intense desire of the author to see the book succeed; self-interest transcends the combination of hurt pride, subjective judgment, stubbornness, and plain weariness that would otherwise cause a flat rejection of such requests, even those coming from respected editors.

This does not mean that authors change their books even though they disagree with the editor's opinion. When they do make important changes it is almost always because they see the merit in the editor's suggestions—with vision cleared by the acute sense of reality referred to above. Of course, the editor is not always right, so the author may refuse to make the changes requested or may make only part of them. There are probably even some (rare) cases where an author has made changes despite strong doubts that the editor was right in requesting them; this *can* happen where there is a strong-willed editor and a compliant author. Major changes at an editor's request are made much more frequently in nonfiction than in fiction. Editors very rarely make important changes in fiction themselves.

What then is the nature of the changes that an author might be asked to make, and by what process are they made? The process is somewhat different for each editor, but here is a typical scenario:

Manuscript editing

The Ms under discussion might be complete or only partially finished. In any case, it is read carefully by the editor in the way that is most favored. This might mean a leisurely reading for pleasure and a general impression, followed by a more critical reading to locate areas of weakness—which is followed by intense study of the parts that seem to need change. Some editors might pick out the trouble spots on the first reading and go directly to work isolating and analyzing them. However the latter stage is reached, it is the prerequisite for a valid recommendation for change.

Once the editor has formed a clear idea of what needs to be done to bring the Ms to optimum quality, the question becomes: Who should do the work? There are 3 possible answers: (a) the author (or ghost), (b) the editor, and (c) the copy editor. In most cases, the work is divided, but the real question is: Who does what? The copy editor's function is usually well defined, but this leaves the problem of agreeing on who will do the remaining work—the author or the editor. There is no easy answer, and the solution varies according to the nature of the author-editor relationship (CH. 34).

Ideally, the editor presents recommendations to the author, who then makes the changes—and does them well. In practice, the author may be unable or unwilling, for a variety of reasons, to do the work and may ask the editor to do it. Where the author is unwilling to relinquish control of the changes but is not able to make them alone, it is usual for author and editor to work together. This generally means that the editor gives detailed guidance and then critically reads the author's changes in relatively short passages. (This is not very different from the ideal situation, in which the author takes the Ms away and returns it days, weeks, or months later with all changes made.) The editor then goes over all of the changes in one reading and gives the author a critical judgment. Obviously, working together is likely to bring a result closer to the editor's ideas, but it is, of course, much harder work for the editor and takes much more time than when the author makes the changes. If the editor alone were to make the changes, the result would probably be most satisfactory, but the time required would probably be more than the editor has available, and there is always the risk of having the editor's work rejected by the author.

This raises the extremely difficult matter of resolving unreconciled editorial differences between author and editor (which in this context means publisher). On one hand, publishers should not have to publish books that contain substandard writing or errors of fact. But it is equally wrong to expect authors to have their names put on books published with material to which they object. In many cases, publishers must choose between accepting whatever the author insists on, or rejecting the manuscript *in toto*—which is sometimes a very hard choice.

It is not uncommon for an author to do the major changes and leave the less important ones to the editor—who in turn delegates some of the work to a freelance editor or a copy editor. The way this work is divided depends largely on how much confidence the author has in the editor, and to some extent on the author's ego, work load, and professional interest in writing.

However the work is divided, the editor must examine the revision as carefully as the original version. The revision may not work, it may be insufficient, or it may create problems that were not there before. If necessary, a second editorial critique and another round of changes will have to be undertaken. At this point, nerves and patience are sometimes overworked, but the good editor will keep a cool head and convince the author of the need for more work. It is best to emphasize how permanent and embarrassing weaknesses are in a published book; how the author would later regret not having taken the opportunity to make changes when there was still time.

Such is the *process* of revising a manuscript. Now we look at the kinds of changes that might be needed, and the kinds of problems that make them necessary. There are 2 categories of problems: writing and substance. Faults in writing are of 2 basic kinds: (a) structure and (b) style. By style we mean all of the characteristics of writing other than structure—which is the plot or architecture of the book. Style includes sentence structure and even paragraph structure, but once the major plan of a chapter is involved we are speaking of structure in the basic sense—certainly if the plan or plot of the whole book is involved.

PROBLEMS OF STRUCTURE

Faults of structure are frequently errors of sequence. Writers sometimes organize a book in an order that works well enough for them, because they have the whole picture in mind, but confuses the reader, who must be informed in a different sequence in order to understand or use the information properly.

Here it seems worth remarking that the most difficult part of writing, and one of the most important parts, is maintaining constant awareness of the reader; more specifically, of the reader's relative ignorance. Whether it is fiction or history or instruction, the writer knows more than the reader (except for scholars who may be reading critically rather than to learn or enjoy) and is constantly in danger of writing on the basis of the *author's* knowledge rather than the *reader's*. When this is done, it leaves a reader confused and irritated because fact C, which followed fact A, can't be easily understood without fact B—which the author omitted because it seemed obvious. Of course it was obvious to the author—who had 20 years of experience in the subject or, in the case of fiction, had knowledge of the whole plot and a clear picture of the scene—but it was not obvious to the reader, who needed it to make sense of the information that came next.

This tendency to overlook the reader's relative lack of knowledge is a major justification for an editor's role, and explains why authors are inclined, against all other inclinations, to accept the help of editors. It is important for a writer to know what happens when the work is read by someone less informed or prepared, and most good writers are aware of this need. At the same time, it is important for an editor who has specialized knowledge to develop an objective point of view when editing works in that subject. If this is not done, the editor cannot properly serve the author's needs for a reader's reaction.

Another major problem in structure is balance. Sometimes a

writer will give an aspect of the work too much or too little space in proportion to its value in relation to the other aspects of the subject. The editor approaches this area with caution, since value judgments are involved and (presumably) the author is more qualified to make these than is the editor. But here, too, the problem of subjective viewpoint arises. Has the author given a topic space in proportion to its *actual* importance or according to a personal interest in it? This is not to say that a writer is not entitled to emphasize what seems to be important. It is to suggest that an editor must be alert to situations where an author has let enthusiasm—or rage—elevate a point far beyond its proper place in the whole work. In didactic works such exaggerations can damage the reader's confidence in the author's judgment and reliability; in fiction, these imbalances can spoil symmetry and break the delicate thread that joins the reader to a story that inspires belief and involvement.

The most difficult structural defect to correct is *lack* of structure. This usually comes from a lack of planning; when a writer begins writing without a clear idea of what needs to be done to reach a goal. Some writers can think logically as they write, and produce a well-designed text without making an outline, but most have to work out the sequence, flow, and balance of the whole book and its parts in advance of writing. If this is not done sufficiently, the result becomes a disorderly mass of material—all the parts of which may be very good—that fails to hang together or enable the reader to use the information efficiently.

Oddly, major structural faults are often easier to correct than some style problems. With the use of scissors and tape, an author (or editor) can revise the sequence of material while hardly changing a word. Imbalances due to *too much* writing in one part can frequently be corrected by simply lopping off unnecessary sections. Even lack of structure can sometimes be corrected by cutting apart the manuscript and taping the pieces back together in a well-planned order, adding transitional passages when needed.

PROBLEMS OF STYLE Style problems fall into 6 main categories:

(a) poor syntax,
(b) poor paragraph structure,
(c) overwriting,
(d) clichés,
(e) repetition, and
(f) weak logic.

Another, and crucial, style problem is lack of grace or style in the sense of quality. This fault is too pervasive to be corrected by anything short of rewriting, so it is not treated here as an editorial problem.

■ *Poor syntax*—This embraces both grammatically incorrect and awkward sentence structure. Correction of these faults is normally left to the copy editor (CH. 36), but where they are very frequent the editor may discuss the problem with the author and ask for improvements. Whether or not this is done depends on what is, and can be, expected of the author. If the editor believes that the author cannot do much better, which is often the case when an expert who is not a professional writer is asked to write a book, or the author is too busy and important to be bothered, which happens with books by major statesmen, industrialists, scientists, etc. then the work is given to a copy editor. If the author is a professional writer, it is proper to send the Ms back with a request that more work be done; but sometimes this is avoided if the author is a big-selling writer who must not be offended.

■ *Poor paragraph structure*—Awkward arrangement of the sentences in a paragraph can be corrected by a copy editor also, but this begins to look like rewriting if it is extensive. The same considerations are involved here as with bad sentence structure, only in greater degree. If too many paragraphs have sentences in the wrong sequence, the author should be asked to revise, if this is at all feasible. If necessary, a very good copy editor can be given the job, but this is accompanied by a heavy responsibility, since such extensive revision of this kind can easily distort the sense and character of the book.

■ *Overwriting*—The most common fault of style is the use of too many words to express a thought. Even good professional writers tend to write too much, but the best ones cut and pare until their expression is economical. This means that it usually takes more time to write less; which explains, partly, why there is so much excess verbiage.

Some cutting can be done by the deletion of sentences, paragraphs, chunks of chapters, or even whole chapters, but sometimes the problem is in the writing of the sentences themselves; the use of roundabout locutions and unnecessary words and phrases, e.g. "it is probable that" instead of "probably", or "due to the fact that" instead of "because", etc. (If the reader should happen to find any such faults of that kind in this book, it is no doubt due to the fact that the author did not have enough time to do better.)

Another kind of overwriting is the use of fancy instead of plain words. Beginners often have the idea that their writing will be more impressive if they use long words or uncommon scholarly words. The opposite is true. Excessive use of fancy words marks the writer as insecure, pretentious, or inept—unless the reader happens also to be one of those. Do not confuse this with the use of fresh and unexpected words—which can be good. The reader should be aware not so much of words as the concepts they convey—and concepts are conveyed more effectively if expressed in a new way.

Overwriting also means using elaborate language instead of simple expressions, and exaggerating qualities, feelings, and occurrences by the use of adjectives that overstate. Perhaps the most offensive form of overwriting is the use of professional and institutional jargon to make the simple appear complex.

Rather than give examples, this writer refers the reader to *The Elements of Style* by William Strunk, Jr., and E. B. White, where this and other aspects of writing are explained briefly but fully. Indeed, if all writers did no more than memorize the "List of Reminders" on the contents page under Chapter V of that book, the need for manuscript editing would nearly disappear.

■ *Clichés*—These are all the worn-out and overworked words, expressions, and rhetorical devices that inexperienced (and some experienced) writers like to use. There are 2 reasons why these chestnuts are so common in writing: (a) they are so familiar they come easily to (a lazy) mind, and (b) they are usually excellent expressions—which is why they became so popular and overused. It is unfortunate that such good words and phrases have to be discarded, but their overuse gives writing a stale, hackneyed sound that is intolerable after a while. Vigorous, effective writing calls for fresh, vital ways of expression that keep the reader alert and indicate a creative mind at work.

■ *Repetition*—Carelessness is the main cause of repetitiveness. Unintentional restatement of thoughts or reuse of expressions often result from the writer's inability to remember what was written a day or a week or a month before, but these understandable defects must be found and corrected before a manuscript is delivered to the editor. Sometimes excessive repetition is due to a writer's overanxious effort to make a point. The temptation to restate a strongly felt idea is resisted by only the most experienced writers. There are, of course, times when reiteration is effective, but too much weakens the impact—just as whipping makes cream thicken, but one whip too many turns it back into liquid.

■ *Weak logic*—This category includes faults such as the use of poor analogies and metaphors, non sequiturs, and failure to present arguments fully or effectively. These are matters of style, but it is a short step from these defects to other faults of logic that are, like inconsistencies and contradictions, matters of substance. Here the editor must be careful not to unintentionally make changes of meaning when only changes of style are intended.

PROBLEMS OF SUBSTANCE

An editor must be careful to respect the writing ability of the author, even when the author is not a professional writer. However, while some nonprofessionals are quite protective of their writing, many recognize their limitations and will take almost unlimited direction and criticism from a respected editor. But this compliant attitude rarely extends to subject matter. Unless the editor is a specialist whose knowledge equals that of the author, the latter is likely to resist any attempts to change the facts or ideas presented in the manuscript—or even the way they are presented, if the nature of their thought is affected.

Nevertheless, it is customary to have nonfiction manuscripts read by experts other than the author, and differences of opinion often arise. Differences that are strictly matters of opinion are usually reconciled in favor of the author, unless the expert reader is very much more qualified than the author by experience and professional standing. In such cases, the author can sometimes be persuaded to modify, or at least soften, the opinion in question. There are, however, differences of opinion about matters of fact where no authority can be cited to settle the matter, and both author and reader insist they are right. This often arises where historical or scientific points of fact are based on personal knowledge, and each party has good reason to claim the truth. Such disputes can sometimes be settled by reference to a third expert, but the author is usually granted the point unless it seems clear to the editor that the others are right. When the latter occurs, the publisher again faces the unhappy alternatives of printing what are believed to be errors or rejecting the book. The second choice is likely only in extreme cases.

Inconsistencies and contradictions are usually easier to handle. Some authors out of pride resist such criticism, but with persistence and diplomacy the editor can usually get the author to make the necessary changes—which are usually small enough for the writer to make. It is best to let the author make them to be sure that no misinterpretation or shade of meaning alters the author's intention.

The worst problems of substance are the *lack* of essential values—plot, tension, drama, information, advice, facts. These problems are sometimes insoluble because of the author's limitations. It is important to recognize such basic faults at an early stage so the project can be rejected rather than become a terrible burden.

Manuscript preparation

Having gone as far as is considered necessary to insure the adequacy, if not the excellence, of the Ms, the editor turns it over to the copy editor for finishing. As explained earlier, the extent of this work varies from house to house, and even among editors in the same company. The nature of the work is discussed in CH. 36.

Where there is a staff copy editor, close coordination with the editor is customary. Freelance copy editors are less likely to communicate with the editor, but do so when questions of policy appear. In cases where the Ms is very complicated and needs a lot of work, a freelance copy editor may temporarily move into the publisher's offices, where the editor is more accessible.

After the substantive editorial questions are settled with the author by the editor, the manuscript goes directly to the design department (or the production department, if that is the channel in the house) via the editor. (In some companies, it goes through the managing editor for traffic control, from both copy editor to editor and from editor to design.) The editor gives the copy-edited Ms a once-over to be sure that the job was properly done. If the copy editing was extensive, the editor may refer some questions to the author before releasing the Ms for design and production. In some houses, unless the schedule is too tight, the copy-edited Ms is shown to the author to preclude major problems at the galley proof stage.

Most professional writers, particularly fiction writers, tend to object to any tampering with their work and frequently complain about the copy editing. However, copy editing is a professional procedure that is in the province of the publisher, as are design and production, so the author is expected to accept the publisher's judgment of its quality. It is the editor's responsibility to see that a high standard of performance is maintained in the copy editing —which includes maintenance of respect for the integrity of the author's work while making it conform to the standards of the house.

41 | Working with design & production

In a general way, the progress of a book through a publishing house is from (a) editorial to (b) design to (c) production to (d) sales. This is a true picture in the sense that those 4 departments carry the ball in that sequence, but in practice, all 4 are actively involved throughout the process. Thus, the editor continues work on a book after the Ms has been delivered to design, and sometimes even after the books have been shipped from the bindery and are being sold. (Administratively, the progress might be (b) production (c) design because the design department is often part of the production department, but functionally the order is always as above.) This chapter deals with the editor's participation in the design and production of the book, but with the assumption that the reader understands those functions as they are explained in Part I —particularly CHS. 3, 5, 6, 8, 14 through 24, and 28.

Editors are involved with the design/production process in 2 ways: (a) contributing knowledge of the book to design, and (b) checking the preparation of the book for accuracy.

Contributing to design

In CHS. 38 and 39, the editor's role in developing a design concept for the book was discussed, as this related to acquisition and marketing plans. Once the final Ms has been turned over to design, the editor resumes the earlier dialogue with the designer or design director, but in more specific terms. By this time, the final character and content of the book have been determined and the house's perception of the book—its quality and sales potential—has been crystalized.

With the marked Ms, the editor sends to the designer an information sheet giving: (a) all of the basic publishing facts—list price, quantity to be printed and bound, basic marketing plans for hardbound, paperback, or other editions, subsidiary sales, if any, descriptions of competing books, and any format specifications that were previously determined, such as trim-size, number of pages, etc., (b) a summary of the book as it finally developed, and (c) the editor's thoughts on the design problems and any special editorial problems that require a design solution.

By this time, the illustrations, if any, have been obtained (CH. 7) and are delivered to design with the Ms. These should be accompanied by a list of illustrations with numbers corresponding to identification numbers on the pictures. Whoever receives the original illustrations should count them, check them against the list, and sign a dated receipt for them. The loss of original pictures, particularly color transparencies, can be catastrophic in terms of time as well as money. Receipts may not enable lost pictures to be found, but they do make the signers more careful.

If the illustrations are related to specific passages in the text, the editor should indicate on the master copy of the Ms exactly where each one belongs. This is done by writing and encircling the appropriate illustration number in the margin of the Ms directly opposite the most relevant line of text.

The interaction of editor and designer is described in CH. 39 ("Book & jacket design"). If the design concept was formulated in the acquisition or marketing-plan stages, it is checked and refined by the designer when the manuscript is completed and released for design. The design is checked by the editor in the sample pages (CH. 18). If it fails to solve the editorial problem (CH. 15), the editor should discuss the matter with the designer at this point, and ask for revised samples if (a) a radical revision is needed and (b) there is enough time. If revised samples are not feasible, the composition may be started—provided the basic type specifications are OK—and the first galley made-up into pages to show the new design.

If no design concept was formed previously, the editor-designer conferences described in CH. 39 take place after the designer has studied the manuscript and the information sheet; the subsequent procedure is the same as described above.

Only rarely, and then only as a courtesy, are sample pages and layouts shown to the author. If they *are* shown, any constructive comments should be passed to the designer, but the design of the book is a publisher's prerogative and the author should be expected to observe this custom. Alfred Knopf firmly put down authors' incursions into this domain because he respected his designers and recognized their special qualifications, but many publishers and editors are inclined to cave in when an author takes a strong position on design. Be as firm as you can. If the author's demands involve extra expenses, a suggestion that they would require a lower royalty can be very effective.

When the design of an unillustrated book is approved, the editor has no further work in this area until galley proofs are received

(CH. 20). If a book is illustrated, and particularly if the illustrations are within the text (as opposed to being in a separate section), the editor, and sometimes the author, check the layouts for editorial flaws (see "Layouts" below).

Checking for accuracy

The editor may have as many as 8 opportunities to check the production for errors, or as few as one. The number depends on the kind of book and the method of production. The largest number occurs when the book is illustrated with full-color illustrations placed within the text. The sequence is as follows:

(a) galley proofs,
(b) layouts,
(c) page proofs,
(d) repro proofs,
(e) color proofs,
(f) mechanicals,
(g) blueprints, and (sometimes)
(h) press proofs.

This number might increase if the volume of galley corrections—and available time—warrant revised galleys.

The other extreme may occur when a book with no illustrations is produced in a system that provides only galley proofs (or a *line-printer printout*) which are corrected on an editing terminal to produce a tape that drives a machine that corrects the type, makes up pages, and, with the aid of a laser beam, automatically makes printing plates, all in one operation (CH. 5). This high-speed production is obviously not feasible where editorial quality is an important consideration. It does, however, have its uses for producing reprints, instant books, and cheap popular fiction, and it can be very economical.

Following is a discussion of the editorial procedures and practices involved in handling the various kinds of materials to be checked. See also CHS. 4, 8, 9, 18, 20, 24, 25, 36, and 37.

As explained in CH. 5, galley proofs are so called because they were originally the proofs of metal type assembled in continuous lines on a long metal tray called a *galley*. These were the first proofs, and were pulled before the type was divided into pages. This is still done to some extent, but most typesetting is now done with *photo-setters*, which produce not metal type but printed images of type on paper or film. The equivalent of a galley proof in *photocomposition* is a photographic print—still unpaged—produced by the machine. The original print is very high in quality, but copies must be made by a photocopying machine, and sometimes these copies are not very good (CH. 5).

When the Ms is sent to design or production, the editor should

GALLEY PROOFS

indicate how many sets of galleys are wanted. As noted elsewhere (CH. 5), the printer supplies a certain number of sets (usually 3) which are included in the price of composition; additional sets cost extra. It is customary to get a set for the author, the proofreader, and the editor—who gets the *Master* set. Additional sets are ordered if there are to be two separate but simultaneous readings and/or if a layout is required. Other sets may be required to send to experts, endorsers, reviewers, and/or book clubs. (It always costs more if more sets are ordered after the initial number are made, but this is particularly true in metal type composition.) Sometimes the managing editor is responsible for distributing (and retrieving) the various sets of galleys, but often they are sent directly from production to the readers.

Presumably, all those who read the galleys finish at about the same time, but often the author takes longer. This may be true for one or more of a number of reasons, but it is usually because changes are being made. In any case, once all copies are returned, the editor goes over them so that all important questions are resolved. Then the copy editor *collates* them and the net result is marked on the Master set. The latter should never be handled by anyone but the editor, the copy editor, and the design/production people; it is the only complete and correct set and must be properly marked.

If any set is marked by more than one person, all should be cautioned to use a different colored pencil. All readers should initial every proof they have read.

Under exceptional pressure of time, publishers will sometimes bypass checking galley proofs and have the compositor make up pages as soon as the type is set. The page proofs are then handled as described above. This procedure does not save much reading time (see discussion under "Page proofs" later in this chapter), but it does cut down a little on the handling time. The practice of going directly into pages is increasing with the general speed-up of publishing, but very few publishers do it as a routine procedure. Obviously, it would be unwise to use this method if there is any reason to believe that the author will make extensive corrections.

LAYOUTS When layouts of the entire book—or a section—are made because there are illustrations (CH. 21), the editor should check the layouts for editorial errors. Ordinarily, layouts are brought to the editor's office by the designer, who goes over them with the editor, answering questions and making some corrections in the process. Sometimes it is impractical to move the layouts, and the editor goes to the designer's desk, or even to the studio of a freelance designer. This is necessary when it is important to have the original illustrations at hand (which is usual) and they are too fragile or bulky to be moved easily.

There are 2 kinds of editorial flaws to be checked: (a) factual errors, such as the wrong caption on a picture, a *flopped* [inverted] picture, or two pictures confused with each other, and (b) faults of editorial judgment by the designer: an unimportant picture made too large, a picture out of sequence, or an editorially significant element cropped off a photograph. Here, as with the other aspects of design, the editor should refrain from imposing esthetic, as distinct from editorial, opinions on the designer.

When the layouts have been checked, the designer makes the changes required and sends the galleys through production for either paging or *repros*, depending on the kind of layout. Sometimes layout changes require corrections on the galleys. These are made by the designer if they involve only space adjustments or very minor changes in the type, but any substantial type changes are made by the editor on the Master proof. Presumably, the Master galleys are ready to be returned to design/production by the time the layouts are completed. If not, there is likely to be a delay in the book's schedule.

It is important, incidentally, for the editor to give design an estimate of the amount of correction likely to be made by the author. If this is expected to be substantial, the layout will not be done until revised galleys are received. Even if revised proofs are not necessary, if the layout is a very tight one, i.e. there will be little extra space, the layout will not be started until the corrections have been received from the author. If these are not too extensive, the designer can calculate their effect on the layout and proceed. Otherwise, it may be necessary to get corrected proofs of the galleys that have the most changes. Since these decisions can involve weeks of work or waiting time, it pays to go after an accurate estimate by the author of the amount of correction anticipated.

Respect for the production schedule is *extremely important*. Once the Ms is received, a publication schedule is made based on the production schedule. By this time, the house is committed to a publication date, and any substantial loss of time in production causes a delay in publication. Postponements of pub dates are not unknown, but they are very disruptive and expensive. They are to be avoided if at all possible.

When galleys are returned, state the number of page proofs required, if there are to be such.

Page proofs are not always made for books with complicated layouts, as it is usually easier to paste the various elements into position on the *mechanical* (CH.8) than to have the compositor make them up into pages. However, page proofs are usual for other books (CH.24).

PAGE PROOFS

The only purpose to checking page proofs should be to find printers' errors—either in the corrections made in galleys or in the makeup of the pages. Checking the latter is done by the designer, although it is customary for the copy editor to check for missing or duplicated lines (*slugging*), or for pages that are too long or too short. Page proofs are sometimes sent to the author to check, but with the understanding that there are to be no author's changes. Obviously, any changes—even the length of a line—at this point can disrupt the entire makeup from that point on, and this can be very expensive.

Page proofs with light corrections are usually read in house, even if the galleys were read outside. Do not, however, make the assumption that only corrected lines need be checked when photocomposition is used. Although it is theoretically impossible for changes to occur in running a tape through a typesetting machine, mistakes do happen—a dropped character is not uncommon, and dropped lines or even paragraphs are possible—so these proofs should be scanned, at least. In *Linotype* composition, the only error that can occur in uncorrected material is the dropping or transposition of lines; there can be no changes within a line because only the corrected lines go through the machine.

When the Ms goes directly into pages without a reading of galleys, the page proofs are read as described for galleys, but with the additional necessity of checking the makeup. If any author's corrections would seriously disrupt the makeup, it is necessary to ask the author for compensatory changes that will enable retaining the existing page arrangement, or to accept the considerable cost in money and time of re-makeup.

REPRO PROOFS The final proof, fully corrected and ready for camera, is called a repro (reproduction) proof (CHS. 5,8). In metal typesetting, this is a new proof pulled on high-grade paper for maximum sharpness. In photocomposition, the normal output is a photographic print which is of reproduction quality, so no special proofing is needed. Here again, the actual practice does not always work as it should in theory. Any photographic print can vary according to the exposure and development. While these are supposed to be perfectly uniform in a typesetting machine, some variations do occur, so that all or part of a proof may be too light or too dark. In light prints, fine *serifs* on the type (CH. 5) sometimes get lost. In dark prints, small spaces inside letters sometimes close up. Any such proofs should be rejected by the production department, but if they reach the editor they should be sent back.

As in page proofs, only the corrected lines, if any, are to be checked and there should always be a check for new errors in uncorrected lines. Repros are not normally sent to the author. However, when the Ms has gone directly into pages, the repros provide the only opportunity to check author's corrections. When the latter are substantial, it would be best to have the author read the repros. There may be a need for revised repros to check printer's errors in setting the corrections in pages.

The checking of color proofs for accuracy of color reproduction is a special technique—perhaps art is a better word—best left to specialists (CH.8). This area is full of booby traps and pitfalls. The intensity and color of the light in which the copy and the proof are viewed can make significant differences, the proof paper is a factor, as is the inking, and even the position of the various pictures on the proof sheet. Even when a decision has been made to make certain changes in color, the question of how to accomplish these changes is not easily answered. Remember that the color is an illusion created by the way that four colors are balanced, so any change in one affects the other three. It is extremely difficult to predict the result when a specific change in one color is requested. Again, only a qualified specialist should correct color where accurate reproduction is needed. If, however, there is no need to match the copy, the editor may be justified in asking that color be changed in some way that seems desirable. But this is likely to be an esthetic judgment and should ordinarily be left to the designer or color specialist.

The editorial correction of color proofs would involve checking: (a) pictures, to see if they are all present, (b) that no errors were made in the cropping or silhouetting (CH.8)—a common fault in silhouetting is to leave in the background in small areas within a figure, e.g. a space between arm and body or between legs, and (c) that no flopping has occurred. The latter is fairly common, since film can easily be turned over at the wrong time and left that way if the picture does not *look* wrong. The designer will also be looking for such errors, but an editorial check is desirable.

Color proofs may appear at any point in the sequence of production, but they should come in early enough so that the separation films are OK'd by the time the mechanicals are finished. Some printers send color proofs made up in position with captions. These should be checked carefully.

When the repro proofs are ready and the illustrations have either been shot by the printer (in the case of black & whites a blueprint of the individual pictures will be provided; for color illustrations there will be color proofs), or a photoprint made to size, if the book is to be printed with photomechanical plates (CH.9), all of the elements are pasted down in their correct position on a sheet of heavy paper. This paste-up is called a mechanical (CH.8). The mechanical is photographed by the printer and printing plates are made from the resulting negative (or positive) film (CH.9).

At this stage, there is no question of editorial changes except to correct errors that might have been missed in previous readings of the proofs. The purpose of editorial checking of mechanicals is to see that no errors were made in the placement of the various pieces of text or illustrations. The arrangement itself was settled in the layout, so no position changes are to be made. Nevertheless, this *is* the last chance to catch serious errors and deficiencies of content or arrangement, particularly in the contents page and the pagination, so if there is anything found that should not be in the printed book, and the deficiency is correctable by moving pieces on the mechanical, speak up now.

BLUEPRINTS These are proofs of the films that were produced by photographing the mechanical (see above and CHS. 5, 8). They are customarily folded and trimmed so that they look much like a printed book (they are then called *book blues*).

The blueprint is *not* to be criticized for printing quality. It is a relatively crude photoprint and cannot be controlled past a certain point. It may be too light or too dark in part or whole, but these are not indications of the printed result to come. Correction of these aspects of blueprints should be left to the design and production people.

The editorial checking of blueprints involves the search for errors in the sequence of pages, the dropping of elements, such as folios or running heads—which happens frequently due to the masking techniques that are used—the accidental cutting of a piece of film, the flopping of film, the misplacement or transposition of illustrations, etc. Remember that only the black & white type and *line* illustrations (CH. 8) are pasted in place on the mechanicals. The *halftones* (CH. 8) and the color illustrations are *stripped* into position in the film, and the blueprint is the first opportunity to see that these have been placed properly.

It has been stated that the mechanical provides the last chance to make vital corrections. This is true in the sense that editorial changes in blueprints are unthinkable. They are very expensive, if possible at all, and involve a change in the production schedule. Having said this, it would be wrong not to point out that *really* vital changes can sometimes be made at the blueprint stage. If they are, expect a battle with the production department, and be prepared to make a very strong case.

PRESS PROOFS It is very unusual to pull press proofs. In fact, it is a rare occurrence since to do so requires spending 3 or 4 hours setting up the production press just as though the whole edition of, say, 10,000 were going to be run, and then stopping it after a hundred or so copies (perhaps 2 or 3 minutes), in order to get one or 2 good ones. This is an expensive procedure that is justified only if the book has very critical printing problems (usually in color illustrations) and is a very important book. Sometimes the procedure is used if, for sales reasons, the great expense of press proofs is justified in order to give printed sheets, in advance of the production run, to the sales-people. This value may be combined with the production reasons to justify the cost. (It is also possible to pull press proofs of only one sheet as a compromise for both sales and production purposes.)

Press proofs would not ordinarily be shown to the editor except for general interest. Certainly, if some *disastrous* error were to be discovered in these proofs it would still be possible, perhaps, to make a correction. This would be even harder to justify to production than blueprint corrections, so the error would have to be correspondingly more serious. If, however, the editor has qualifications to evaluate the quality of illustration printing, a check of the press proofs either with or instead of an art director would be in order.

Once all the proofs have been checked and the book has gone to press, the editor can only pray that all will go well, and that the reviewers will not notice (and mention) the errors that will almost certainly remain.

PART **III** Useful information

Sources of information

BOOKS

Books and Printing—Paul A. Bennett, ed. World (paperback). 1963.　**General**
    (Reprint of 1951 collection of essays by typographers and designers;
    includes some famous statements.)

Graphic Forms—György Kepes, and others. Harvard University Press.
    1949. (Top graphic artists of the era—among them, Conkwright,
    Dwiggins, the Beilensons, Rand, Armitage, Hofer—discuss the arts
    as related to the book.)

Handbook for Graphic Communications—Stanley Lasday. Graphic Arts
    Technical Foundation, 1972–74. (Nine volumes, sold together in
    slipcase, or separately. Topics of volumes are: Art and Copy Prepara-
    tion, Composition, Conversion Processes; Illumination; Photog-
    raphy; Letterpress, Screen Printing, Gravure, Flexography; Ink, Pa-
    per, Binding; Handling of Chemicals Safely; Related Data; Compo-
    site Index.)

Into Print: A Practical Guide to Printing, Illustrating and Publishing
    —Mary Hill, Wendell Cochran. Wm. Kaufman, 1977. (Authors'
    and illustrators' standpoint; includes self-publishing.)

Manufacturing Standards and Specifications—National Association of
    State Textbook Administrators. 1976. (Prepared and published by
    the Association "in consultation with" the Association of American
    Publishers and Book Manufacturers' Institute. Available at BMI.
    Looseleaf format, allowing revisions to be inserted.)

One Book, Five Ways—Association of American University Presses, ed. Wm. Kaufman (paperback). 1978. (Each of five university publishers provides papers and documents showing every step in how it would edit, design, plan, and produce a hypothetical book from the same manuscript.)

Penrose Annual. Lund Humphries (London), Hastings House (New York). (A yearly international survey of graphic arts—design, technology, current and past; edited in England.)

Pocket Pal—Michael H. Bruno, ed. Paperback. International Paper Company. 11th ed. 1974. (Practical, alphabetical, voluminous, illustrated guide to graphic arts practice and backgrounds.)

Printing in the 20th Century—James Moran. Hastings House. 1974. (Articles from 50 years of the *Penrose Annual*.)

Production for the Graphic Designer—James Craig. Watson-Guptill. 1974. (Composition, printing, paper, inks, color, imposition, folding, binding, mechanicals; major glossary.)

Publishing

BACKGROUNDS

At Random—Bennett A. Cerf. Random House. 1977. (Edited oral reminiscences of the widely-known late publisher.)

The Bantam Story—Clarence Petersen. Bantam (paperback). 1975. (On the growth of Bantam and other mass-market paperback publishers.)

The Book in America—Hellmut Lehmann-Haupt, Lawrence C. Wroth, Rollo G. Silver. Bowker. Revised ed. 1951. (Comprehensive one-volume history, 1630–1950; original edition, 1939.)

Book Publishing in America—Charles A. Madison. McGraw-Hill. 1966. (Later sold by Bowker. Highlights of 300 years of history.)

Book Publishing, Inside Views—Jean Spencer Kujoth, compiler. Scarecrow Press. 1971. (Anthology of 50 articles, 1962–1970.)

Eighty Years of Best Sellers, 1895–1975—Alice Payne Hackett, Henry James Burke. Bowker. 1977. (Year-by-year listings and comment; useful category lists.)

Golden Multitudes—Frank Luther Mott. Bowker. 1960. (Reprint of Mott's 1947 Macmillan classic about the books that became American best sellers.)

A *History of Book Publishing in the United States*—Vol. 1, 1630–1865; Vol. 2, 1865–1919; Vol. 3 1919–1940; Vol. 4, in preparation—John A. Tebbel. Bowker. 1972, 1975, 1978. (The most comprehensive history.)

The House of Harper—Eugene Exman. Harper & Row. 1967. (Lively, surprisingly unbiased account of the firm's first 150 years.)

Published in Paris—Hugh Ford. Macmillan. 1975. (About the young American writers who did their own publishing and printing in Paris in the 1920s and 1930s.)

Publishing and Bookselling: A History from the Earliest Time to the Present Day.—F.A. Mumby. Bowker. Revised, 5th ed. 1974. (British emphasis.)

OPERATIONS

The American Reading Public—Roger H. Smith, ed. Bowker. 1967. (Symposium on readers and their relation to the book industry.)

The Art and Science of Book Publishing—Herbert S. Bailey, Jr. Harper & Row. 1970. (Applying management science.)

Book Publishing: What It Is and What It Does—John P. Dessauer. Bowker. 1974; rev. ed. (hardcover & paperback) 1979. (Concise, comprehensive.)

Books from Writer to Reader—Howard Greenfield. Crown. 1974. (Every step in general book publishing described; extensively illustrated.)

The Bowker Lectures on Book Publishing—Bowker. 1957. (The first 17 R. R. Bowker Memorial Lectures, by authorities.)

The Business of Publishing: A PW Anthology. Arnold W. Ehrlich, ed., intro. Bowker. 1976. (Operations of publishing in the 1970s.)

A Candid Critique of Book Publishing—Curtis G. Benjamin. Bowker. 1977. (A top executive's views on publishing operations.)

Editor to Author: The Letters of Maxwell E. Perkins—John Hall Wheelock, ed. Scribners (paperback). 1950. (Correspondence with Hemingway, Wolfe, Fitzgerald, Galsworthy, and others.)

Editors on Editing—Gerald Gross, ed. Grosset & Dunlap (paperback). 1962. (Writings by various editors; good source of information on editorial functions.)

Getting Into Book Publishing—Chandler B. Grannis. Bowker (pamphlet [Gratis]). 1977. (For students and other prospective members of the book industry.)

A Guide to Book Publishing—Datus C. Smith, Jr. Bowker. 1966. (The basics, with special emphasis on third-world publishing.)

Guide to Women's Publishing—Polly Joan and Andria Chesman. Dust Books (Paradise, Calif.). 1978. (Describes a wide range of publishing enterprises and related facilities.)

How to Get Happily Published—Judith Applebaum, Nancy Evans. Harper & Row. 1978. *A Writer's Guide to Book Publishing*—Richard Balkin. Hawthorn. 1978. (Two up-to-date books for writers, describing the needs, wants, and ways of publishers.)

Literary Agents: A Complete Guide—Judith Johnson Sherwin. New York. Poets & Writers, Inc. 1978. (Full account of how literary agencies work; relations with writers and publishers; directory information.)

Max Perkins, Editor of Genius—A. Scott Berg. Dutton. 1978. (Biography of a great 20th-century editor at Scribners.)

Now Barabbas—William Jovanovich. Harper & Row. 1964. (Essays on the principal varieties of publishing, and on reading, writing, and learning.)

Paperback Parnassus—Roger H. Smith. Westview Press. 1976. (Structure and operations on the paperback industry.)

Perspectives on Publishing—Philip G. Altback, Sheila McVey, eds. Lexington Books. 1976. (Symposium on current trends.)

Publishers on Publishing—Gerald Gross, ed. Grosset & Dunlap (paperback). 1961. (Reprint of Bowker anthology of publishers' writings; enlightening, amusing.)

Publishing Children's Books in America, 1919–1976. Robin Gottlieb, compiler. Children's Book Council. 1978. (Annotated lists of 1,709 articles, books, pamphlets.)

Publishing: The Creative Business—Harald Bohne and Harry Van Ierssel. University of Toronto Press (paperback). 1973. (Manual of the business operations.)

To Advance Knowledge—Gene R. Hawes. American University Press Services (paperback). 1967. (Handbook on American university press procedures, problems, backgrounds.)

The Truth About Publishing—Sir Stanley Unwin. Bowker. 7th ed. 1970. (An outspoken English publisher's views on sound practice.)

What Happens in Book Publishing—Chandler B. Grannis, ed. Columbia University Press. 2nd ed. 1967. (Chapters by 20 experts on the functions and fields of book publishing.)

What Is an Editor? Saxe Commins at Work—Dorothy Commins. University of Chicago Press. 1978. (A great editor's editorial reports, correspondence, and notebooks.)

Writing, Illustrating, and Editing Children's Books—Jean Poindexter Colby. Hastings House. 1967. (Standard how-to account.)

Design & Typography

Books for Our Time—Marshall Lee, ed. Oxford University Press. 1951. (Essays and specimens by leading innovative designers; 150 books illustrated.)

From Cover to Cover: The Occasional Papers of a Book Designer—Stefan Salter. Prentice-Hall. 1969. (The author found his eyesight failing, but then dictated many articles about his craft, and kept on designing.)

Printing Design and Production from Seven Countries: Singapore to Istanbul. —American Institute of Graphic Arts (paper cover). 1962. (Record and commentary on an exhibition collected on a production consultation tour by Milton B. and Evelyn Harter Glick.)

Printing Types: An Introduction—Alexander S. Lawson. Beacon Press. 1974. (By an outstanding teacher of graphic arts.)

Type Design and Typography—Frederic W. Goudy. Myriade Press (hardcover and paperback). 1978. (New edition of the prolific type designer's essays originally issued by the Typophiles in 1946.)

Typologia—Frederic W. Goudy. University of California Press. 1970. (Collection of studies and comments on the design, making, history, and legibility of types, and on fine printing.)

American Book Design and William Morris—Susan Otis Thompson. Bowker. 1977. (Roots of the 20th-century revolution in book design; much history of design-conscious U.S. publishers.)

The Art of the Printed Book, 1455–1955—Joseph Blumenthal. Godine and Morgan Library. 1973. (Essays and 125 reproductions from a Morgan Library exhibition.)

The Book: The Story of Printing & Bookmaking—Douglas C. McMurtrie. Oxford University Press. 1943. (The classic tradition.)

Book Typography, 1815–1965—Kenneth Day, ed. University of Chicago Press. 1966. (A big book, showing developments in Europe and the United States.)

Five Hundred Years of Printing—S. H. Steinberg. Penguin (paperback). Revised ed. 1974. (The leading concise, one-volume account.)

Four Centuries of Fine Printing—Stanley Morison. Barnes & Noble. Revised ed. 1960. (Short essay by the great English typographer and historian; 192 reproductions of book pages from 1465 to 1924.)

A *History of the Printed Book*—Lawrence C. Wroth, ed. Limited Editions Club *(The Dolphin*, vol. 3). 1938. (Large, well-illustrated study by experts on various aspects.)

History of Printing in America—Isaiah Thomas (Marcus A. McCorison, ed.) University Press of Virginia, distr. 1975. (Originally published in 1810 by the prominent Revolutionary-era printer.)

Modern Book Design from William Morris to the Present Day—Ruari McLean. Oxford University Press. 1959. (Survey by a top British authority.)

Printing and the Mind of Man: The Impact of Print on Five Centuries of Western Civilization—John Carter, Percy H. Muir, eds. Holt, Rinehart & Winston. 1967. (Heavily illustrated descriptive account, based on a famous exhibition.)

Printing Presses: History and Development from the 15th Century to Modern Times—James Moran. University of California Press (paperback). 1973.

Printing 1770–1970: An Illustrated History of Its Uses and Development—Michael Twyman. Bowker. 1970.

Daniel Berkeley Updike. Harvard University Press. 2 vols. 3rd ed.
1962. (An essential classic; original edition, 1922.)
The Shaping of Our Alphabet—Frank Denman. Knopf. 1955. (Interesting, well-illustrated history of letters and type.)
A Short History of the Printed Word—Warren Chappell. Knopf. 1970.
(Handsomely illustrated account by a famous illustrator and designer.)
The 26 Letters—Oscar Ogg. Crowell. Revised ed. 1971. (Development of the Roman alphabet; extensively and charmingly illustrated by the author-designer; splendid introduction for the general reader.)
The Typographic Book, 1450–1935—Stanley Morison, Kenneth Day.
University of Chicago Press. 1964. (Massive illustrated study.)

Asymmetrical Typography—Jan Tschichold. Van Nostrand-Reinhold.   APPLICATION
1967. (Brilliant statement of "modern" typography, first written in German many years before.)
Basic Course in Graphic Design—Richard Taylor. Van Nostrand-Reinhold. (paperback). 1971.
Book Design—Vol. 1, Systematic Aspects; Vol. 2, Text Format Design—Stanley Rice. Bowker. 1978. (How to deal systematically with a full range of typographic problems under present-day technology; alternative models for every element of virtually all kinds of books.)
Comprehensive Graphic Arts—Ervin A. Dennis, John D. Jenkins. Sams.
1974. For high-school and technical-school students and other newcomers; gives working knowledge of graphic arts technologies.)
The Design of Books—Adrian Wilson. Peregrine Smith (paperback).
1974. (Reprint of 1967 Reinhold original; design approaches and problems described and fully illustrated.)
Design Through Discovery—Marjorie Elliot Bevlin. Holt, Rinehart and Winston. 3rd ed. 1978.
Design with Type—Carl Dair. University of Toronto Press. 1967. (Guidance by an outstanding Canadian designer.)
Designing Books—Jan Tschichold. Wittenborn. 1951. Rules for conventional typography; written after the author of *Asymmetric Typography* changed his views.)
Designing Instructional Text—James Hartley. Nichols Publishing Company. 1978. (Many format models; guide by a British educator.)
Designing with Type: A Basic Course in Typography—James Craig.
Watson-Guptill. 1971. (Said to be the most widely used textbook.)
Editing by Design: Word- and Picture-Communication for Editors and Designers—Jan White. Bowker. 1974. (How-to and why-to.)
Estimating Standards for Printers—Fred W. Heck. Revised ed. 1971.
Available from Printing Industries of Metropolitan New York.
(Called the bible in its field.)
Graphic Arts Encyclopedia—George A. Stevenson, ed. McGraw-Hill.
1968.
Graphic Arts Management—Victor Strauss. Presentation Press, PIA, and Bowker. 1973. (For users as well as suppliers.)
Graphic Design for the Computer Age—Edward A. Hamilton. Van Nostrand-Reinhold. 1970. (Contemporary visual communication applied to books and other media; author directed design of Time-Life Books.)
Introduction to Typography—Oliver Simon. Paperback. Transatlantic Arts. (Reprint of Harvard, 1949, original.)
Methods of Book Design: The Practice of an Industrial Craft—Hugh

Williamson. Oxford University Press. 2nd ed. 1966. (Detailed guide to book production in Britain.)

Production for the Graphic Designer—James Craig. Watson-Guptill. 1974. (What the designer needs to know about production; includes comparisons of composition systems.)

Typography: Design and Practice—John Lewis. Taplinger (Pentalic). 1978. (Foundations and development of letter forms, and practical application in film and electronic technology; emphasis on book design; by a British authority.)

Typography for Photocomposition—A. S. Lawson, Archie Provan. (Available from Typographers Association of New York.)

Visual Communication and the Graphic Arts—Estelle Jussim. Bowker. 1975. (Photography's impact on the graphic arts; contemporary application and terminology.)

TYPE SPECIMENS   *About Alphabets*—Hermann Zapf. M.I.T. Press (paperback). 1970. (Designs and comment by a leading contemporary type designer.)

The Alphabet and Elements of Lettering—Frederic W. Goudy. Dover (paperback). (Reprint of 1918 and 1922 essays, revised and enlarged for 1942 book published by the University of California Press.)

Manuale Typographicum—Hermann Zapf. M.I.T. Press (paperback). 1970. (100 pages selected and designed by the famous typographer; quotations on types and printing.)

Treasury of Alphabets and Lettering—Jan Tschichold. Reinhold. 1966. (Source book; 150 fine alphabets, with incisive comment by a classical typographer.)

Type and Lettering—William Longyear. Watson-Guptill (paperback). Revised, 4th ed. 1966. (A widely used source book.)

Type Specimen Book. Van Nostrand-Reinhold (paperback). 1974.

Types of Typefaces—J. Ben Lieberman. Myriade Press. Revised ed. 1978. (How letters and typefaces have developed since ancient times; samples of hundreds of faces in letterpress and photocomposition designs.)

Typographic Variations—Hermann Zapf. Myriade Press. New ed. 1978.

NOTE: Manufacturers and distributors of composition systems and typeface designs provide specimen books showing their designs in various sizes and forms. Many typesetting companies and book manufacturers also have substantial specimen books. These specimen books, covering photocomposition and metal typefaces, are available on request by users or are for sale.

Illustration   *American Picturebooks from 'Noah's Ark' to 'The Beast Within'*—Barbara
HISTORY   Bader. Macmillan. 1976. (Definitive history of the illustrating and publishing of picture books for children over the past century. Profuse reproductions, many in color.)

The Artist and the Book, 1860–1960. Boston Museum of Fine Arts. 1961. (Excellent survey of book illustration.)

500 Years of Book Illustration—Howard Simon. Garden City. 1949.

A History of Book Illustration: The Illuminated Manuscript and the Printed Book—David Bland. University of California Press. Revised, 2nd ed. 1969. (Comprehensive, extensively illustrated; a major work.)

The Illustrated Book—Frank Weitenkampf. Harvard University Press. 1938. (Thorough, scholarly history.)

The Illustrator in America, 1900–1960s—Walt Reed, ed. Van Nostrand-Reinhold. 1967. (Careers of 350 artists; 600 illustrations.)

An Introduction to the History of Woodcuts—A. M. Hind. 2 vols. Dover (paperback). 1963. (Reprint of definitive, 1935 work.)

The Art of Art for Children's Books—Diana Klemin. Potter; distr. by Crown. 1966. (How the artist illuminates the text; 60 examples shown.)

Artists' and Illustrators' Encyclopedia—John Quick. McGraw-Hill. 1969. (All methods and materials commonly used in graphic arts.)

The Illustrated Book: Its Art and Craft—Diana Klemin. Crown. 1970. (Work and methods of 74 book artists.)

Illustrating Children's Books; Writing Children's Books—Children's Book Council (brochures). 1977. (Brief outlines; includes lists for further reading.)

Photography Market Place—Fred W. McDarrah, ed. Bowker. 2nd ed. 1977. (Comprehensive directory of the photo industry.)

The Picture Researcher's Handbook—Andra Nelki and others. Scribners. 1975. (Agencies, other sources, methods of search.)

Picture Searching: Tools and Techniques—Renata V. Shaw, compiler. Special Libraries Association (paperback). 1973.

Stock Photo and Assignment Source Book—Fred W. McDarrah, ed. Bowker. 1977 (Hundreds of agencies, and other sources—international and domestic, public, professional, and commercial.)

The Careful Writer: A Modern Guide to English Usage—Theodore M. Bernstein. Atheneum. 1965. (Author was for many years the *New York Times* copy chief.)

Manuscript preparation

Copy Editing: The Cambridge Handbook—Judith Butcher. Cambridge University Press. 1975. (Up-to-date, British, scholarly.)

Copy Preparation for Printing—John F. Cabbi. Paperback. McGraw-Hill. 1973.

The Elements of Style—William Strunk, Jr., E. B. White. Macmillan. Revised 2nd ed. 1972. (The widely respected guide to precision and clarity in English writing.)

A Manual of Style—University of Chicago Press. 18th ed. The Press. 1979. (Major authority used in book publishing.)

Manual of Style and Usage—Lewis Jordan. New York Times Books (Quadrangle). 1976. (A leading authority.)

Proofreading and Copy Preparation: A Textbook for the Graphic Arts Industry—Joseph Lasky. Mentor Press. 1954.

Proofreading and Copyediting: A Practical Guide to Style for the 1970s—Henry M. Mc Naughton. Hastings House. 1973.

United States Government Printing Office Style Manual—GPO. Revised ed. 1973. (Order from Supt. of Documents.)

Words Into Type—M. E. Skillin, R. M. Gay. Appleton. Revised, 3rd ed. 1974. (A standby in many publishing houses.)

Complete Guide to Pasteup—Walter B. Graham. North American Publishing Co. 1975.

Preparation of camera copy

Preparing Art for Printing—Bernard Stone, A. Eckstein. Van Nostrand-Reinhold. 1964. (Planning, assembly, tools, materials, and all operations.)

Automated Typesetting: The Basic Course—Frank J. Romano. (Available from Typographers Association of New York.)

Composition

Book Composition—National Composition Association. (Available from Typographers Association of New York.)

Electronic Composition: Guide to the Revolution in Typesetting—N. Edward Berg. Graphic Arts Technical Foundation. 1975. (For printers and publishers.)

Fundamentals of Modern Composition—John W. Seybold. Seybold Publications, Inc. (Media, Pa.). 1977. (Thorough instructional survey by the field's foremost authority; focus on editorial-typesetting relations.)

How to Evaluate and Specify a Computer Typesetting and Data Management System—Frank J. Romano. (Available from Typographers Association of New York.)

Photo Type Setting: A Design Manual—James Craig. Watson-Guptill, 1978. (Comprehensive, heavily illustrated, up-to-date guide; explains different equipment and systems.)

Printing

Dramatic Color by Overprinting—Donald E. Cooke. North American Publishing Co. 1974. (Original ed., Winston, 1955.)

How to Estimate Offset Lithography—Fred W. Heck. Available from Printing Industries of Metropolitan New York (pamphlet). (Guide for printers and buyers of printing.)

An Introduction to Color—R. M. Evans. Wiley. 1948. (Properties: physical, psychological.)

The Lithographers Manual—Charles Shapiro, ed. Graphic Arts Technical Foundation. 5th ed. 1974. (Massive, comprehensive volume; 882 illus.; the basic reference.)

Planning for Better Imposition—Daniel Melcher, Nancy Larrick. North American Publishing Company. 1977.

The Printing Industry—Victor Strauss. Printing Industry of America and Bowker. 1967. (An encyclopedic introduction.)

Paper

Dictionary of Paper—American Paper Institute.

Handbook of Pulp and Paper Technology—Kenneth W. Britt. Van Nostrand-Reinhold. 1970.

History of Paper Making in the United States—David C. Smith. Vance Publishing Corp.

Paper and Paper Manufacture—American Paper Institute (pamphlet).

Paper Industry in the United States—American Paper Institute (pamphlet).

Paper Making: The History and Technique of an Ancient Craft—Dard Hunter. Knopf. 2nd ed. 1957. (Classic in its field.)

Pulp and Paper: Science and Technology—C. Earl Libby, ed. 2 vols. McGraw-Hill. 1962.

The Story of Papermaking—Edwin Sutermeister. Bowker. 1954. (Technical but readable review of the process.)

Working with Papers: A Guide for Printers—Michael Bruno, Leonard Schlosser. National Association of Printers and Lithographers (pamphlet). 1977. (Technical; useful also for publishers.)

Binding

Bookbinder—Jack Rudman. (paperback) National Learning. (Civil service examination guide.)

Bookbinding in America—Hellmut Lehmann-Haupt and others. Bowker. 1967. (Reprint of 1941 edition; bookbinding in both aspects, commercial and handcraft.)

Bookbinding: Its Background and Techniques—Edith Diehl. Kennikat Press. 1965. (Originally Rinehart, 1946; definitive.)

Books for the Millions—Frank E. Comparato. Stackpole. 1971. (History of book manufacturing, especially binding; inventions, equipment, companies, trends.)

The Conservation of Books and Documents—William H. Langwell.
Greenwood. 1974. (Reprint of 1957 edition.)

Creative Bookbinding—Pauline Johnson. University of Washington Press (paperback). 1975. (Handcraft.)

Development of Performance Standards in Bindings Used in Libraries. American Library Association (paperback). 1961, 1966. (Studies by the Library Technology Project.)

New Directions in Bookbinding—Philip Smith. Van Nostrand-Reinhold. 1974. (The high art of decorative, colorful leather binding, by an innovative, modern master.)

A Copyright Handbook—Donald Johnston. Bowker. 1978. (Detailed guide based on the new, 1976 copyright law.) **Copyright**

New Copyright Law Primer—Susan Wagner. *Publishers Weekly* (pamphlet). 1978. (Reprint of articles.)

Overview of the New Copyright Law—Charles H. Lieb. Association of American Publishers (pamphlet). 1976.

Photocopying by Academic, Public and Nonprofit Research Libraries— Association of American Publishers and Authors League. 1978. (Statement of authors' and publishers' position; questions and answers.)

Photocopying by Corporate Libraries—Association of American Publishers and Authors League. 1978 (Questions and answers.)

Visual Artist's Guide to the New Copyright Law. Tad Crawford. New York, Graphic Artists Guild. 1978. (Advantages, pitfalls, "work for hire" aspects and other necessary information for the artist.)

Audiovisual Market Place. Bowker. Annual. Guide to hundreds of producers and distributors of a-v materials and equipment, reference sources, and much other information; glossary.) **Reference**

The Bookman's Glossary—Jean Peters, ed. Bowker. 5th ed. 1975. (Much revised and enlarged; editorial, design, mechanical, collecting, selling, and other terminology of the book world.)

Bowker Annual—Bowker. (Yearly volume of statistics and other information about the library world and the book industry.)

Elzevier's Dictionary of the Printing and Allied Industries in . . . English, French, German, Dutch—F. J. M. Wijnekus. Elsevier. 1967. (More than 8100 terms, four languages per entry, with precise technical definitions in English; also cross-indexes by language; nine appendices.)

An Encyclopedia of the Book—G. A. Glaister. World. 1960. (People, processes, terms, history, technology.)

Encyclopedia of Contemporary Typesetting—Charles Shapiro. Graphic Arts Technical Foundation. 1977. (Extensive glossary, with directories of manufacturers, equipment, acronyms, model numbers, trade names.)

Fine Arts Market Place—Bowker. Annual. (Directory of firms, organizations, persons.)

Graphic Arts Encyclopedia—George A. Stevens. McGraw-Hill. 1968. (Illustrated compendium.)

Guide to Reference Books, 9th ed.—Eugene P. Sheey, ed. American Library Association. 1976. (Librarians call it the bible of reference to references.)

Literary Marketplace with Names and Numbers—Janice Blaufox, ed. Bowker. Annual. (Directory, including personnel, of publishers, agencies, associations, suppliers, manufacturers, book-trade services, review media, etc.; also alphabetical telephone list.)

The Reader's Adviser—Sally Prakken, ed. Revised and enlarged, 12th ed. 1974–77. (Vol. 1 of this 3-volume "Layman's Guide to Literature" includes extensive annotated listings of books about books, printing and bibliography.)

Roget's International Thesaurus, Fourth Edition—Robert L. Chapman, ed. T. Y. Crowell. 1977. (Topical arrangement, following principles of the original work, but thoroughly updated; widely recommended. Among works in alphabetical order, but also using the Roget name, The Doubleday Roget's Thesaurus edited by Landau and Bogus is most up to date.)

Technical Terms of the Printing Industry—Rudolf Hostettler. Wittenborn (New York). 1959. (Pocket-size reference; more than 1300 equivalent terms in English, French, German, Italian, Dutch; tables, diagrams, on composition, presswork, binding.)

PERIODICALS

Book Production Industry—21 Charles Street, Westport, Conn. 06880. (Bi-monthly journal about book manufacturing and its machines and materials.)

The Bookseller—London, Eng. (Weekly journal of the British book trade.)

Fine Print—2224 Baker Street, San Francisco, Calif. 94115. (Quarterly "review for the arts of the book"; the makers and products of fine printing; output of fine presses; reviews of literature in this field.)

Graphics—Zurich, Switzerland, and P.O. Box 320, New York, N.Y. 10005. (Luxurious bi-monthly about commercial graphic design throughout the world; lavish illustrations, many in color; text in English, German, French.)

Inland Printer/American Lithographer—300 W. Adams Street, Chicago, Ill. 60608. (Monthly; long-established journal for producers and users of printing.)

Print—355 Lexington Avenue, New York, N.Y. 10017. (Monthly; contemporary graphic design and production including book work.)

Printing Impressions—North American Publishing. 401 N. Broad St., Philadelphia, Pa. 19108. (Monthly; all facets of printing—practice, equipment, methods, trends.)

Publishers Weekly—1180 Avenue of the Americas, New York, N.Y. 10036. (News and trends of the book industry, people, forecasts of new books; monthly section on bookmaking.)

Publishing History—Michael Turner, ed. Chadwick-Healy, Cambridge, Cambridgeshire, England; Somerset House, Teaneck, N.J. 07666. (Illustrated scholarly journal; two issues a year.)

Quill & Quire—Susan Walker, ed. and pub. 59 Front St. East, Toronto, Ont. M5E-1B3. (Tabloid-size journal of the Canadian book industry.)

U and l c—International Typographic Corp., 216 East 45th Street, New York, N.Y. 10017. (Quarterly; tabloid-size; types and typographics for contemporary technology.)

FILMS & FILM STRIPS

The Book of Kells—Color, 20 min. Pictura Films Distr. Corp., New York.   **Backgrounds**
(The famous 9th-century Irish masterpiece of manuscript lettering
and illumination.)

Graphic Communications—We Used to Call It Printing—16mm,
sound, color, 23 min. DuPont. 1969. From Public Relations Photo
Products Div., E.I. DuPont de Nemours & Co., Wilmington, Del.,
or Graphic Arts Technical Foundation. (Free for loan.)

History of Printing—Sound, color, 22 min. Blondheim Productions.
1975.

Ideas Won't Keep—80 35mm slides with script and tape. Eastman Kodak
Co. 1970. From Eastman Kodak A-V Service, Rochester, N.Y., or
Graphic Arts Technical Foundation. (Graphic arts as visual com-
munications technology; career opportunities.)

The Making of a Renaissance Book—25 min. 1969. From American
Friends of the Plantin-Moretus Museum, New York City.

Messages. 16mm, sound, color, 7 min. International Typographic Composition Ass'n. From Graphic Arts Technical Foundation.

Careers in Illustration—Sound filmstrip, 35 min. Educational Dimen-   **Illustration**
sions Corp., Great Neck, N.Y.

Etching and Engraving—Sound filmstrip. Educational Audio Visual,
Inc., Thornwood, N.Y. 1977. (History and techniques.)

Basic Reproduction Processes in the Graphic Arts—Sound, color, 25   **Printing**
min. Farrell. 1964. From A-V Services, Penn. State University.

Cold Type Makeup Techniques—Filmstrip. 1971. From Scholastic Press
Ass'n.

Graphic Arts—Series of filmstrips with cassettes. Prentice-Hall Media.
1978. (Units include "Planning and Preparation of Copy" and "An
Introduction to Printing".)

The Graphic Arts: An Introduction—Sound filmstrip. Educational
Audio Visual, Inc., Thornwood, N.Y. 1977. (Current technical,
commercial and artistic aspects.)

Lithography—14 min. Amalgamated Lithographers of America. 1961.
From Laura Singer, Ed.D., New York. (Short history of lithography
and lithographic methods.)

Lithography or Offset Printing—16mm, sound, color, 22 min. Graphic
Arts Films, Inc. 1968. From Graphic Arts Technical Foundation.

The Offset Press—35mm slides; color, with script or cassette. From
Graphic Arts Technical Foundation. (How the modern offset press
works.)

The Offset Story—25 min. Canadian Film Institute, Ottawa, Ont.

Silk Screen—Sound filmstrip. Educational Audio Visual, Inc.,
Thornwood, N.Y. 1976. (Art history and techniques.)

Silkscreen Fundamentals—14 min. BFA Educational Media, Santa Monica, Calif. 1969. (Manual process.)

Binding   A *Book by Its Cover*—Motion picture. Iowa State University. Film Production Unit, Ames, Iowa. 1969.

Introduction to: Bindery Operations; Bookbinding—Case Binding; Unsewn Magazine and Pamphlet Binding; Adhesion and Adhesives; Papermaking—Series of slide sets with scripts. PIRA, Randalls Road, Leatherhead, Surrey, Eng.

Paper   *Paper: The Prologue*—Sound, color, 17 min. American Paper Institute, New York. 1972. (History and making of paper.)

OTHER SOURCES

Associations   The organizations listed below are only some of the more important business or professional groups active in the book industry. A few of the largest are able to carry on some informational activities; many have newsletters for members; some confine informational efforts to their meetings, workshops and seminars. Details about these organizations, and about many others, including numerous specialized and local or area groups, are given in each annual volume of the *Literary Market Place* (Bowker).

Organizations concerned largely with standards and appreciation of the book arts.

American Institute of Graphic Arts (AIGA)—New York (*Bulletin*; incorporates catalogues of AIGA exhibitions; fully illustrated.)
American Printing History Association—New York. (*APHA Letter*).
Bookbuilders of Boston
Bookbuilders West—San Francisco
Chicago Book Clinic
Philadelphia Book Clinic
The Typophiles—New York

Business and technical associations.

American Booksellers Association—New York (*American Bookseller* magazines; also many service publications.)
American Paper Institute—New York (Economic and technical reports.)
American Society of Magazine Photographers (ASMP)—New York
Association of American Publishers—New York, Washington. (Numerous reports and service publications; information on education for publishing.)
Association of American University Presses—New York (Service publications.)

Book Manufacturers' Institute—Stamford, Conn. (Information on standards.)

Book Industry Study Group, Inc.—New York (Reports.)

Canadian Book Publishers Council—Toronto

Association of Canadian Publishers—Toronto

Canadian Graphic Arts Industries Association—Ottawa

Children's Book Council—New York (Quarterly bulletin; service publications.)

Christian Booksellers Association—Colorado Springs (Service publications.)

Edition Bookbinders of New York

Graphic Arts Technical Foundation—Pittsburgh (Extensive publications.)

Graphic Communications Computer Association, Division of Printing Industries of America—Arlington, Va.

Information Industries Association—Bethesda, Md. (Newsletter.)

Library Binding Institute—Boston

National Association of College Stores—Oberlin, Ohio (*The College Store*; many service publications.)

National Composition Association, Division of Printing Industries of America.

Printing Industries of America, Inc.—Arlington, Va. (Extensive publications.)

Research and Engineering Council of the Graphic Arts Industries, Inc.—McLean, Va. (Reports and publications.)

Technical Association of the Pulp and Paper Industry (TAAPI)—Atlanta, Ga. (Technical reports.)

Professional and craft associations.

Authors League of America—New York

Bookbinders Guild of New York

Copyright Society of the U.S.A.—New York

Guild of Bookworkers—New York (Affiliated with AIGA)

International Association of Printing House Craftsmen, Inc.—Cincinnati, Ohio

National Critics Circle—New York

New York Rights and Permissions Group

P.E.N. American Center—New York

Publishers Ad Club—New York

Publishers Library Promotion Group—New York

Society of Scribes—New York

Any major library contains items of bookmaking interest. The following are some of those that have important specialized collections and exhibitions in the fields of printing, publishing, design, and the history of the book.

Book Club of California—San Francisco

Brown University—Providence, R.I.

Columbia University—New York City

Dartmouth College—Hanover, N.H.

R. R. Donnelley & Sons Co.—Chicago

Grolier Club—New York City

Harvard University—Cambridge, Mass.

Henry E. Huntington Library—San Marino, Calif.

Hunter College—New York City

Libraries

Kansas State University—Emporia
Library of Congress—Washington, D.C.
Museum of Fine Arts—Boston
Museum of Science and Industry (Smithsonian Institution)—Washington, D.C.
New York City Community College
Newberry Library—Chicago
The Pierpont Morgan Library—New York City
Princeton University Library—Princeton, N.J.
Rochester Institute of Technology—Rochester, N.Y.
Syracuse University—Syracuse, N.Y.
University of California—Berkeley
University of California—Los Angeles
University of Indiana—Bloomington
University of Kentucky—Lexington
University of Texas—Austin
University of Wyoming—Laramie
Williams College—Williamstown, Mass.
Yale University—New Haven, Conn.

Metric system conversion tables

INCH/CENTIMETER CONVERSION TABLE

Inches		Centimeters	Inches		Centimeters
1/16	=	.1588	(1 Foot) 12	=	30.48
1/8	=	.3175	13	=	33.02
3/16	=	.4763	14	=	35.56
1/4	=	.635	15	=	38.10
5/16	=	.7938	16	=	40.64
3/8	=	.9525	17	=	43.18
7/16	=	1.1113	18	=	45.72
1/2	=	1.27	19	=	48.26
9/16	=	1.4288	20	=	50.80
5/8	=	1.5875	21	=	53.34
11/16	=	1.7463	22	=	55.88
3/4	=	1.905	23	=	58.42
13/16	=	2.0638	(2 Feet) 24	=	60.96
7/8	=	2.2225	25	=	63.50
15/16	=	2.3815	26	=	66.04
1	=	2.54	27	=	68.58
2	=	5.08	28	=	71.12
3	=	7.62	29	=	73.66
4	=	10.16	30	=	76.20
5	=	12.70	31	=	78.74
6	=	15.24	32	=	81.28
7	=	17.78	33	=	83.82
8	=	20.32	34	=	86.36
9	=	22.86	35	=	88.9
10	=	25.40	(1 Yard) 36	=	91.44
11	=	27.94	39.37	=	100.0 (1 Meter)

FREQUENTLY USED
INCH DIMENSIONS AND SIZES
CONVERTED INTO CENTIMETERS

PAGE SIZES

Inches		Centimeters
$5\frac{3}{8} \times 8$	=	13.65×20.32
$5\frac{5}{8} \times 8\frac{3}{8}$	=	14.29×21.27
$5\frac{1}{2} \times 8\frac{1}{4}$	=	13.97×20.96
$6\frac{1}{8} \times 9\frac{1}{4}$	=	15.56×23.5
$8\frac{1}{2} \times 11$	=	21.59×27.94
9×12	=	22.86×30.48
12×18	=	30.48×45.72

SHEET SIZES

Inches		Centimeters
$17\frac{1}{2} \times 22\frac{1}{2}$	=	44.45×57.15
19×25	=	48.26×66.04
20×26	=	50.8×66.04
$22\frac{1}{2} \times 35$	=	57.15×88.9
25×38	=	63.5×96.52
30×44	=	76.20×111.76
35×45	=	88.9×114.3
38×50	=	96.52×127
41×61	=	104.14×154.94
44×66	=	111.76×167.64
50×76	=	127×193.04

METRIC WEIGHT CONVERSION
AND EQUIVALENTS

Pounds	Kilograms	Equivalents in grams for text paper weights
1	.4536	
30	13.61	44.4
40	18.14	59.1
45	20.41	66.5
50	22.68	73.9
60	27.22	88.7
70	31.75	103.5
80	36.29	118.3
90	40.82	133.1
100	45.36	147.9
120	54.43	177.4
150	68.04	
300	136.08	

The column headed kilograms gives the actual *conversion* of avoirdupois weight to metric measure. (To convert kilograms to grams simply move the decimal point 3 places to the right, i.e. 1 kilogram = 1000 grams). The right hand column gives the *equivalent* gram weights of paper measured by the metric system. These weights are based on one sheet one square meter in size. The pound weights in the left hand column are U.S. basis weights for text papers (500 sheets 25 × 38″).

U.S.*/Didot point equivalent table

U.S.		DIDOT	U.S.		DIDOT
1	=	.935	18	=	16.823
2	=	1.869	19	=	17.757
3	=	2.804	20	=	18.692
4	=	3.738	21	=	19.627
5	=	4.673	22	=	20.561
6	=	5.608	23	=	21.496
7	=	6.542	24	=	22.430
8	=	7.477	30	=	28.038
9	=	8.411	36	=	33.646
10	=	9.346	42	=	39.253
11	=	10.281	48	=	44.861
12	=	11.215	54	=	50.468
13	=	12.150	60	=	56.074
14	=	13.084	66	=	61.684
15	=	14.019	72	=	67.291
16	=	14.954	84	=	78.506
17	=	15.888	96	=	89.722

*The same point system is used by the United States and Great Britain.

Glossary-Index

This index was planned to be used in conjunction with the detailed Contents pages—which are, in effect, a subject index. Terms that appear only once in the text are defined at that time. Definitions are given here for terms mentioned on more than one page if the meaning of the term is not defined or made clear by the context in each case.

G

BOOKMAKING: *The illustrated guide to design/production/editing*

This book was designed by the author and
produced by BALANCE HOUSE, LTD., New York.
Composition was done by Printworks, Inc., Norwalk, Connecticut.
The text type—11 on 13 Electra—was set on a
Mergenthaler V.I.P. phototypesetter.
The printing and binding were done by
Kingsport Press, Inc., Kingsport, Tennessee.
The text paper is Warren's Old Style wove, 60 lb.
For the cover, Joanna Western's Arrestox was printed
by Reehl Litho, New York. The front endpaper was
printed by Philips Offset Inc., Mamaroneck, New York.
The back endpaper is Canfield's Colortext.

NOTES & CLIPPINGS

NOTES & CLIPPINGS

NOTES & CLIPPINGS

Lee, Marshall, 1921-
    Bookmaking : the illustrated guide
to design/production/editing /
Marshall Lee. -- 2d ed. completely
rev. and expanded. -- New York :
Bowker, c1979.
    485 p. : ill. ; 26 cm. -- (A Balance
House book)

    Includes index.
    Bibliography: p. [449]-464.
    ISBN 0-8352-1097-9 : $25.00

1. Books. 2. Book industries and trade. I.
Title.